D1521447

CASUAL SLAUGHTERS AND ACCIDENTAL JUDGMENTS

PATRONS OF THE SOCIETY

Aird & Berlis

Blake, Cassels & Graydon

Borden & Elliot

Davies, Ward & Beck

Gowling, Strathy & Henderson

McCarthy Tétrault

Osler, Hoskin & Harcourt

The Harweg Foundation

Tory Tory DesLauriers & Binnington

Weir & Foulds

BENEFACTORS OF THE SOCIETY

Bastedo Stewart & Smith

Roger T. Hughes, QC

The Society also thanks The Law Foundation of Ontario and
The Law Society of Upper Canada
for their continuing support.

Casual Slaughters and Accidental Judgments

CANADIAN WAR CRIMES PROSECUTIONS,
1944–1948

PATRICK BRODE

Published for The Osgoode Society for Canadian Legal History by
University of Toronto Press
Toronto   Buffalo   London

© The Osgoode Society for Canadian Legal History 1997
Printed in Canada

ISBN 0-8020-4204-X (cloth)

Printed on acid-free paper

Canadian Cataloguing in Publication Data

Brode, Patrick, 1950–
Casual slaughters and accidental judgments : Canadian
war crimes prosecutions, 1944–1948

Includes index.
ISBN 0-8020-4204-X

1. War crime trials – Canada.   2. World War, 1939–1945 –
Atrocities.   3. War criminals – Germany.   4. War criminals –
Japan.   I. Osgoode Society for Canadian Legal History.
II. Title.

D803.B76 1977   341.6'9   C97-930894-1

This book has been published with the help of a grant from the Humanities
and Social Sciences Federation of Canada, using funds provided by the
Social Sciences and Humanities Research Council of Canada.

University of Toronto Press acknowledges the financial assistance to its
publishing program of the Canada Council for the Arts and the
Ontario Arts Council.

Contents

Foreword   vii
Abbreviations   ix
Preface   xi
Introduction   xv

 1 Rumours of Murder   3
 2 Murder Division   17
 3 Indifference to the 'War Crimes Business'   30
 4 Questions of Partiality   54
 5 Brigadeführer on Trial   67
 6 But for the Grace of God   102
 7 Shot like Wild Animals   116
 8 Opladen: The Forgotten Case   136
 9 Hong Kong: The Law of the Imperial Japanese Army   157
10 The Japanese Trials: Camp Guards and the Architects of War   178
11 'Siegergericht'   200
12 Canadian War Crimes and the Consequences   217

Appendix   Charge Sheet of Kurt Meyer   231
Notes   233
Photo Credits   275
Index   277

Foreword

THE OSGOODE SOCIETY FOR CANADIAN LEGAL HISTORY

The purpose of The Osgoode Society for Canadian Legal History is to encourage research and writing in the history of Canadian law. The Society, which was incorporated in 1979 and is registered as a charity, was founded at the initiative of the Honourable R. Roy McMurtry, a former attorney general for Ontario, now chief justice of Ontario, and officials of the Law Society of Upper Canada. Its efforts to stimulate the study of legal history in Canada include a research-support program, a graduate student research-assistance program, and work in the fields of oral history and legal archives. The Society publishes volumes of interest to its members that contribute to legal-historical scholarship in Canada, including studies of the courts, the judiciary, and the legal profession, biographies, collections of doocuments, studies in criminology and penology, accounts of significant trials, and work in the social and economic history of the law.

Current directors of The Osgoode Society for Canadian Legal History are Jane Banfield, Tom Bastedo, Brian Bucknall, Archie Campbell, Susan Elliott, J. Douglas Ewart, Martin Friedland, Charles Harnick, John Honsberger, Kenneth Jarvis, Allen Linden, Virginia MacLean, Wendy Matheson, Colin McKinnon, Roy McMurtry, Brendan O'Brien, Peter Oliver, Paul Reinhardt, Joel Richler, James Spence, and Richard Tinsley.

The annual report and information about membership may be obtained by writing to The Osgoode Society for Canadian Legal History, Osgoode Hall, 130 Queen Street West, Toronto, Ontario, M5H 2N6.

Casual Slaughters and Accidental Judgments: Canadian War Crimes Prosecu-

tions, 1944–1948 is Patrick Brode's third publication with The Osgoode Society and furthers his already considerable reputation for combining sound scholarship with readability.

The prosecution after the Second World War of German and Japanese war criminals by the Canadian military was a new venture for Canadians, a break from Canada's colonial past and an entry into world affairs. In one of the most sensational trials, SS General Kurt Meyer was prosecuted for the massacre of Canadian prisoners. Meyer's reprieve, only days before he faced a firing squad, remains one of the most contentious post-war decisions. Throughout these trials, which included the trials of Germans accused of murdering Canadian airmen as well as of Japanese guards who allegedly tortured Canadian prisoners from Hong Kong, evolving standards of international law were applied by military tribunals. This fascinating and disturbing study demonstrates the efforts of military tribunals to apply the law of war against those who had acknowledged no law.

R. Roy McMurtry
President

Peter N. Oliver
Editor-in-Chief

Abbreviations

ALFSEA	Allied Land Forces South East Asia (British and other Allied forces in India, southeast Asia, and China)
CMHQ	Canadian Military Headquarters (London, England)
DND	Department of National Defence
HQ	Headquarters
IMT	International Military Tribunal (Nuremberg Trial)
IMTFE	International Military Tribunal for the Far East (Tokyo Trial)
IPS	International Prosecution Staff (Tokyo)
JAG	Judge Advocate General
PGR	Panzer Grenadier Regiment
RCAF	Royal Canadian Air Force
SHAEF	Supreme Headquarters Allied Expeditionary Force
SCAP	Supreme Commander for the Allied Powers (Douglas MacArthur's title in the occupation of Japan)
UNWCC	United Nations War Crimes Commission

Preface

The world wars of this century have left a sense that unrestrained violence is a permanent feature of the human condition. Against this background, it seems absurd to look for legal order when the destruction of the enemy is the first objective of the state. Yet, to most modern combatants, there are, to greater or lesser degrees, recognized rules of conduct. The armies of the Second World War acknowledged limits on their destructiveness, and the exceeding of these limits constituted a criminal act. But rules are meaningless if there are no means of enforcement. By the end of the war, the Canadian military, not far removed from being colonial auxiliaries, seized the initiative and applied the laws of war against those who had acknowledged no law. This was a new venture for Canadians, marking a break from the past and an entry onto the world stage. It was also a venture begun with great reluctance by hesitant leaders who could not imagine a self-reliant Canada taking control of its own affairs.

When finally initiated by men of great perseverance, the Canadian war crimes prosecutions were marked by painstaking investigation and scrupulous judicial process. The most remarkable case in these prosecutions was that of SS Brigadeführer Kurt Meyer in December 1945. This still controversial trial publicized the extent of Waffen SS atrocities against Canadians in 1944 and aroused shrill passions in the Canadian public. Overshadowed by Meyer's case, the other prosecutions passed without much comment. However, they showed, perhaps even more than Meyer's case, the pitfalls of prosecuting the defeated.

While Canada's war crimes trials were few in number, their impact on the consciousness of the nation became apparent years later. In 1951 the government was preoccupied by a new war in Korea and seeking rapprochement with a revived Germany. There were rumours that war criminals were about to be freed, and this mere suggestion caused hundreds of telegrams of protest to be sent to the Department of Justice. A typical message deplored any display of leniency as 'an insult to the revered memory of the thousands who died to free the world of Nazi enslavement.'[1] Succeeding generations may be unable to appreciate the depths of sorrow caused by the loss of these young men, and especially of those lost after capture when the laws of war should have guaranteed their lives.

Canadians may not have cared that these prosecutions were not retribution for the thousands who had died but rather punishment for specific war crimes. Those responsible had tried to apply legal standards concerning a commander's responsibility for his troops and a soldier's duty to refuse illegal orders. The Canadian war crimes prosecutions did not establish new standards in these areas, but they were part of a process (still very much under way) that would set standards for soldierly conduct in Vietnam, the Middle East, and Somalia. While far from perfect, these prosecutions were a part of the evolving standards of international law.

The military leaders of the Second World War were products of their time. They saw such great evil in their enemy that their own misdeeds were often left unpunished. To what extent should the prosecution of war crimes have included Canadians as well? Insisting on norms of conduct in the midst of war becomes mere retribution if these norms are selectively applied. If, as Oliver Wendell Holmes suggested, the life of the law is experience, not logic, then experience should tell us that the prosecution of war criminals is valid only if a nation is willing to prosecute its own war criminals, if breaches of the laws of war are recognized irrespective of the uniform of the offender.

Throughout the writing of this book, I was assisted and enriched by an extraordinary group of men: the officers of the No. 1 Canadian War Crimes Investigation Unit. John Blain, John Page, Wady Lehmann, and Raymond Robichaud regularly gave me the benefit of their recollections and comments. In my early research, I was greatly assisted by Bill Rawling, William H. Wiley, and Mark Walsh. Glenn Wright, the staff historian of the RCMP, directed my research on police involvement in war crimes investigations.

A major influence, not adequately recognized by this acknowledgment, was Dr Charles G. Roland, of McMaster Medical School. His comprehensive knowledge and advice regarding the trials of Japanese war criminals were invaluable.

A book such as this is made up of stray but vital bits of information, and in assembling those bits I am indebted to Sheila and Shelly Burke, Susan Binnie, and Ken Boland.

Of all the institutions consulted in the writing of this book, the Windsor Municipal Archives was indispensable. Linda Chakmak and Janet Brown were unfailingly helpful. I was also assisted by Dr Elizabeth Sinn and Au Yeung Chi Ying of the University of Hong Kong. D. Matignon of the Depôt Central d'Archives de la Justice Militaire provided vital information on French military records.

As always at the Osgoode Society, Peter Oliver believed in and fostered this work while Marilyn MacFarlane helped make it possible. My editor, Curtis Fahey, patiently erased my more flagrant mistakes. Lastly, I owe an enduring debt to my three girls for their subtle contribution.

Introduction

'To introduce the principles of moderation into the theory of war itself would always lead to logical absurdity.'
Karl von Clausewitz, *On War*[1]

The intent of the Canadian war crimes trials was to show that, notwithstanding Clausewitz, there are restraints on warfare. These trials restated the principle that military excesses are morally unjustified and should be punished. Such notions of justice are by no means unique to Canada; rather, they may be viewed as part of a modern trend to compel soldiers to bear responsibility for their actions, to demonstrate that force is controlled not only by treaties but also by actions.

Recognized rules of warfare have existed since ancient Greece and Rome, but they rarely seem to have extended beyond the occasional humanitarian gesture. Neither was there much compassion on the medieval battlefield. The defeated enemy could be enslaved or slaughtered. Armies took plunder, lived off the country, and had little reason to keep prisoners.[2] The only mitigation occurred when noble prisoners were held for ransom.[3] To a limited extent, the Church moderated soldierly ferocity against peasants and non-combatants. Yet religion could be an excuse for even greater barbarity. The slaughter of the 24,000 inhabitants of Magdeburg during the Thirty Years' War shocked Europe and spurred scholarly writers such as Grotius and Suarez to seek 'due proportion' to the violence of war. Grotius asserted that there was a *temperamenta belli* that provided for humanity towards captives and civilians.[4] In his 1625 study *On the Laws of War and Peace*, Grotius set out general precepts that nations should follow. Yet even in Grotius's view these rules did little for prisoners: 'So far as the law of nations is concerned, the right of killing such slaves, that is, captives taken in war, is not precluded at any time, although it is restricted, now more, now less, by the laws of states.'[5]

After Grotius's time, the taking and keeping of prisoners became, if not the rule, the accepted practice. It was recognized that minimum rules of conduct could benefit even hostile parties. This was especially true by the eighteenth century, when armies became uniformed, provisioned, and disciplined far better than their predecessors. A 1785 treaty between Russia and the United States was the first international agreement to stipulate decent treatment for prisoners of war.[6] When the French revolutionary government ordered its soldiers to refuse quarter to British and Hanoverian troops in 1794, this order was so contrary to accepted standards of conduct that it was ignored by French officers.[7] By the time of the American Civil War it was considered appropriate to publish the rules relating to the conduct of war, and the code drafted by Francis Lieber became the first manual on the subject.[8] The Lieber code documented the existing customary law, but it said little about enforcement or the duty of officers to control their men. Nevertheless, the Lieber code was used by several European armies and there was consideration of making it an international tool binding on all nations. The Geneva (Red Cross) Convention of 1864[9] partially fulfilled this objective by providing new rules to humanize warfare by protecting non-combatants.

The technology of the late nineteenth century vastly increased the ability of armies to destroy and better communications carried this dire news to the public. During the Franco-Prussian War of 1870–1, violations of the laws of war such as the shooting of Red Cross workers strengthened international resolve to enact comprehensive codes of conduct. Conferences at the Hague in 1899 and 1907 did that by providing regulations to protect the wounded, those trying to surrender, or those already taken prisoner. Prisoners were now to be considered wards of a hostile government and not the personal property of their captors. While progress was made, military leaders at the Hague cared little about the fate of captives. British Admiral Sir John Fisher sniffed at the concern for the lives of prisoners, claiming that such rules would soon force victors into putting 'their prisoners' feet in hot water and giving them gruel.'[10] There remained, despite the Hague Convention, the inherent conflict between attempts to humanize war and the generals' duty to use massive force to guarantee victory.

While the First World War saw a general deference to the Hague Convention, lapses in conduct were apparent on all sides. It was not until January 1919, after the end of the war, that an allied commission was struck to examine war crimes. Germany, for its part, was obliged by the Treaty of Versailles to surrender all war criminals. However, when the list of the accused was sent to Germany, the authorities refused to act. Eventually, Germany proposed to try some of the accused at Leipzig and the list of suspects was trimmed from 896 to 45. In the end, there were only six convictions resulting in only a few months' imprisonment. An example of Leipzig justice was the trial of General Karl Stenger. Despite clear evidence from German soldiers that Stenger had ordered the killing of prisoners in 1914, he was acquitted amid bouquets, applause, and public acclaim.[11] The travesty of the Leipzig trials was adequate proof that the nation that employs soldiers is unlikely to punish them for atrocities. On the other side of the trenches, allied misconduct had been documented by the Prussian Bureau of Investigation and, using information supplied by neutrals and allied servicemen, the bureau had prepared a list of suspects. In one case, it had substantial evidence from neutral sources that a British naval captain had murdered helpless German seamen. None of these suspects was ever brought to trial.[12]

After the horrors of the First World War, nations resolved to try and prevent future wars and to mitigate the effects of future ones. In 1929 a new Geneva Convention supplemented the Hague Regulations and improved the prospects of prisoners of war by requiring neutral countries to inspect the prisoners' camps and living conditions.[13] Fine as these provisions sounded, they bound only the contracting countries and had no impact on those who ignored them. There was also the practical problem of translating the Geneva Convention into domestic military law. In the United States, the *Law of Land Warfare* effectively incorporated the Geneva Convention's requirements to treat prisoners humanely, as did the *Manual of Military Law* in Britain. Yet even in these countries, there was confusion as to how to prosecute individuals who breached the convention and it remained up to the national military codes to provide sanctions against soldiers who breached the laws of war.[14] For example, the German army's *Kriegesgebrauch im Landkriege* listed international provisions and provided that 'whoever breaks these rules shall be prosecuted by his State. If he is taken prisoner, he is subject to punishment by (foreign) court-martial.'[15]

Canadian experience with war crimes was necessarily limited. During the War of 1812, one American commander was summarily dismissed after his men burned a civilian encampment.[16] Canadians were also aware of American outrage following the horrific massacre of American prisoners after the battle of Frenchtown in 1813.[17] Long before the Geneva conventions, legalities were of great importance in nineteenth-century warfare. Canadians were infuriated when one group of American irregulars, the 'Canadian Volunteers,' bypassed military positions and instead raided Upper Canadian farms and villages. However, when a number of the raiders were tried for treason in 1814, the province's acting attorney general, John Beverley Robinson, was careful to see that the law was fairly applied. One convicted rebel was granted a reprieve on Robinson's recommendation that, although he was technically guilty, 'he behaved with humanity to prisoners taken by the party and expresses his regret at some of their outrages while together.'[18] Those Canadians who failed to apply the laws of war could earn the opprobrium of their fellows. During the patriot raids of 1837–8, Colonel John Prince seized and summarily executed five prisoners at the Battle of Windsor. His superior, Sir George Arthur, was incensed at this 'most unjustifiable' act and even the House of Lords debated whether he should be court-martialed.[19] In the circumstances, however, Prince's action was celebrated instead of condemned by the populace and he escaped official censure.

After that, Canadians saw little of warfare until 1914. Many of the allegations arising during the First World War seemed more propaganda than reality. In *Canada in Flanders*, a masterpiece of jingoism, Max Aitken mentioned an incident, without citing specifics, of wounded Canadians being bayoneted by the 'Hun.'[20] Perhaps one of the most vivid legends of the war was that of the 'crucified Canadian.' According to the story (probably a camp rumour that eventually spread to the press), a captured Canadian was spreadeagled in front of his comrades, his hands and feet pierced by bayonets. He died slowly as German soldiers watched with sadistic glee.[21]

It seemed that after 1929 new standards of morality had taken hold among the armies. At the beginning of the Second World War, Germany advertised its strict adherence to the laws of war. If anything, Germans themselves felt aggrieved when they discovered an order left in the remains of a vehicle abandoned after the tragic Dieppe raid of August 1942 that called for the tying up of German captives. In retaliation, German authorities ordered Canadian prisoners bound and eventually shackled.[22] Conditions for these men were deplorable, although they were somewhat heartened to learn that in retaliation German prisoners were also being bound. It was not until Canada's high commissioner to Britain, Vincent Massey, protested to the British about the consequences of retaliation for Canadian prisoners of war that the British relented. The Germans eventually ceased the practice as well. The desire to retaliate was replaced by the reality that reciprocity was not in the prisoners' interests.[23]

The 'shackling' incident had shown that Germany was sensitive to the laws of war being applied to its men and in its own way had applied those laws to the captured enemy. Given these facts, the fathers and mothers of Canada's servicemen could have some confidence that the laws of war would protect their sons. But their confidence began to be shaken by news coming out of Europe in March 1944.

U.S. Army pathologist performs autopsy on Canadian war crime victim at Verneuil, Normandy, October 1945.

Canadian war crimes investigation vehicle at Dutch border crossing.

Meyer's assigned defence lawyers, Lt. Col. Maurice Andrew (left) and
Capt. Frank Plourde.

Official portrait of Lt. Col. Bruce J.S. Macdonald.

Exhibit T-31 to the trial of Kurt Meyer, showing Jan Jesionek standing at the entrance to the garden.

L'Ancienne Abbaye d'Ardenne as it appeared at the end of the Second World War. Note the towers Meyer used as observation points.

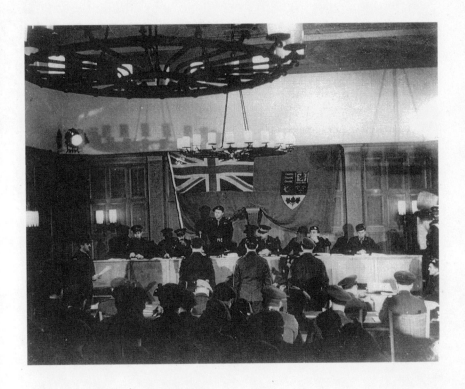

Commencement of the trial of Kurt Meyer. Lt. Col. W. Bredin is standing with
the assembled generals. Meyer is standing with his back to the camera, flanked
by his officer guards.

Brigadeführer Kurt Meyer in his cell
in Aurich during his trial.

A reluctant Meyer poses for a
Canadian Army photographer,
December 1945.

Prosecution team assembled outside Marine barracks, Aurich, Germany, December 1945. Centre front is Bruce Macdonald, with Dalton Dean on his left and Clarence Campbell on his right.

Accused Japanese war criminals in the dock in Hong Kong. Second from right is medical officer Capt. S. Saito; third from left is POW camp commandant Col. Isao Tokunaga.

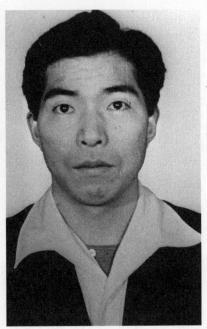

Lt. Kosaku Hazama,
commandant of the POW camp at
Oeyama, Japan.

Col. Isao Tokunaga in custody.

Major G.B. Puddicombe, standing at right, conducts the trial of Col. Tokunaga. Sergeant-Major H.B. Shepherd of the Canadian War Crimes Liaison Detachment sits on his right.

Casual Slaughters and Accidental Judgments

1

Rumours of Murder

The first official notice of German atrocities against Canadians came from Prime Minister Mackenzie King's announcement in Parliament that six RCAF officers had been shot after an attempted escape from Stalag Luft III. During the 'Great Escape' of 24–5 March 1944, seventy-seven men had broken out of the Luftwaffe prison camp. Some of the escapees were recaptured and held at the Gestapo prison at Görlitz. There, the guards told them that they could be executed at any time: 'You are wearing civilian clothes,' they said, 'and we can do what we like with you. You can disappear.'[1] Some officers seen alive at Görlitz were later shot. On 6 June, a Swiss representative was given a note which stated that thirty-seven British and thirteen non-British officers had been killed. None had been wounded. It surpassed belief that fifty men could be shot while escaping and none injured. All circumstances indicated that the officers had been shot after their recapture.

King promised the House that 'those who have been responsible for this crime, whenever they may fall into allied hands, are brought to trial and punished.'[2] According to reporters, the House received the news 'in grim and stony silence.'[3] British reaction was similar as the Foreign Secretary Anthony Eden assured Parliament that the 'foul criminals' would be tracked down and punished. The Toronto *Globe and Mail* reflected the public outrage in its editorial 'Crown of German Infamy.' Using vivid religious imagery, the editorial accused the German nation of abandoning Christian principles for paganism and promised 'exemplary justice in the form of severe punishment' not only on the perpetrators but on 'the whole German people.'[4]

A few days later the leader of the Opposition, Gordon Graydon, noted a report from a former French prisoner regarding the killing of two Canadians at Stalag IIB. 'It makes one's blood boil,' Graydon pronounced, 'and calls loudly for the kind of punishment that these murderous vandals so richly deserve.'[5] Missing from the parliamentary debate was the French prisoner's other report on the deliberate extermination of Russian and Polish prisoners. Of the 33,000 that had arrived in 1941, 27,000 had been starved or killed. He had seen prisoners forced to dig a mass grave for 500 bodies following which the diggers were themselves shot and thrown in. While British and French prisoners were treated correctly 'Russians and Poles were treated worse than animals.'[6] This report detailed only a fraction of the slaughter of East Europeans in the German camps. In response to a German enquiry, Stalin had indicated that he would not obey the Geneva Convention for prisoners of war and thereby insured that the laws of war would not be applied to his own men. Neutral observers were shocked by the contrast between the relatively healthy camps for western prisoners and the Russian charnel houses. Of the 5.7 million Soviet prisoners, approximately 3.7 million died in captivity.[7]

However, Canadian concerns were centred on the safety of their own servicemen. By 1944 crippled prisoners were being repatriated and new incidents were recounted. One soldier described how a comrade had been killed at Dieppe after capture in August 1942. The Canadian had raised his arms but still held a clasp knife. One German guard said something to him that he did not understand. Another guard called out to the prisoner and, as the latter turned around, the first guard shot him. The two guards berated each other as the remaining Canadians stood by, uncomprehending, over the fatally wounded man. In 1944 CMHQ, the central command for the Canadian forces in Europe, made an official remonstrance to Germany through Swiss intermediaries, but the only response was that the passage of time had made it impossible to determine the facts.[8] The killing was most likely an accident, a misunderstanding between the prisoner and the guards. While considered serious in early 1944, it would pale when compared with the later deliberate executions of scores of prisoners.

In contrast to the situation in the First World War, the Allies had begun planning for war crimes trials during the course of the conflict. As early as January 1942 Winston Churchill was promising eventual retribution for 'Nazi butcheries.'[9] Speaking in Parliament in February 1943, Churchill declared that 'justice must be done against the wicked and the guilty.'[10]

Nothing was added to this amorphous statement until the Moscow conference of October 1943, when a manifesto from the United States, the United
Kingdom, and the Soviet Union announced that Axis troops implicated in
atrocities would be tried according to the laws of the place where the
offence occurred. There would also exist an umbrella organization to
supervise national courts. The United Nations War Crimes Commission
(UNWCC) was established on 20 October 1943 and would draw up lists
and exchange information on war crimes suspects.[11] While each country
would have its own investigative agency, all information would be available through the UNWCC.

Some wondered why these commissions had to exist at all. The arch-
bishop of York was reported to have suggested that 'Hitler and Himmler
and his gang should be killed on the spot when captured.' Many in the
Allied countries agreed. U.S. Secretary of State Cordell Hull's preference
was to bring the Axis leaders 'before a drumhead court-martial' and shoot
them the following dawn.[12] Harvard professor Sheldon Glueck warned in
1944 that strict adherence to form was dangerous. 'The same technicalities
in the prosecution of war criminals that they observe in the domestic
administration of criminal justice may seriously weaken the program for
dealing with Nazi-Fascist malefactors.'[13] Taken in context – the extent of
Nazi atrocities was just beginning to emerge – Glueck's call for quick
action against 'ruthless gangsters' was understandable. But, in the end,
legality overrode rage; procedure diluted vengeance.

Canada's interest in war crimes prosecutions would arise out of the
events occurring after the D-Day landing on 6 June 1944. To understand
these events, it is necessary to have an overview of the 3rd Canadian
Infantry Division's operations from 7 to 17 June. The Canadians had
landed on Juno Beach with orders to attack the gap between the Norman
cities of Caen and Bayeux. Hours after the landing, lead elements of the 9th
Infantry Brigade, including troops of the North Nova Scotia Highlanders,
supported by tanks from the Sherbrooke Fusilliers, had advanced almost
to Caen. By the afternoon of 7 June, 'C' Company of the North Novas was
in Authie, the tip of the Canadian spearhead.[14]

At mid-afternoon, the exposed Canadians were attacked by soldiers
from the 12th SS Panzer Division (Hitler Jugend). Supported by tanks and
artillery, the young soldiers of the Hitler Youth shouted encouragement to
each other as they moved in to attack the Canadians. The historian of the
North Novas describes what happened next: 'There was never a wilder
melee than that in Authie amid the smoke and dust and shooting ...
Captain Fraser kept shooting until he was killed. So did the North Novas

with him, and the Sherbrooke Fusilliers and Cameron Highlanders who elected to fight to the finish. They took a dreadful toll of the fanatical SS troops.'[15]

There was vicious, swirling combat around Authie until, as the panzers moved into the town, the Canadians were forced to fight their way out. By late evening, the 12th SS had pushed north into Buron and captured a number of Canadians there. However, this was the high-water mark of their advance, and they fell well short of driving the Canadians back to the beaches.

On the following day, it was the turn of the 7th Infantry Brigade. The lead infantry of the 7th, the Royal Winnipeg Rifles, had advanced as far as the Caen-Bayeux road to the town of Putot-en-Bessin. On the morning of 8 June they were also attacked by the 12th SS. After hand-to-hand fighting, the Winnipegers were encircled and 256 men were killed or captured.[16] That night, a counter-attack mounted by the Canadian Scottish and the 1st Hussars recaptured the position. It was now essential to push inland and advance to the west of Caen. On 11 June the 6th Armoured Regiment and the Queen's Own Rifles of Canada attacked at Le Mesnil-Patry into an area held by the 12th SS. The Canadians were repulsed with heavy losses, and for the next two weeks the front line stalled on the Caen-Bayeux road.

A press report, issued barely two weeks after the invasion, gave the story of two tank sergeants, Tom Johnson and Ernie Payne. Together with another soldier, they had been captured shortly after the landing, and while they were being marched away their guard had suddenly, and without warning, fired on them. One soldier fell, and Payne and Johnson ran for their lives. Johnson recognized the soldiers who had captured and then tried to kill them. 'Most of the Germans he saw were extremely young and fought fanatically. They wore the hip length camouflaged jackets and tucked in trousers of the Hitler Youth Division.'[17]

Bad as this incident was, it could have been an isolated case of one sadistic guard. Worse was to follow.

Canadian involvement in war crimes investigations began with reports from a Frenchwoman, Beatrice Delafon, of incidents occurring at the Chateau d'Audrieu on 8 June. Philippe Level, the owner of the chateau, was away in the Free French air force, and he had left his niece Beatrice in charge. The chateau itself was a large, attractive country mansion where the Delafons and their cousins the Levels presided as the local gentry. The area around the chateau was seized by British troops on 9 June, and Beatrice wasted no time in contacting a medical officer, Captain J.F. Neil, to tell him of the slaughter of Canadian prisoners. As proof, she showed him the bodies of thirteen Canadians lying in a row against a fence. Neil examined the bodies and concluded that the nature of the head wounds confirmed Beatrice's story.[18] Word of this passed quickly to CMHQ in London and Brigadier W.H.S. Macklin, the commanding officer of the 13th Infantry Brigade, assembled officers to look into the report. Lieutenant-Colonel J.W. McClain and an RCMP officer attached to special investigations, Captain Morrison, were sent to France on 1 July. On 4 July they reported to Lieutenant-General H.D.G. Crerar, the commander of the First Canadian Army, that an atrocity had occurred and should be investigated by a court of inquiry. In Crerar's view, a thorough investigation would carry great authority and could well serve a larger political purpose. 'If these cases are substantiated,' he said, 'the document may well prove an important political instrument in the peace settlement, and may quite likely represent one of the very few thoroughly authenticated charges of war atrocities.'[19]

CMHQ agreed that an issue of this importance could not be handled by a subordinate formation but should be sent up to army headquarters, or even to 21st Army Group. However any notion of a cordial investigation among Allies was quickly dispelled. On 6 July a CMHQ representative was discussing the massacre at the chateau with Crerar when he confided that U.S. military police had informed him that American paratroopers had reportedly shot German prisoners. That evening, a British officer, Lieutenant-Colonel W. Blackhurst of 21st Army Group staff informed Crerar that an American general, Raymond W. Barker, the assistant chief of staff of the Supreme Headquarters of the Allied Expeditionary Force (SHAEF), had been appointed by General Eisenhower as president of the court of inquiry.[20]

No Canadians had been consulted. Crerar was outraged, first because he considered this to be a 'Commonwealth' matter and also because it would taint the process to have an American officer involved if the Americans themselves were implicated in atrocities. However, there was little that Crerar could do about it, other than to advise the British that he was 'profoundly disturbed' that an issue that should have been reserved to the 21st Army Group had been sent to SHAEF and the Americans, and that 'the matter had been put on an inter-allied plane, rather than a Common-

wealth one, all this without consultation with responsible Cdn. authori-
ties.'[21] This first arrangement for war crimes prefigured later events where
American and British interests would overwhelm attempts at significant
Canadian involvement.

The SHAEF court of inquiry would have limited Canadian input. One of
the first Canadians contacted to assist the court was Major John Page, a
highly capable staff officer who had done much of the work in setting up a
Canadian intelligence establishment.[22] He was joined by an army pathologist, Lieutenant-Colonel R.A.H. MacKeen. A 1924 medical graduate of
McGill University, MacKeen had taught pathology and bacteriology at
Dalhousie University before becoming the provincial pathologist of New
Brunswick. His ability in pathology would put the forensic reports beyond
dispute. MacKeen exhumed the twenty-six bodies removed from the chateau and the nature of the wounds (almost all had been shot in the head)
was not consistent with battle casualties. Shortly after the court was sworn
in, its members travelled to the chateau on 11 July and the president,
Major-General Barker, took control of the investigation. A former artillery
officer, Barker had been one of the senior planners for the D-Day landings.
He would be assisted by two British officers, Brigadier G.W.B. Tarleton
and Lieutenant-Colonel W. Blackhurst. Considering that it was operating
in the middle of a battle, the court of inquiry conducted its investigations
with remarkable thoroughness. Photographers took pictures of the site,
and all bodies were exhumed for forensic examination. A prime source of
information was the residents of the chateau themselves. For this task,
Barker was indispensable, for the Delafons and Levels were highly conscious of their social rank and they appreciated being the object of attention of a senior American general.[23] Their stories would give a chilling
account of Waffen SS operations.

At the time of the incident, the Chateau d'Audrieu was far removed
from the fighting. About noon on June 8 a detachment of 50 men of the 12th
SS's reconnaissance battalion arrived and set up a command post under a
large, low-hanging sycamore tree. By about 2 o'clock prisoners were coming in from the fighting at Putot-en-Bessin. Beatrice Delafon, Monique
Level, and a gardener and his son stood and watched while SS guards
marched three unarmed prisoners into the local woods. An officer waved
them on their way. Monique, more curious than the rest, followed the
party into the forest. Losing sight of them, she turned back until she heard
a series of shots. Shortly thereafter she saw the SS guards return without
the prisoners. One of the guards returned to the chateau kitchen where he
bragged of now having 'Tommy cigarettes.'[24]

A short time later, Beatrice Delafon saw another group of about four prisoners marched away. 'As soon as they disappeared I heard shots; I counted them and there were as many shots as there were British soldiers.'[25] Still later that day, civilians saw a group of about thirteen prisoners sitting by a roadhouse. When the gardener's son looked for stray pigs near the hen house he was horrified to find these men lying dead in a row. He was reluctant to come near the still bleeding bodies, but an SS guard signalled for him to approach, saying, 'Komm hier, Tommy kaput.' He then made a gesture with his revolver indicating that the prisoners had been shot and said 'Tommy tat-tat-tat-tat.'[26] The prisoners knew that they were about to be executed for one of the dead still clutched a rosary, another a family photograph. Of the twenty-four Canadians (almost all from the Winnipeg Rifles) and two British soldiers found at the Chateau d'Audrieu, MacKeen confirmed that nineteen had been executed by pistol shots at close range. The other seven had likely been murdered but the forensic results were inconclusive.[27]

At almost the same time as the court of inquiry was assembling at the chateau, word of another atrocity reached Crerar's HQ. On 10 July he sent Barker a notice of the killing of seven Canadian prisoners near the town of Mouen. SHAEF promptly assembled another court (composed of the same personnel) to examine this incident.[28] On 17 June seven Canadians had been captured after the fighting at Le Mesnil-Patry and taken to a command post of the 12th SS's engineering battalion. A civilian was suspicious that fourteen Germans were detailed to guard the seven and decided to follow them as the prisoners were marched to a hill. There, he reported, 'the Germans stood them up in one straight line ... The Germans went back a few metres, formed in a line facing the Canadians and shot them.'[29] The following day, one member of the firing squad approached a French civilian and raised the topic of the killings. 'Do you know why we have done this?' he asked, almost eager to explain why they had killed unarmed prisoners. 'We have found an order on British soldiers directing them not to take SS prisoners.'[30] Along with the fact of the killings, a motive was emerging. However, the only clue as to the officer in charge of the Mouen killings was a sign-post marker 'Muller P.' that had been left at the scene. Without question, units of the 12th SS were murdering prisoners, although exactly which units and under whose orders remained difficult to ascertain. General Barker reported these findings to SHAEF on 28 July 1944.

Even before these reports, word of the atrocities had been leaked to the English press. As early as 21 June the London *Daily Mirror* published an article under the headline 'Huns shooting Canadian prisoners' that described the Chateau d'Audrieu killings. By the end of July, there was concern that rumours and gossip were about to overwhelm the facts. Ottawa instructed the high commissioner's office in London to dispel these rumours for 'the Canadian public are being misled and General Crerar is seriously afraid that Canadian troops will commit acts of vengeance on German prisoners.'[31] Representatives from the British and Canadian governments met in London on 25 July, and the Canadians announced that they would issue a statement. The British preferred to wait, for the SHAEF findings were only interim reports. Brigadier M.H.S. Penhale of CMHQ disagreed and advised the British that an official report would be made shortly.[32]

On 1 August 1944 Crerar issued a statement based on the report to the 21st Army Group on the Chateau d'Audrieu killings. Read to all troops and posted on orderly-room bulletin boards, the statement declared that a court of inquiry 'assembled at my request' had concluded that nineteen Canadian soldiers had been deliberately murdered 'in clear violation of the well-recognized laws and usages of war.'[33] According to reporter Ralph Allen, this terse report was already common knowledge among the front-line troops and that word of it had not spread to Canada only because of the request of the Allied commanders.[34] In his statement, Crerar cautioned his soldiers that they 'must not, under any circumstances, take the form of retaliation in kind.' This restrained response must have been made in the knowledge that revenge by Canadian troops would lead only to greater escalation of atrocities. On 2 August Prime Minister King told the House of Commons about the killings, declaring that Canadians had been 'wilfully murdered by the enemy's forces.'[35] According to press reports, 'Instantly the atmosphere of the House congealed into a cold hatred.'[36] It was bad enough that so many men were being lost in the brutal fighting in Normandy. It was worse to learn that unarmed prisoners were being murdered far behind enemy lines. Given the intense public feelings that could be expected at such a revelation, King's response was muted yet determined. Further investigations would be carried out by the Swiss government as the protecting power. The Swiss would send a protest to the German government and request further details. Leaflets were dropped on German soldiers in Normandy telling them of Allied knowledge of the atrocities and warning them that the guilty faced punishment.

Crerar sent a message to SHAEF that there were undoubtedly further incidents and that the First Canadian Army was 'extremely anxious that these atrocities should be proved up to the hilt when they take place so that after the war, there may be no question as to their verification.'[37] While

SHAEF insisted on controlling the investigation, the question arose as to who would supply the staff. Barker proposed to SHAEF's chief of staff, Bedell Smith, that a special investigating team be formed.[38] Once again, Barker was appointed overall head of the court, and another American officer, Colonel Paul Tombaugh, was named president. Lieutenant-Colonel J.H. Boraston, a barrister and former military secretary to Field Marshal Douglas Haig, represented Britain. Although the inquiry was of prime concern to Canadians, SHAEF was determined that the process would be objective and not beholden to any one army. Canadian participation would be limited to two officers, Captain J.R. Gauthier and another officer fresh from the Normandy fighting, Lieutenant-Colonel Bruce Macdonald.

In group photographs of military units, Macdonald's out-thrust jaw and wire-rimmed glasses make him particularly conspicuous. His tenacious character would eventually justify his selection to sit on the Permanent Court of Inquiry. Born in Nova Scotia in 1902, he grew up in Alberta and did post-graduate studies in law at Harvard. He had practised law in Windsor, Ontario, since 1927. An avid militiaman since 1929, Macdonald had volunteered for active service at the outbreak of the war. He missed the Dieppe raid, where most his regiment, the Essex Scottish, were killed or captured. Macdonald helped rebuild the regiment and led it into Normandy in July 1944. In their first action, his troops were held in reserve in an assault on the Verrières Ridge when the 1st SS Panzer Division broke the Canadian front. Looking down on the Essex Scottish, the panzers poured fire on their position. On the following morning the panzers exploited their success and again the weight of their assault fell on the Essex Scots. The regiment was soundly whipped and had to be withdrawn.[39] Macdonald was fired and, despite his protests that he had conducted the fight as well as his resources allowed, he seemed doomed to return to Canada in ignominy. However, his dismissal coincided with Canadian determination to take part in SHAEF's war crimes investigations, and his legal experience and five years' army service made him an ideal representative for the court of inquiry. Given his circumstances, he needed the assignment almost as badly as the Canadian authorities needed him.[40]

The court received formal orders from Eisenhower on 21 August and assembled at the end of the month near Granville, France. While indelibly American in orientation, the special inquiries branch of SHAEF did its best to operate as an inter-Allied body. The members appreciated American efficiency in supplying transport, food, and lodging, but they also recalled being treated as part of one unit drawn together for the purpose of identifying war criminals.[41] It was left to a Canadian, John Page, to run the court's day-to-day administration and arrange for the small army of pathologists, interpreters, drivers, and provost marshals who were essential to the investigation. Remembered by one former colleague as 'a first rate staff officer, with a little of the school master about him,' Page saw little need for military formalities among this fraternity of capable staff officers.

By September, the special inquiries branch was operating out of the Grandes Écuries at Versailles. The building, formerly the stable for Louis XIV's *chevaux de main*, accommodated the war crimes staff, which was itself only a small part of the vast SHAEF administration. Macdonald made it a bit more Canadian. On a trip to London he recruited a French translator, Lieutenant Raymond Robichaud, an RCMP constable, Sergeant Prevost, and another Canadian officer, Lieutenant-Colonel J.H. Mothersill. Eventually, the court would expand its staff to include French and Belgian officers.

Initial reports were coming into the court from the armies in the fields; however, these reports were sketchy and teams were dispatched to talk with local citizens and get statements. Raymond Robichaud later recalled talking with gendarmerie, who during the occupation had usually kept a discreet watch on the local Gestapo. 'Going about from witness to witness I would take down their statements, read them back to them and have them sign. Invariably too, I would, with them, visit the scene of the crime.' Once a report was received in Versailles, senior officers would decide whether it was worthwhile to assemble a court of inquiry to take sworn statements. If it was decided to do so, then a formal court would be convened at the local *mairie* or schoolhouse to interrogate everyone who was familiar with the allegations. The main purpose was to preserve evidence, and the administrative instructions to 21st Army Group investigators conceded that 'it is not necessary that the evidence obtained be strictly admissible in English courts.' Any statements likely to assist the investigations were welcome.[42]

One of the first incidents brought to the court's attention was the 1940 massacre of eighty British soldiers at Wormhout, France. The French police had carefully kept records of the incident which they now released to the Allies.[43] One of the Waffen SS officers implicated in this report, Wilhelm Mohnke, would later be a prominent figure in the atrocities committed against the Canadians. However, for the autumn of 1944, the investigations focused on the 12th SS and the Canadians.

Of the many incidents being reported to the court, three stood out. One of the first cases dealt with the discovery by a chaplain and a graves-registration unit on 3 July of a suspicious mound at Le Mesnil-Patry containing the bodies of several Canadian dead. On the advice of a legal officer, the mound was left intact for investigation. As there were no witnesses to what had occurred, the pathological evidence was crucial. Six of the seven bodies exhumed from the mound had died from small-calibre bullet wounds to the head. Even with this limited evidence, the court concluded that, because of the nature of the wounds and the location of the bodies a half-kilometre from the fighting, the men had been murdered after capture.[44] This was only the beginning of the court's inquiries. On 8 September Macdonald described his work to his wife Norma: 'We have been busy all week trying to establish whether atrocities occurred and it certainly looks as if they did. We have had three full sessions of the Court and were busy the rest of the time preparing and going over typed copies of the evidence.'[45]

As the representative of one of the smaller Allied armies, Macdonald might have been expected to keep discreetly in the background. While he got along well with the American officers, he did have some 'terrific arguments' with his British counterpart, Lieutenant-Colonel Boraston. Boraston, as a barrister of the Chancery Court and the author of several legal texts, may have considered himself the legal light of the court. John Page noticed the difference in approach between the two men. Boraston was a stickler for form, while Macdonald had a more freewheeling 'let's get the evidence' approach.[46] By November, Macdonald had established himself as a presence; he wrote to his wife that 'after three complete defeats on all points my Oxford trained British colleague [Boraston] now has lost most of his superior manners and seeks my opinion first, before he expresses his own views.'[47] In addition to the Le Mesnil-Patry graves case, the court reported on the shooting of the three soldiers on 11 June. They went over the already familiar story of Sergeant Ernie Payne, who described how the guard had opened fire on the three men as they were being marched away.[48] At the time, this incident had created a sensation in Canada. Now, it was of a piece with many other incidents.

Most of the court's time was spent in resolving what had occurred in Authie and Buron on the savage night of 7 June. For this investigation, the Americans stayed in the background and interrogations were conducted by Boraston or Macdonald. Together with their staff, they travelled to the towns on 30 August to interview civilians. For the first time, escaped Canadian prisoners were brought back to the site to identify where atrocities had occurred. Throughout September and October, full pathological reports were received on dozens of suspected victims. As the Allied armies ranged across Europe the court travelled to the Netherlands, where on 17–18 October it examined British officers who had discovered Canadian graves in the area. A French civilian in Authie testified that, after the town had been retaken, SS men had gathered around a wounded Canadian in the town square. 'About 5 or 6 of them pierced this wounded man with bayonet thrusts. Then, having scoffed at him for some minutes, they finished him off with light machine gun and revolver fire.'[49] Another civilian, Clément Faucon, saw wounded Canadians shot dead as the Germans regained the town.[50]

One entire group of Canadian prisoners had been summarily executed. The witness to the atrocity, Lance Corporal W.L. Mackay, had been shot in the face during the fighting and had passed out. He regained consciousness to see a comrade trying to surrender: 'He just got up on one hand and his knees when a Jerry stepped on the back of his neck and shoved him hard to the ground ... I think it broke his neck ... [his] commando knife was strapped to the side of his trouser leg. The German took the knife and stuck it into [his] body 3 times and left it there sticking into the body.'[51] Mackay was so covered in blood that he was ignored by the killer until he was taken under guard. As he was led down a street he saw eight prisoners, without helmets or rifles, lined up by the side of the road. Without warning, the guards fired on them. Mackay's guard, perhaps to spare his life, had pushed him into a doorway where he avoided the slaughter but had a clear view of the execution. The bodies were deliberately dragged into the street to be destroyed by tank and truck traffic. Major John D. Learment recalled that, after his group of prisoners was marched to Buron, they were lined up against a wall. The guards moved back in preparation to fire when 'a German soldier, who I took to be an NCO of some description, arrived on the scene and from his actions I judged he prevented the shootings.'[52] Some Germans, it appeared, were trying to stop the wholesale slaughter of the captives.

Eventually, the court heard extensive testimony from Lance Sergeant Stanley Dudka. An exceptionally durable survivor, Dudka escaped and hid out with French civilians until his recapture. Eventually, he was sent to Stalag 221 near Rennes. Shortly thereafter the prisoners were sent farther east where, during an air raid, Dudka escaped again. With the assistance of the French underground, he returned to Allied lines and by the last week of August was back with the North Novas. He told his colonel, D.F. Forbes, what had occurred on 7 June and Forbes in turn contacted SHAEF. After learning of the availability of a survivor of the Authie battle, Macdonald immediately requested that Dudka go to Paris for interrogation. There, Dudka described how his platoon had been driven out of Authie and fallen back to Buron where they had been captured. One prisoner in his group was found to be in possession of a grenade (the prisoners had not been searched nor told to give up weapons) and was shot on the spot. He did not die outright. Dudka described how the guard 'would go over and kick M. and when his nerves moved he would laugh and be right happy.' Eventually, the guard finished him off.[53] As they were marched away, another prisoner was injured by shellfire. He could not keep up, and so the guard simply shot him and left the body on the road. As the prisoners passed through Authie, Dudka saw 'seven of our men from our company lined up in the street. Every one of them was shot through the head.'[54] As they marched to Caen, Dudka also related how a German truck had deliberately swerved into the prisoners, killing two of them. Occasionally, the guards berated the Canadians for the Allied bombing campaign. 'There was one fellow who said it in English. He said that we were bombing their wives and mothers back home.' As was later discovered, the bombing campaign may have been the justification for scores of executions. The identification of the bodies and the determination of the cause of death were especially difficult because, as French civilians reported, the SS had deliberately tried to destroy the corpses. Despite civilian attempts to retrieve the bodies for burial, they were dragged into the roadway to be pulverized by traffic. Eventually, the corpses were so badly crushed that most were unrecognizable as human remains.[55]

In its report to SHAEF, the court concluded that in the area of Authie-Buron at least twenty-eight Canadian prisoners had been murdered in thirteen separate incidents, and that these incidents 'were of such common occurrence in the enemy unit concerned as to suggest the existence of an order directing, or approval authorized by higher enemy formation for such execution of prisoners.'[56] While the solid fact of atrocities was beyond question, exactly who was the higher authority ordering them remained unknown. As the court concluded, the key could be provided only by captured Germans.

During their 1944 investigations, the court came across one minute piece of evidence that was almost passed by. On 27 September, as the members toured Authie with Lance Sergeant Dudka, they received a message that a cache of identification papers belonging to Canadian soldiers had been found elsewhere. Lieutenant Robichaud went with a young Frenchman, Jean-Marie Vico, to a pit where a pile of papers, insignia, and equipment of Canadian soldiers had been hidden.[57] The pit was located at the Ancienne Abbaye d'Ardenne, the former HQ of the 25th Panzer Grenadier Regiment.[58]

The court reconvened in London at the end of November under Boraston's leadership to hear from more Canadians who had escaped from the 12th SS. One incident was particularly vivid. A Winnipeg rifleman, W.R. Lebar, had been captured on 8 June and was being led away for interrogation when he stopped with his guard by a roadside. Suddenly, he saw about seventeen to twenty prisoners run from the woods into a field. When the prisoners were formed up, the guards fired on them with machine-guns. As Lebar recounted, the victims 'just collapsed, you could hear them screaming.'[59] At least two prisoners saw what was about to happen and ran for their lives. Lebar was hurried from the scene although later on he met two of the survivors. Lieutenant D.A. James also met a survivor, Corporal McLean, in a Caen hospital and McLean related the incident much as Lebar had described it.

While this eyewitness evidence was persuasive, no bodies were recovered and the court was 'unable to say with finality that the facts as alleged are true, until bodies have been found.'[60] There were so many different stories that at times it must have seemed impossible to recreate what had happened. Were these isolated incidents, the work of a few sadistic officers or NCOs? Or were they consistent with a general plan, devised by senior officers, to exterminate Allied prisoners? Everything now hinged on getting more and better information from returning Canadians and from captured Germans. Yet all the evidence gathered so far seemed to point inevitably to one German formation, the 12th SS Panzer Division 'Hitler Youth.'

2

Murder Division

Self-sacrifice, comradeship, and an intense devotion to Nazi ideology were the foundations of the Hitler Youth movement. Its main purpose was to 'mobilize and to discipline an entire generation of German youth in the spirit of National Socialism; to loosen their ties to the Church, the family and to the past; to inculcate the ideal that the State was everything and the individual nothing.'[1] In the pre-war years, the movement offered a popular athletic, patriotic, and social forum for young people, but during the war it became increasingly militaristic as youths trained for combat and acted as auxiliaries for the regular army. The Waffen SS began to look hungrily at this potential source of recruits.

Under Heinrich Himmler, the SS (Schutzstaffel) had become a pervasive branch of government dedicated to racial purity, police control of local affairs, and Nazi control of the state. The Waffen SS, the armed elite of this organization, provided an army at the personal disposal of the Nazi party. The 1st SS Division, Leibstandarte SS Adolf Hitler, had its origins in Hitler's desire for a household guard and was expanded thereafter with men who met Himmler's rigid racial and physical standards.[2] While in the first years of the conflict the Waffen SS constituted only a small fraction of Germany's armed forces, by the end of the war 40 SS divisions numbering 900,000 men constituted one tenth of the field army. Unlike the regular army, the Waffen SS welcomed officers from the lower social ranks and to that extent was an egalitarian organization in which officers and men competed in endless soccer, boxing, and track-and-field competitions.

Also, unlike comparable army units, the Waffen SS stressed *Härte* (harshness or severity) in its training. Because SS men were fighting for the nation and the race, they were expected to go to ruthless extremes to achieve victory.[3] The SS were intended to act as shock troops, their purpose being not to defend positions but to attack and overwhelm the enemy.[4] Such attitudes made the SS the spearheads for offensives, and by 1943 these tough divisions had been bled white.

Desperate for manpower, Himmler seized the idea of transferring Hitler Youth directly into a separate SS division. In February 1943 Hitler approved the idea and authorized the recruitment of seventeen- and eighteen-year-olds into the 12th SS division. Officers and NCOs would be transferred from the 1st SS and a father-son relationship established between the two divisions. Training for the 12th SS was unique. Recruits arriving at the HQ at Beverloo, Belgium, were spared the endless drill and route marches of the regular army. Instead, the young soldiers were conditioned by sports and practised real battle situations with live ammunition. While toughening and dangerous, this regime avoided the drudgery that is the usual lot of young soldiers. Recruits responded to the training by showing an eagerness to learn, a fascination with their weapons, and pride in their distinctive camouflage uniforms.[5]

The core of the 12th SS was its two Panzer Grenadier Regiments (PGRs), and the personnel records of the two regimental commanders were almost identical. Wilhelm Mohnke, the commanding officer of the 26th PGR, had been a clerk before joining the 1st SS in 1933. Fighting in Poland, France, and the Balkans, he had been wounded and decorated repeatedly. A brave, hard man, Mohnke had little sympathy for his young troops. Unpopular among them, he was described as 'harsh and austere in appearance ... a man of violent emotions, distant and even brutal.'[6] In contrast to Mohnke, at least in popularity, was the commanding officer of the 25th PGR, Kurt Meyer. Meyer was born in 1910 and had grown up with a fascination for the military. But, owing to its strict size requirements, he was unable to join the post-Versailles German army. Without any vent for his powerful ambitions, Meyer, a strident nationalist, joined the Hitler Youth and become a street brawler with Communists. By the late 1920s he had joined both the police and the SS. Unquestioning in his obedience to Nazi ideology, Meyer fitted into the mould of a perfect SS man.

Once he was transferred to the 1st SS, Meyer's drive and ability came to the forefront. Wounded and decorated in Poland, he led his troops into the Netherlands where he acquired the nickname 'Schneller-Meyer' for his ability to overwhelm the enemy rapidly. In battle, Meyer was always a man on the go, seeing for himself what was going on at the front and directing the battle from there. During the invasion of Greece in 1941, Meyer's battalion became bogged down in a mountain pass. Personally taking over an assault group, Meyer headed the attack until machine-gun fire pinned his men down. Sizing up the situation, Meyer pulled out a hand grenade and threw it just behind the last of his troops. The men got the message and went on to overwhelm the stubborn Greeks.[7] In the Soviet Union he displayed the same aggressiveness, taking units far behind enemy lines and then fighting his way out again. At the age of thirty-two, his face had appeared on the front of newspapers as one of the Reich's most revered heroes.

This chivalrous image did not match the murderous record the court of inquiry was uncovering. Yet it was questionable whether any real action would be taken. By the beginning of 1945, two standing courts of inquiry, one headed by Boraston and the other by Macdonald, were functioning. Canadians were now taking responsibility for investigating many Allied cases. In June 1945 Robichaud would conduct extensive inquiries into the execution of French SAS (Special Air Service) paratroopers in the Moribhan. The first evidence of a massacre at Malmédy would come from a transcription of tape recordings at the Canadian embassy in Paris.[8] The inspector general's section of the 1st American Army uncovered seventy-two bodies at Malmédy and the SHAEF court examined American survivors in England. Boraston, Macdonald, and an American officer, Lieutenant-Colonel John Voorhees, heard how on the morning of 17 December 1944 a group of about 100 U.S. prisoners had been machine-gunned by their Waffen SS guards. Once again, the court could reconstruct what had happened but found it almost impossible to ascribe responsibility.[9] The American public was outraged by the massacre and demanded prompt justice. Moreover, the Americans were determined to make Malmédy a priority. 'Now the US War Department however has decided to take over the whole subject of War Crimes through their own Judge Advocate's General Dept. in each army,' Macdonald observed, adding that 'we will be out of a job in a couple of months.'[10]

Among the unfinished business at SHAEF was the examination of the first SS prisoners. In January 1945 Boraston interrogated Friederich Torbanisch, a reluctant SS man who had deserted from the 12th SS and joined the Belgian resistance. He described a 'secret order' given to the troops in April 1944 while they were drawn up in a tight square in the town of Montague, Belgium. A sergeant-major, or *Speiss*, read out a series of orders and one in particular caught the interrogator's attention: 'SS troops shall take no prisoners. Prisoners are to be executed after interrogation.'[11] After his desertion, Torbanisch had notified his Belgian comrades of this order.

Another SS man confirmed that they were told that the Allies were not taking German prisoners. He also reported that, within the German army, the 12th SS had the reputation of being a 'Murder Division' and that 'during the invasion period they had committed atrocities.'[12] Other prisoners gave a glimpse into the SS mindset. One company commander told his men that 'in this sector the enemy would take or was not taking any prisoners.' This was intended to discourage German troops from surrendering and to force them to fight to the end. The soldiers who heard their commander's admonition talked among themselves as they left the parade square and many felt, with some justification, that if the Allies did not take prisoners, then neither would they.[13] These thoughts reflected the subculture within the Waffen SS that existed apart from international conventions. If the enemy was ruthless, the obvious response from the SS was even greater ruthlessness; more violence, more *Härte*, would ensure victory.[14] Even regular German troops seemed shocked by SS brutality. CMHQ received a report in September 1944 from a German prisoner who had seen five Allied prisoners, including two Canadians, shot at Les Hogues by guards from the 1st SS. The prisoners' crime had been their slow response to orders in German.[15]

Another recent prisoner described an incident at a training course in early 1944 where some 'SS Sheiks' had mingled with Wehrmacht officers. During an evening's relaxation, one of the SS men had described with great relish how he had taken a reconnaissance company into the Russian village of Jefremovka. When he was forced to pull out, he wiped out the entire town, men, women, and children. 'If it were not for the Supreme Command,' the officer bragged, these tactics would surely have brought victory. The officer was Kurt Meyer.[16]

The first real breakthrough for the investigators in identifying a war criminal came from the affidavit of a Polish conscript, Withold Stangenberg. The Pole had been at the HQ of the 26th PGR on 11 June when he saw three prisoners brought before the regimental commander, Mohnke. Along with four other soldiers, Stangenberg witnessed the proceedings. 'The interrogation lasted about 15–20 minutes and Mohnke shouted and gesticulated the whole time.' Taken away by military police, the prisoners were led about 27 metres away from the HQ and all identity discs and cards were removed from them. They were led to the edge of a bomb crater and shot; their bodies were dumped into the bottom of the crater. Mohnke and his officers had watched the entire proceedings. Stangenberg described the area in detail and even described his comrades' reactions. As they realized the prisoners were about to be shot, one turned away, unable to watch. Two others were pleased and said, 'the Tommies are no good anyway.' Stangenberg asked those who had approved, 'When we are taken prisoner, should we expect the same treatment?'[17] In the summer of 1945, Stangenberg travelled with the court to the site of the former regimental HQ and the bodies were found at the bottom of the crater exactly as he had described. This was reliable proof that a senior Waffen SS officer, Wilhelm Mohnke, had personally ordered and supervised the execution of Canadian prisoners. Gratifying as this was, Mohnke had disappeared but was thought to be in Soviet hands.

The other commander, Kurt Meyer, was readily available. On D-Day, while the 3rd Canadian Infantry Division had moved south from the beaches, the 12th SS was held south of Caen in the panzer reserve. A cautious High Command refused to release the reserve until late on 6 June. By midnight, Meyer's 25th PGR was in contact with the remains of General Wilhelm Richter's 716th Infantry Division. Richter explained how his division had been annihilated by the invasion forces. With boundless enthusiasm, Meyer assured him that the 'little fishes' would be thrown back into the sea. Meyer drove northwest of Caen and selected the Abbaye Ardenne as a regimental command post. The Abbaye's high turrets provided a fine observation post for the coming battle. While his 25th PGR moved into position, Mohnke's 26th PGR, which was to cover the left, was still far away. From the tower, Meyer could see the tanks of the 9th Canadian Infantry Brigade passing across his front and headed for the vital Carpiquet airport. Meyer determined to strike. His third battalion, supported by tanks from the 12th Panzer SS Regiment, would attack the exposed Canadian flanks. It was these grenadiers who smashed into the North Novas and Sherbrooke Fusilliers on the afternoon of 7 June, and drove them back from Authie and Buron. However, an artillery barrage halted the counter-attack. The official Canadian history of the battle concedes that the German attack had been well coordinated, but the little fish were not about to be thrown into the sea.

After the death of division commander Fritz Witt on 16 June, Meyer became the commanding officer of the 12th SS and the youngest division commander in the German army. His men were the rock that hindered the Allies from taking Caen in the early fighting. Finally forced back from Caen, the 12th SS faced three Canadian and eventually three British divisions in a bid to keep the Falaise Gap open to cover the German army's retreat.[18] At one point, Meyer had personally gone to the front to confront troops of the 89th division who had broken under the Canadian assault. He rallied the men, calmly lit a cigar and asked them whether they were going to force him to fight the Canadians single-handed. Sheepishly, the men re-formed and moved back to the front. Meyer had become, in the words of his corps commander, 'the soul of fanatical resistance.'[19] Escaping with the remnants of his division, he came close to being lynched by Belgian partisans before he was captured by Americans in September. When located by military intelligence, Meyer was in a prisoners' compound for regular soldiers and was not wearing any rank badges. However, it was apparent from the deference paid to him by other prisoners that he was a senior officer. He was quickly removed and his identity established.

Given the importance of this interrogation, Major-General Barker himself decided to question Meyer on 25 March 1945. A disappointed Macdonald confided to his wife that 'I will not have the opportunity to put the Hun over the jumps myself. However I have been busy preparing the case and the questions etc. for him.'[20] In the end, Macdonald ended up conducting substantially all of the examination. Assisting him was a remarkable British officer, Lieutenant-Colonel A.P. Scotland. Able to speak idiomatic German, Scotland had spent years interrogating German soldiers and was familiar with all aspects of the German army.[21]

At the beginning, there appeared to be little reason to press Meyer for he seemed honest and forthright. He went through his military career and his command of the 25th PGR. When Macdonald pointed out that at the time of his capture he was wearing ordinary army insignia, Meyer denied trying to hide his identity, saying, 'Many of my friends have fallen and I am not ashamed to wear those badges.'[22] However, when the questions turned to the treatment of prisoners, Macdonald found the answers increasingly suspect. Meyer denied that Russian prisoners were shot on the Eastern Front, even when Macdonald confronted him with the German High Command's admission that this was so. Meyer claimed to have ordered his troops to send prisoners back for interrogation as soon as possible. It was a serious breach of discipline to shoot prisoners, he noted, and 'if discipline is abandoned then a soldier is useless.'[23]

As a measure of how international law operates in wartime, German army legal officers had received by way of Switzerland the Canadian government's protest concerning the murder of prisoners. They, in turn, had forwarded the enquiry to all front-line commanders. All generals responded in the negative; Berlin accepted this at face value, and in

December 1944 Germany advised the Swiss that the accusations were groundless, a mere 'defamation of the Wehrmacht.'[24] In his interrogation, Meyer recalled receiving this enquiry and responded that he had 'never heard of it [atrocities] in any case.'[25]

Near the end of the first day, Macdonald confronted Meyer with the charge that, between 6 and 17 June 1944, in 30 separate incidents, his division had murdered 106 Allied prisoners, most of them Canadians. Meyer professed bewilderment and replied: 'I can only say that I am deeply shocked by this and I would like to add that in July we captured a whole Canadian staff, including the commander and the adjutant, and I spoke to them in quite a friendly way and they were sent back by my troops.'[26] Meyer added that he had one of his own men shot for the rape of a French girl. If there were atrocities, this was the first he had heard of it. A sceptical Macdonald noted in the margin of his transcript 'untrue.' Lieutenant-Colonel Scotland was impatient with Macdonald's gentlemanly conduct of the examination, and he decided to join in with some rapid-fire questions in German. Shouting at Meyer, Scotland demanded immediate answers. 'Come on Meyer, let's hear it and no nonsense.' During his interrogations, Scotland had personally taken some prisoners to mock executions in order to extract information; on another occasion he had used the 'gestapo stance' by stripping a prisoner half naked and making him talk while kneeling.[27] In this instance, Scotland urged the court simply to take Meyer back to France where he could be summarily court- martialled.[28]

On the following day, Macdonald, in his plodding, non-threatening way, went through the accusations against the 12th SS. The secret order to kill prisoners was, according to Meyer, a mere 'piece of folly' that no officer under his command would even think of issuing, and 'anyway, secret orders are never read out to the whole troops.' Meyer also continued to deny any knowledge of atrocities. He felt it impossible that Karl Heinz Milius, the commanding officer of the 3rd battalion that had attacked Authie, had given any orders to kill prisoners. While Milius was lacking in experience, Meyer refused to believe that he issued any such orders. When confronted with growing proof of war crimes, Meyer went on the defensive: 'From my division? In what sector can these things have taken place? I find it impossible to believe.' He followed this with another disclaimer of great significance: 'I can only say that I gave no orders in connection with any such thing and have never heard anything of these atrocities, nor has any official report been made to me about them.'[29] Next to this answer, Macdonald noted, 'nice acting.'

Meyer was also questioned on any knowledge he might have of Canadian war crimes against German troops. 'There were many cases in which [German] prisoners came back,' Meyer answered, 'and the fact that they came back alive was the best proof that there was no fooling of this sort.'[30] However, he did recall finding a number of dead German troops from another division whose position suggested that they might have been killed after capture. Macdonald followed up on this report, but Meyer had few other details.

At the end of the examination, the court returned to Versailles to complete its supplementary report to SHAEF. Macdonald was satisfied that 'I had the complete conduct of the examination in London of the SS General. I had him on the grill for 2 days.'[31] It was his hope that the report would be finished before he was transferred out of war crimes to the military administration of occupied Germany.

The court's supplementary report of March 1945, canvassed all information on the 12th SS. This was no ordinary division, it concluded, but one of 'distinctive uniforms, ranks and insignia and not only felt themselves to be better soldiers than those of the Wehrmacht, but made that feeling very evident to all.'[32] Going through the division's Normandy battles one by one, the court listed the atrocities. At Authie-Buron there were 12 proven incidents in which 27 Canadian prisoners had been murdered. At the Château d'Audrieu 19 prisoners had been executed. There were also isolated incidents such as one where 12th SS men shot a wounded American flyer. In total, there were 31 confirmed incidents in which 107 Allied soldiers, almost all of them Canadian, had died. Taken together, these facts led the court to state that 'the conduct of the 12 SS Panzer Division (Hitler Jugend) presented a consistent pattern of brutality and ruthlessness.' Yet there was no direct evidence implicating divisional commanders Witt or Meyer. And, although there was strong circumstantial evidence, there was no corroboration against regimental commanders Mohnke or Milius. But, even without corroborative evidence, the sheer number of cases indicated that 'the conclusion is irresistible that it was understood throughout the Division, if not actually ordered, that a policy of denying quarter or executing prisoners after interrogation was impliedly if not openly approved by the Regimental and Divisional Commanders.'[33] The supplementary report was a vast source of information on war crimes, and it was now up to the respective armies to prosecute.

Even before the report was issued, Macdonald reported privately to General Barker on 7 April. He felt it likely that the senior officers were guilty, but 'at the present time ... the evidence in the opinion of the court is insufficient to ensure a conviction in a court of law against any of them. This is also true as to Meyer, insofar as direct proof is concerned.'[34] The most that could be said against Meyer was that atrocities had been committed by his division and that as commander he was responsible. It was imperative, Macdonald urged, that the German prisoners now becoming available in large numbers be interrogated and the whole story brought forward. The Normandy tragedy was of special concern to Canada for 'it would appear that at least 100 Canadian prisoners in 30 different incidents were killed while prisoners of war, by this Division, while only 3 victims were British and 1 American.' If interrogations were not conducted soon by trained personnel, 'the significance of available evidence might not be appreciated, and the whole effort prove a waste of time.'

The supplementary report was submitted to SHAEF on 19 April and the various members prepared for other duties. By then, Barker and Page had gone to Halle, Germany, to negotiate the release of Allied troops held by the Russians. The court was anticipating being moved to Frankfurt and a HQ had already been selected in the former I.G. Farben factory. However, before the move, the court was disbanded. After all this effort, nothing had been proven against any individual; no evidence strong enough to stand up in a court had been uncovered.

By the end of April 1945, the Queen's Own Rifles of Canada had fought their way to the north German town of Aurich, and on 8 May Germany surrendered to the Allied Forces. A Canadian officer, Major H.A. Hanson, had been attached to the Canadian echelon of 21st Army Group and he was not impressed with British willingness to pursue Canadian war crimes. There was a proposal to set up a British court of inquiry with a Canadian representative. It was never implemented.[35] For their part, the British considered the SHAEF courts inefficient and instead sent out teams of investigators to gather information. At a meeting on 21 April, a new section was set up at 21st Army Group to examine war crimes and Hanson was posted Canadian liaison officer. He was given four cases dealing with Canadians, but war crimes was only one aspect of his duties. The Canadians, the prime victims of the 12th SS, made no plans to continue the investigations.

It took the intervention of the Americans, through Major-General Barker, to keep Canadian war crimes investigations alive. Near the middle of April, Barker phoned CMHQ and told them that it was vital to keep Macdonald working on the 12th SS files.[36] SHAEF formally requested the Canadian army to continue the case 'as the prosecution of this case will presumably rest with the Canadian authorities.' It suggested that CMHQ 'assume responsibility for the completion of all necessary further investigation.'[37] Macdonald's transfer to I Corps was cancelled.

Three days after the release of the court of inquiry's supplementary report, a young Polish conscript in the 12th SS asked to talk with his jailers at the American POW camp at Chartres, France. As were all Allied nationals, the Poles were kept apart from German prisoners. Jan Jesionek had served with the 15th reconnaissance company of the 25th PGR and he voluntarily approached the Americans to make a statement. With no love lost for his former commanders, Jesionek told Sergeant Sigmund Stern of events he had witnessed at the Abbaye Ardenne on 8 June 1944:

In the morning of June 18 1944, I escorted 7 (seven) English soldiers which were taken prisoners by the 15th Reconnaissance Co. of the 25th Rgt. SS–Div. 'Hitlerjugend' back to our CP. CP was located in the vicinity of Bretteville near Caen.

As I reported the above prisoners to the Regimental Commander he hollered at me and asked me: 'Why do you bring prisoners to the rear, those murderers only eat off our rations.' Immediately after he gave the order to the Executive Officer to have the prisoners shot.

I myself received the order to return to my unit. Because there was a waterpump in the yard, I washed up before I left. As I was standing near the waterpump I saw the following:

An Unteroffizier of the SS 'Hitlerjugend' whose name is not known to me, went into a barn, where the prisoners were kept then. He took away all papers from the prisoners there.

After that the prisoners were sent, one by one, through an opening which is leading to a park. Every time a prisoner passed that opening, he was shot from behind.

When the shooting was over I convinced myself of the cruelties, which were committed on those seven prisoners by looking at their dead bodies.

The name of the regimental commander who gave the order was Standartenfuehrer Meyer – also called 'Panzermeyer.'[38]

Stern had difficulty understanding Jesionek's German, and he had called in another German prisoner to write down the statement in German. After the words were transcribed, Stern translated them into English. The attempt was rough indeed, since Stern wrote down 18 June instead of 8 June as Jesionek had stated. There were numerous other inconsistencies between the German version and Stern's English copy. Jesionek was not given the chance to review the statement and make corrections. To further confuse matters, mid-way through his statement, Jesionek recalled that another American sergeant had entered the room, noticed Jesionek's SS flashes, and commented that all SS men were going to hang.[39]

While confused, and possibly tainted, Jan Jesionek's story was an explosive piece of evidence, the first direct testimony incriminating a high SS general. Yet it seemed likely that this affidavit was doomed to be lost among the vast records of the American army. No one took any particular note of it at Chartres, and, in any case, Jesionek was due to be transferred to the Polish army in Italy.

By chance, Boraston and Macdonald were in Chartres a few days after Jesionek's interrogation to interview other prisoners on an unrelated incident. Stern told them of Jesionek's story and his sketch of the Abbaye. While both officers were intrigued, Jesionek was no longer available for on that same day he had been dispatched to the Polish camp at Chalons. Fortunately, he was pulled from the transfer. If he had disappeared into the mass of troops moving about Europe, the single most important actor in the coming drama might have been lost. On 28 May Jesionek was brought to Paris to be interrogated. At first suspicious of the Polish SS man, Macdonald felt that he might have made up the story for his own purposes. However, Macdonald became convinced during the intense examination that Jesionek was telling the truth and, further, that he was an intelligent witness with a superb recall of places and events.

Jesionek was taken back to the Normandy battlefield and located the Abbaye Ardenne without difficulty. When he saw the Abbaye towers, Jesionek excitedly directed the driver to go in that direction. The ancient abbey consisted of a chapel that had been unused for centuries but still possessed high towers overlooking the countryside. Around the chapel were several stone buildings surrounded by a wall. Farmers used the buildings for residences or for storage of equipment. Jesionek took the investigators to the chapel where, on 8 June, he had seen Meyer discuss the prisoners. He guided them to the stable where the seven Canadians were held and showed them the entrance to the park where the prisoners were shot. As the Canadian officers went over the grounds of the park, they discovered that the earth had recently been disturbed. To their surprise, the French residents informed them that only a few weeks previously they had discovered part of a body protruding from the earth. They had notified Canadian authorities, who located eighteen bodies in five different graves. Most strangely for a battlefield situation, the graves had been concealed by making them level and covering them with sod. Macdonald and company next went to the local graves-registration unit where they ordered the bodies exhumed for examination. All had been reported as missing on 7–8 June 1944, fully a month before any fighting occurred near the Abbaye. All had died of head wounds, most from a single shot to the base of the skull.[40] Jesionek's story and the concealed graves with their harvest of victims were all direct evidence implicating one man, Kurt Meyer.

Even before finding this critical evidence, Macdonald had been charged with a sense of purpose and determined to keep a Canadian war crimes investigation apparatus alive. In that quest, he had an ally at CMHQ in the deputy adjutant general, Brigadier B. Matthews, who summoned him to London on 24 April to discuss how Canadian interests could be protected. In a lengthy memo to Matthews dated 8 May, Macdonald outlined how that might be done. The Judge Advocate General's Department at CMHQ should create a separate war crimes investigation unit. This unit, in coordination with SHAEF, 21st Army Group, and the UNWCC, would exchange information on cases of concern to Canada. Specifically, 'it is agreed that the case against the 12 SS Div (HJ) will be so regarded as a Canadian responsibility.'[41] Investigations would parallel the British system of teams of pathologists, interpreters, and examiners gathering evidence. If at the end of an examination a trial was warranted, a recommendation would go to the UNWCC. If this recommendation was approved, the case would be returned to the army's Judge Advocate General's Department (JAG) for prosecution.

In preparing this outline, Macdonald had already met with his British counterparts, including Brigadier H. Shapcott of the Judge Advocate General's Department and the treasury solicitor, Sir Thomas Barnes. On 12 May he took his case directly to Canada's high commissioner in London, Vincent Massey. Massey had already met on 24 April with Macdonald, Colonel W. Anglin, and other service heads and appreciated the military view that a 'peripatetic court ... might meet Canadian needs.'[42] Massey approved Macdonald's plan and CMHQ officially created the No. 1 Canadian War Crimes Investigation Unit (CWCIU) on 4 June 1945. The unit was instructed to undertake the investigation of all cases 'reported against Canadian nationals and members of Canadian Armed Forces and to prepare cases for trial in which sufficient evidence is available.'[43] Macdonald became the new unit's commanding officer, and he had at his command two other officers and two other ranks. But investigation without prosecution would be a futile effort, and so Macdonald and Massey met in early

June with British officials to map out a system for trials. The British pressed them to put Meyer on trial 'as a means of establishing [a] general case against major war criminals.'[44] This expeditious procedure appealed to Macdonald, who was gaining more confidence in the case against Meyer. In order to establish a framework for the proceedings, External Affairs asked the high commissioner's office to 'ascertain informally' from United Kingdom officials the authority for the British royal warrant for war crimes trials.[45] The response may have surprised the Canadians. There was no statute or order-in-council, nothing but the king's command. The British warrant had been approved under the royal prerogative and provided that it was the king's 'will and pleasure' that war criminals be prosecuted by his forces.[46] This may have satisfied the British, but it offended Canadian notions of responsible government. Eventually, an order-in-council and a statute would be the legal foundation for the Canadian war crimes prosecutions.[47]

Arrangements were made for Macdonald to return to Canada and bring his proposals directly to Ottawa. Frustrated by the slow pace of the proceedings, Macdonald confided to his wife that the creation of the No. 1 CWCIU had been 'a child born of much anguish ... we are wasting so much time and losing the benefit of all the preparation that I did at SHAEF.'[48] Unbeknown to him, several more hurdles remained before war crimes prosecutions would become a reality.

3

Indifference to the
'War Crimes Business'

Bureaucracies, even in time of conflict, proceed at a stately pace, and the arrangements for war crimes prosecutions were no exception to this rule. After the United States and Britain had created the United Nations War Crimes Commission in November 1942, Canada was asked to participate. It declined. The diplomatic view, expressed by External Affairs officer Marcel Cadieux in April 1943, was that because Canada was far removed from the conflict it should content itself with looking after its nationals and prisoners of war.[1] War crimes investigations could be useful, he suggested, as a 'weapon of political warfare' to rally the people against the enemy. Cadieux had no objection in theory to a Canadian representative on the UNWCC but he felt that body was unlikely to be effective. While Canada should cooperate with the major powers, he concluded that this issue was of no great moment: 'In summary, it seems that the question of war crimes is not of great importance for Canada. We have a moral interest in seeing that rules of international law are respected and that this question is ably used as a political weapon, but clearly our policy should be one of moderation in both cases.'[2]

Throughout 1943 and 1944, Ottawa carried moderation to an extreme. Prime Minister King's one action was to appoint the MP for Parry Sound, Arthur G. Slaght, as an honourary consul charged with examining crimes against Canadian servicemen and nationals.[3] Slaght, an outstanding criminal defence lawyer and a pillar of the Liberal Party in Ontario, had no reputation or expertise in international affairs. This did not bother the government. As the legal adviser of External Affairs noted at the time of Slaght's appointment, 'Canadian contact with the War Crimes problem will necessarily be slight.'[4] To assist Slaght, an advisory committee, the Canadian War Crimes Advisory Committee (CWCAC), was created. An interdepartmental body based in Ottawa. CWCAC had armed-forces representation from the Judge Advocate General's Department, a Justice Department official, and perhaps the key figure in the committee, John Read, the legal counsel of External Affairs. Read, a former law dean at Dalhousie Law School, exerted considerable influence in External Affairs and beyond to the Prime Minister's Office. A junior member of the committee, Lieutenant-Commander R.E. Curran, was responsible for interviewing repatriated servicemen in order to preserve and assemble evidence.

At a December 1943 meeting, CWCAC established its intention to limit its investigations to acts against Canadian servicemen and nationals. Only Justice Department representative Charles Stein 'raised for consideration the question of execution of Jews in Germany.' The committee was not interested in the question for it 'felt that atrocities against Jews in Germany could not be considered war crimes.' Even with regard to the punishment of crimes committed against Canadians, Slaght was content to wait until 'guidance could be expected from Great Britain and decision as to Canada's procedure could be deferred until Great Britain and the United States had formulated their policy.'[5] Having so limited its function, there was little for CWCAC to do. It is a fair observation that the creation of CWCAC constituted 'a modest attempt to collect evidence for crimes'[6] and little else.

Most of the incidents coming to Curran's file cabinet concerned the Japanese. The exchange ship *Gripsholm* had brought back civilian internees from Asia in December 1943 and they gave reporters horrific stories of rape and murder. One Canadian soldier, who had slipped away from Hong Kong as a civilian, described Japanese troops breaking into a compound intent on bayonetting the wounded and only being prevented by the intervention of a nurse. As well, he had heard of the bayonetting of sixty-three wounded men at St Stephen's College and of the rape and murder of three nurses.[7] The first report of CWCAC included cases such as that of Captain John Hickey, who had died at St Stephen's trying to protect a wounded soldier, and of Rifleman William Sweet, who had lost his arm trying to protect a comrade. A Toronto report described how a Canadian businessman in Singapore had attempted in vain to prevent Japanese troops from raping and murdering his eleven-year-old daughter. Only by falling unconscious on his seven-year-old had he saved her.[8] Curran followed up on this report and established that the older girl, although repeatedly raped, had not died. He also discovered that three French-Canadian missionaries had been brutally murdered at a China mission.[9] However, as far as Europe was concerned, CWCAC found little of interest. Repatriated prisoners from Germany did not report any pattern of mistreatment. A group of former prisoners spoke in Toronto in January 1944 and praised their treatment in the German camps.[10] This resulted in CWCAC concluding in its May 1944 report that 'the number of atrocities involving Canadians is much less than original reports would have led one to expect.'[11]

In January 1944 Sir Cecil Hurst, chairman of the UNWCC, called on Vincent Massey to urge that Canada join the body or at the very least send an observer.[12] By then, some Ottawa officials were disturbed by the fact that, while Australia, New Zealand, and India were full members of the international war crimes organization, Canada's interests were still represented by Britain. It seemed appropriate for a sovereign country, a significant member of the Allied cause, to be a part of the UNWCC: 'If Luxembourg-in-exile could afford to contribute £400 a year, so could Canada.'[13] King was unmoved. Hurst again met with Massey in December 1944 to press his case. For his part, Massey was unimpressed, since he was aware that at one meeting of the UNWCC the United States had been represented by a mere lieutenant.[14] It was not until April 1945 that Canada became associated with the UNWCC and Massey was appointed Canada's representative.

However, Canadian participation was derisory at best. This was partly because of a fixed opinion in Ottawa that the UNWCC would never accomplish anything,[15] and partly because of wider strategic considerations. Since 1943 External Affairs had been dealing with the creation of the Permanent Court of International Justice and had been compelled to agree to Soviet demands that, if the USSR republics could not have standing, then neither would the dominions. The same sensitivity to Soviet concerns led the department to view war crimes as an area in which Canada should remain in the background.[16] Indeed, war crimes were such a low priority in Ottawa that CWCAC secretary, Lieutenant-Commander Curran, was reassigned in December 1944 just as he was about to travel to Europe. Despite several protests, his reassignment was confirmed and CWCAC was deprived of its most informed officer just as war crimes were fast becoming an issue.[17]

External Affair's studied indifference to war crimes may well have originated in the office of John Read. In the summer of 1943, he had advised the under-secretary of state for External Affairs, Norman Robertson, that the UNWCC was bound to fail. Captivated by the past, Read maintained that 'the present plans will have little more success than the "Hang the Kaiser" moves at the end of the last conflict.'[18] Detachment, however, soon began to prejudice any Canadian involvement: the high commissioner's office informed Ottawa on 17 May 1944 that, because Canada was unrepresented on the UNWCC, it was unable to find out what the body was doing. In November 1944 John Page, one of the senior officers working in SHAEF, was astounded to learn that none of the cases he was working on was going to the UNWCC and as a result 'this absence of representation might mean that the perpetrators of crimes against Canadian nationals might go unpunished.'[19] But even in the face of Page's protest, Slaght reported to the prime minister on 8 November 1944 that no practical results were likely to come from the UNWCC and perhaps it was just as well that Canada was not represented.[20] In much the same vein, Read advised Norman Robertson in January 1945 (six months after the widely reported stories of the Normandy massacres) that 'it is now almost certain that the war crimes business will be a fiasco,' and in any event 'it also seems to be certain that the war crimes in which there is a Canadian interest will be insignificant.' According to Read, therefore, it was vital 'to avoid criticism of the Canadian Government for failure to deliver a lot of non-existent war criminals.'[21] This failure of will may be explained by the growth of the Anglo-American partnership, which had greatly diminished Canada's wartime role to the extent that often the United States and the United Kingdom felt no need for Canadian participation.[22] It has been suggested that during the war Canada changed 'from a timid Dominion to a sometimes aggressive and nationalistic middle power.'[23] But as the government's dithering over war crimes policy showed, the timid dominion remained much in evidence on this issue. Canada still did not consider itself a figure on the international stage with independent interests to be protected and promoted.

Even if Canada could not discard the habits of the colonial era, other Allied powers were quick to seize the initiative. At Kharkov, the Soviets tried three German soldiers for killing civilians in mobile gas vans. The three were hanged on 19 December 1943 before British and American journalists.[24] The United States, for its part, created the Central Registry of War Criminals and Security Suspects (CROWCASS) in January 1945 to record the location, identity, and evidence against suspected war criminals. It was time for Canada to take action. At least Massey had been converted to the cause of war crimes, for in a telegram on 8 June 1945 he reported to External Affairs that he had learned from British officials that the 'new war crimes section at CMHQ have now obtained very complete evidence of personal guilt of S.S. Divisional Commander Kurt Meyer, now prisoner in British hands, and case should be ready for trial shortly.' These high British officials had impressed on Massey that 'it would be helpful if this trial could take place as soon as possible as a means of establishing general case against major war criminals.'[25]

Ottawa remained unswayed. Massey's telegram was relayed to John Read, who reported privately to King. While Read agreed that the Meyer case was important, he also made it clear that he was leery of the enterprise: 'Personally, I am not enthusiastic about the whole war crimes business,'[26] he advised the prime minister. Furthermore, Read wanted to dispense with Macdonald and the existing staff and use new prosecutors drawn from the Ottawa establishment. He suggested the chief of staff, Lieutenant-General Price Montague, as president of the court martial. For his part, Slaght was even opposed to the trial of major war criminals by international tribunals and instead urged speedy military trials. As part of the 'Armistice terms' he proposed that 'crimes of Germans against Germans, whether Jewish or otherwise, should be dealt with by domestic German courts.'[27] It seems a bizarre notion that German courts in 1945 could possibly deal justice to the architects of the 'Final Solution.' Read's memorandum and Slaght's comments were indications that Bruce Macdonald was flying back to a government whose establishment was seriously out of touch with the situation in Europe. But even if Read viewed war crimes as a potential embarrassment, Macdonald had been immersed in the investigation of numerous killings of Canadian prisoners and he was not about to let perpetrators escape justice just to spare the government any inconvenience.

CWCAC's new secretary, Wing Commander Hopkins, provided a much needed link between Ottawa and Europe. Hopkins visited London in March 1945 and noted that Massey was most interested in war crimes but had no staff – 'in the European theatre we have a number of Queen Bees, together with an inadequate number of Worker Bees.' In fact, during the course of his inspection, Hopkins was drafted by the chairman of the UNWCC, Lord Wright, to assist in preparing lists of war criminals. Hopkins was impressed by Macdonald and thought 'it was to my mind a very great stroke of fortune that Canadian officers have played so important a part in the SHAEF Court of Inquiry, and that they are now available for a straight Canadian effort.' Upon his return to Ottawa, Hopkins prepared a full report and recommended that Macdonald's war crimes section be put into action. Hopkins was pessimistic that Canada, despite its wartime contribution, would play any role other than observer in the trial of the major war criminals, and he further noted that 'personally, I do not believe that we should strive to participate officially or assume responsibility in this matter.' He gave no reason for this retiring view. He even seemed reticent in advocating action in cases involving Canadian servicemen: 'In this connection, I would suggest that the British military authorities should, by arrangement, try by military court any enemy war criminals in their custody who have committed crimes against United Kingdom nationals and Canadians jointly, with a proviso covering Canadian representation on such courts. Where, however a straight Canadian case is concerned, then it seems to me that the case should be tried by Canadian military courts in the British zone of occupation.'[28] Canadian interests in war crimes were not extensive, he felt, and 'on the whole, Canadian prisoners of war appear to have received treatment at least as favourable as that accorded to the nationals of any other country.' Hopkins failed to account for the now documented fact that over 100 Canadians had been murdered in 30 separate incidents in Normandy, an atrocity in size and extent not visited on either the British or American armies and one in which Canadians might be said to have a keen interest.

The prospect of speedy trials pursuant to the British royal warrant were rejected by CWCAC, which instead instructed the Judge Advocate General to draft regulations under Canada's War Measures Act of 1939.[29] As events would show, proceeding under this statute would have near disastrous consequences. When Macdonald appeared before CWCAC at an extraordinary meeting on 3 July 1945, he found no sense of urgency among the members. He described the formation of the No. 1 Canadian War Crimes Investigation Unit and reported that it had recently obtained 'important corroborative evidence' of Meyer's guilt.[30] While CWCAC agreed to file the Meyer case with the UNWCC, it was distinctly cool towards Macdonald's suggestion that the army certify Meyer's case as approved for trial. No such certification could take place, the committee ruled, until Canada's war crimes regulations became law.

Even if the expected trials were delayed, the investigations proceeded in Europe and in America. Headquartered in London, near CMHQ, Macdonald established a British office for his investigations which became the 'UK Detachment.' He tried to staff the new detachment with men from the SHAEF courts of inquiry. However, most veterans, such as John Page, were eligible for demobilization and were returning to Canada. Major

G.K.M. Johnston replaced Page as chief administrative officer. A fresh source of staff was the legally or police-trained men of the combat forces. Major Clarence Campbell, a lawyer, Rhodes scholar, and university friend of Macdonald's, joined the unit and eventually became second-in-command. Beginning the war as a private, Campbell had eventually become a major in an anti-tank regiment. Officers such as lieutenant-colonels Ken Morden and J.W. Walker served until they were eligible for demobilization, while others such as majors H.H. Griffin and W.D.S. Morden served for the unit's duration. An urbane New Yorker, Major J.J. Stonborough, became a leading interpreter for the unit, as did another former intelligence officer, Captain Ernest Skutezky. Throughout 1945, the U.K. Detachment would be absorbed by the Meyer case and the other allegations against the 12th SS.

On 2 July 1945 a further subunit, the North-West Europe Detachment (NWE), was created in Bad Salzuflen, Germany.[31] This group, formed by majors Neil Fraser and L.S. Eckhardt, had few experienced investigators. Lieutenant Raymond Robichaud had been snapped up by a British war crimes investigations team when the SHAEF courts had ceased to exist, and it took some manoeuvring by Macdonald to transfer him to the NWE detachment.[32] For the most part, the unit took its staff from the combat forces. An example was Captain John Blain, a Toronto lawyer who until recently had served in the 23rd Field Regiment of the artillery. In June 1945 he jumped at the offer to join the unit for it seemed to him that the Canadian occupation force would remain in Europe indefinitely and war crimes would be by far the most interesting way to serve out his time overseas.[33] George Drynan, another lawyer, formerly of the Irish Regiment of Canada, joined the unit in the summer of 1945. The addition of combat soldiers may have given the unit a different perspective from the SHAEF courts of inquiry. Robichaud recalled one incident when, on a drive through northern France, he and Boraston had stopped by a roadside where they could hear the flutter of American artillery shells passing overhead towards a German-held fortification. Boraston, whose staff positions in both world wars made it unlikely that he had ever been that close to deadly fire, was distinctly nervous and suggested they move along. To the younger officers and men in the unit, artillery fire had long been an unpleasant fact of life. Transfers also came from the intelligence corps. Captain Wady Lehmann had interrogated hundreds of German prisoners in Italy and had a thorough understanding of the German army. Raised in Vancouver in a cosmopolitan family in which German was as readily spoken as English, he typified the bright individuals who made up Canada's war crimes investigation teams.

More wide ranging than its U.K. counterpart, the North-West Europe Detachment examined reports on a variety of cases across the continent. Originally commanded by a soldier, Neil Fraser, the detachment increasingly concentrated on crimes against airmen. It was therefore appropriate that Fraser's successor, Wing Commander Oliver 'Pat' Durdin, would investigate and eventually prosecute a number of cases concerning Canadian airmen. So concerned was Durdin with making the NWE detachment familiar with air force issues that on 1 October 1945 he sought authority from the U.K. detachment for 'obtaining RCAF investigators and substaff.'[34] Durdin was assisted by Flight Lieutenant Jennings, who had himself been shot down over France and narrowly escaped capture. A former Spitfire pilot, Flight Lieutenant Mike Einhorn also joined the unit as interrogator and interpreter.[35] Invaluable to the unit's work were two police officers, Squadron Leader M. Carmichael and Captain Harold Hunter of the RCMP. Hunter had volunteered from the RCMP to serve overseas with intelligence and for a time had commanded a field-security unit. Described by a police supervisor as a 'keen investigator, aggressive, and shows good judgment,'[36] he would bring meticulous police techniques to the investigations.

Bad Salzuflen was a glorious location for so grim a task. Before the war, it had been a spa much frequented by liverish Rhine industrialists. As a result, it had a number of villas and pensions available for billeting. The unit had its own facilities and transport and shared the mess of the 1st Echelon of the 21st Army Group. As Robichaud observed, 'There was a good deal of pleasant mess life ... *la table était excellente.*'[37] In the evenings, the staff could repair to the *Kurhaus* (spa) across the street from their offices where the champagne (labelled *Reserviet für Wehrmacht*) was served, all to the strains of an excellent string orchestra. The work, however, was serious, and the Unit members travelled about Europe following up on reports of missing airmen or executed prisoners. There was a regular exchange of information with the British war crimes unit at Bad Oyenhausen and many cases came from British sources. Whenever an incident was to be examined, a team usually consisting of two interrogators, an interpreter, driver, and a shorthand reporter would be assembled to go to the area. As Macdonald described the procedure, a senior officer, usually a lieutenant-colonel, would be the main interrogator while a major might cross-examine on behalf of any person implicated by the witness. Acting as a devil's advocate, the major would try to draw out points to assist the suspect.[38] Whenever possible, a team would endeavour to visit several towns on one trip to cover a number of unrelated incidents. Occasionally, it could be the driver who was the most valuable member on an expedition. One driver, Corporal D.J. Guegueirre, spoke excellent Dutch, and another, Corporal A. Klassen, a German-speaking Mennonite from northern Saskatchewan, was so capable that he was remembered by the officers as a military version of the 'Admirable Crichton.' Often, the services of Guegueirre and Klassen went far beyond merely getting the officers to their destination.

Investigations were not as systematic as those conducted by SHAEF. Fraser had divided the NWE detachment into two three-man teams, each with a list of assigned cases. The legal officer in each team (the others would be police or interpreters) would conduct the examination. Since only lawyers could examine, they would borrow a lawyer from the other team to cross-examine.[39] There would likely be no preliminary searches for information. Upon arrival at a given site, unit members would immediately interrogate known witnesses. On other occasions, they would 'wander about a little, speaking to people here and there before deciding to sit down with them somewhere to receive their evidence.'[40] On their return, they would prepare a report to be filed with CMHQ, and higher authorities would determine whether there should be further investigation or arrangements for a prosecution.

The staff recalled that German civilians could be surprisingly cooperative. 'I think some were truly horrified when they finally realized what had taken place,' John Blain recalled, 'while others, of course, were anxious to curry a certain amount of favour from the occupying authorities.'[41] Cooperation had its limits. Wady Lehmann remembered that after being sworn in, some civilians would invariably repeat, 'That I can no longer remember today,' leaving the interpreter caught 'between a perplexed witness and an infuriated legal interrogator.'[42] The trips, several to the American sector where the messes were well stocked, could be quite enjoyable. Other tasks, such as the examination of bodies to determine identity and cause of death, could be draining. One unit member recalled trying to find the identification tags in the chest cavity of a badly decomposed body, a job that, though horrifying in retrospect, was merely routine at the time. On at least one occasion, unit members used the Allied Control Commission pass to travel to the Soviet sector in an attempt to locate a crashed bomber near Berlin. Not much information was obtained, and the staff began to attract the unwelcome attention of Russian patrols. The Canadians spent an uneasy night in Berlin, where refugees and soldiers in tattered uniforms and feet wrapped in rags drifted about the wretched metropolis. As Lehmann recalled, 'at night rubble in the darkened streets lay in huge mounds etched against the starry sky. Yet in the shell-pocked opera house

I sat in a capacity audience of survived Berliners and Allied service people alike taking in a performance of Fidelio.'[43]

Although diligently pursued, most investigations were fruitless. During the summer of 1945, investigators went on an extended trip to Bavaria, northern Italy, and, eventually, southern France. 'It was a venture,' Wady Lehmann later recounted, 'more memorable for its beauty than our achievement.'[44] In the unit's comprehensive report of March 1946, Macdonald concluded that there were 106 cases which could not be prosecuted. Either there was no evidence of a war crime, the events were trivial, the victims were not Canadian, or the perpetrators were unknown or had disappeared. On the first criterion, it had to be determined whether the killing was even a violation of the recognized laws of war. Early in the investigations, the high commissioner's office in London had reported that two Canadian officers, Frank Pickersgill and Romeo Sabourin, had been executed at Buchenwald concentration camp. Arrested while in civilian clothes, they were unable to claim the protection of the Geneva Convention. The killings were thoroughly investigated by John Blain, who discovered that the two had been saboteurs assisting the French resistance as part of the Robert Benoist group. He found a surviving prisoner who had seen the Canadians arrive at the camp in civilian attire. While men of exemplary bravery, Pickersgill and Sabourin had volunteered for duty that placed them outside the protection of international law. Macdonald personally reported to Vincent Massey that the officers 'acted as saboteurs and as such had forfeited rights to treatment as PsW and we are therefore, not in a position to criticize their execution.'[45]

A similar case concerned a Canadian paratrooper caught behind German lines after D-Day. He had joined a patrol of the Forces Français de l'Intérieur (FFI) but at the time of his capture he was not wearing an FFI armband that would have marked him as a combatant. Raymond Robichaud interviewed people in the town of Verneuil who had seen the Canadian and his FFI comrades marched to the German *Kommandatur* (HQ) and then to their execution.[46] Allegations of torture were not proven, even after an American doctor examined the body. By the Geneva Convention, even saboteurs deserve a trial before execution, but there was no way to prove that a summary trial had not taken place at the *Kommandatur*. In cases such as this, Macdonald tended to bring a regular soldier's attitude to the issue. As he confided to Robichaud, 'What would you do if you found partisans operating in your sector?'[47] It was decided that no war crime had occurred.

On other occasions, the allegations were found to be completely false.

Typical of these cases was an accusation made against a German officer (by one of his own men) that he had killed Canadian prisoners. According to the witness, the officer had control of the prisoners, and on his return to his own lines he had boasted, 'Die habe ich umgelet' (I made them kick the bucket). However, the officer insisted that he had released the Canadians, and further research proved his story. Both Canadians captured that night confirmed that they had been released.[48] The report was dismissed as a fabrication, as was a case in Dunkirk where a German prisoner accused one of their doctors of killing a Canadian prisoner. An autopsy confirmed that the Canadian had died of wounds and that the 'bullet hole' in the skull was really the *foramen ovale*, the opening for the spinal chord. Such wild-goose chases could be exceedingly frustrating. In the Dunkirk case, Macdonald consoled Blain for his efforts in examing many witnesses to no result: 'It is unfortunate that we have been put to this trouble but you have apparently made a thorough investigation and we can regard the matter as closed.'[49]

Other cases could not be dismissed so easily. Technically, many of the incidents the unit was uncovering constituted war crimes according to the criteria set out by the leading text of the day, Oppenheim's *International Law*, which took the view that 'combatants may only be killed or wounded if they are able and willing to fight and to resist capture ... Further, such combatants as lay down their arms and surrender or do not resist ... may neither be killed or wounded but must be given quarter.'[50] In the heat of battle, Oppenheim's words counted for little. During a sharp fight at Kalkar, Germany, three soldiers of the Canadian Scottish had been cornered in a basement. As they walked up a staircase, a German paratrooper fired on them, killing one of the surrendering troops. Macdonald decided not to press the issue, one reason being that 'hand to hand fighting had only just ceased.'[51] Neither was it necessarily a war crime for Germans to apply their own severe military code to Canadians. One Canadian prisoner who had helped in the clean-up of Dresden took eight ounces of meat, and for this he was tried and executed; a sign was put over his grave reading 'A prisoner of war shot for looting.' One captured Canadian soldier had in his possession a cache of watches, rings, and other jewellery apparently looted from German civilians. The senior German officer, Lieutenant-General Wolfgang Erdmann, ordered his execution. After reflecting that the German army regularly shot looters in its own ranks, Macdonald decided not to proceed.[52]

All reports concerning the maltreatment of prisoners were examined, but again little turned up. One Canadian prisoner at Stalag VIII B had been stabbed by a guard. However, the prisoner admitted, almost to the point of bragging, that he was a provocative type who had gone on a 'slow down' strike.[53] One prisoner managed a brief escape from Stalag II D but was later captured and shot by a guard. Upon liberation, the Canadians identified the guard to Russian troops who, with no appreciation for legalities, promptly shot him. The unit's disposition of the case displays a curious regard for correctness: 'It has not been established beyond all doubt that a war crime was in fact committed. However, inasmuch as the party responsible for the death of Johnston has himself paid the penalty for the act, no other action is indicated and the file has been closed.'[54] Other allegations were examined, but nothing improper was disclosed. While the Canadian navy was concerned about the treatment of sailors lost after the sinking of the HMCS *Athabascan*, no evidence of atrocities was ever found.[55] Similarly, on the Italian front, the Royal 22nd Regiment reported a case in which the Germans had used the ruse of appearing under a red cross to capture a platoon and perhaps kill one of the troops. However, there was no proof of a killing, and it was impossible to identify the soldiers who had misused the red cross.[56]

Back in London at the U.K. Detachment, Clarence Campbell was now acquiring a steady stream of SS men to interrogate, and through them he was aquiring a greater appreciation of the thinking of the 12th SS. One junior officer, Paul Kuret, told him that they had fully expected to be shot if captured. His superior had informed him that 'on this front the Canadians are taking no prisoners.'[57] Next, Campbell interviewed a typical SS trooper, Walter Nimmerfroh, who had served in Kuret's platoon. According to him, while Kuret had passed on the news that the Canadians took no prisoners, he also told his men that they were to take prisoners for interrogation. The soldiers grumbled at this double standard and 'some believed that the Allies would take no prisoners and thought that they, likewise, should not take any.'[58]

At times, the investigators seemed tantalizingly close to making a match. In August 1945 Campbell interrogated Karl Walter Becker of the 12th SS Reconnaissance Battalion, the same unit that had slaughtered twenty-six captives at the Chateau d'Audrieu. Becker had not been with them at the time, but he had had the chance to discuss what had happened with another officer, an Oberleutnant Palm, who had been present. Palm explained how the unit's commander, Gerhard Bremer, had been killed (in fact only wounded) in an artillery barrage. The men were enraged by the tremendous volume of fire, their severe losses, and the difficulty in transporting the wounded to the rear. The acting commander, Gerd von

Reitzenstein, ordered that as an act of revenge all prisoners were to be shot. 'The deed was carried out by Osschf (sergeant) Leopold Stun whose brutal personality well qualified him for a deed of this sort.' Stun was considered by fellow SS soldiers to be a sadist, 'a man without conscience or scruples who in Russia had several brutalities on his conscience.'[59]

This new evidence substantiated the earlier observations of French civilians and also held up under Major Morden's cross-examination. Acting as devil's advocate, Morden tried to get Becker to admit that Palm might have exaggerated. Becker insisted that their conversation was most candid and that he had repeated it much as he had heard it.[60] Despite this new information, none of those implicated in the killings – Bremer, von Reitzenstein, Stun, or any of the other soldiers – was ever put on trial. The unit's final report in March 1946 concluded that 'nothing further can be done in this case until the apprehension of the alleged perpetrators.'[61] Gerhard Bremer, the man who most likely ordered the murder of twenty-six Canadian and British soldiers at the Chateau d'Audrieu, was in a French prison until 1948. Inexplicably, he was never put on trial.[62]

By 16 July, Clarence Campbell was personally trudging through the Norman countryside examining the sites where alleged war crimes had occurred in order to get an appreciation for the events.[63] One priceless tool the investigators hoped to find was the war diary, the day-by-day account of operations, of the 12th SS. This was thought to be in Soviet hands, but even after Blain had been dispatched to the Soviet military mission to the British Army of the Rhine, no diary was ever forthcoming.[64] In addition to this problem, many of the suspects had been killed in the intense fighting in Normandy. Others had merely changed identity and faded into the masses of German prisoners in the Allied camps. As John Blain noted, 'Germany was in a chaotic mess. Many major cities had been extensively damaged by bombing, records were incomplete and perhaps non-existent and people, particularly those who had something to fear, simply melted away.'[65] One of the most galling failures to Bruce Macdonald was his inability to locate the killers of Chaplain W.L. Brown. His jeep had run into a German patrol on the evening of 7 June and another soldier had seen the chaplain approach the Germans with his arms raised. A month later, his bayoneted body was found near the same spot. It was even questionable whether a war crime had occurred, for the light was poor and the chaplain could have been mistaken for a combatant. His case keenly affected Macdonald, who had known Brown in Windsor where he had been chaplain of the Essex Scottish. Chaplain Brown had not even been eligible for overseas duty, but he had persevered in order to be with the fighting troops. A fine man and soldier, he may well have been killed while trying to surrender. But, in the end, his case was also left unresolved.[66]

At times, the information the unit uncovered seemed to put some cases close to resolution. In October 1945 Blain interviewed Germaine Saint-Martin, the owner of a farmhouse near Le Mesnil-Patry. Her pantry had been taken over as an aid station, and on 9 June 1944 she had observed three wounded Canadians brought in. All three received treatment, and Mme. Saint-Germain had given one Canadian with a foot injury a wooden clog. German orderlies shared cigarettes with the prisoners, and a medical officer obtained milk for them. However, shortly after they had been interrogated, an officer arrived and ordered all three out of the pantry and into the garden. Although she dreaded what was to come, Mme. Saint-Germain was ordered into the garden as well. There, the same medical orderlies who a short time ago had been treating the Canadians were now covering them with submachine-guns. At a given order, the orderlies shot the Canadians and the officer gave the *coup de grâce*.[67] Her account tallied exactly with the finding of three bodies in the garden. All had been wounded and then shot in the head, and one was still wearing a wooden clog. Mme. Saint-Germain's nephew Henri had witnessed another execution. Early that morning he had seen a group of about five Allied soldiers marched under guard into a field where all were shot. A number of German troops, including about ten officers, had watched the execution. Aghast at what he had just seen, Henri was seized by some SS officers who were not pleased to leave any witnesses to the incident. Henri described the officers as in a 'happy mood' and, after the intervention of the medical officer, Henri was released. While the grave of these soldiers was not discovered, another four bodies were located in the Saint-Germains' garden.[68] Other evidence indicated that the Saint-Germains' farmhouse was the aid post of the 2nd battalion of the 26th PGR. Both the medical officer and the battalion commander, Bernhard Siebken, were implicated in the killings. In its November report, the unit concluded that these were not isolated incidents 'but rather the results of a general order eminating [sic] from Bn [Battalion] HQ or possibly even higher authority.'[69] However, there was no proof that Siebken, or for that matter any officer, had sanctioned the murders.

The killing of seven Canadians at Mouen by the Pioneer battalion, one of the first known atrocities, also went unresolved. A few tantalizing clues came from Wilhelm Stremme, a platoon officer in the Pioneer battalion who had been located in a camp in Alva, Oklahoma. In the early fighting he recalled that one of his troopers had flushed out four Canadians.

Stremme had taken them back to the battalion command post; however, when he had tried to watch the interrogation, he was hurried back to the front. When he was told that the company commander, Bischoff, had likely killed the prisoners, Stremme became upset for 'I firmly believe that, as a human being, a prisoner once taken should have his life and if I can be of any assistance I will give it.'[70] On another occasion, Stremme had carried a Canadian prisoner with his platoon and shared rations with him. Stremme was by no means alone among the Waffen SS in showing humanity towards prisoners. But on the other extreme were officers such as Bischoff, whom Stremme described as 'robust and hard, unjust even to his own men,' adding, I regard him capable of shooting prisoners.'

Nothing was more disappointing for Macdonald and his investigators than their failure to ascribe responsibility for the most horrific massacre of Canadian troops in the Second World War. Repatriated soldiers gave the unit bits and pieces of a story about the mass slaughter of Canadians after the battle at Putot-en-Bessin. Lieutenant D.A. James recalled a conversation he had in a German hospital with a Corporal H.C. McLean. McLean told him how his group of prisoners had been taken to a field where they had been told to huddle together. Afraid that something was up, McLean moved to the rear. A short time later, the guards opened fire on them, and McLean was hit as he ran for his life.[71]

As more survivors were located, the full story emerged. On the morning of 8 June, the 2nd battalion of the 26th PGR had overwhelmed Putot-en-Bessin and scores of prisoners were taken. Most were from the Royal Winnipeg Rifles. The one officer captured, Lieutenant Bill Ferguson, was perhaps typical of the combat leaders in the 3rd Division. An athlete and RCMP constable before the war, he hoped that a decent war record would stand him in good stead. On departing Canada, he was miserable over leaving his wife and infant daughter but he steeled himself 'not to think of that and [to] do such a good job that the sacrifice Sala [his wife] and I are making will be worth all the heartaches.' Ferguson was one of about thirty prisoners (several of them wounded) marched south from Putot-en-Bessin. Another group of about ten prisoners joined them, and all were herded to the battalion HQ at Le Mesnil-Patry where they were 'looked over' by some officers. Although they were kept in a barn for several hours, the prisoners were not mistreated or even interrogated. In the late afternoon they continued south until their column was halted by an officer in a vehicle. He began to berate the sergeant in charge, and one prisoner who understood German thought the sergeant had been instructed 'to get rid of us.'

About dusk, the column came within sight of the Caen-Fontenay-le-Pesnel road and the men were moved to a grassy field and told to sit down with the wounded in the middle. They watched as a convoy of field artillery and armoured vehicles passed along the road. One of the guards who could speak a little English commented reassuringly that it was only another three-quarters of a mile to the camp. But ominously, one of the field pieces was left behind and trained on the massed prisoners. They watched with even greater alarm as the guards pressed the men to sit closer to each other. Suddenly a vehicle pulled up and another nine soldiers joined the guards. As two soldiers dismounted from the vehicle, they were saluted. In the presence of these officers, a line of guards, automatic rifles at the ready, approached the huddled prisoners. One Canadian, Weldon Clark, realized that they were poised for slaughter, and he prepared to run. Ferguson and another officer, Lieutenant R.D. Barker, cautioned the men to hold fast while they tried to reason with the guards. Barker called out, 'It looks as if we are going to get the gun. Stand steady and I will try and talk them out of it.'[72] He never had the chance. Moments later rifle fire poured into the massed Canadians. Those that could ran. As Clark fled he looked back and 'saw the Germans going among our fellows and shooting as fast as they could.' As well, he heard the screams of men being finished off as the Germans went through the dead and dying prisoners.[73]

On 3 May 1945 a mass grave containing the bodies of thirty-one Canadian soldiers was found near the area. Four more bodies were located in shallow graves nearby. While the identities of the participants in the killings was never established, once again the battalion commander, Siebken, could have been responsible for what became known as the 'Canadian Malmédy.' Indeed, in the deliberate, staged manner of the slaughter, the killings at Fontenay-le-Pesnel were acutely similar to the massacre of American troops at Malmédy. In a harsh judgment, British writers have noted that 'why the Canadian authorities failed to follow up this Canadian "Malmédy" – the worst crime ever inflicted against their armed forces at any time in their history – remains unknown to the present day.'[74] Perhaps the answer lay in the near impossibility of locating the culprits and matching them with sufficient evidence for conviction. In the case of Siebken, however, justice would be delayed but, in the end, not denied.

In case after case, the investigators had shown that troops of the 12th SS had systematically killed Canadian prisoners far behind the lines. These were no 'heat of battle' killings but planned, deliberate butchery. And yet the investigators seemed always a step away from laying responsibility on a specific individual. As Macdonald observed, suspects took advantage of 'the great anonymity into which perpetrators eventually disappear among millions of fellow prisoners' and those who were implicated disclaimed everything.[75] Occasionally, frustration surfaced during the interrogations, as when Campbell asked an SS officer (who *pro forma* denied the slightest knowledge of atrocities) why his patrols were never able to capture prisoners for questioning:

Q. But your company never took prisoners?
A. No.
Q. What did you do? Kill them all?[76]

The one case where it was possible to put the 12th SS on trial was that of Kurt Meyer. And yet, as he had admitted in the spring, Macdonald knew that the case was far from conclusive. After his meeting with CWCAC in Ottawa, Macdonald, along with Major H.H. Griffin and translator J.J. Stonborough, spent the summer of 1945 touring prisoner camps in Canada and the United States. On 3 July he travelled to Hull, Quebec, and there came upon an unexpected find in Alfred Helzel. Helzel, a tall, blonde, Sudeten German, described how his company commander, von Beuttner, was introduced to his troops by Meyer. In his remarks, Meyer had said that 'my regiment takes no prisoners' and von Buettner had later repeated the admonition.[77] Helzel's recollections would be the link between the atrocities and the officers who had encouraged them. Buoyed by this vital evidence, the investigators continued on to Gravenhurst, Ontario, to examine twenty-six more prisoners. There they found, in Macdonald's words, 'hundreds of bronzed, well-fed and fine looking physical specimens of the "master race" swimming, boating and living the life of Riley at what appeared to be, except for a few fences, an exclusive summer camp on the lake.'[78]

From Canada the investigators travelled to Washington D.C., where they conferred with the American War Crimes Branch. The investigators went through CROWCASS records of suspected war criminals and the FBI compiled a list of likely prisoners to be examined at American camps. Macdonald and company then flew to Colorado and interviewed prisoners at two camps. Afterwards, they moved on to Alva, Oklahoma, and it was there that fortune struck again in the discovery of the young officer who described, from the German perspective, what had occurred at the Chateau d'Audrieu. During these interrogations (ninety-nine full investigations and forty to fifty shorter exams) no compulsion was used to obtain evidence. 'We made no effort to force them [prisoners] to answer questions if they did not wish to do so,' Macdonald recalled. 'If they knew anything of importance, we wanted them later as witnesses and their testimony would be of little value if given unwillingly.'[79] After Macdonald finished with a witness, Griffin would then examine 'on behalf of anyone who may be adversely affected by any of the evidence you have given today.'[80] This cautious, non-threatening approach was much in contrast to Scotland's bullying tactics at the London 'Prisoner's Cage'. It also seemed the opposite to the beatings and death threats used by American investigators on suspects in the Malmédy massacre. In the Malmédy case, the beatings had the effect that Macdonald feared. Evidence obtained under duress was tainted and the entire prosecution became discredited.[81]

Despite the useful information they had gathered, Macdonald remained apprehensive. It was now the beginning of August and no substantial action had been taken to formalize the war crimes regulations. In July the Judge Advocate General's Department had redrafted the proposals, but nothing had been completed. During the first week in August, meetings were scheduled by CWCAC to get this tedious but necessary process out of the way. As the blueprint for the upcoming trials, Canadians would look to the British royal warrant. British jurists noted that the warrant contained unprecedented procedures and that, even though it followed the process for the general field court martial, unique provisions had been added to ensure speed and avoid technical objections to the extent that 'To a criminal lawyer looking at these innovations in an Old Bailey light, they appear quite at variance with our own traditions.'[82] According to the royal warrant, the accused could not object to the president or any member of the court. Rules of evidence were altered to permit the court to accept any oral statement or document appearing on its face to be authentic. The court could accept 'hearsay' evidence, that is, statements made by a person who was not testifying before the court. Ordinarily, hearsay was not permitted in criminal trials except in rare circumstances. In that regard, courts martial under the royal warrant imitated continental procedure where hearsay was admitted in order to determine the truth; the warrant was 'an approximation to Continental rules of procedure in which what is sacrosanct at the Old Bailey is dismissed as obstructive technicality.'[83]

A subcommittee of CWCAC composed of Wing Commander Hopkins, Group Captain C.M.A. Strathy of the JAG office, and Macdonald was directed to commence the drafting of the Canadian war crimes regulations. It was a process only a lawyer could love. The draft rules would be based on the British precedent and make no attempt to break new ground.

Despite a suggestion that the regulations also include an offence for breachs of the 'laws of humanity,'[84] it was finally decided that the staple of international law, violations of the 'laws and usages of war,' would be the only offences to be punished. Unlike the major powers, Canada was not about to embark on a prosecution of crimes against humanity. The procedures, on the other hand, varied widely from Anglo-American legal tradition.

The court could take into consideration any oral statement or document appearing to be authentic, including previous sworn depositions, evidence before any of the courts of inquiry, and even letters or diaries.[85] Macdonald wanted to make this provision even more emphatic by changing the phrase 'take into consideration' to 'admit as evidence.' Even if by civilian standards the regulations gave an extraordinarily wide discretion in the admission of evidence, the underlying intent was to provide an unfettered search for the truth. Operating within the military framework, the regulations provided certain safeguards. Any charge first had to be reviewed and certified as ready for trial by the Judge Advocate General's Department. A convening officer, being the senior army or RCAF commander of Canadian occupation forces, would then authorize the military court. The court was to consist of not less than two and not more than six officers of equal or superior rank to the accused. At least one officer had to belong to the same branch of service as the accused. The president of the court was to have legal training, but, if this was impractical, a judge advocate (a military lawyer) would assist the court. To preclude jurisdictional arguments, section 8 provided that 'the accused shall not be entitled to object to the president or any member of the court or the judge advocate or to offer any special plea to the jurisdiction of the court.' Bearing in mind the extraordinary nature of the proceedings, such a blanket clause was probably warranted. To civilian eyes, it was a strange situation to have lay persons, some of whom were probably involved in the events related to the charge, deciding life-and-death questions concerning their recently defeated enemies. However, this was military justice, and it provided an expeditious way for soldiers to hear a soldier's plea.

In a formal representation on the draft wording, Macdonald had insightful comments from the prosecutor's perspective. He wanted to be able to present evidence by way of depositions because of the great difficulty in keeping witnesses: 'Many of these witnesses, civilian and military, will be required in more than one trial, and it would be necessary to tie them up for months in Europe awaiting each trial.'[86] One of the reasons for the courts of inquiry had been to amass evidence for later use. Using depositions had other benefits since 'the effect of this would be clearly to admit such evidence as the interrogation of Kurt Meyer and other prisoners. This having the effect indirectly of compelling the accused to give evidence.' Macdonald apparently saw no great sanctity in the principle that an accused had a right to remain silent. Instead, if an accused did not respond to a charge, his previous interrogation could be used against him.

One area of concern to the prosecution lay in the gray area of crimes committed by groups of men with no known person in charge. Section 10(4) of the draft regulations provided that, where more than one war crime was committed by a 'unit or group,' the commander was *prima facie* responsible. This was inadequate, Macdonald argued, for the term unit or group would be applied only to small formations and not to regimental or divisional commands (such as Meyer's) which were removed from the actual fighting. 'Should not such responsibility of a commander also be inferred where it is shown that a war crime has been carried out in an organized manner, apparently pursuant to orders of an officer or non-commissioned officer present at or immediately before the time when such offence was committed.'[87] Macdonald was perhaps more familiar with situations where deliberate executions, supervised by officers, had occurred and the prosecution was severely handicapped by being unable to demonstrate exactly who was responsible. However, CWCAC wanted to delete subsection 10(3), which implied guilt on the part of all members of a formation who had been present during the commission of a war crime. Imputing guilt to those who may not have committed a crime apparently went against the committee's notion of impartial justice. Macdonald fought hard to reinstate the clause. As the investigations had shown, it was frequently difficult to determine who had taken part in or ordered an atrocity. Therefore, a provision implying group guilt would, in Macdonald's view, 'enable pressure to be exerted in members of the group to identify the actual offenders,' and he added by way of justification that 'It is understood that such a policy has been accepted by the representatives of the four major prosecuting governments.' It was unlikely that defence lawyers would share his philosophical serenity that this was in the best interests of justice. Nor would they have been mollified by another of his arguments. At the end of his comments, Macdonald stated that 'it is assumed that these regulations are equally applicable to the trial of a Canadian against whom any German might prefer a charge.' Of course, it was naive for anyone to expect that some among the millions of cowed captives in the allied prisoner camps might be about to lay charges against their conquerors.

In their final form, the regulations addressed some of the prosecution's concerns. The meaning of 'unit or group' was extended to include any military formation. Subsection 10(3) was reinstated, and all members of a formation that had committed a war crime were presumed jointly responsible. The Canadian regulations went well beyond the standards set by the British royal warrant in holding a commander responsible for his men's crimes. Two additional subsections, 10(4) and 10(5), deemed a commander responsible where there had been multiple atrocities or where an atrocity been committed in the presence of an officer or non-commissioned officer.[88] To Meyer and his partisans, the regulations were a travesty, violations of international law intended by the victor to justify revenge on the defeated. As Meyer would later argue, 'The selection of the President and his co-judges alone was an impossibility according to international law.'[89] According to one of Meyer's partisans, 'through a succession of wordy self-serving platitudes, the rules were changed to accommodate the proposed acts of vengeance.'[90] Macdonald, in a response to later charges, gave the best refutation to the notion that the regulations were the legitimation of vengeance: 'Without such provisions it would in many cases be completely futile to attempt to convict admitted war criminals and the guilty would escape just retribution. One is inclined to lose patience with impractical persons who would prefer to see the cowardly perpetrators of war crimes against helpless prisoners escape justice, than any deviation from the strict rules of evidence in ordinary criminal cases should take place.'[91]

Interestingly enough, Macdonald had tried to get the views of captured German army legal officers. Two of them, colonels von der Hydte and Wildermuth, gave a lecture in military law for the edification of their fellow officers in April 1945. Laws of war applied, von der Hydte held, only if incorporated into domestic military law. This German view varied from the 'Anglo-Saxon interpretation' where 'international law applied to the individual soldier as well as to the state.' The end result was 'unfortunately very unpleasant for us ... the Armed Forces have therefore never been instructed on a number of subjects and this was 'the reason why the average German soldier has heard very little or nothing about the Hague convention concerning land fighting.'[92] Both officers agreed that even in war there were dictates of humanity that governed both Allied and Axis troops.

This was unquestionably so, for since the beginning of the war the German army had maintained a war crimes bureau that paralleled the later work of the No. 1 Canadian War Crimes Investigation Unit. In the Polish campaign of 1939, Germans had been reported murdered and the bureau had sent out officers to investigate. This led to a number of trials, and in the largest case thirty-eight Polish soldiers were tried for killing ethnic Germans; twenty-two were convicted and sixteen acquitted. The military court rendered a careful decision that went on for 177 pages.[93] The Wehrmacht War Crimes Bureau rejected proposals from more fanatical Nazis that collective penalties be imposed against all Polish soldiers who were in an area where a war crime had been committed. In addition to the bureau, strict military justice followed the Wehrmacht. Standards of discipline were extremely severe, and soldiers were executed for petty larceny in rear areas. It has been estimated that over 33,000 German soldiers were executed during the war, a state of discipline that made it unthinkable for the average soldier even to consider disobeying an order.[94] The bureau also had a mandate to investigate accusations against German troops. However, of the 226 volumes of its records, only one is devoted to German war crimes.[95] Like most armies, the German one tended to dwell on its enemies' wrongdoings while ignoring its own. An example is the Canadian protest through Swiss intermediaries that the 12th SS was killing prisoners in Normandy. Perhaps to avoid a thorough investigation, this protest had been deliberately forwarded to army Intelligence rather than to the War Crimes Bureau. As we have seen, after a few perfunctory enquiries (such as the one Meyer had received), the intelligence branch whitewashed the affair. This enabled the German government to reply in December 1944 that the Canadian charges were a mere 'defamation of the Wehrmacht,' although somewhat ambivalently the reply went on to state that 'the investigations of the alleged killings near Chateau Audrieux could not be completed because the majority of the 12th SS Panzer Division had been either killed or captured.'[96] While the intelligence branch's search had yielded nothing, the principle that war crimes applied to all troops was clearly acknowledged.

In the meanwhile the time consumed in drafting the regulations seemed endless. The glacial pace of the review maddened Macdonald and on 10 August his frustrations burst forth in a provocative memorandum to CWCAC. Only two days previously, the major Allied powers had agreed to create the International Military Tribunal for the trial of war criminals. This initiated the Nuremberg trials, a process in which Canada would play no part. 'Aggressive action,' Macdonald noted ruefully, 'is being taken in which the views of smaller nations are not being requested or considered.'[97] The one case of major concern to Canadians was that of Kurt Meyer and there was a strong possibility of it being given short shrift by the other Allies. The full extent of the 12th SS's atrocities in Normandy had never been revealed to the Canadian public. Macdonald viewed the trial of Kurt Meyer as a national cleansing in which all of these incidents would be revealed and in which one of the main perpetrators would be judged. He urged CWCAC to proceed forthwith in getting Meyer released to Canadian custody (he was still in a British prison) and in arranging for his trial: 'Every effort should be made to see that the members of this Division responsible for these crimes against Canadian soldiers are punished by a Canadian court.'

It was not long afterwards that the fine-tuning of the regulations ceased. The bureaucratic knot was severed and on 14 August the Department of Justice accepted the third draft of the regulations.[98] As the way cleared towards trial, Macdonald spent the rest of August surmounting other obstacles. He prepared an abstract of evidence and submitted it to the Judge Advocate General's Department. From the latter he received preliminary consent to begin the Meyer prosecution. On 18 August Prime Minister King approved the regulations and, after the cabinet followed suit, an order-in-council put them into effect. Cabinet approved on 29 August, and contacts were made with the British to arrange for the surrender of Meyer into Canadian custody. British officers advised Macdonald that, for several reasons, the war crimes trials should be held in Germany. Punishment of these men would likely have a useful psychological effect on Germans and serve as a tangible sign of their defeat. There were legal considerations as well. If Meyer were tried in England the extraordinary nature of the proceedings could be challenged in court and it was even possible for someone to bring a writ of habeas corpus on his behalf.[99] No such legalistic notions would trouble the occupation authorities.

On 1 September, Macdonald flew back to London to put the preparations for trial into high gear. Two weeks later, King formally introduced the War Crimes Regulations to the House of Commons. King stressed that they were identical in substance to those used by the other Allies and that all accused would have full opportunity for defence. Referring to the relaxation of normal procedures, the prime minister conceded that 'in view of the impossibility of assembling all of the witnesses, some of whom may have been demobilized and many of whom will have been repatriated, there are some modifications to the rigid rules of evidence applicable under an ordinary criminal procedure.' The courts themselves would be run by soldiers 'experienced in the law and usages of war; and the proceedings will be conducted with dignity, fairness and justice.' He further announced (what had been fact for some time) that Macdonald would head the war crimes section at CMHQ and that 'Colonel Macdonald and his associates will then undertake the prosecution of the accused.'[100]

Having devoted so much of himself to war crimes, Macdonald had a real dread of someone else being selected to undertake the prosecutions. While his own experience in criminal law was limited, Macdonald unhesitatingly thrust himself forward as the preferred prosecutor. In a memo to Brigadier R.J. Orde, Macdonald urged that only an officer with extensive first-hand knowledge of the Normandy campaign and its personalities (such as himself) should prosecute Meyer. 'I trust I will not be considered immodest,' he proposed to Orde, 'when I say that with my experience in these matters and with valuable civilian, legal as well as military experience, I feel better equipped successfully to prosecute this particular case than some more brilliant counsel who is not so familiar with all the matters mentioned above.'[101] Delighted by his selection, Macdonald (a lifelong Conservative) wrote to his wife, 'My opinion of Mackenzie King's judgment is certainly high.'[102]

4

Questions of Partiality

Back in England the prosecution team was being assembled and Macdonald selected Clarence Campbell as his assistant. Dalton Dean, an expert in military law from the Judge Advocate General's Department, was also assigned to the prosecution. The rest of the unit's staff would help the prosecutors gather witnesses and evidence. The translation load promised to be enormous, and Major J.J. Stonborough would act as chief interpreter with other officers as alternates. While the unit had collected the evidence and would prosecute, JAG would continue to perform a separate function. As the armed forces' legal professionals, JAG staff would ensure that the conduct of the court martial would comply with proper legal norms. In fact, as impartial advisers to the court, their conduct varied from that of American judge advocates, who actively participated in prosecuting cases. For his part, Macdonald suggested that no judge advocate would be necessary if a legal officer sat on the court, since 'the trial is not intended to involve legal technicalities, guilt or innocence being largely determined as a matter of common sense based on the practical experience of the members of the court.'[1] However, CMHQ decided that it was prudent to have a judge advocate and Lieutenant-Colonel W.B. Bredin was appointed.

If a citizen is entitled to a jury of his peers, officers are to be judged by soldiers of equivalent rank; in Meyer's case, this meant that the Canadian army had to find enough general officers to make up a court. At a meeting held at the HQ of the Canadian army at Bad Zwischenahn, it was decided to offer Macdonald a selection of six brigadiers and three major-generals. Major-General Harry Foster was named president and was to preside with

Major-General R.H. Keefler and brigadiers H.A. Sparling, Ian S. Johnston, and H.P. (Budge) Bell-Irving. Keefler made an objection to sitting and was replaced by Brigadier J.A. Roberts. Macdonald described the court members as 'a tough looking bunch of fighting soldiers,'[2] as indeed they were. Harry Foster had taken the 7th Infantry Brigade through heavy fighting in Normandy and had later commanded the 4th Armoured Division. Bell-Irving had won a DSO leading a company of the Seaforth Highlanders in Sicily, while Johnston, a Toronto lawyer, had led the 48th Highlanders through the fighting in Italy and had ended the campaign with a DSO and the command of the 11th Brigade.[3] That Meyer would be tried by his Canadian counterparts was a factor that was likely to work to his advantage. As Foster admitted in later life, he considered all sides guilty of atrocities: 'We are all guilty. But the enemy appears more guilty than we because any evidence of our excesses remains buried safely behind our advance.'[4] Macdonald was fully aware that this sentiment might sway the court. He confided to his wife, 'The trial should be fair enough because each [member] will be wondering whether we would like to be found guilty in the same circumstances.'[5]

As the players were put into place, the stage needed to be set. Coincidentally, the site of the trial was to be Aurich, the small German town by the North Sea where the war had ended for the Canadian army. And fittingly enough, the garrison troops were from the Winnipeg Rifles. Major D.J. Leach of the Canadian Scottish was in charge of the layout, and he and Captain Smedmor rearranged the naval-barracks conference area into a courtroom. Over 100 persons could watch the trial, including representatives of the Winnipeg Rifles, North Novas, Sherbrooke Fusilliers, and Queen's Own Rifles of Canada, the regiments that had suffered the most from the 12th SS. German civilians would also be invited to attend. The conference room was beautifully panelled in wood and was now adorned with a huge Canadian Red Ensign. If Canada was excluded from Nuremberg, its military justice would be on conspicuous display in Aurich.[6]

In his pre-trial brief, Macdonald had an invaluable reference in Meyer's debriefing by Canadian intelligence in August 1945. The report revealed a man unswerving in his Nazi loyalties who described the slaughter of ('Brown Shirts') officers in the 1934 purge as a 'dignified military performance' in which the victims were 'shot like officers.' As a measure of his stunted sense of morality, Meyer's reaction to the horror of the Nazi death camps was to respond that Allied soldiers had stolen rings and watches from his men. When asked if this was a reasonable comparison he could make no reply. Moreover, while Meyer's record as a soldier was exceptional, his propensity to lie was manifest. He explained his regiment's failed counter-attack of 7–8 June as being caused by a shortage of gasoline and ammunition. This was nonsense, scoffed the commander of the adjacent 21 Panzer division. If Meyer's assault had succeeded, he could have had all the fuel and ammunition he wanted. As a result of the debriefing, Macdonald was assured that he could portray the accused as an arrogant, unrepentant Nazi with a reluctance to speak the truth.[7]

Meyer was about to be tried by a code of conduct quite different than that which regulated the trial of civilians. In British law, a separate court-martial jurisdiction had existed since the first Mutiny Act of 1689. Long before then, however, it had been recognized that the military required a special code dictated by the necessity to maintain a rigid adherence to discipline. Alex Cattanach, a legal officer who would advise the RCAF courts martial, would later say when he was a judge on the Federal Court that military discipline would be ineffective 'without equipping the armed forces with its own Courts for enforcing those breaches.'[8] Moreover, it was appropriate that soldiers be judged by their officers. As Justice Ritchie would observe in the same case, an officer 'whose career in the army must have made him familiar with what service life entails would ... be a more suitable candidate for president of a court martial than a barrister or a judge who has spent his working life in the practice of non-military law.'[9] Yet safeguards existed in Canadian courts martial that would be transferred to the war crimes trials. All decisions would be subject to review by the judge advocate and the convening officer; legally trained officers would be made available to advise the court. Even though the process under courts martial varied considerably from civilian trials, Macdonald concluded that a court martial was appropriate to Meyer's circumstances. 'There was no intention to try him as if he were in an ordinary criminal court, but as a soldier charged with an offence for which he could be sentenced to death by a court martial in the field.'[10]

On 15 October, Macdonald conducted his last interrogation of Meyer and told him the grounds for the court martial. One final set of questions was put to the accused. Asked whether he knew if wounded prisoners had died at his HQ, Meyer gave an answer that was to haunt him at trial:

Q.184 Was it reported to you by anyone that Allied prisoners had died at your
       headquarters and that it was necessary to bury them?
A.184 No.[11]

Meyer was put on notice of Jesionek's statement and of the fact that Canadian bodies had been found at the Abbaye. In response to Jesionek's accusation, Meyer replied, 'Of that I know nothing. What the Colonel has said I do not know anything nor was I ever so stupid as to give an order to shoot prisoners.' Two days later, he reviewed the transcript, made minor changes, and added to his previous comments:

Q.19 None of your officers or NCOs or even private soldiers ever reported atroci-
       ties to you?
A.19 No.
Q.20 And so it is correct to say that, by reason of the fact you never had to, you
       therefore did not at any time discipline any of your officers or men for
       committing such offences?
A.20 I did not need to punish anyone for I did not know anything about it.[12]

To his wife, Macdonald confided that the brigadeführer would be difficult to break: 'He is going to be most difficult to convict. Cool, poised, polite and now disconcertingly frank about most things.' Even Macdonald betrayed a growing fascination with his prey. He would later describe Meyer as of average height, with a sturdy, athletic build, a dark complexion, and cold blue-grey eyes 'with which he fixed one with a stare when talking.'[13] Meyer's claims of innocence also seemed to be affecting Macdonald for he now conceded that 'I don't like this business of going after a fellow deliberately and cold bloodedly to do him in, even if he is responsible indirectly for shooting prisoners.' He added equivocally, 'It is so hard to be really positive that your story is 100% correct.'[14]

Positive or not, less than a week after writing these words, Macdonald filed his request with JAG to approve the charge sheet. In public, Macdonald was full of confidence, advising Brigadier R.J. Orde that 'I am of the opinion that we have a good case and that convictions on all charges should be obtained.'[15] But there were flaws in the case. On the first charge of issuing orders to refuse quarter, three of Meyer's men would swear that they were instructed not to take prisoners, while eight others denied ever receiving such orders. The troops who had murdered prisoners at Authie and Buron on 7 June were under Meyer's command, but Macdonald conceded that 'there is no positive connection with Meyer.' As to the indignities to the bodies in Authie, Meyer denied ever seeing anything or, for that matter, ever driving through Authie. The killing of seven men at Mouen on 17 June was, Macdonald admitted, 'somewhat remote' from Meyer's command. There was not enough in these charges to prove guilt, but Macdonald wished to lay them anyway in order to create 'a background ... against which the court can judge as to the sincerity of Meyer's denials.' If the judge advocate would let him, he also wished to examine Meyer's career in the Nazi party and allegations that he committed atrocities against the Russians.

The heart of the prosecution was Jesionek's recollection of Meyer's part in the killing of seven prisoners at the Abbaye on the morning of 8 June. Undoubtedly, there were problems with the case. 'The evidence, however, is only circumstantially corroborated and has not been consistent throughout.' Macdonald stressed to Orde that Jesionek was a strong, reliable witness, and while his story was not entirely in harmony 'he has very good powers of observation, a reliable memory and an unwillingness to be influenced into changing any of his story in its essential aspects.' Everything hinged on Jesionek; his story was the 'smoking gun' that directly linked Kurt Meyer to the murder of prisoners.

Orde wished to meet with Macdonald before he approved the trial, and accordingly Macdonald flew to Ottawa on 21 October. Orde had one concern, namely that the draft charges alleged a 'responsibility for a war crime' while the regulations only prescribed 'committing a war crime' as an offence. Orde also insisted that Macdonald concentrate on the most serious issues and that the charges of mutilation of bodies be removed.[16] Ultimately, it was decided to proceed with five charges. The first covered the period when Meyer was training the 25th PGR in Belgium and France and alleged that the troops were incited to deny quarter to Allied soldiers. The second related to the killing of twenty-three prisoners after the fighting at Authie and Buron. The remaining three charges dealt with the killings at the Abbaye Ardenne. The third charge, by far the most damning, alleged that he had given orders to troops under his command to kill seven prisoners. The last two charges were in the alternative, that as the commander of the soldiers at the Abbaye he was responsible for the atrocity (see appendix A). There was a second charge sheet alleging that Meyer was also responsible for the killings at Mouen, but this was held in abeyance. With Orde's approval, and a certificate approving the charges for trial in his briefcase, Macdonald returned to Germany. He left unaware that the Meyer case was about to go through some bizarre twists that threatened to derail the prosecution before Meyer even pleaded to the charges.

On the morning of 26 October, Meyer approached prison officials about making another statement. Campbell was summoned and did his best to dissuade Meyer from talking. Afraid of anything that might prejudice the prosecution while Macdonald was in Ottawa, Campbell held a brief, uneasy meeting with the prisoner. Meyer agreed that he would wait until Macdonald returned to clarify 'new facts.'[17] Upon his return on Sunday, 28 October, Macdonald also tried to discourage Meyer from speaking since he had been charged but did not yet have a defence lawyer. However, Meyer had been talking with a fellow prisoner, the Berlin law professor von der Heydte, and on his advice he wished to change his previous explanations. He began, cooperatively enough, by correcting some of the operational information he had given to the military debriefers. Meyer's greatest concern, however, was to correct part of the interrogation of 15 October. At this examination, and the previous one in March, he had insisted that he had never seen any dead Allied soldiers at his headquarters. Now he told Macdonald: 'From the statement I wish to make tell the Lieutenant-Colonel a lot depends and at any rate it would clarify the matter so that we approach the trial with open cards, because the point raised in question 184 is not 100% correct and I don't want to be regarded as a perjurer at trial.'[18] His adviser, von der Heydte, added: 'It is not a negation of previous testimony but only an amendment.' Meyer then proceeded to give a radically different version of the events at the Abbaye Ardenne.

On 10 or 11 June, two officers had reported to him that there were a number of unburied bodies of Canadian soldiers at the headquarters. At first incredulous, Meyer ordered his adjutant to investigate. When he went to see for himself, he found the bodies of eighteen or nineteen soldiers in the garden. All of them had been shot through the head. Outraged, Meyer ordered the adjutant, Scheumann, and the regimental legal officer, Dr Tiray, to investigate. In his turn, Meyer advised the divisional commander, Fritz Witt, who ordered him to find out who was responsible. Meyer's wrath focused on the adjutant, who was responsible for everything that occurred at the HQ. Scheumann was relieved and sent to a front-line unit where, shortly thereafter, he was killed. Dr Tiray also died in the fighting. Nothing came of the investigation, but Meyer sent orders to his battalion commanders warning against killing prisoners. As to why he had lied at his previous examinations, he explained that he had been ashamed that German soldiers, especially men from his own regiment, could have committed such deeds.[19]

This new version caused the prosecution to re-evaluate its evidence. On the eve of trial, the nature of the case was evolving, as Macdonald confided to John Page: 'We are busy getting ready for the Meyer case and from all the conflicting material which now comes in the Lord only knows what the result will be. However, fortunately, we now have his own admission that eighteen Canadians were killed at his regimental headquarters and no matter how much he disclaims responsibility for that he will have to do a lot of fast talking to escape some of the proper consequences.'[20] Meyer's admission that prisoners had been murdered at his HQ and that he had known of it all along might spell his downfall. Much now depended on how the court accepted Jesionek's inference that it was Meyer himself who had ordered these killings.

With the charge sheet approved, Macdonald arranged on 31 October to have Meyer flown from England to the German airfield at Jever where a milling crowd of soldiers, photographers, and reporters waited on the tarmac. Cameras recorded the scene as Meyer left the aircraft and saluted the two waiting officers. No one returned his respects. Instead, as his hand came down, it was handcuffed to one of the guards. Upon his arrival, Meyer's status changed from that of a prisoner of war to a prisoner charged with a crime. This was reinforced when the guard drove him to the marine-school barracks (now the Maple Leaf Barracks) where Meyer was stripped and searched. A medical officer ensured that he had no poisons hidden on his body; for Kurt Meyer there would be no escape by way of suicide. His uniform was removed and he was given boots without laces and blankets sewn to the edge to prevent unravelling. Extensive precautions were warranted for, before his uniform was returned to him for trial, a razor blade was found under a badge.

Barely had Meyer settled into his cell than he was marched out to be formally charged. The commander of the Winnipeg Rifles, Lieutenant-Colonel R.P. Clark, read out the five charges and told Meyer that his trial was set for 28 November. According to reporter Ross Munro, Meyer stood 'sturdy, poker faced and erect.' His only response was to ask for von der Heydte's assistance.[21] Meyer later recalled his feelings on this occasion: 'So now I know with what I am to be accused and for what I am to be sentenced. I feel a certain sense of relief having received this information despite the hardly pleasant situation as now I can prepare myself for the accusers' charges and refute them with corresponding evidence.'[22]

The Germany Kurt Meyer returned to was a prostrate nation lying uneasily under Allied occupation. Food was in desperately short supply and it was questionable whether there would be sufficient fuel for the coming winter. The 'denazification' program under which anyone who had Nazi affiliations had to explain themselves before a court, was proceeding fitfully. In October 1945 Eisenhower was trying vigorously to enforce denazification in the American sector and to 'uproot Nazism in every shape and form.'[23] Dr Wilhelm Hoegner, the minister-president of Bavaria, stated his primary object to be 'the summary punishment of German criminals who have so far escaped punishment.' But this attitude did not necessarily extend to the lower ranks of the Waffen SS. Pastor Martin Niemoeller, the highly respected survivor of a concentration camp, warned against a blanket condemnation of the SS: 'Many young Germans who were drafted merely as soldiers were thrown into SS and SA units without their consent.'[24] For most Germans, however, the shock of bereavement and the daily struggle to survive overrode any concern for the fate of one SS general.

If the proceedings were of little interest in Germany, they had created a sensation in Canada. The charge sheet was the first revelation of the extent of the Normandy atrocities and the effect in Canada was electric. The front pages of Canadian newspapers carried the story that 144 prisoners had been murdered in 33 incidents. The magnitude of the crimes, previously known to only a few officers at CMHQ, focused national attention on Aurich.[25] The No. 1 Canadian War Crimes Investigation unit emerged from the shadows to become known to a wider public. Although its work had been quietly progressing since May, the investigations of Macdonald, Campbell, and Durdin (described by Ross Munro as carried out 'on a purely Canadian basis') were now of national interest. The unit's work was described in detail in the *Globe and Mail*. Featuring especially the investigative unit at Bad Salzuflen, 'whence they travel all over Europe with investigating teams,' the *Globe* reported that as a result of these efforts 104 cases were almost ready for trial.[26] Other Allied nations were closely watching the Meyer case. The Nuremberg proceedings had not yet begun, and Meyer's court martial would be a trial run for the prosecution of the major war criminals.

A display of fair, impartial justice was vital to the success of the Meyer prosecution. However, this was made all the more difficult when another twist threatened the trial's integrity. In mid-October, Macdonald told Meyer that he was entitled to a lawyer and Meyer's first reaction was to ask, 'Could the Colonel act for me?'[27] Macdonald may have struck him as an intelligent, fair-minded man, or he may simply have wished to deprive the prosecution of his services. In any case, Macdonald would prosecute, not defend. Meyer then discussed his situation with two fellow prisoners, von der Heydte and General Eberbach. Von der Heydte's experience had been limited to academe, and he declined to participate actively. Meyer indicated that his first preference was an English civilian barrister assisted by a German military officer. If this was not possible, he preferred a

German lawyer assisted by a Canadian officer. But the Canadian government was not about to pay for lawyers. One of Meyer's confidants, the English officer Lieutenant-Colonel Chater, advised that no English barrister would work gratis on a case which would involve 'considerable risk of loss of goodwill and professional reputation.'[28] Neither was it possible to find a German lawyer. Enquiries were made in Aurich and no lawyer would work for Meyer for compensation or otherwise.[29] A number of Canadian officers were considered to act for Meyer, and Lieutenant-Colonel Maurice Andrew of the Perth Regiment seemed the most likely choice. However, Andrew was scheduled to return to Canada, and instead Lieutenant-Colonel Peter Wright was assigned to Meyer's defence.[30] Shortly after Meyer was charged, Macdonald briefed Wright on the nature of the prosecution's evidence and witnesses. He was then asked if he wanted to see Meyer. To Macdonald's surprise, he declined, saying that he had no wish to set eyes on Meyer and then adding, 'I won't have anything to do with the bastard.'[31] Outside the room the press was waiting to talk to the lawyers and Macdonald's mind raced with the implications of the news that Meyer's appointed counsel heartily endorsed his client's demise. This threatened to destroy everything, and so Macdonald hurriedly ushered Wright out a side door. The reporters were told that acting for the defence interfered with Wright's repatriation plan and instead Maurice Andrew was being assigned to the defence.

As Macdonald delicately explained to his superiors, Wright's attitude to the defence was 'one which could have caused misunderstanding and ill will on all sides.'[32] Kurt Meyer's principal defender, Maurice Andrew, had achieved a solid reputation and a DSO as commander of the Perths in Italy. A skilled lawyer, he had anticipated returning to his law practice in Stratford, Ontario, until the army's legal demands intervened. Though his feints and dodges in the trial would match Macdonald's dogged perseverance, he did not have an easy case or client. At their first meeting, Meyer asked Andrew, 'Why are you wasting your time on all this – why not just shoot me?'[33] After Andrew assured Meyer that he would get a fair trial, the prisoner's attitude changed to one of cooperation. According to one account of the trial, Andrew came to respect Meyer and even trust in his innocence; he 'couldn't believe that he [Meyer] ordered the executions for which he was charged.'[34] Andrew, assisted by Captain Frank Plourde, guaranteed that the accused would have a vigorous defence.

Andrew notified Macdonald that he wished to call a number of witnesses including the commanding officer of Panzer Group West, General Geyr von Schweppenberg, Karl Milius, the commanding officer of the 3rd battalion of the 25th PGR, and two French civilians. Macdonald put the unit at his disposal to locate these persons.[35] In the meantime, it was becoming increasingly unrealistic to consider 28 November as a trial date. The lawyers agreed to a delay, and General Vokes was advised to set 10 December for the beginning of the trial.[36] This determination to be fair was also a boon to the prosecution, for they were by no means ready to proceed. Robichaud was still in Normandy collecting civilian witnesses at the Abbaye, and the rest of the staff was trying to get Canadian witnesses (most of whom were now civilians back in Canada) to return to Europe to testify.[37] The next problem was one of communication. CMHQ was unwilling to supply Meyer with a personal interpreter, and so Macdonald was compelled to assign one of his own staff, Wady Lehmann, to the task. It was an awkward arrangement, but Lehmann had no previous connection with the Meyer investigation and Macdonald made it clear that from now on he worked for the defence and should avoid contact with unit staff.[38] This requirement was scrupulously observed in order to avoid any suggestion that 'the prosecution may be in a position to unduly influence the conduct of the defense.'[39] During hours of discussion and preparation, Lehmann would come to know Kurt Meyer as well as any Canadian could. In mid-November he was dispatched by Andrew to see Meyer's family and give them the chance to attend the trial. Lehmann drove to the town of Offleben and (somewhat to their surprise) offered to drive Kate Meyer, her four daughters, and infant son to Aurich. The family's reunion with Meyer, even if it was closely watched by guards, was an intensely emotional one, made all the more poignant in that in a few days he would stand trial for his life.

While the trial was delayed, Macdonald took stock of new difficulties. He had learned that Meyer was likely to refer to an incident in which a German reconnaissance patrol was allegedly killed after capture by Canadian troops near La Villeneuve.[40] A check of reference maps indicated that the area in question had been held by 'D' Company of the Regina Rifles. 'As prosecutor,' Macdonald noted, 'it is my duty to place all information impartially before the court.' Pinning down exactly what had occurred proved most difficult since the only remaining officers from 'D' Company were touring somewhere in Ireland. But there was an even more troubling aspect to the La Villeneuve incident. The Canadians had been part of the 7th Infantry Brigade, commanded by the court's president, Harry Foster. Was he also to be charged with responsibility for troops who had killed prisoners? In something of a panic, Macdonald telephoned Brigadier Orde (who had at last arrived by ship) to get the opinion of Canada's ranking military lawyer. Macdonald asked if he should call Foster to ask whether his troops had been involved in any way 'so he would not be embarrassed as President of the Court.'[41] Orde did not think it necessary but mentioned in passing that it was likely that an officer would be partial towards the prosecution only if his troops had been the victims of atrocities. A number of the troops murdered in Normandy had belonged to the 7th Infantry Brigade.

Questions concerning the partiality of the court and whether Canadian troops had also killed prisoners would have to be addressed at trial. The prosecution had defused the problem of providing a defence lawyer for Meyer, and it was preparing a response to his change in evidence. There remained one final twist in the pre-trial preparations that threatened to destroy the case before Meyer even stood before his accusers.

The judge advocate assigned to the case, Lieutenant-Colonel Bredin, noticed that the regulations were made pursuant to the War Measures Act and that section 4 of that act provided a maximum penalty of five years' imprisonment. Yet section 11 of the regulations empowered a court mar-tial to order sentence of death. Bredin's warning about this contradiction set off alarm bells at CMHQ London and in several ministries throughout Ottawa. Orde conferred with his British counterpart, Sir Henry MacGeagh, and was reassured that the regulations were 'merely declaratory of the punishments recognized by international law.'[42] Back in Ottawa, John Read canvassed the constitutional perils of the issue and in his report to the acting External Affairs minister, Louis St Laurent, he listed the govern-ment's options. The British royal warrant could not apply to Canada's military because this would be inconsistent with national sovereignty. Neither could the governor general as commander-in-chief make regula-tions except through his council. Therefore, if the government desired (and it appeared to have little choice) to eliminate the War Measures Act as the basis for the regulations, it could do so by reissuing the regulations as an order-in-council under the prerogative power.[43] After this report, there was a meeting of CWCAC in Ottawa after which Read transmitted its opinion to Orde that the purpose of the regulations had merely been to provide a procedure for the application of international law and that a belligerent state was entitled to establish courts to punish enemy offend-ers. Admittedly, there remained some residual doubt as to the validity of the regulations (Read added reassuringly that legal opinion was three to one in favour of validity) but it was too late to refer the issue to the Supreme Court. As of 17 November, Read still hoped to 'find some resolution within the next day or so which will avoid the possibility of abandoning the proceedings and making a fresh start.'[44]

The embarrassment of having to start over again was narrowly avoided when the departments of Justice and External Affairs decided on 19 November that the Meyer trial could proceed under the existing regulations.[45] St Laurent sent an amending order-in-council to the governor general in which all references to the War Measures Act were removed and the regulations were reissued under the prerogative power of the crown. The amendment was back dated to 10 September.[46] Orde wrote to Bredin on 21 November advising him of these changes and strongly impressing upon him that this resolved the issue and that 'should this question arise during the course of the trial you will, please, as my representative thereat be guided by the opinions in question with which I concur and advise the Court in the sense thereof.'[47] That is, comply or else.

Macdonald had watched these high-level manoeuvrings with mounting anxiety that could not be allayed by Orde's laying down the law to Bredin. He was amazed to learn that copies of the papers questioning the constitutionality of the regulations had been given to Bredin to give to Andrew. By so doing, 'a rather potent weapon has thereby been put into his hands ... Col. Andrew may feel it his duty to read these communications to the court, and the effect of it may be to give the appearance of a conspiracy in high places to ensure Meyer's conviction.'[48] Macdonald warned that these documents would 'supply ammunition to the critics of this trial which might be very hard to meet.' At the last minute, Bredin was ordered not to give the documents to Andrew, and a major embarrassment was thereby avoided. Or, from another perspective, was a vital legal issue deliberately withheld from the defence?

Macdonald suspected sinister motives in the near release of this material. 'There are officers,' he cautioned Orde, 'some of whom are in your own branch, who are opposed to the whole principle of war crimes trials' and such officers would likely criticize the legality of the upcoming trials. He had sufficient difficulty in prosecuting Meyer without having to fight JAG staff at the same time. Accusing his superiors of deliberate obstruction was harsh indeed but reflected the strain Macdonald endured in preparing for trial. The pressure was showing. Only four weeks before the trial was to begin, Macdonald was still trying to find evidence to tie Meyer conclusively to the killings at the Abbaye. He advised his superiors: 'I should like it to be thoroughly understood at this time, as it has been by the JAG, that while a prima facie case exists against Meyer and I think convictions will be obtained, nevertheless, on the more serious charge of direct responsibility for the shooting of prisoners, the issue rests largely on a question of credibility. If Meyer can locate the witnesses mentioned by him, for whom we are also searching, and they are able to corroborate his story, it is unlikely that a conviction on this charge is possible.'[49] The case was by no means open and shut, and since to a great extent the prosecution evidence was of a 'circumstantial character, one would be foolish to make any certain predictions about the outcome.'

By way of an apology for his failure to write, Macdonald explained to his wife that he had been working late every night and that 'many unexpected difficulties had arisen.' There were enormous expectations on the prosecution, both from the government and the people of Canada, to present the evidence in the most damning light. As Macdonald advised his wife, 'I also realize that I've got to convict this bird or all hell will break loose.'[50]

5

Brigadeführer on Trial

On Saturday, 8 December, camera crews took over the courtroom to test their equipment. With a Canadian soldier substituting for Kurt Meyer, they conducted a rehearsal of the opening formalities. The following Monday, with the camera recording the scene, the judicial theatre was officially convened. Wearing a plain German army uniform with gold general's epaulettes, Meyer, flanked by his officer guards, was marched into the courtroom. Passing through a gauntlet of journalists and photographers, he walked confidently to the front of the courtroom and bowed to the generals. He was determined to demonstrate 'the firm will to prove myself in front of the tribunal and to be a model for my soldiers.' The five charges on the first charge sheet were read out, and Meyer pleaded 'not guilty' to each. As he scanned the bench, Meyer considered it a bitter irony that his 'opponent on the battlefield of 1944 [Foster] was designated President of the court to pass judgement on me ... The victor was now chosen to administer "justice" over the vanquished after they had fought each other with every fibre of their being ... All of these gentlemen had fought against me and were thus involved in the case.' Meyer ignored the German practice of trying Allied troops with far fewer formalities. And yet Meyer saw reason for hope in Foster's selection as president: 'I looked to discover understanding and sympathy in Foster's eyes. At any event, I felt I was standing in front of a soldier and not a mere uniform bearer.'[1] More than Meyer may have realized, Foster would indeed sympathize with his position.

Of the English and Canadian correspondents covering the trial, Ralph Allen of the Toronto *Globe and Mail* gave the most vivid account of the court's convening. To Allen, Meyer's sang-froid was notable: the 'stocky blackhaired prisoner might have been a private soldier facing nothing more serious than a possible three months detention for a protracted absence without leave.' Giving a deferential bow to the court, Meyer seated himself next to his lawyers. The accused was uniformly respectful, Allen noted, and in contrast to the arrogant defendants at Nuremberg he 'appeared to find nothing either amusing or particularly depressing in the proceedings.'[2] The former brigadeführer sat clasping and unclasping his wiry hands, occasionally consulting with the interpreter Lehmann and paying close attention to all that was said. As the proceedings were conducted in English and then translated into German, the pace became excessively ponderous.

After the formalities and the swearing in of the court, Macdonald outlined the prosecution's case. Jan Jesionek's eyewitness account of Meyer giving the order to kill Canadian prisoners would be critical and would be supplemented by pathological reports. As well, French civilians would confirm the fact that the graves at the Abbaye had been concealed to hide the crime. Further reliance would be placed on Meyer's deception at his initial interrogation. Finally, the prosecution would rely on comments from German soldiers themselves that they had received orders from their commanders to deny quarter. Macdonald chose to stake much of the prosecution's case on these statements that Meyer was, through his subordinates, urging his men to kill prisoners.

In addition to outlining the facts, Macdonald also presented a grander vision of what the trial entailed. This was the first case of its kind ever to be tried by a Canadian military court, and it was also the first case in Europe to try and establish the responsibility of a ranking officer for atrocities committed by his troops. These crimes were violations of the military codes of both Germany and Canada and the only novelty in this respect was the number of incidents and the total of victims. Macdonald was interrupted by Bredin (as he was at several points during his address) and asked whether he was going to prove the latter point, to which Macdonald replied: 'I took it that this was common knowledge.' Macdonald persisted that the various incidents were all relevant to Meyer's guilt as a commander for 'if more than one forbidden act occurs in a unit or formation, that is some evidence that the commander has been at least negligent in his duty, if not directly responsible.'[3]

The prosecution's first witness, Major Stonborough, set out the organizational chart identifying Waffen SS units. Then Macdonald read into the record Torbanisch's statement that his company had been given the 'secret order' to eliminate prisoners in April 1944. After Torbanisch had deserted to the Belgian resistance (he had decamped yet again and could not be found for trial), he dictated a copy of these secret orders in German. This had been translated into Flemish, and an English translation was put before the court. The orders stressed the bonds among SS troops and declared that 'traitors will be executed even after the war.' The fourth paragraph read: 'Attitude at the front: The SS troops shall take no prisoners. Prisoners are to be executed after having been interrogated. The SS soldiers shall not give themselves up and must commit suicide if there is no other choice left. The officers have stated that the British do not take prisoners as far as SS soldiers are concerned.'[4] All the men then signed to show that they understood the order.

Proving the secret orders through a live witness would be much more effective, and so Macdonald proceeded to call Alfred Helzel to testify. While a prisoner in Canada, Helzel had had no difficulty remembering that his company had orders to kill prisoners. But in Aurich, with his legendary commander confronting him, Helzel's confidence evaporated. Macdonald's first mistake may have been to ask Helzel to identify Meyer. Ralph Allen described what happened next: 'As Helzel pointed a long finger across the courtroom to identify his former regimental commander the two men stared at each other and then dropped their eyes as though on a single impulse ... from the moment he and Meyer looked at each other any value Helzel might have had for the prosecution was lost.'[5] Macdonald reviewed Helzel's previous statement that the company commander, von Buettner, had passed along Meyer's direct order that 'my Regiment takes no prisoners.' Now, as Helzel slumped in his chair, nervous and evasive, the story changed:

Q. And what did he [von Beuttner] say to you?
A. That if prisoners are taken they are immediately to be brought back to be treated decently as it is of great value if the prisoners make statements.

He agreed that secret orders had been given, but he disputed Torbanisch's recollection of paragraph four: Paragraph four is also not quite correct ... SS troops were to take prisoners. Also the prisoners were not to be executed after interrogation.'[6]

Macdonald's face reflected his incredulity as he walked slowly back to the prosecution table and wondered what to do next. It was then that he noticed that Meyer had transfixed Helzel with a vitriolic glare that fairly electrified the courtroom. This was, as Macdonald recalled, 'an amazing demonstration of the tremendous disciplinary hold that this S.S. officer still had on a former soldier, and of the fear inspired by his presence.'[7] Hoping to salvage something, Macdonald stepped between Meyer and the witness. He hoped that Helzel, no longer able to see Meyer, would regain his composure. Picking up a copy of Helzel's examination at Hull, Quebec, Macdonald asked him to confirm that previously he had said under oath that von Beuttner had instructed his company not to take prisoners. Helzel confirmed this. Then Macdonald read another portion of the examination where Helzel had indicated that Meyer himself had given the same order. He confirmed this as well. Recapping, Macdonald asked him if von Buettner had told his soldiers not to take prisoners. Helzel promptly went back on all he had just said by replying, 'I cannot remember that Hauptsturmfuhrer von Beuttner said such a thing.' Vacillating back and forth between confirming his previous comments and then denying them, Helzel had destroyed his own credibility.

On the second day, the proceedings became stranger still. Macdonald began by telling the court that, after he had left the witness stand, Helzel had talked with the interpreter Stonborough, and Helzel had told him that he had misunderstood the questions. Bredin stopped Macdonald and informed the court that it was wildly improper to refer to a witness's out-of-court comments as if they were evidence. The comments were struck and Foster refused to let Macdonald recall Helzel. The next witness, Horst Heyer, testified that as his unit moved up to the battle area their company commander had said that they should not take prisoners. At an assembly in Beverloo, Belgium, Meyer had also remarked that 'my regiment takes no prisoners.' Under cross-examination, Heyer did not dispute Andrew's suggestion that perhaps what Meyer had said was that his troops should not be taken prisoner. Heyer also confirmed that there was an offer of leave to soldiers who brought prisoners in for interrogation. This ended Macdonald's attempt to prove that SS troops had been instructed to kill prisoners. It seemed far from convincing.

The prosecution now switched to painting a broader picture of SS atrocities in Normandy. Lieutenant-Colonel Charles Petch of the North Novas described the battles at Authie and Buron, and a French civilian, Constance Guilbert, described the harrowing aftermath. From his window, Guilbert saw a Canadian soldier trying to surrender but 'as he was crossing Madame Godet's garden and when he had got within three or four metres of the Germans, he was shot down. The Canadian soldier had his arms up in the air.' Minutes later, Guilbert saw a wounded Canadian move, and 'one of the German soldiers who wore a gaberdine took a bayonet and hit him, opening his head.'[8] Guilbert had a fine eye for the terrible detail of the German re-occupation, but none of this directly implicated Meyer. Macdonald conceded the oblique nature of this evidence: 'We are not proposing to adduce any evidence of a direct order that prisoners should be shot because our case rests largely on circumstantial evidence.' The grim stories continued the next day as three of the North Novas described what they had seen. Unaccustomed to addressing such senior officers, they testified quietly, occasionally glancing dispassionately at Meyer. Ralph Allen described the growing tension in the courtroom as the trial 'ceased to be a delicate problem in international law and became a plea for the comrades they watched die by order of the 12th SS.'[9]

Stanley Dudka had ended the war with two wound stripes and the Military Medal, and he had agreed to return to Europe to testify. He described the unprovoked killing of Private John Metcalfe: of his being dragged out of the ranks and shot, and his wounded body left on the ground until sometime later when a smiling guard finished him off. He testified of the killing of a wounded soldier, Private John Hargraves, for the offence of not being able to keep up with the others. In Authie, Dudka had seen Canadian bodies lined up in a row, all without weapons or helmets. Eventually, his column of prisoners had arrived at the Abbaye where military police had asked for ten volunteers. No one stepped forward. Ten men were dragged out, including Private J.A. Moss from Dudka's hometown of Stellarton, Nova Scotia. Moss was one of the men later identified as executed at the Abbaye. In cross-examination, Dudka denied Andrew's suggestion that the prisoners were decently treated at the Abbaye. 'They weren't killing our fellows at the time if that is what you mean.' The next witness, Sergeant William McKay, had seen a good deal more. In the space of a half-hour, he had observed ten unarmed prisoners shot by their captors. From a doorway, McKay had seen SS men execute eight Canadian prisoners who were lined up, sitting on the side of the road.[10]

On 12 December, Ottawa released the names of 125 Canadian soldiers known to have been murdered in Normandy. The lists were published in newspapers and chaplains were dispatched to warn families that their son's or husband's name might come up at the trial. Canadians were transfixed by the Aurich trial, and this latest revelation of 125 victims of 'Meyer's SS Division' only seemed to confirm his irrefutable guilt. Simultaneously, the Nuremberg trial was examining evidence of concentration camp SS men using the skins of their victims for lampshades and of 'human beings hunted down in wild manhunts by the SS.'[11] Photographs of a scowling Meyer looking like a caged tiger in his cell added to the feeling that here was another Nazi butcher, the only difference being that his victims were not Jews or Gypsies but disarmed Canadian prisoners.

However brutal the conduct of some SS men, the prosecution's evidence showed that it was by no means universal. Major John Learment's affidavit described how his group of eighteen to twenty North Novas was herded against a wall and about to be shot when an SS officer or NCO intervened and prevented the shooting.[12] Private Gordon Talbot also described an officer halting the imminent execution of his section: 'The German soldiers began to shift about uneasily while this man came right up to them and appeared to be reprimanding them.'[13] At least some officers and NCO were trying to prevent the summary killing of prisoners and this was hardly consistent with a regimental policy of annihilation.

The fourth day of trial was a repetition of North Novas describing the killing of disarmed prisoners. Corporal John Campbell graphically recounted the end of one wounded Canadian: 'The German that shot at A. deliberately walked across the road and pointed at his head and pulled the trigger.' But all this was only a prelude to the most crucial phase of the trial. At the end of the day, Macdonald advised the court that Jan Jesionek would testify the following morning. Macdonald prepared the way by reading into the record Jesionek's statement to Sergeant Stern. In this the prosecution faced a formidable hurdle, for the statement was filled with inconsistencies and inaccuracies. However, Macdonald would try to show that these errors were a result of the translator's haste and sloppiness, not Jesionek's duplicity.

On Friday morning, 14 December, Jan Jesionek took the stand. The case against Kurt Meyer would either be proven or fail on the words of the slim nineteen-year-old Pole. A native of Upper Silesia, he had apprenticed at a steel factory when Waffen SS officers had visited and asked for volunteers. Of 200 apprentices, 4 stepped forward. The rest were given fifteen minutes to think it over, and two more stepped forward. After that, all youths who met the requirement for height and Nordic appearance (including Jesionek) were drafted into the SS. Jesionek's conscription was a great help to his family. His father, a Polish nationalist and co-founder of the Polish league 'SOKOL,' had once been greeted by a German neighbour with 'Heil Hitler' and had had the temerity to reply in Polish, 'Zin Dobre' (Good Day). This action had earned him a prison term until his son's assignment to the Waffen SS resulted in his release.

Unlike other German witnesses, Jesionek was not wearing a Wehrmacht or SS uniform. This may have been a prosecution ploy to curry favour with the court. But it was not well received and Macdonald had to have Jesionek explain that he was wearing a naval uniform given to him by the Red Cross. At the beginning of his service he was a dutiful recruit, selected to serve in the 15th Reconnaissance Company of the 25th PGR. By coincidence, he had been in the 4th platoon with Frederich Torbanisch and also recalled the secret order. Though he no longer remembered the contents, he did remember that when Meyer addressed the troops, informing them of Germany's marvellous new V-rockets, he also told them that they, too, were instruments of Germany's revenge and that 'we ourselves should make the reprisals on English prisoners of war.' After the speech, the soldiers talked among themselves and Jesionek recalled that 'there were quite different opinions. Many said that an enemy who has weapons no more is no enemy.'[14] Sometime thereafter, their company commander, von Buettner, a former comrade of Meyer's, told them: 'May the others do what they please; our Company takes no prisoners.'

At the beginning of the Normandy campaign, Jesionek's platoon had been on a reconnaissance patrol when they strayed into a minefield; a vehicle blew up and the men retreated in haste. They returned to the regimental HQ at the Abbaye on the morning of 8 June and Jesionek was temporarily left at the HQ with no duties to perform. About noon, he saw seven Canadian prisoners marched in under guard, and one of the guards asked him where they could find the commander. Together, they went to the chapel, into which, on Meyer's order following an air raid only fifteen minutes before, all vehicles had been moved. It was there, amid the motorcycles and jeeps, that the guard reported in. Kurt Meyer rounded on him and in a loud voice asked, 'What should we do with these prisoners; they only eat up our rations.' 'Meyer then turned to a tall, slim officer and spoke to him in half-tones. Speaking again out loud for the benefit of all soldiers in the chapel, Meyer called out, 'In future no more prisoners are to be taken.' The tall officer then left with the guard to the stable where the prisoners were confined.[15]

Jesionek wished to clean up and went to a pump at the entrance to a garden. From there, he could still see events going on in the stable. While Jesionek could not understand English, it was clear that the officer was berating the Canadians. He laughed and sneered at them, and Jesionek noted that the Canadians looked grim and one was crying. Paybooks were taken from the prisoners and, one by one, they were called out of the stable. They were marched along a guarded path to an enclosed passageway and guided up a few steps to a small park. As each man entered the park, he turned left and an *Unterscharführer* (corporal) from Meyer's HQ shot him in the back of the head. In addition to the pistol shots, Jesionek heard the occasional scream. The men knew that they faced death for, as each man's name was called out, he shook hands with his comrades. After the seven were killed, the corporal emerged from the park and unloaded his pistol. Along with other soldiers from the HQ, Jesionek was drawn to the park where he saw the seven Canadian bodies lying in a heap. The soldiers walked around the pile in awe 'because the whole place was full of blood.'[16]

The following day Jesionek was wounded in the attack on Bretteville and in March 1945 he deserted. None of his American captors knew of his involvement in the Abbaye killings, and so Macdonald asked him why he had come forward with his story. Despite Meyer's fierce glare, the Pole replied, 'I made the statement from a purely soldierly or military point of view. In my eyes Meyer was no longer an officer.'

On cross-examination, there was little that Maurice Andrew could do to attack directly this evidence. Instead, he initiated a series of sorties to discredit Jesionek's credibility. He raised the threat by the U.S. sergeant to hang all SS prisoners. Had this motivated Jesionek to save himself by turning in his former commander? He admitted that this had rattled him, but it had not diverted him from giving a true statement. Errors were the result of the American going too rapidly and failing to note accurately what was said. A major discrepancy between Jesionek's April statement and his current testimony was his comment in April that, immediately after Meyer said that there were to be no more prisoners, 'he gave the order to the Executive Officer to have the prisoners shot.' Now he denied ever hearing a direct order from Meyer to kill the prisoners. When Andrew pressed him on this inconsistency, Jesionek told him that he had brought the errors to the attention of the American sergeant and had been told that he could correct the document later. He was never given the chance. Perhaps unwisely, Andrew pressed him on what he understood Meyer to have said in the chapel:

Q. What is the kernel of that statement?
A. That I strongly suspected that Meyer gave the officer the order to shoot the prisoners.
Q. And is not the whole thing something in your mind connected with Meyer?
A. Such a story one cannot invent.[17]

Yet Jesionek might be discredited on other details. He had originally deposed that his father had written to get him deferred from service in the SS. This was false, since his father was in prison at the time; his mother had written the letter. When Andrew confronted him with this lie, he responded that 'I remained silent about the fact that my father was imprisoned, not to arouse any suspicion that because of my father I sought revenge on Meyer.' Andrew read back part of a 30 October 1945 statement in which Jesionek described Meyer wearing a rubber motorcycle coat. Now he was not certain. Just how clear was his recollection?

Q. Now, am I correct in saying that the details – the details as you call them of the eighth of June in the morning, are not clear in your mind?
A. That is not correct. It is hard to say, as I said before what a man had on – whether he had gloves on at this moment. One doesn't look at such things.

Another line of attack was to press Jesionek on why, at his interrogation on 28 May, he had failed to mention Meyer's comment that in the future no more prisoners were to be taken:

A. Yes, there is lacking there the part that he then said to all those assembled there that 'in future no prisoners are to be taken.' That was by error not written down.
Q. Am I correct in classing this as one of your errors in minor detail?
A. No because the Lieutenant Colonel here [Macdonald] could be a witness himself to that.[18]

Macdonald interjected that Jesionek had said the words and the stenographer had failed to note them. The omission had been corrected at the next interrogation. Jesionek's recollection of that morning, while not perfect, seemed remarkably clear and consistent. The Pole remained adamant that he had given an accurate account, even when Andrew pressed him:

Q. At the time you gave that evidence you were not quite sure as to what Meyer did say, were you?
A. The sense I know but not the precise arrangement of words. If the Defending Officer was there he too after one year would not have known the precise language.
Q. I can assure you of that. Now, Jesionek, will you say that the words as you gave in this courtroom today as coming from Meyer on the morning of the 8th were the exact words that Meyer said on that occasion?
A. As far as I know they are right.

Q. Are you sure?
A. Yes.
Q. Positive – no doubt?
A. Without a doubt that it is the right meaning.[19]

Reporters noted that Andrew reddened after this sally, while Jesionek merely smiled.

On other details, Andrew did succeed in tripping up the prosecution's main witness. Jesionek insisted that Meyer's driver was a Russian while all other evidence indicated that the driver was German. But, except for minor points, Jesionek's story was unshaken after three hours of cross-examination. 'At times the tug of wills between the witness and Meyer's counsel, Lieutenant-Colonel M.W. Andrew, became so intense that the story Jesionek told this morning was almost forgotten' and even Meyer, glaring at his accuser, 'seemed a minor figure.' Also gone was any cordiality between the counsel tables. Objections became commonplace, and once Foster had to separate the lawyers with a crisp 'Quit arguing.'

Andrew's zeal impressed the reporters, who found him 'fighting as hard and as conscientiously for his client's life today as though they had never been enemies.'[20] Though Jesionek's testimony, the keystone of the prosecution's case, had survived intact, he had not impressed the generals; Foster recalled him as a 'young smart aleck who possessed a remarkable memory.'[21] As for Meyer, even as his defenders fought, he seemed to become detached from the proceedings. Ross Monro noted that Meyer had lost his keenness and at times during Jesionek's testimony 'he sat back, with his eyes closed in an attitude of resignation.'[22]

Jesionek's testimony was the high point of Macdonald's case. The following days only added the final touches to a finished landscape. Together with the interpreter Stonborough, Macdonald went through Jesionek's initial deposition and showed how the translation from German into English had been inaccurate on many points. Another translator, Captain R.J. Pootmans, described how the unit had taken Jesionek back to Normandy and how he had led the way to the Abbaye. As one of the only two German speakers, Jesionek had guided Pootmans step by step through the site and shown him where and how the events had transpired. Photographs were taken of Jesionek at the stable, the water pump, and in the park. Throughout all this, he had exhibited a superb recollection of the incident and at no time had he been prompted to make any statements. Two residents of the Abbaye, Françine and Jean-Marie Vico, described the discovery of the bodies in the park in January 1945. Unlike other hastily prepared battlefield graves, these had been carefully dug to leave little suggestion of burials. There were no mounds of dirt, and the sods had been carefully placed over the dead. The Vicos also found two clubs (one of which was bloodstained) in the park. The final phase of the prosecution was the pathologist's report. Six of the bodies were discovered buried together in one grave, and all of these victims had been shot in the head. There were four more graves as well, one with one victim and the others with five, four, and two victims respectively. One unidentified body, bearing the insignia of the Stormont, Dundas and Glengarry Highlanders was found outside the garden. Lieutenant-Colonel R.A.H. MacKeen, who had been on the trail of the war criminals since July 1944, was recalled from New Brunswick to testify. His examination showed that all the soldiers buried in the garden had died of head wounds. Of these, eight had been shot in the back of the head. As for the others, a projectile or blunt instrument had severely damaged the skull. The court adjourned that Saturday afternoon, 15 December, until the following Monday. Even with most of the prosecution evidence in, Ralph Allen observed that 'the case against Meyer does not appear so strong that a conviction can yet be considered certain.'[23]

For the defence lawyers, Andrew and Plourde, this was an intense period of activity. In addition to discussing strategy, Wady Lehmann had the opportunity for more philosophical discussions. Meyer remained, despite Lehmann's remonstrances, a committed Nazi. As Lehmann later recalled, 'his life really meant very little to him. His only regret was that he hadn't died in battle. He still idolized Hitler and became vehement in his support of the Fuhrer when I suggested that all he'd done was lead Germany into destruction.'[24] As for the generals, most of their battle stories had been retold in the officer's mess, and they were becoming restless at their confinement. Foster seemed to think that by this point they had a complete picture of what had happened at Authie, Buron, and the Abbaye. Years later, Foster recounted to his son that he was reminded of an occasion in Italy when his operations officer, Scott Murdoch, was notified by a battalion commander that they had captured some Germans and wanted to know what to do with them. Foster heard Murdoch order him to 'shoot the buggers.' Then Foster remembered that 'a day earlier I'd said that we wanted no more prisoners. They were a nuisance to feed and look after.' Murdoch was only passing along his superior's orders. As Foster listened to the testimony in Aurich, he was left to ponder, 'How many prisoners did that battalion commander shoot? I never knew, neither did Scott. Was I guilty of a war crime; was Scott; was Meyer? Probably.'[25] Foster shared none of these thoughts with the rest of the court or the lawyers and he made no attempt to disqualify himself. In the back of his mind there unquestionably lurked a sympathy for Meyer; while in command both had given orders that in peacetime seemed absolutely damning.

Monday, 17 December, was a dreary day of arguments on points of evidence. Macdonald did introduce the affidavit of Private Marcel Dagenais who, along with Lieutenant Tom Windsor and three other soldiers, was captured on 7 June. On the way to the Abbaye, Dagenais saw SS men shoot wounded men who were unable to walk. Arriving at the Abbaye, he observed an SS sergeant slap Windsor when he called out that 'he had only three words to say to them; his name, his rank and his number.' Because he was francophone, Dagenais was separated from the others and taken to Caen. Windsor would be among the murdered at the Abbaye. It has been suggested on the basis of Dagenais's report that Canadians were being executed for failure to divulge vital information. Yet it seems unlikely that the victims, most of whom were privates, had any real information to disclose. While it may be inferred that some of the prisoners were shot for not cooperating, the motivation for the killings seems to have primarily been revenge or bloodlust. Neither the Abbaye, Mouen, or the Chateau d'Audrieu were intelligence-gathering areas where prisoners would normally be interrogated. Witnesses recalled Germans defending the murders as justice for civilians killed in the air raids or as revenge for their comrades killed in the battle, and not for any failure to give information.[26]

As if he did not have enough to work with, Macdonald now tried to prove that another murder had been commited at the Abbaye a week after the others. This evidence related to the unknown body wearing the insignia of the Stormonts that had been buried apart from the others. It was now known that this was the body of Lieutenant Fred Williams, who had been wounded and captured on 16 June. However, the defence had been given no notice of this fact, and the killing had not been mentioned in the charge sheet. In Andrew's view, the defence was being ambushed. Dalton Dean replied for the prosecution that the evidence was admissible under paragraph 10(4) of the regulations whereby the court could receive evidence of the responsibility of a commander for crimes committed by his men. This did not require, Dean noted, that each offence be listed. Judge advocate Bredin agreed that section 10(4) cast a wide net, but there was still an issue of fairness to the accused. Andrew protested the prosecution's tactics: 'It is not only a question of surprise but it is introducing something different – absolutely new. I have had four weeks to prepare this case and my friend has had fifteen months.'[27] After an adjournment, the court decided to permit the prosecution to proceed on the understanding that they must prove that Meyer was actually the commander at the time of the killing.

A staff officer of the 12th SS confirmed that Meyer had succeeded Fritz Witt as division commander at noon on 17 June. However, another witness, who was at the Abbaye at the time the prisoner was killed, recalled that Meyer had already left to assume his new post. In support of his case, Macdonald presented the Stormonts' war diary, which showed that Lieutenant Williams and two other soldiers had been lost on the night of 16 June. An SS man remembered hearing a shot as he drove up to the Abbaye on the night of 16 or 17 June and a guard told him in a matter-of-fact way that 'perhaps it is a prisoner has been shot who would make no statement.' An army officer, Fritz Steger, commanded the 3rd battalion of the 25th PGR after 1 July and he heard from two of his platoon commanders that prisoners had been shot at the regimental HQ. Yet there was no direct evidence that Lieutenant Williams or the other captured soldier, Lance Corporal Pollard, had been murdered.[28] There were strong suspicions that they had been shot after capture but nothing could be proved, and the attempt had perhaps detracted from more persuasive evidence.

The prosecution ended with the reading into the record of part of Meyer's previous sworn statements in which he had confirmed that Scheumann, a tall thin officer who spoke English, had been his adjutant in June. The implication was that it was Scheumann whom Meyer had talked to in half-tones in the chapel. When asked when Scheumann had been relieved as adjutant Meyer had given a careful response: 'He was a few more days adjutant once I took over the Division and then he was relieved.' That is, after 16 June, Meyer's successor as commanding officer of the 25th PGR wanted his own man as adjutant. In these interviews, Meyer also agreed that it was likely that he gave the order to move the vehicles into the chapel, that he was probably at the Abbaye on the morning of 8 June, and that an air attack had occurred that morning. As well, he stated that on 7 June he had ordered prisoners to be sent to Division HQ for interrogation. Perhaps this explained why ten men were selected on that night. Only two were sent by staff car to the Division HQ and Macdonald inferred that the others had been shot at the Abbaye because it was unlikely that they would talk.

On the afternoon of 18 December, Maurice Andrew began the defence of Kurt Meyer. He declined to make an opening statement and instead directly called Meyer to testify. Speaking clearly, with no hesitation, Meyer described the formation of the 12th SS, the rigorous training given to the youngsters, and the aim to make them warriors of high moral character. He recounted for the court the speeches he had given to the recruits, in which he urged them never to let themselves be captured and reminded them that if they faced captivity 'the last shot belongs to you.' Never had he told them to kill prisoners. In a voice that was 'clear and confident, and sometimes close to ranting,' Meyer relived his addresses to the Hitler youth until some of the reporters had the erie feeling of being transported back to Meyer's training command. Meyer recounted his address to the 15th Reconnaissance Company at Le Sap, France. Having served as a reconnaissance officer himself, Meyer was partial to this company and shared his experiences with them. 'The deserter Jesionek,' he spat out, had misconstrued his meaning. At Le Sap, Meyer had referred to the V, *Vernichtung*, weapons and had told his recruits that they were to be 'weapons of the German people ... destined to effect the annihilation of the enemy forces.'[29] The defence interpreter Lehmann interjected that the term *Vernichtung* in German military parlance meant 'destructive attack' and not 'annihilation' with its connotation of killing all the enemy, those who resisted and those who did not. The court was cautioned that, in the translation of German into English, meanings could be given to words that tended to colour what was said in the other language.

Parts of the prosecution case Meyer dismissed as patently absurd. The so-called 'secret order' was really a quarterly order read to troops concerning the prevention of espionage and desertion. There was nothing sinister in this, nothing that advocated the killing of prisoners, and the inference that it was an illegal order was, in Meyer's view, 'the product of the imagination of a deserter.' Andrew then took his witness through the opening battles in Normandy. With mounting enthusiasm, Meyer, a man unmalleable for any purpose but war, recounted the desperate situation he had faced and how he had given the orders for the counter-attack that had stemmed the Allied invasion. To the reporters it seemed as if Meyer had taken over his own defence; when Andrew tried to end one of his soliloquies, Meyer dismissed him with 'I would like to proceed logically with my description.' Meyer looked confidently about the courtroom, more like an actor sizing up his audience than an accused man on trial. After the battle on 7 June, he had encountered about 100 prisoners at the Abbaye and gave orders to move them out to Division HQ. Seeing one older prisoner he took to be an officer, Meyer went over to him and asked, 'Why do you fight us? ... is it not ridiculous that we crush each other's skulls?' To Meyer it seemed absurd that western Europeans should fight each other when they should be making common cause against Bolsheviks. This did not seem consistent with a man about to order the murder of these prisoners.

The rest of the night of 7 June was spent checking on positions north of Saint Contest and at Cambes. During the entire time he wore his SS camouflage uniform. At one point, he was in the rear with a group of Canadian prisoners when he came under SS fire. Desperately waving a map to indicate that they were not enemy, Meyer tried to stop the firing. 'At that moment I was on my feet,' he recalled, bringing some knowing smiles from the bench of generals, 'that is to say, I crawled on my stomach.'[30] While there was some confusion about when he returned to the Abbaye on the 8th, it was early enough to have lunch with his officers. He did not recall seeing any vehicles in the chapel, and he had told his staff to remove them so that the Abbaye could not be identified as a HQ. After a nap, he awoke at 9:00 P.M. to prepare for the 15th Reconnaissance Company's attack on Bretteville. His other battalions had fought the previous day, and the 15th was the only fresh unit available to renew the counter-attack.

Meyer's vivid description of the attack on 9 June said much about the man in the prisoner's dock. Previously, Meyer had promised the 15th that he would go into battle with them. Early in the battle, the company commander, von Buettner, was killed and Meyer himself was engaged by a machine-gun position. Meyer's driver was fatally shot through the stomach, and their motorcycle was engulfed in flames that ignited Meyer's uniform. After troops doused the fire, Meyer, his uniform still smouldering, again took up his weapon and renewed the attack. This Wagnerian zeal went for nothing, for the SS could not hold Bretteville and were forced back. Yet the sight of a senior officer personally taking on enemy machine-gun positions was an example to the soldiers of *Härte* and was as well a measure of Meyer's audacity and courage. In giving this testimony, Ralph Allen reported, the brigadeführer 'exhorted the ghosts of his dead battalions, refought old battles, invoked his Nazi gods ...'[31] Ironically, it was at this battle at Bretteville that both Meyer and his chief accuser, Jesionek, were wounded.

The following morning, Meyer checked his positions at Authie and saw dead Canadians and one dead German soldier by the roadside. He berated the battalion commander Milius and ordered him to bury the bodies. In the end result, Meyer's account of what occurred on 10 June would decide the issue. After meeting with General Geyr that morning, Meyer was approached by two staff officers, the regimental surgeon Dr Gatternig and the dentist Dr Stift. They reported that the bodies of several dead Canadians were laying in the park just outside the HQ. 'I laughed and said "that is impossible. You must be crazy." Both officers confirmed to me, "Yes we have the impression it is so."'[32] A startled Meyer ordered the adjutant

Scheumann to check on this report and the latter confirmed it. Meyer himself went to the park and verified the situation. Taking the adjutant aside, Meyer soundly excoriated him: 'How does it come that you have not been informed of such a deed here at Regimental H.Q.? It is out of the question that here at Regimental H.Q. conditions are reported to me by other officers.' Scheumann was ordered to see to the burial of the bodies and to start breaking in a replacement since he would be returning to the front. While he was on his way to the 2nd battalion where the legal officer, Dr Tiray served, Meyer encountered the division commander, Witt, and told him of the situation. Witt was outraged and ordered Meyer, 'Well, we have to stop this swinishness.' Noting that perhaps these were reprisals for the rumoured killing of German prisoners, he said, 'This taking the law into one's own hand must be stopped ... This could only have been men who heard about the shooting of our own comrades.' Meyer defended his Hitler Youth and thought it unlikely that they were responsible, but he promised to submit a written report.

Perhaps by way of justification, Meyer elaborated on the rumours of German prisoners being shot by Canadians. Near La Villeneuve, Meyer had come across a line of dead Germans, each one shot through the head. The insinuation was that the killings at the Abbaye might have been reprisals for an earlier atrocity against Germans. Meyer continued that, despite Witt's insistence, he had never gotten around to issuing a written report on the incident because he had 'found no clues as to the guilty.'[33] It had been a seductive performance. Meyer had convincingly portrayed himself as a leader so preoccupied with the demands of command that he could not be bothered with prisoners or plotted their murder. By the afternoon of the 19th, Andrew had finished and Macdonald rose to cross-examine.

The first sallies were inconclusive. Meyer merely repeated his previous testimony by denying any knowledge of the killing of prisoners. Macdonald finally made some headway when he recounted how a decorated Wehrmacht officer, Hauptmann (Captain) Fritz Steger, recalled that Meyer had bragged about killing prisoners. For diplomatic reasons, the court would not let Macdonald refer to Russia but instead made him describe 'another theatre.' Nevertheless, he received a surprisingly frank answer:

Q. Now did you say in the Officer's Mess to Capt. Steger and other officers in Beverloo that when you were in another theatre you frequently had to shoot prisoners?

A. It is possible that I have said that. I can't recall it but it is completely possible. I can recall at that time I had a Recce [Reconnaissance] Company Battle Group that operated up to a one hundred and fifty kilometers behind enemy lines.[34]

Meyer's sudden candour might have been explained by Steger's presence in the courtroom and his willingness to remember the conversation if Meyer did not.

Yet Meyer distinguished what happened in the Soviet Union from the Normandy fighting. He denied ever giving orders to kill British prisoners and in a moment that broke much of the tension he mentioned that 'my last fight with Englishmen ended with a couple of bottles of champagne and it was together with your officers after being taken prisoner.' For his part, Macdonald found the cross-examination a grind because every question had to be translated from English to German and the answer from German to English. This allowed Meyer considerable time to reflect on his answers, especially since, as Macdonald observed, he could understand English. Added to this was the fact that, 'when faced with any embarrassment, he would launch into long irrelevant speeches.'[35] The prosecution increasingly found straight answers a scarce commodity.

As the cross-examination wore on, the atmosphere in the courtroom became more tense. Reporters described how Meyer and Macdonald 'raised their voices often and frequently they glared straight into each other's eyes with unmasked hostility.'[36] Macdonald chided Meyer for urging his seventeen-year-olds to 'save the last bullet for themselves' but allowing himself to be captured. 'It sounded good in a speech,' Macdonald jibed, 'but when it came to carrying it out yourself it was a different thing.' Meyer flushed at this attack on his courage and shot back, 'I do not have to defend in this room my soldierly bearing.' Macdonald also challenged him on whether he had ever worn a rubber coat as Jesionek had observed. Meyer replied that 'from the first to the last day, I during no battle activity wore a coat.' The brigadeführer easily surmounted all challenges.

A year and a half of investigations and countless hours of work and anxiety would conclude with one final afternoon of cross-examination. Bruce Macdonald also carried a weight of personal responsibility. If his own war had been a few hours of confused disaster in Normandy, he could redeem himself by conclusively proving Meyer's guilt. And he would do so by showing the direct conflict between Meyer's previous statements and his testimony in court. The road to victory lay in convincing the generals that Meyer had consistently lied to protect himself. The first step was to take Meyer back to the interrogation of 15 October in London. On that occasion, after he was told that the Canadian army had verified that eighteen bodies had been secretly buried at the Abbaye, Meyer was asked if any wounded prisoners had died at his HQ:

A.183 I heard nothing of that, I must also say that I did not pay much attention to that. I had a lot of things to do at the time.
Q.184 Was it reported to you by anyone that Allied prisoners had died at your headquarters and that it was necessary to bury them there?
A.184 No.

As well, on 15 October, Meyer had been confronted with Jesionek's story and had responded: 'Of that I know nothing. What the colonel has said I do not know anything nor was I ever so stupid as to give an order to shoot prisoners.' He also categorically denied any knowledge of the execution of prisoners at his HQ:

Q.196 This member of your unit who saw them and heard what I have just repeated took us to the place where the execution is supposed to have occurred and eighteen bodies of Canadian soldiers were recovered from that spot, everyone of whom had died from a bullet in the head, or from other head injuries.
A.196 Tell the lieutenant-colonel that I have never heard of this thing until I have just been told of it, and if that happened it is swinishness. I can tell the lieutenant-colonel that I did not give that order whether he believes it or not.[37]

Two days later, on 17 October, when he was given a chance to review his statement, Meyer made minor changes but repeated that he had never heard of atrocities:

Q.19 ... but none of your officers or NCOs or even private soldiers ever reported atrocities to you?
A.19 No.
Q.20 And so it is correct to say that, by reason of the fact you never had to, you therefore did not at any time discipline any of your officers or men for committing such offences?
A.20 I did not need to punish anyone for I did not know anything about it.[38]

At his trial Meyer was asking the court to accept a radically different story, that the medical officers had reported the killings to him and that he had tried to find the guilty parties. This version had first emerged when

Meyer sought to make a further statement on 2 October. But the contradictions between this statement and Meyer's previous sworn statements were too stark to leave unchallenged. Macdonald moved in for the kill and the resulting exchanges were not pleasant. Macdonald pounded on the counsel table while Meyer responded with 'silent but equally angry little movements of his hands':[39]

Q. I don't care anything about giving the orders or who did it, you knew on the 11th June that Canadian prisoners had been shot at your Headquarters and when you gave these statements on the 15th and 17th October 1945 that knowledge was present in your mind.

A. In the question I was asked whether any of my soldiers had been shot and I said 'No.' Then I was asked whether it had been reported to me that my soldiers had shot Canadians and I denied that.

Q. You said you didn't know anything about the whole business?

A. That my soldiers were supposed to have shot soldiers I did not know.

Q. Alright, if you think by evading the question that way you are convincing anyone that you are telling the truth you are seriously misled.

A. Of that I can only say the following, I do not know today who really committed the deed and I have no idea of incriminating my Regiment without exact information.

Q. I put to you the next question, Question 196. See if you can get around this one. 'Q.196 This member of your unit who saw this and heard what I have just repeated took us to the place where the execution is supposed to have occurred and 18 bodies of Canadian soldiers were recovered from this spot –'
And let me say here that unless there were a large number of spots where 18 bodies were buried you knew what I was talking about –
'every one of whom have died from bullets in the head or other head injuries.'
Is there the remotest possibility you didn't know what I was talking about on that occasion – did you know what I was talking about on that occasion?

A. Yes.

Q. Now, let's hear what your answer is,
'A. Tell the Lt-Col that I have never heard of this thing until I have just been told of it.'
Now, is that a truthful answer? Answer yes or no.

A. I cannot answer yes or no. I must say more.

Q. You answer yes or no.

A. I cannot.[40]

There was no mercy left for the witness. In Macdonald's eyes, Meyer was clearly both a murderer and a liar; the contradictions had only to be underlined. After one evasive answer, Macdonald noted sarcastically that Meyer might want to wait on the translation to think up an answer. 'I don't need any time to think this over,' he snapped back. By this time, Meyer was glaring furiously at Macdonald and the prosecutor began to experience the hypnotic sensation that had overcome Helzel, noting that 'under his [Meyer's] amazingly fierce and frightening glare I began to feel a little giddy.'[41] He decided to retaliate: 'And glaring at me isn't going to answer anything either ... You are not going to intimidate me with your glares I can assure you.' Meyer dropped his eyes; the competition was over.

Macdonald also ferreted out other deceptions. Meyer had lied to his own superiors when they had asked if he knew of any atrocities in his sector. However, he now evaded the accusation by maintaining that he never knew who had killed the prisoners at his headquarters. In exasperation, Macdonald could only retort, 'It would be pretty difficult to get it any closer to you unless it was done right in your own command post.' The truth, in Macdonald's view, was a rare commodity to Kurt Meyer, for he had maintained his complete ignorance of the killings until 15 October, when he realized that the weight of the evidence was against him. It was only later that he came up with the new version that seemed to lay the blame on the conveniently deceased Scheumann. Macdonald confronted him:

Q. Nine or eleven days later [from October 15] you decided it was high time for you to get on the right side when you found out that we knew much more about this than you thought we did, and that you had better come and make a statement fast before the trial, and despite the fact that we did everything we could to dissuade you from making this statement we could not stop you. Now, what is your comment on that?

A. You are right but with these differences. It was not nine or eleven days later but in the first twenty four hours but I could not get in touch – I could not reach any officer and the commandant of the house when I reported to him the following day said that no officer could be reached and that you yourself were enroute and that he would look after the matter – within a reasonable time an officer would look after the matter and as far as my silence up to that point, I can tell you that every commander has silence when there is no clarity in the matter – remains silent as long as he can.

Q. You mean until you discover that you are for it you keep silent –[42]

At this point, Foster broke in and told Macdonald to rein in his sarcasm.

But, in any event, the prosecution's case was running down. Macdonald finished with a flourish, going through the litany of atrocities committed by the 12th SS: the slaughter of three prisoners at Haut du Bosq by Mohnke, the murder of five Canadians at Le Mesnil-Patry as ten officers watched, the mass execution of thirty-five prisoners at Fontenay-le-Pesnel, and, lastly, the killing of nineteen prisoners at the Chateau d'Audrieu. Meyer maintained that he had never heard of any of these incidents.

At 4:28 that afternoon, Macdonald closed his loose-leaf binder and sat down. Meyer rubbed his hand under his jaw and stared impassively at the courtroom wall. It had been a draining battle for both men. As Ralph Allen observed, 'no court in the world could render a verdict on the clash of wills and personalities that filled the courtroom today with fireworks redolent of a Hollywood melodrama.'[43] Later, Meyer's recollection of his cross-examination was his typical mixture of bravado and self-pity:

I sat alone. Hundreds of eyes watched my every movement and every expression on my face. I was unable to relax for a moment. A group of men with total authority, spurred by honour and professional ambition against one man deprived of his rights ... Annihilating fire behind the front line, no grenades or valiant combat, but destruction simply using malicious words, distorted statements and questions, confusing allusions and distorted pictures of the past. It was in this way that MacDonald tried to force a victory over me but I refused to capitulate.[44]

Despite all that had passed, there would be several more twists to come in the trial of Kurt Meyer.

The defence's next witness, Bernhard Meitzel, was characterized by the translator Stonborough as a man who would be a 'willing tool for any future Nazi movement in need of an alert, courteous, crisp and efficient staff officer.'[45] Although he was able to speak fluent English, he gave his testimony in German for Meyer's benefit. The SS soldier, Meitzel advised, was fully briefed on the Geneva Convention and given strict orders to take prisoners. He recalled Meyer being a tough disciplinarian, to the extent that he had had one of his own men executed for raping a French girl. He thought it unlikely that Meyer would shoot prisoners. Meitzel had been captured on 10 August but had escaped and on his return he found Meyer having supper with three captured Canadians. Meitzel also doubted Jesionek's story: there were no minefields in the area, Meyer was not wearing a rubber coat, and there were no vehicles in the chapel. To Macdonald, Meitzel denied ever hearing about atrocities and, when pressed on the issue, he primly replied, 'I cannot imagine that an older officer would brag about such atrocities to me.'[46] However, he did acknowledge having met Meyer at the Abbaye on the morning of 8 June, conclusive proof that he was present as Jesionek had said.

Another defence witness, Max Wunsche, was the most flamboyant individual to face the court. Dressed in dark trousers with a high-collared, mustard-coloured tunic, adorned with his many decorations, including the Knight's Cross, he impressed Harry Foster as 'young, tall, slender, blond and blue-eyed with his hair combed straight back and unbelievably handsome. He should have been a movie star.'[47] To the sardonic Stonborough, Wunsche was an 'SS pin-up type ... with a vigorous loyalty complex.' Turning the witness chair so that he stared directly at the court president, Wunsche gave his evidence glaring unblinkingly at Foster. After a few moments, Foster gave up trying to match Wunsche in this Prussian staring match. Despite his display of bravado, Wunsche had little new to add. Two points did emerge, almost by chance. In passing, Wunsche noted that he told Meyer of the proposed Bretteville attack on the evening of 8 June, although the latter had testified that he had spent the morning doing reconnaissance for the attack, an attack he did not even know about till later. The other point concerned Jesionek's patrol losing a jeep in the minefield. Foster (who presumed that Jesionek was in the jeep) asked Wunsche if he had ever seen a vehicle blown up by a mine. The latter replied. 'According to my experience in Russia nothing remained of the occupants.' Last to testify for the defence was Kurt Bergman, adjutant of the 3rd battalion of the 25th PGR, who noted that the killing of prisoners was a deliberate breach of army regulations. This completed Andrew's case, although he felt compelled to have the court note that the defence was handicapped by the number of witnesses who had died or (such as the medical officers) seemed unavailable.

Before Macdonald began his reply evidence, he asked the court's permission to rebut the charges of murder against the Canadian army in connection with the La Villeneuve incident. It was a strange reversal of position: the prosecution wished to assume the defensive. Two witnesses were standing by to refute Meyer's story. One of them, Major H.S. Roberts of the Regina Rifles, entered the court and saluted the bench, only to be told that his presence was unnecessary. Foster refused to permit Macdonald to address the issue or to call evidence. This refusal only kindled further interest in the incident, or, as the newspapers called it, the 'obdurate secret' of Canadian war crimes. It took almost a further week before Macdonald convinced the generals at least to release the information on the incident to the press. Through affidavits, Roberts stated that three German vehicles had attempted to penetrate Canadian positions at this juncture. The vehicles were knocked out by anti-tank guns and the troops killed in the subsequent fighting.[47] Publicly at least, Meyer's charges were answered.

The court's final day of evidence, 22 December, was one of the most dramatic in the entire trial. Daniel Lachèvre, a sixteen-year-old Norman, had been discussing the case with the trial's French translator, Raymond Robichaud, and the youngster had revealed further information that Robichaud hurriedly brought to Clarence Campbell's attention. Startled, Campbell advised Macdonald to explore the new information with Lachèvre.[48] When called to the witness stand, the boy testified that he recalled the night of D-Day when German troops first came to his home at the Abbaye. Along with other boys, he had gone to the Abbaye's garden around 8:00 P.M. on the evening of 8 June to play on the swings, and they all had continued to play there after the Germans' arrival. There were no bodies in the park. On three subsequent evenings, no bodies were visible. How could this be reconciled with Meyer's story? Or with Jesionek's?

Confusion deepened when the young Norman described an air-raid shelter in the passageway that led to the garden. It was an impromptu shelter, made of rock and earth, and was in place by the evening of 8 June. If it had existed that morning, it would surely have obstructed Jesionek's view into the garden. How could the blood and disruption caused by so many killings not have been apparent in the garden? One answer, of course, would be that the bodies had already been buried and the sods placed over them. Months had passed before the Vicos had even suspected that there were graves in their garden. If the bodies were in the garden on the morning of 11 June, as Meyer had said, then surely Lachèvre must have seen them at some time. For Macdonald, Lachèvre's observations were 'one of the decisive turning points of the trial. It disproved completely, if it had ever been believed, Meyer's last minute explanation of the discovery of the bodies by him on June 11th.'[49] Ralph Allen wrote that this new evidence added 'a note of mystery that might well have come straight out of the second-last chapter of any detective novel.'[50]

Recalled to the stand, Jesionek refuted several points raised by the defence. In a prodigious display of memory, he recalled the patrol where one of their jeeps (not the one he was in) was destroyed by a mine. Jesionek was able to recount the incident in vivid detail; he even located the minefield by relating it on a map to a wrecked British tank. Foster was impressed, for he remembered that tank and had also used it as a marker. Jesionek's ability to use two maps he had never seen before to locate the exact point of the minefield was an impressive display of intelligence and credibility.[51] Macdonald's final submission was to read into the record Meyer's unsworn examination by SHAEF officers in March 1945, when Macdonald had confronted him with reams of material on atrocities committed by the 12th SS. Time and again, Meyer had denied any knowledge of the killing of prisoners. 'In which sectors can these things have taken place? I find it impossible to believe,' he had innocently responded. Macdonald had then asked:

Q. Can you quote any single example where you took action to restrain any members of your division from the improper treatment of prisoners of war?
A. I have had no experience, have not been and have had no reports of improper treatment of prisoners of war.

At his trial, this same man was saying that he had lied to Allied interrogators in March and October 1945, and had even lied to his own superiors about the killing of prisoners, but now should be believed. Feeling that he had accomplished his purpose, Macdonald sat down. General Foster decided to adjourn the court for four days over Christmas. This break would also give the reporters time to prepare a transcript for the use of the lawyers in their summations.

'The evidence has gone in even better than we hoped for,' Macdonald confided to his wife, 'and nothing has been brought out that we did not anticipate.'[52] Win or lose, he sensed that Meyer's guilt had been demonstrated and it was now up to the court to deal with it. Christmas Day found the prosecutor having a quiet dinner with the officers of the Loyal Edmonton Regiment. He excused himself early to work on his summation.

In contrast to the blaze of publicity in Canada, few Germans were aware of the Meyer trial. One former Wehrmacht officer, the manager of the Aurich officers' club, did observe the trial briefly and was quite amazed. He had expected to see a show trial with the guilt of the accused already presumed. Instead, he was stunned to see the court accord Meyer military courtesies, even returning his salute every morning. 'We were dumbfounded at the utterly unexpected impartially neutral or, shall we say, benevolently correct atmosphere. Frankly, we expected to see a victor's privilege exercised of brow-beating a defeated enemy.' He felt it most unfortunate that the few German newspapers that were operating did not cover the case. If they had, the correct behaviour of all present, the manifest integrity of the trial, would have given 'an entirely new slant on the Allied military government.'[53]

For Meyer, the interlude was bittersweet. On 23 December, his thirty-fifth birthday, he was suddenly removed from his cell by an officer and two sergeants with submachine-guns. 'Sensing nothing good I allowed myself to be led into a well lit room.' An officer removed his handcuffs, and he was asked to give his word of honour that he would not try to escape. Then Meyer was led into another room. 'I thought I was dreaming. Before me stood a festively decorated table which could hardly bear the weight of the food and drink it was carrying.' The officers burst into 'Happy Birthday' and Meyer stood petrified. 'My enemies had arranged a birthday party for me ... I was unable to prevent the tears coursing down my face.' During this celebration with the Canadians, he was surprised to learn that many were sympathetic; according to them, 'if you are found guilty ... then the Canadian Army will have no generals tomorrow.' Meyer was particularly amused by one officer who had little good to say about Macdonald and who passed along the prosecutor's comments in the officers' mess as he 'drowned his anger with whisky at the bar after the daily proceedings.'[54] On Christmas Eve, Meyer had a visit from his wife Kate and daughter Ursula. They talked of everything but the trial.

Because the accused had testified, the defence gave the first summation. Maurice Andrew carefully detailed the facts that supported his case, including the accusations that Meyer had incited his troops to deny quarter. The evidence of the 'secret order' was simply absurd. It rested on the evidence of Torbanisch, himself a deserter, who was anxious to ingratiate himself with the Belgian Resistance. As for Meyer's speeches to his troops, what he had actually said was that his soldiers had to rely on their own courage to defeat the enemy. He never directed them to kill prisoners. Von Buettner or others may have done so, but they were not on trial. With regard to the killings at Authie and Buron, Andrew pointed out that on several occasions German officers or NCOs had intervened to prevent killings. This was hardly consistent with a general plan to eliminate captives. Moreover, troops were present from other units, including the Luftwaffe and the 21st Panzer Division. About 150 Canadians captured on the night of 7 June were sent to Division HQ. If standing orders were to kill prisoners, why had so many survived? Andrew steered clear of Jesionek's testimony and stressed peripheral issues. He used the latter's evidence on the rubber coat, the minefield, even who had written to the SS when he was conscripted, his mother or his father, to suggest that Jesionek was inconsistent and a liar. Andrew's main attack on Jesionek lay through the boy Lachèvre, who had seen no disturbance in the garden, a place where only a few hours earlier (according to Jesionek) the dead had been heaped up and blood pooled under their bodies. 'All traces of graves and blood had vanished – no loose earth – just completely normal. I submit that this is just a bit far-fetched.'[55]

In his turn, Macdonald asked the court to consider the charges as interlocking and mutually supportive. A general who would incite his troops to deny quarter would also be likely to direct the execution of prisoners. He carefully pieced together various threads of evidence, including the testimony of faithful SS men who candidly admitted that they considered themselves under orders to shoot enemy captives. There was no doubt in Jesionek's mind when he left the parade square in Le Sap that he had been instructed by Meyer to kill prisoners. This rhetoric bore fruit at many places in Normandy where prisoners, either individually or in groups, were subdued and then shot. 'Is it possible,' Macdonald asked, 'that such things could occur without incitement or counsel?'

On the all-important third charge, that Meyer himself had ordered the killings, Macdonald urged the court to accept Jesionek's story. He bore no personal grudge against Meyer and it was conceded that he had a telling eye for detail. After only one visit to the Abbaye, he was able, almost a year later, to render a detailed sketch of the grounds. Moreover, he had been painstaking in his recollection of Meyer's words. It would have been easy for him to say that Meyer had ordered the prisoners' execution. Rather, Jesionek had reported only what he had heard and did not guess at what Meyer had said to the other officer in low tones. As to whether he was wearing a rubber coat, Meyer had just returned from visiting his battalions and could have been wearing such a coat. In any event, Jesionek knew who his commander was.

Meyer, on the other hand, was a well-scripted character, capable of evasions or denials as the occasion required. Even when confronted with evidence of the killings he had denied knowledge of them. The most recent story, that Meyer was told of the killings on 11 June, could not stand scrutiny:

If this story is to be believed, it means that whoever shot these eighteen prisoners was so little concerned about the risk of disciplinary action that he was prepared to carry it out openly at the Headquarters, within earshot of the Commander, and more than that he was prepared to leave the bodies lying around for several days to be eventually discovered. Does this sound like a reasonable story with fifty civilians about the place? Does it sound probable that if the whole eighteen were buried at one time that they would be buried in five separate graves? Does it not sound more reasonable that they were buried after each shooting and that four separate shootings or killings took place?[56]

The Lachèvre testimony had shown that there were no piles of bodies lying about the Abbaye on 8, 9, or 10 June, and 'he [Meyer] is completely and finally exposed I say by this fabrication, and herein lies the solution to the whole case,' which was that the ten men selected for interrogation on the night of 7 June (six of whom were known to be among the eighteen murdered) had probably been murdered that night after their interrogation. Other groups, such as the one seen by Jesionek, had been shot the following day. Macdonald suggested that the SS decided to solve two problems simultaneously by using the excess soil from the carefully concealed graves to construct the air-raid shelter in the passageway. Young Lachèvre had seen the pile of dirt on 8 June and presumed that it was the completed shelter. 'We cannot produce,' Macdonald conceded, 'a photograph of the accused standing over the dead bodies of prisoners with a smoking pistol in his hand.' Beyond any doubt, Kurt Meyer was an inspiring leader, but the result of his leadership was Authie, Buron, and the Abbaye. Macdonald's voice rose, displaying the passion that had marked his cross-examination of Meyer: 'the cowardly murders of helpless, unarmed prisoners' should not go unpunished. Instead of Meyer, the court should keep before it the image of Lieutenant Tom Windsor, wounded and captured but unwilling to betray his comrades. He and the others went to their deaths defying their captors and it was now the duty of the court to see these foul murders punished.

Far less emotional was Bredin's instruction to the court on the law. The test of criminal responsibility for war crimes was not, as it is in civil law, intent or malice, but rather whether the accused had violated the laws and usages of war. A soldier may do a very praiseworthy act, such as spy on the enemy. However, to the enemy this is a serious crime and justifies the soldier's execution. Bredin reminded the generals that Meyer was to have all the advantages of British justice and was to be presumed innocent until proven guilty. The court had admitted hearsay evidence but should carefully gauge its value. Yet perhaps the most weighty legal issue was Meyer's liability as a commander. Sections 10(4) and 10(5) detailed the legal parameters:

10(4) Where there is evidence that more than one war crime has been committed by members of a formation, unit, body, or group while under the command of a single commander, the court may receive that evidence as *prima facie* evidence of the responsibility of the commander for those crimes.

10(5) Where there is evidence that a war crime has been committed by members of a formation, unit, body or group and that an officer or non-commissioned officer was present at or immediately before the time when such offence was committed the court may receive that evidence as *prima facie* evidence of the responsibility of such officer or non-commissioned officer, and of the commander of such formation, unit, body, or group, for that crime.

A comparison of section 10 with the comparable section of the British royal warrant shows how much farther the Canadians took the concept of command responsibility. The British section[57] only provided that, when a war crime was the result of concerted action, then this was prima facie evidence against each member of that unit. However, in addition to the British clause, the Canadian regulations provided that the number of crimes or the presence of officers or NCOs was also prima facie evidence of the commander's guilt.

The legal definition of command responsibility was still evolving, and the Meyer case would be its first application in post-war Europe. In trying to describe the law, Bredin had few modern precedents to draw on. During the Glorious Revolution of 1689, Count Rosen was severely reprobated by King James II for the murder of non-combatants at the seige of Londonderry. More than two centuries later, Brigadier J.H. Smith was court martialled by the U.S. Army for inciting his subordinates to commit war crimes during the Philippine insurrection. In approving his conviction, President Theodore Roosevelt cautioned his commanders to be prudent in what they said: 'It is impossible to tell exactly how much influence language like that used by General Smith may have had in preparing the minds of those under him for the commission of deeds which we regret.'[58] By the time of the Meyer case, the U.S. Pacific forces had rendered another precedent on command responsibility. General Masaharu Homma had been a senior officer in charge of the troops who conducted the infamous 'Bataan Death March.' His HQ was only 450 metres from the road along which hundreds of American captives were being bayoneted to death. He frequently drove along the road and must have witnessed the routine murder of prisoners. Although he personally had never killed anyone, he was found guilty by reason of his command position and was executed.[59]

However, it was not until the *Yamashita* trial (concluded on 7 December 1945, only three days before the Meyer trial began) that the standards of command responsibility were thoroughly reviewed. Yamashita had commanded the Japanese forces in the Philippines during the American offensive to retake the island of Luzon in early 1945. During February 1945, his soldiers had committed appalling atrocities, killing over 8,000 unarmed civilians. These killings were carried out under written orders and under the supervision of army or navy officers. Outside Manila, entire villages, including women and children, were exterminated.[60] In his defence, Yamashita alleged that he had not inspected the camps or villages where the atrocities had occurred. Moreover, the effectiveness of the American advance had cut his communications. But his command was never as disrupted as he alleged, and the U.S. military commission trying him concluded that 'the crimes were so extensive and widespread, both as to time and area, that they must have been wilfully permitted by the Accused, or secretly ordered by the Accused.' The commission did not claim that a commander was responsible for every tainted act of his troops, but it did conclude that where, as in the Philippines, atrocities were so widespread and 'there is no effective attempt by a commander to discover and control the criminal acts, such a commander may be held responsible, even criminally liable for the lawless acts of his troops.'[61] Yamashita was executed and a new doctrine (in the words of one writer, an 'awesome standard'[62]) emerged, one that held a general responsible when he 'must have known' that his troops were committing atrocities.

In his opening address, Macdonald hinted that he would look to *Yamashita* as a precedent. He urged the court, 'as similar American courts have, [to] arrive at the same conclusions as to a commander's responsibility. In the last few days in the *Yamashita* case, one almost the same as to its facts as this one ...' Foster cut him short. 'Let us not be influenced by that [the *Yamashita* case] at this stage.'[63] In his description of a leader's responsibility, Bredin was not inclined to go as far as the U.S. commission. Cautiously, he noted that the question of when a commander was responsible for his men's actions was not easily answered. Despite the broad phrases of section 10, which considered certain circumstances as prima facie evidence of a commander's guilt, Bredin stated that 'if an explanation is given by or on behalf of the accused which raises in the mind of the Court a reasonable doubt as to his responsibility as military commander, he is entitled to an acquittal.' After the prosecution had established the accused's responsibility for his men's actions, the burden shifted to the accused; the latter had to show that, even if a war crime was committed, he was not implicated in the crimes. Bredin defined command responsibility this way:

As I have endeavoured to explain, the Regulations do not mean that a military commander is in every case liable to be punished as a war criminal for every war crime committed by his subordinates but once certain facts have been proved by the Prosecution, there is an onus cast upon the accused to adduce evidence to negative or rebut the inference of responsibility which the Court is entitled to make. All the facts and circumstances must then be considered to determine whether the accused was in fact responsible for the killing of prisoners referred to in the various charges. The rank of the accused, the duties and responsibilities of the accused by virtue of the command he held, the training of the men under his command, their age and experience, anything relating to the question whether the accused either ordered, encouraged or verbally or tacitly acquiesced in the killing of prisoners, or wilfully failed in his duty as a military commander to prevent, or to take such action as the circumstances required to endeavour to prevent, the killing of prisoners, are matters affecting the question of the accused's responsibility. In the last analysis it is for the Court, using its wide knowledge and experience of military matters, to determine, in the light of all the relevant factors and the provisions of the Regulations, the responsibility of an accused in any particular case.[64]

Bredin's analysis suggested that, for guilt to be proved, either the facts or the issues of rank or responsibility must link the commander to the criminal act.

On the third charge, of whether Meyer had ordered the killing of seven prisoners on 8 June, the court's duty was clear. 'The Court must decide,' Bredin advised, 'whether Jesionek is a truthful witness ... similarly, you must test the accuracy of the accused's evidence.' The generals were obliged to compare and contrast the two stories and arrive at the truth. Lastly, Bredin reminded them that 'this Court is not trying the German nation, nor the Nazi Party, nor the Hitler Jugend, it is trying Kurt Meyer.' The generals and Bredin adjourned to consider a verdict.

No reasons for judgment were ever given, and the only knowledge of what occurred came from later recollections.[65] Unlike a civilian jury, a court martial acts collegially, and a conviction requires merely agreement among a majority of the five members.

With deference to rank, voting on the charges began with the junior officers and went up to the most senior. Of the generals, Johnston and Sparling took a hard line and considered Meyer guilty on all charges. Roberts and Bell-Irving were inclined towards leniency. None of them had any doubt that Meyer had encouraged his men to kill prisoners and he was unanimously convicted on that charge. Whether he bore any responsibility for the killings at Authie and Buron was questionable and Foster cast the deciding vote to acquit. The third charge, that Meyer had personally ordered the killing of prisoners at the Abbaye, remained the principal issue before them. Despite Jesionek's personal account and Meyer's prevarications, Foster 'was not satisfied that he [Meyer] had actually given the order for executing the seven at his headquarters. He may have done so but no evidence was offered by anyone to prove that he did.'[66] This breathtaking observation either discounted or ignored Jesionek's eyewitness account. There was direct, credible evidence before Foster that Meyer had ordered the execution of prisoners, and yet he seemed determined to disregard it. He cast the deciding vote against Johnston and Sparling to acquit on the third charge.

Having rejected the heart of the prosecution's case, the court then considered one of its weakest claims. Turning to the charges that Meyer had failed in his duties as a commander, the generals concluded that he was guilty. They decided that he probably knew of the murders at the Abbaye. 'It was inconceivable,' Foster concluded, 'how he, sitting in his headquarters, could have heard a succession of regularly spaced pistol shots less than 150 feet away and not sent someone off to investigate ... He didn't because he knew what was going on – even if he hadn't given the order.'[67] Moreover, Foster had a peculiar view of command responsibility. 'The laws and regulations governing war crimes were broad and definite. There was nothing for it. Under these laws, Meyer was guilty.' This was highly inaccurate, for Bredin had gone to great pains to instruct the generals that a commander was not responsible for every war crime committed by his men but rather was liable only in those instances where he had encouraged or tacitly acquiesced in the killing of prisoners. This comment would indicate that Foster either did not understand the judge advocate's instructions or chose to ignore them.

Late that afternoon, the court reassembled to give its verdict. Meyer was acquitted on the second and third charges but convicted on the first charge of inciting his troops to commit murder and on the fourth and fifth charges of being responsible as a commander for the killings at the Abbaye. It was an unusual and inconsistent verdict. Having rejected Jesionek's evidence, the court was left with Meyer's version in which he asserted that he was unaware of any killings until long after the fact. To hold Meyer responsible as the unit commander for the killings seemed to indicate that the court accepted a portion of the prosecution's case, a strange selectivity that indicated an attempt at compromise rather than a determination to arrive at the truth. Some of the generals on the bench appeared to be torn between making a finding on the facts and striking a fair policy towards the defeated enemy. As Bell-Irving later conceded, he 'had misgivings about the legality of what they were doing ... We all knew that our troops at various times were guilty of similar conduct. Whenever it happened we looked the other way.'[68] If the court members felt themselves guilty, it was that much harder to condemn Meyer. On the other hand, those members who favoured acquittal must have felt uneasy about exonerating the leader of a division that had callously murdered so many Canadian prisoners, as well as about the explosive reaction such an exoneration was bound to have in Canada.

Surprisingly, prosecutor Macdonald was not upset at the result. Apparently satisfied to get any conviction he felt that the verdict was 'quite reasonable' and believed that the conviction on the lesser charges would render Meyer liable to, at most, a sentence of life imprisonment.[70]

Whatever its merits on the facts, the *Meyer* case became Canada's one contribution to war crimes precedents. Because there was no judgment, Bredin's instruction to the court on command responsibility was later published in the *Law Reports of the Trials of War Criminals*.[71] While *Meyer* was overshadowed by *Yamashita*, Bredin's attempt to link the commander to the actual crime was probably a more accurate assessment of accepted law than the reasons given in *Yamashita*. L.C. Green has observed that 'the Canadian judge advocate required a closer link with the crime than did the American court,'[72] and Bredin's interpretation seems closer to subsequent decisions on command responsibility. At the Nuremberg trial of Field Marshal von Leeb and others for depredations committed in the Soviet Union, the tribunal rejected any notion of strict liability: 'Criminality does not attach to every individual in this chain of command from that fact [atrocities] alone. There must be personal dereliction. That can occur only where the act is directly traceable to him.'[73] For example, von Leeb recognized that Hitler's 'Commissar Order' mandating the summary execution of captured political officers was directly contrary to international law, and he advised his subordinates of his position and that he would prosecute any of his soldiers who committed war crimes. Consequently, von Leeb was not held responsible for his subordinates' crimes. This view was reaffirmed at the 'Hostage Case Trial' where again a Nuremberg tribunal held that there must be proof of 'a causative overt act or omission from which a guilty intent can be inferred.' While the court conceded that modern war creates such a large measure of decentralization as to make it impossible for a commander to be aware of every administrative act, a commander could nevertheless be liable if there was personal dereliction.[74] If *Yamashita* had drawn a broad brush over the doctrine of command responsibility, cases such as *Meyer* and *von Leeb* restricted the doctrine to make the commander liable for what he should reasonably have known.[75]

On the evening of the verdict, Maurice Andrew was cleared to return to Canada and turned the case over to his assistant, Captain Frank Plourde. The following day, the court reassembled to consider the sentence.

Macdonald advised the generals that General Vokes had authorized him not to proceed with the second charge sheet. The court had already dismissed any responsibility on Meyer's part for the killings at Authie-Buron, and so any liability for the later killings at Mouen was even less likely. Character evidence was submitted on Meyer's behalf. General Heinrich Eberbach, the former commander of Panzer Group West, considered Meyer an idealist who had moulded his young men into warriors, not murderers. As a soldier, Meyer was of the highest quality: 'an outstanding soldier, caring well for his young soldiers, brave, good trainer ... as far as we knew without hate against Canadians; murder of prisoners not in his line.'[76] For Meyer to kill prisoners would have been absurd since the Germans had no air reconnaissance and prisoners were their main source of information. Even one Canadian officer, Captain J.A. Renwick, spoke on Meyer's behalf. Captured on 9 August 1944, Renwick had been shown a copy of the *Maple Leaf* (armed forces') newspaper that contained Crerar's announcement of the Chateau d'Audrieu massacre. Renwick's interrogation officer protested that the accusations were unfair and that the German army 'did not wage war this way.' Meyer watched the interrogation and when it was over he talked with Renwick for a few minutes. He expressed his astonishment that Canadians had come all this way to fight Germans and that there should be no quarrel between the two countries. Renwick was left with the impression that Meyer was an idealist who had acted completely within the proper laws of war.

Perhaps the most poignant moment in the trial occurred when Kate Meyer stepped forward on behalf of her husband. They had been married for eleven years and had five children, including a ten-month-old boy. Devoted to her husband, Kate Meyer had sat in the same chair throughout the trial, but now the strain was beginning to show on her. Pale and bareheaded, surrounded by be-medalled strangers, she was ill at ease and could only say that 'I have a very good husband ... and I have been happily married.' She paused helplessly and turned to Plourde and then Foster, as if there was something else she should say. When they gave no reaction, she continued with a forced smile: 'I cannot say anything else – just that I am supremely happy with my husband and the children are very much attached to him.' For the first time, Meyer's poise seemed to break, and he leaned forward, clasping and unclasping his hands, his head bowed, unwilling to look at his wife as she begged for his life.[77]

Finally, Kurt Meyer was permitted to address the generals on his own behalf. Instead of asking for the court's favour, he gave one last vindication of his division, a testament to the fortitude and steadfastness of his men:

It was my objective to form for my nation a hard-hitting fight-willing Grenadier Regiment. I endeavoured to train them in a spirit closely resembling actual battle conditions and drawing on the experiences which we made in battle. I wished with this Regiment to give an example to the youthful power of a people. I have asked much of my young soldiers and I think I gave much to my young soldiers. I worked during the time of training in Belgium and France and trained them according to the international soldierly ordinances. To train a troop to become a band of murderers is a crime against one's own people. Such a troop becomes a total loss to one's own nation; every single individual becomes a total loss. I endeavoured to train my men, not only as soldiers, but to give them a backbone for their entire life. The battles in Normandy, the battles of the invasion showed that the spirit of those troops was good. These young people of 17, 18 years fought for three whole months without any relief, without a night of sleep ... The divisional sector became not smaller but became bigger. The burden on the individual soldier and the individual officer grew day to day ... If a troop can stand a quarter of a year of such attacks and also air attacks, then the mass of this troop must consist of good soldiers.[78]

As for the atrocities, he still refused to believe that his Hitler Youth were responsible. Admittedly, the division had been tainted by men who had been brutalized on the Eastern Front. But as for himself, Meyer denied any complicity in the crimes for 'I lived and fought as a soldier.' With a nod towards command responsibility, and a shrewd assessment of his judges, Meyer added: 'How far a commander can be held responsible for individual misdeeds of individual members of his troop the court should decide as it consists of old soldiers.' And lastly, he conceded the fairness of the proceedings: 'I, here, in front of the German public, wish to say that by the Canadian Army I was treated as a soldier and that the proceedings were fairly conducted.'

The generals withdrew again to consider the sentence. Meyer, Plourde, and the guard of officers waited in a sideroom. The Canadian observers seemed to think that Meyer would most likely be sentenced to several years' imprisonment 'to satisfy the outraged public.'[79] Both Foster and Bell-Irving felt a kinship to Meyer; they 'knew how hard it must have been for Meyer trying to run a one-man show with a bunch of green kids and battle-hardened NCOs.' Both he and Foster also seemed to misunderstand the nature of the legal parameters, imagining them to be much more limited than they were. Bell-Irving later commented that 'the legal restraints under which we were placed allowed for no other verdict than guilty. And it was a verdict that required the death penalty.'[80] In this he was mistaken for the court clearly retained the authority to levy a penalty appropriate to the offence. Having convicted Meyer of the lesser offence of silently condoning the murders instead of actually ordering them, a prison sentence was (as even prosecutor Macdonald thought) a likely punishment. The generals did not seem to expend much effort trying to match the severity of the offence with the right sentence.

After only twenty-five minutes, the generals returned and Meyer and his guards were marched back before the court; accused and guards came to attention. Harry Foster was visibly disturbed by what he was about to do. While it was one thing for men to die in battle, the cold reckoning of a death sentence in peacetime was another. He trembled and hid his tension behind a gruff voice that read out the court's decision: 'Brigadeführer Kurt Meyer, the court has found you guilty of the First, Fourth and Fifth Charges in the First Charge Sheet. The sentence of the court is that you suffer death by being shot. The findings of Guilty and the sentence are subject to confirmation. The proceedings are now closed.' As the words sank in, Meyer seemed to redden but he kept his hands clutched firmly by his side. Even Macdonald was impressed with his bearing, remarking that 'there is no doubt of his ability and bravery.'[81] At the end of the sentence Meyer bowed to the court and turned to go.

As he left, he glanced at the spot where his wife had sat through every day of the trial. She was not there. Upon hearing the sentence of death she had fled from the courtroom.

6

But for the Grace of God

On New Year's Day, 1946, Wady Lehmann visited Kurt Meyer for the last time. He carried with him confirmation that Meyer was to be shot by firing squad on 7 January. As Lehmann was leaving, he inadvertently wished the condemned man a happy New Year. He quickly apologized, but Meyer waved off his thoughtless comment. Death did not upset him for he had seen many fine men die and was not about to make an exception for himself.[1]

In the days following the conviction, both Lehmann and Plourde urged Meyer to frame an appeal. At first he refused to even consider it, so reconciled was he to death: 'So, this is how my life is to end. A volley will crack out in a sandpit somewhere and my body will disappear into a nameless grave!'[2] But the pressure from the lawyer and his wife was too much and Meyer agreed to assist with a petition for clemency. Meyer's family gathered in Aurich and obtained the services of a German lawyer, Dr Wilhelm Schapp, to help draft the appeal. Schapp convinced Clemens August Graf von Galen, the highly respected Catholic bishop of Munster, to write a letter of support. The appeal for clemency was delivered to the HQ of the Canadian army of occupation at Bad Zwischenahn. Brigadier Orde reviewed the trial and reported that everything had been done properly. The convening officer of the court, Major-General Chris Vokes, dismissed the appeal and noted on the document: 'I have considered this appeal and cannot see my way clear to mitigate the punishment awarded by the Court.'[3] As he later explained, he did this 'somewhat reluctantly.

But after making my decision I wanted no time wasted in getting on with the business.'[4] The 'business' was postponed in order to permit U.S. and British intelligence to interrogate Meyer further. Why he should cooperate at this point was a mystery.

On 5 January, Meyer had a last meeting with his wife and their five children and for the first time he held his ten-month-old son, Kurt Jr. In addition to the farewells, he left instructions with his wife on how the children were to be raised. The following day his four daughters returned to their home in Offleben to sew mourning dresses.

Both the prosecution and defence lawyers had spent New Year's Day in Amsterdam. There was subdued satisfaction in the prosecution camp at the result. An exhausted Macdonald wrote to his wife that 'I doubt whether I will ever engage in a more interesting or important criminal case. It is the culmination of many months of work.'[5] To Colonel Scotland, he wrote that the prosecutors 'have the satisfaction of having had him [Meyer] convicted and sentenced to death by a very experienced court of senior field commanders.'[6] The Canadian conduct of the Meyer case stood in favourable contrast to the later American trial of Jochen Peiper and seventy-three soldiers of his battle group charged with the murder of U.S. troops at Malmédy. In the Malmédy case, all defendants were tried together (with numbered placards hung about their necks to differentiate one from another) and evidence from one incident was used to implicate all. It was later revealed that statements had been obtained by way of 'mock trials' to intimidate witnesses and that other witnesses had been beaten about the face and testicles. As noted earlier, while some of the defendants were likely guilty, the use of tainted evidence discredited the process.[7] By contrast, Meyer's investigation and trial was, as even he admitted, scrupulously fair.

Curiously, Meyer's fate attracted little notice in Canada. News of his death sentence was carried on front pages, but only the London *Free Press* commented on the outcome. Perhaps one reason for the indifference was that, as the *Free Press* noted, the result was so expected. Canadian readers had been inundated with information about Meyer's guilt, mixed in with reports on the trial and execution of the commandant and staff of the Bergen-Belsen concentration camp. On the day that Macdonald presented evidence about the killings at Authie, Canadians also read about the hanging of Irme Grese, the blonde 'Queen of Belsen' who had set dogs to tear out the throats of prisoners. Any punishment short of execution for these monsters seemed ludicrous. According to the *Free Press*, there was still a lesson to be learned from Meyer's execution: 'Certainly war criminals who are charged with specific violations of accepted military codes are faring worse this time than after the last war when their punishment was left to the German courts, and most of them got off. It is a step forward when German generals learn that crime does not pay.'[8]

Ironically, Canadian troops in Europe seemed ambivalent about Meyer's fate. Three infantry officers wrote to the *Maple Leaf* that the trial had 'caused a lot of discussion as to whether a commander can be held responsible for the actions of his men' and that they were amazed at the strict standard to which Meyer had been held. They recalled their own training had instructed them to 'get the ... and don't be too particular how you do it,' and they asked, 'Are we such innocent little angels with respect to the same charges that this man was condemned to death?'[9] The officers' letter touched off a flurry of comment among the occupation troops. Some felt it appropriate to shoot this 'dangerous mad dog.' Yet other soldiers felt that even life imprisonment was too harsh. One writer reminded D-Day survivors that 'they won't forget the secret huddles "off the record" where German prisoners were killed on the beaches. 'You've got to have been through it to understand a soldier's feelings, there ain't no give and take when the going's rough.'[10]

One final matter bothered Bruce Macdonald. In all the excitement over the trial, death sentence, and preparations for execution, one section of the regulations had been overlooked. Months ago, when he had drafted the regulations, Macdonald had provided for a final appeal to an authority unconnected to the court martial itself: 'I thought that in the hysteria of war there was a good possibility of something being done in the heat of action and battle that ought to be reviewed.'[11] Therefore, section 14 provided that the senior combatant officer in the theatre 'shall have the power to mitigate or remit the punishment thereby awarded, or to commute such punishment for any lesser punishment.' Curious as to whether the review under section 14 had been completed, Macdonald contacted a friend at CMHQ, Lieutenant-Colonel Lorne McDonald. Not only had the review not been done, no one was even aware that it was necessary.[12] After some confusion, it was settled that Major-General Vokes, the court's convening officer and the same man who had just dismissed Meyer's appeal, was also the commander of the Canadian army in Germany. Vokes ordered a further postponement of the execution while the question of Kurt Meyer's sentence was finally resolved.

Tough, determined, pugnacious, Chris Vokes was every inch a regular soldier. One of the ironies of the Meyer case was that the man who ultimately determined his fate was like him in so many ways. Voluble and opinionated, Vokes had no hesitation in telling others what he thought of them. Reporter Ross Munro thought him 'a roughneck. I never knew a more profane man in my life.'[13] In 1943, while commanding the 2nd brigade of Canada's invasion force of Sicily, he had wished his troops 'good scalping' – a bloodthirsty exhortation that might have come from Meyer. Nor was this just rhetoric. On passing through Ragusa, three of Vokes's men were killed by civilian snipers. After capturing them, Vokes hurriedly ordered the snipers' execution. Only the division commander's intervention prevented him from carrying through with the killings.[14] Vokes had to content himself with having the men beaten up before being sent to the rear. In November 1943 Vokes was promoted to Major-General and commanding officer of the 1st Division. Through the bloody fighting in Italy, Vokes led his division to success at Ortona and the Gothic line. While occasionally criticized for limited imagination in his plan of attack,[15] ultimately it was hard, persistent men such as Vokes who made victory a reality.

However, strict adherence to the Geneva Convention was not a high priority. While he was mulling Meyer's plea for clemency, Vokes confided to another officer that 'as far as counselling them [soldiers] not to take prisoners there isn't a general or a colonel on the allied side that I know of who hasn't said "Well, this time we don't want any prisoners."'[16] Perhaps because of this, Vokes seemed to display sympathy for Meyer's predicament. As for the prosecutor, Vokes made it clear that he considered officers such as Macdonald to be pathetic strivers, civilians in uniform, unfit to judge a fighting man such as Meyer. In his memoirs, Vokes thought that Macdonald 'had never seen a shot fired in anger as far as I knew [apparently, he was unaware of Macdonald's part in the attack on the Verrières Ridge] and [he] knew nothing of battle.'[17]

When confronted with the review under section 14, Vokes suddenly seemed unsure about his previous position. On 5 January he ordered a further postponement of the execution and expressed his concerns about an issue that had such sensitive 'German political and other implications.'[18] He asked to meet with senior officials in London. On 9 January 1946, Vokes met with High Commissioner Vincent Massey, CMHQ chief of staff Lieutenant-General J.C. Murchie, Brigadier Orde, and Bredin. Significantly, the meeting also featured the legal adviser to External Affairs (and the prime minister), John Read. Vokes began by going over his previous review and rejection of clemency. Some of those present might have wondered why they were rehashing an appeal that Vokes had already considered and dismissed. None of the evidence had changed. But perhaps the wider significance of the issue had become apparent to Vokes. This was the first time in Europe that a commander had been condemned to death for crimes committed by his men 'where the commander had not given any direct order and had not directly participated in the commission of such crimes.' There were serious implications to this decision to shoot commanders whose men had breached the laws of war; Vokes drew the group's attention to the effect this result could have 'on superior commanders in any future war.' A consensus arose that the sentence should be regulated by the degree of the commander's accountability and death would be justified only when he had ordered or condoned the war crimes.[19] After yet another review of the evidence, Vokes concluded that 'nowhere ... could I find that order [to shoot prisoners] to be proved.'[20] As had the military court, Vokes chose to disregard Jesionek's eyewitness account, and reversing his previous decision, he commuted Meyer's sentence to life imprisonment. But even Foster's court had considered Meyer guilty of knowing about the murders at the Abbaye and doing nothing to prevent them. Vokes absolved Meyer of even this level of guilt. He explained in a message to Ottawa that death would have been justified only if 'the offence was conclusively shown to have resulted from the direct act of the commander or by his omission to act.'[21]

Several days later, Vokes wrote to Murchie about the factors that had swayed him. Throughout the trial, Vokes had remained aloof, guided only by advice from JAG staff. But in his own review of Meyer's appeal, Vokes had been most influenced 'by the fact that sentence of death in this case would set a precedent, whereby a commander in the field could be held responsible with his life for the acts of his subordinates ... It was my opinion that Meyer's responsibility on the Fourth and Fifth charges was vicarious in that it was not proved, except by inference, that he gave a direct order for the killing of prisoners, nor was it proved in evidence, to my satisfaction, that he knew that the executions recorded in the charges were taking place.'[22] By so concluding, Vokes effectively dismissed all the evidence that the investigators had accumulated over the past eighteen months.

On 14 January the death sentence was formally commuted to life imprisonment and a stunned Meyer was told that he would shortly be transferred to Canada to serve his sentence. After waiting days for the firing squad, he found this latest twist beyond belief. Meyer sagged into his bunk, completely baffled. 'I did not expect this turn of events,' he recounted. 'The thought that I am to spend my whole life behind bars is a crushing prospect.'[23] His only question was when he might be taken to

Canada. Told of the reprieve, Kate Meyer hurriedly arranged for her photograph to be taken and sent to her husband. After being flown to England, Meyer bided his time in English jails. There was some doubt as to whether he was headed west or east. The Communist Berlin newspaper, *Deutsche Volkszeitung*, editorialized that if the Canadians would not shoot Meyer then the Soviet Union wished to put him on trial for murder at Kharkov.[24] But nothing came of this, and at the end of April Meyer took ship for Canada. To avoid any commotion, he was dressed in the uniform of a Canadian private. After landing in Halifax he was transferred to Dorchester Penitentiary in New Brunswick. Ever resourceful, Meyer became proficient in English and got a job in the prison library. Once there, he was amazed to find that 'newspaper propaganda against me is still running at high speed.'[25]

For his part, Macdonald dismissed any 'rumpus' over the commutation and in a note to Dalton Dean remarked that 'you, Campbell and myself will always have a clear conscience.'[26] Nevertheless, there remained a profound sense of disappointment. To Colonel Scotland he confided that the commutation was thoroughly 'disappointing as that action may be to those of us who had worked for so long a period to pin this responsibility where we know it should properly rest.'[27] Vokes's decision had called into question the 'usefulness of any effort to establish responsibility' and was 'discouraging to all of us who had laboured so arduously over a long period in the field of war crimes.' Macdonald expressed his frustration in a scathing report to his superiors in which he claimed that, as a result of the *Meyer* decision, it was unlikely that any commander would be executed for his crimes: 'The test now laid down to determine the degree of accountability of a commander is a difficult one to meet. As Meyer himself said in evidence at his trial: "I never commit such an order to writing ... when you have enough old comrades in such a company, they know how the commander fights."' That is, subordinate officers such as von Beuttner and Scheumann knew full well without any need for orders on paper that prisoners were to be shot. Macdonald felt that the evidence that Meyer had given instructions to kill prisoners was overwhelming. It was shown that he had called out to his officers, 'In the future no more prisoners will be taken,' and, within minutes, seven Canadians died.

Moreover, if the commander was innocent in these circumstances, that put the entire weight of responsibility on the actual executioner, the common soldier. 'It is to be expected that a death penalty is justifiable, or would be supported against the private soldier or minor official, the "trigger man" where it is not against the real instigator, his commander.'

After this stinging rebuke to his superiors, Macdonald closed with a recommendation that if the war crimes unit was not going to do any good it might as well be closed down. In a handwritten note at the end of the report, Macdonald cited a conversation with Brigadier W.H.S. Macklin and his orders to proceed with the RCAF trials. Laconically, Macdonald remarked: 'Accordingly we continue.'[28] But Macdonald's feelings of dismay were nothing compared to the thunderous outrage that was to come from Canada.

'It is a known fact,' wrote a Canadian Legion officer, 'that Meyer is a vicious murderer and he should either be shot or burned at the stake.'[29] 'Our boys had no chance at all – why should he be given a second chance?' asked the mother of one of the murdered soldiers.[30] 'We fought this war to extinguish Fascism, not to pamper Nazi murderers,' added a labour leader.[31] The Toronto *Globe and Mail* was particularly forceful in condemning what it viewed as misplaced mercy. It published numerous letters from the mothers of dead soldiers who expressed the popular view that 'surely not even one adult Canadian approves the sentimentality of the Kurt Meyer fiasco.'[32] And what would be the effect on the Nuremberg trials? The *Globe* speculated: 'There [Nuremberg] the prosecutors are holding them collectively responsible for war crimes, even though some of the conspirators may not be so deeply involved as others. The decision of the reviewing authority in the Meyer case leaves a splendid opening for Nurnberg defence lawyers.'[33]

Veterans organizations, municipal councils, women's auxiliaries, all thought that execution was a condign punishment for Kurt Meyer. There was further outrage at the thought that Meyer's family might accompany him to Canada and that they would become Canadian citizens. Telegrams of protest flowed into the prime minister's Office, most from veterans but also from labour groups demanding that 'seeds of Fascism must not be harboured in Canada.'[34] The volume of protest seemed to grow in the face of confusion as to who was responsible for the commutation. The news release from Germany had merely stated that the 'confirming authority' had decided to reduce the sentence because Meyer's 'degree of responsibility [was] not such as to warrant the extreme penalty.'[35] It was already known that Vokes had refused one appeal, and so it was presumed by many that Guy Simonds, commander of the Canadian army in the Netherlands, or Murchie had made the decision to commute. The Calgary *Herald* featured the headline 'Just who commuted sentence is puzzle,'[36] a confusion that deepened when even the minister of national defence, Douglas Abbott, appeared uncertain as to who had made the decision.[37] When

Vokes's role was clarified, the next question became whether he had been instructed to make his decision at the meeting on 9 January in London. Fingers of blame began to be pointed towards Ottawa. In an editorial on 18 January, the *Globe* noted that John Read, the trusted adviser to the prime minister, had been present at the fateful meeting. 'An officer of Mr. King's own department was consulted, and surely the prime minister is not maintaining a staff of legal experts ready to tender advice to all who seek it without pausing to consider their position.' The implication was that King himself was a party to this rancid affair. 'General Vokes thus placed the case where it should be – on the Federal Government's doorstep,' the newspaper concluded. 'He [King] is now directly involved, and for him there can be no evasion of responsibility.'[38]

Subsequent editorials hammered away at the political significance of the Meyer commutation and the perceived connecting link was invariably Read. 'It can hardly be argued that Mr. Read has a dual personality, and when giving advice to a military officer can doff his cloak of responsibility as an officer of the prime minister's own department.'[39] The decision to commute after the finding of guilt tainted the war crimes process and was such a serious step that it could only have been willed by Ottawa. 'Nor can it be pleaded that Mr. Read, when consulted by Gen. Vokes, was not speaking as an official of the Government.'[40] In fact, the commutation had been discussed at a cabinet meeting on 16 January, and the unanimous decision was that Vokes had acted within his powers and what had been done could not be undone.[41] Other than a brief press release from National Defence,[42] King's government made no official comment on the controversy. The only discussion in the House of Commons was a request from John Diefenbaker for a copy of the transcript of the evidence taken at trial and the correspondence related to the commutation. Defence Minister Abbott was willing to let him view the evidence but claimed official privilege over departmental communications. In any case, he advised the House that, contrary to the *Globe*'s fulminations, there had not been any contact with Ottawa officials and that 'their advice was neither sought nor given.'[43] No one followed up to ask what role Read had played at the London conference.

Embarrassing his political masters is the worst thing (except perhaps for losing a battle) that a general officer in a democracy can do. Telegraph lines buzzed between London and Ottawa as soldiers and diplomats worked frantically to repair the damage. Massey contacted External Affairs to confirm that Vokes understood at the London meeting that the decision was his and his alone, and he added tartly that the chief of staff,

Murchie, was requesting Vokes to make no further statements.[44] In his defence, Vokes telegrammed Murchie on 21 January denying the implications in the *Globe* editorials, admitting that the responsibility for commuting the sentence was entirely his own, and concluding, 'I would say that this business is [a] nine day press wonder but I am prepared to make a public statement that the commutation of sentence was my responsibility that I merely sought other opinion.'[45] Ottawa requested that Vokes simply make no further comment.[46]

No sooner was one fire stamped out than another flared up. Harry Foster arrived back in Canada and was immediately sought out by reporters. In an offhand comment in Montreal he said that it was 'very unfair to a fellow like that [Meyer] to shut him up in a prison for the rest of his life ... The best thing to do would be to shoot him.' This suggested that there was a division among the generals as to Meyer's proper sentence. Foster rambled on with thoughtless comments that guaranteed further controversy. He considered Meyer to be 'a marvellous soldier, quite the best panzer general they had and a wonderful organizer,' and that he had borne his trial 'splendidly.' The affair was already at a delicate enough stage without one general contradicting another. The press reported that Foster's ill-timed interview 'caused an immediate uproar in the highest army circles in Ottawa.'[47] Even Foster's role in the trial came under new scrutiny when it was revealed that, prior to the proceedings, the *Maple Leaf* had editorialized on the appropriateness of Foster's selection. At the time the *Maple Leaf* had noted that, as the former commanding officer of the 7th Infantry Brigade, one of Meyer's principal victims, Foster would surely be ready to extract justice. CMHQ had instantly clamped down on the *Maple Leaf*, and it was ordered to run a false statement that Foster would not be trying a case involving the murder of his own men. But it was the tone of Foster's comments that most rankled the civilian population for there was a justified suspicion that the generals were sticking together for mutual protection. The *Globe* reminded Foster that war, especially for the lower ranks, was not a football game in which, at the conclusion, one shook hands all around and that 'there is no place for professional admiration where war crimes are involved.'[48]

Back in Europe, Vokes was told of the protests and of the vengeful patter of the editorials. He declared his astonishment: 'How any fair-minded person who read the evidence could find any reasonable ground for protest is beyond me. There was no suggestion that he [Meyer] ordered any of his men to shoot any prisoner.'[49] Had Vokes actually read the evidence? At times it seemed as if Jesionek had never testified. Vokes had evidently convinced himself that the entire trial was suspect for he advised a friend, General Maurice Pope, that 'Meyer's conviction on the charge of having incited his troops to kill Canadian prisoners of war had not done Canada much credit.'[50] Vokes had his supporters in Canada as well. The Peterborough *Examiner* gave credit to him for noting that there was doubt as to whether Meyer had actually given the orders to execute the prisoners, adding that: 'It is not an easy or popular thing to commute the sentence of a man like Meyer to a milder punishment; in doing so General Vokes and his advisors showed great moral courage, and a higher respect for the principles of justice than those who are howling for a hanging.'[51]

Vokes was held in such high regard by the nation that, to many, this alone vindicated the commutation. To the Vancouver *Sun*, Vokes 'was not courting popularity. He preferred to listen to the voice of his own conscience.'[52] The Hamilton *Spectator* even questioned the validity of the trial itself. Was this not a case, it suggested, of the victor punishing a prostrate enemy? 'There might be grave doubts about whether Meyer as a soldier should have been tried in the first place – in fact it is open knowledge that many returned soldiers are not fully in sympathy with these trials. There may also be some doubts as to whether the crime of which he was found guilty was not also practised by some of the Allied armies.'[53]

In an interview with Canadian Press on 21 January, Vokes tried to defuse the situation by advising reporter William Boss that Meyer's conduct did not warrant death and 'therefore it is unjust to hold him [a commander] responsible with his life for every act committed by every soldier.'[54] He added with airy callousness that there was a difference in the degree of guilt between a deliberate murder and Meyer's case, which he described as similar to a motorist who accidentally hit a pedestrian.

Yet there was a strong suspicion in Canada that this explanation was a convenient device for generals to excuse their own deeds. Perhaps Meyer's triers had felt a noose about their own necks for, as another newspaper noted, 'in all this argument about reducing the sentence of death against Major General Kurt Meyer, no one has mentioned what might have been going through a lot of minds. Many years ago, someone said to the effect "There, but for the grace of God go I."'[55]

Debate on the morality of Meyer's commutation could be endless. Perhaps Vokes was more in touch with the reality of warfare, where it is often meaningless to make fine legal distinctions. On the other hand, sparing Meyer might have simply been a way for Vokes to excuse his own conduct. But to the average citizen at the time, especially those who had been told during the trial that their sons or husbands had been murdered after capture, leniency towards Meyer was a profane gesture. 'Canada has so shamefully betrayed her own heroic dead – murdered in cold blood,' wrote the father of one murdered soldier.[56] Recondite arguments on command responsibility meant little to the victims' families. The mother of Rifleman F.W. Holness, one of the prisoners executed at Le Mesnil-Patry, could not fathom why the Canadian military spared Meyer: 'Our boys were innocent – they were taken unawares and shot in cold blood. This man Meyer should be made to suffer in the same way he made them suffer.'[59]

The decision, however, could not be reversed and for the foreseeable future Meyer would be another inmate with the murderers and rapists at Dorchester. The *Globe and Mail*'s raging editorials against the King government's complicity in the commutation fizzled into nothingness. Canadians were becoming intrigued by the mushrooming Gouzenko spy case and the revelation of the extent of the Soviet spy rings in Canada. Concern with this new threat overshadowed interest in the fate of the remnants of the shattered enemy.

In February 1946 Macdonald attended the Nuremberg trials. While Canada had no official role at Nuremberg, Macdonald was graciously welcomed and he found that he 'was unofficially being sponsored by both the British and Americans.'[58] But there was additional unfinished business with the 12th SS. A substantial case could be made out against Wilhelm Mohnke, the commanding officer of the 26th PGR. Macdonald's war crimes unit had six charges of murder against Mohnke filed with the UNWCC and was confident that they had an 'excellent case' against him. The only problem was that they had no defendant. Ending the war as the last commandant of Hitler's Berlin bunker, Mohnke had defended the shrinking Reich until on April 1945, when he personally delivered the news to Hitler that the Russians were only 300 metres away. Taken into Soviet custody, he survived because of his captors' fascination with Hitler's last days and was constantly under interrogation.[59] Macdonald sent an officer to Berlin with orders to demand information about Mohnke. After several days, the Soviets threatened to expel the officer if he persisted.[60] Macdonald could only hope that the Soviets would mete out their own brand of justice to Mohnke.

Near the end of February, the war crimes unit located the two medical officers Meyer said had first told him of the Canadian bodies. One of them, Dr Erich Gatternigg, was being held at a U.S. camp near Salzburg, Austria.

1

Even though the Meyer case was completed, Macdonald decided to pursue these witnesses for any additional information. Gatternigg had served with Meyer on the Eastern Front and during the interrogation he spoke glowingly of him. At his trial, Meyer had insisted that on 10 June both Dr Gatternigg and Stift had reported to him that there were dead Canadian prisoners in the garden. Now Macdonald had a witness to Meyer's story, and he wasted little time putting the question to him:

Q.197 Now, I want you to tell me all that you know about the shooting of Canadian prisoners at the Regimental Headquarters on the 7th and 8th of June?
A.197 None of the Canadian prisoners were shot there.
Q.198 I want you to tell me all you know about Canadian prisoners being killed by any means at Regimental Headquarters on the 7th and 8th of June?
A.198 I don't know. What am I to understand by 'other means of killing.'
Q.199 Beating them to death with rifle butts and clubs?
A.199 It is impossible.

Gatternigg had heard rumours of Canadian prisoners being killed at Authie. Nevertheless, he completely denied Meyer's story of what had occurred at the Abbaye:

Q.209 And do you say then that you know nothing whatever of the shooting of prisoners at the Abbaye Ardenne during the month of June 1944?
A.209 Nobody was killed or shot or beaten to death as far as I know.
Q.210 Did you ever discuss with Meyer the killing of Canadian prisoners at the Abbaye Ardenne?
A.210 No.
Q.211 Did you ever discuss with Dr Stift the killing of Canadian prisoners at the Abbaye Ardenne during the month of June 1944?
A.211 No.
Q.212 I want you to be very sure of this now because I have questioned Meyer and he says that you did know about the shooting of prisoners.
A.212 No.[61]

The doctor's demeanour made Macdonald suspicious. He fidgeted throughout the examination and kept biting his lip until it bled profusely. Macdonald sensed that he 'was holding something back and knew much more than he was willing to tell.'[62] If he had something favourable to say Gatternigg had no reason to withhold it. However, he may have felt that

Meyer was responsible for the killings and decided that a blanket denial was the safest course. The salient point, however, was that an eyewitness, who was also a friend and comrade, denied the events as Meyer had described them.

The other medical officer, the dentist Dr Erich Stift, was located in Hungary and flown to London for examination. Much more at ease than Gatternigg, he, too, emphatically denied that he had reported the finding of Canadian bodies to Meyer:

Q.62   Did you at any time while you were at the Abbaye Ardenne see the bodies of any Canadian prisoners?

A.62   No.

Q.71   Now, if Meyer says that you saw some 18 or 19 bodies of Canadian soldiers in that garden and reported that to him, is that true or not true?

A.71   That is not true.[63]

This seemed to destroy what little credibility Meyer's account had. And yet Stift added a postscript that intrigued Macdonald. In February 1946 Stift and Gatternigg had been together in a camp and begun to discuss the Meyer trial. News of the events were circulating throughout POW camps in Germany, and Stift was curious to know if Gatternigg could confirm Meyer's testimony. At that time, Gatternigg told him that he had seen bodies at the HQ and that he had reported this to the commander. Macdonald read to Stift Gatternigg's statement in which he denied all knowledge of the killings. Yet Stift insisted that their February conversation had taken place.

Puzzling as these conflicting stories were, Macdonald concluded that 'the evidence of these two witnesses does not support Meyer's explanation nor absolve him from responsibility.'[64] Forever self-serving, Meyer maintained in his memoirs that Stift and Gatternigg had been deliberately prevented from testifying and that they could have been 'the main witnesses for the defence.'[65] In fact, as the record of their interrogations shows, their testimony would have put Kurt Meyer several paces closer to the firing squad. Still, even if there was further, damning evidence against Meyer, it was beside the point for the proceedings were concluded and, in view of the recent controversy, no officials would dare risk reopening the case.

In a newspaper interview in early January, Macdonald conceded that the number of cases the unit was considering for trial had been pared down from sixty-five to about fifty. The majority of these would never come to trial for the suspects had disappeared into prison camps or the Soviet zone. However, the trials of the killers of RCAF aircrew were about to begin and Macdonald, in the words of a newspaper report, believed that these 'new cases represent the next step by the people of Canada in their effort to punish war criminals.'[66] Officialdom no doubt hoped that it was a step that could be taken quietly and with a minimum of tumult.

7

Shot like Wild Animals

Maria Hirsch was at her hairdresser in March 1945 when an air-raid alarm sounded and she ran for shelter. What happened next was typical of the surreal existence of wartime Germany. The raid's target was elsewhere, but before Hirsch left the shelter a soldier came in and called out, 'Are some strong men here? We have a Canadian soldier out there. We may not lay hands on him.' The soldier's intent was plain. He was recruiting a civilian murder squad. Some suggested that the police do it, but the soldier explained that the police could not be involved. Maria Hirsch spoke up and asked why he wanted to kill a fellow soldier, and 'because of that I was abused by the people.' When the all-clear sounded she left to buy a loaf of bread and passed by the screeching mob who were now beating the airman to death. A youngster witnessed the same scene. He saw an officer lead the wounded airman to a main street and berate 'the populace because so far no one had laid hands on the flier.' With this encouragement, some bystanders proceeded to beat the prisoner with spades and hoes until the officer finished him off with a pistol shot.[1] As happened in many cases, the military and police had not taken a direct part in the killing but had overseen and encouraged it.

During the early war years, German propaganda had minimized the effect of British bombing. However, the American reporter William Shirer noted a change in view after the August 1940 raids on Berlin; propaganda minister Joseph Goebbels encouraged hysteria by accusing the RAF of attempting to 'massacre the population of Berlin.'[2] The air war largely bypassed the German civilian population until a decisive turn in the strategic-bombing campaign in 1942. Studies had shown that the RAF's night bombing of specific industrial and military targets had failed and that the only likely way to achieve results would be the 'area bombing' of entire cities.[3] On 30 October 1942, the British chiefs of staff endorsed a strategic review in which the Allies would make 'the aim of the bomber offensive ... the progressive destruction of the enemy's war, industrial and economic system.' Details of the review were provided by Air Marshal Sir Charles Portal, who concluded that 'twenty-five million Germans would be rendered homeless, 900,000 would be killed and one million seriously injured.'[4] Chilling as these figures sounded, they ensured that 'the real contest was between the Allied air forces and the German cities themselves.'[5] Portal's strategy was, in the words of one RAF historian, 'a prescription for massacre, nothing more nor less.'[6] During the battle of the Ruhr in the spring of 1943, approximately 32,000 German civilians died. During a series of raids in July 1943 Hamburg was engulfed in a firestorm, and by war's end 55,000 of its citizens had been killed in the air raids.[7]

To the average German, who had no control over Hitler or his policies, the strategy of targeting women and children was criminal and inhumane. Yet, since the bomber offensive was the only way for the western Allies to engage Germany directly, abandoning this weapon was unthinkable. Part of the difficulty, as Bomber Command's Sir Arthur Harris observed, was that 'in this matter of the use of aircraft in war there is, it so happens, no international law at all.' Neither international law nor moral thinking had adjusted to the startling technological changes in air power.[8] By contrast, the laws of war governing the treatment of prisoners were well defined and, in the main, would be rigorously applied, but laws of war are most effective in familiar situations. For example, Napoleonic armies acknowledged humane conduct in warfare except when confronted with the 'people's war' in Spain when soldiers reacted to guerilla raids with a deadly spiral of retribution and atrocities.[9] By 1943 the air war against Germany had reached such a superheated state that bombers were killing thousands of women and children. The human targets of this campaign considered it barbaric and the airmen who carried it out *terrorflieger* or air pirates, not warriors. Those who survived the bombing were not inclined to accept the laws of war as applying to captured airmen.

In August 1943 SS leader Himmler gave orders to police not to interfere in clashes between downed airmen and civilians. Goebbels, for his part, all but declared war on the airmen in a lead editorial in the *Volkischer Beobachter* on 29 May 1944:

It is only by the use of firearms that we can protect the lives of enemy pilots shot down during bombing attacks; otherwise these men would be killed by the sorely tried population.

Who is right here? The murderers who, after their cowardly misdeeds expect humane treatment from their victims, or the victims who wish to defend themselves on the principle of 'an eye for an eye and a tooth for a tooth.' This question is not difficult to answer. It appears to us intolerable to use our soldiers and police against the German people who are only treating child murderers as they deserve.[10]

In early 1945 Goebbels proposed the mass execution of Allied aircrew prisoners in retaliation for the Dresden firestorm, and it took the military's persuasion to forestall this abandonment of the laws of war.[11] Germans could develop an intense hatred of the bombers without official prompting. After the Hamburg firestorm, a policeman found a little girl dragging her dead little brother behind her. She had been wandering aimlessly for a couple of days, and the side of her brother's face had been scraped smooth. The policeman was outraged: 'I would have shot any enemy airman who had parachuted down. I also think that any English or American person would have felt the same way.[12] Numerous Canadian airmen would bear witness to this German rage.

During his interrogation, one Canadian airman was suddenly attacked by his interrogation officer. After several blows the officer stopped, regained his composure, and explained that his wife had recently been killed in an air raid.[13] One group of American fliers was held in a train station in Frankfurt, where they were confronted by a mob of factory girls. With pure hatred in their eyes, the girls surrounded the fliers and asked that they be turned over to them. When the guards refused, they shrieked, 'Just give us one!' Eventually, the guards had to use their guns to clear the crowd away.[14] Spontaneous civilian outbursts were one thing, but killings planned and sanctioned by the authorities was quite another. Investigators would increasingly concentrate on premeditated incidents.

The official history of the RCAF indicates that the 'number [of downed airmen] believed to have died in unacceptable circumstances is very low – perhaps about a dozen ... Given the horrific conditions that existed in German cities after the heavier and more successful raids, that is a remarkable statistic.'[15] It would be remarkable, if true. However, the real number of murdered airmen is almost double the figure given, and this, too, represents only a fraction of the total. Many murders and likely many criminals were never discovered. Fearful of Allied retaliation, Germans hid unpleasant incidents and those who were prosecuted were discovered almost by accident.

As Maria Hirsch had witnessed, Nazi party officials could be instrumental in whipping up the 'sorely tried population.' For example, seven American airmen were held on Borkum Island in August 1944 while their captors discussed Goebbel's decree. An officer made an inflammatory speech to a crowd: 'Knock them down, kill them, they kill our brothers, sisters and children,' he urged. The Americans were marched around the island, beaten, and eventually killed.[16] Word of the campaign against the captured airmen had reached the Allies and was common talk in RCAF messes. As early as June 1944, the *Globe and Mail* was reporting that it was 'lynch law for British and American flyers.'[17] While there are no accurate statistics, the vast number of reports indicates that the summary execution of Allied airmen was widespread and frequently committed on the orders of superior officers. One early case to come to the attention of the investigators was that of Dr Ferdinand Mahr, the senior medical officer at Diest, Belgium. On 28 April 1944 a Canadian bomber had crashed in the vicinity and the one survivor was taken to Mahr's hospital. There, he was denied all medical attention as well as food or drink and was left on a cot to die. Investigators learned that he was 'bleeding from the mouth, nose and ears and blood formed under him, which, in the unventilated room with the windows closed, shades drawn and door locked, caused a nauseating smell.'[18] The local gravedigger was told to prepare seven graves and advised that the wounded Canadian, the very image of wretchedness, would shortly be joining his comrades. Mahr was put on a UNWCC wanted list.

Unit investigators uncovered many atrocities against airmen, some spontaneous, others on command. In Woltersdorf in April 1945, a Canadian airman was dragged from his crashed bomber 'like a dog to the wood' and shot. The perpetrators, an SS officer cadet and a farmer, were being held in the case.[19] In Italy, an airman who was evading capture was seized by a German officer and a fascist and shot. Both were put on the CROWCASS wanted list.[20] In many cases Nazi officials deliberately engineered the murders. Captain E. Skutezky detailed the Wassertrudingen killing in which an injured flyer had been taken to Nazi party headquarters. Once there, the local leader, Gattinger, arranged for the execution, while his wife announced that 'tonight I shall have the women come to the *Rathaus* and have this chap whistled and spit at.' After being investigated by U.S. authorities, Gattinger killed his wife and children and then took his own life.[21]

Many of the RCAF investigations would be dead ends. A Canadian pilot shot down over Frankfurt had died of wounds and it was suspected that he had been denied treatment. However, a British serviceman and fellow captive informed the investigators that the Canadian had been treated but, because his wounds were so severe, had died nonetheless. The case was closed.[22] In other RCAF cases, the task of finding the perpetrators or sufficient evidence to convict them was even more difficult than in the Normandy cases of the 12th SS. In October 1943 two RCAF prisoners were told that one of their crewmen had been lynched in Kassel. There was no further information.[23] One German female, Stellmach, was being held on information that she had killed a Canadian airman with a pitchfork. But later she denied the incident and her original confession to the U.S. military had been lost.[24] In the town of Frankenberg, five soldiers disguised as civilians beat a captured Canadian airman to death. A civilian witness reported that the deed was done at the direction of 'the whole staff of officers.' Yet it was not possible to identify the individual assailants and, because Frankenberg lay east of the Elbe River, the investigation was delayed until authority to enter the Soviet zone was obtained. It was never forthcoming. In all, seven cases had to be abandoned as the events had occurred in eastern Germany.[25]

Though evidence was hard to come by, the fact of widespread killing of Allied airmen was inescapable. The unit obtained depositions from German witnesses in Lüttringhausen who knew of two RAF and two RCAF airmen held at the local town hall. When a Luftwaffe officer arrived to take them away, Nazi leaders incited an angry crowd who shot the four men before they could be removed.[26] Knowledge of these incidents made RCAF staff resolute that justice would eventually be done.

At the time he drafted his plea for separate Canadian war crimes trials, Macdonald was aware of crimes against airmen and had suggested that the army be responsible for these cases in addition to those of the 12th SS.[27] However, the RCAF was anxious to look after its own. On 10 January 1946, Orde visited Bad Salzuflen to discuss the RCAF trials and it was agreed that they were to be conducted 'by RCAF personnel, Col. Macdonald to remain generally responsible nevertheless for preparation of cases.'[28] Wing Commander T.W. O'Brien became the commander of the RCAF War Crimes Administration Unit in Aurich. As the time of trial drew closer, the affair became indelibly air force. On 4 March, the unit war diary noted that all provost guards were RCAF and that 'no demands would be made on army authorities for any personnel for any purpose other than liaison during the trials.'[29] On one occasion, Macdonald attended the RCAF trials (which were conducted in the same courtroom as the Meyer trial), only to have his presence challenged. 'The President took a very dim view of my presence there, that he wasn't going to have any Brown bodies interfering with an Air Force trial.' Macdonald was sent a message reading 'I think you had better not continue in your presence here because the President is thinking of having you ejected if you do.'[30] Mindful that he had been appointed by the prime minister, Macdonald was tempted to challenge him, but in the end he left the RCAF to handle its own affairs.

At one point, it was questionable whether the trials would be run by Canadians of any service. After the Meyer trial, Ottawa seemed satisfied with its fling in the world of international law and there was a feeling that Canada should now disengage itself from war crimes. In February, the minister of national defence for air suggested that no RCAF personnel be sent to Europe to constitute the court and instead 'RAF courts should be used for this purpose.'[31] However, there was enough proof of atrocities against Canadian airmen for the RCAF to insist on its own courts. The officers appointed to hear the cases were among the most renowned in the RCAF. Wing commanders Park and Brown had been leading bomber and fighter pilots respectively. Group Captain Nelles Timmerman had achieved fame early in the war both as a bomber and as a fighter. Another group captain, F.M. Newsom, had served in 408 Bomber Squadron and on two occasions had aircraft badly damaged in combat but returned with his crew. Awarded the DSO, DFC, and bar, by war's end Newsom commanded a squadron of the elite Pathfinders.[32] Even an army observer conceded that 'these guys were real Air Force.'[33] Somewhat in contrast to his bemedalled colleagues, the court president, Air Vice-Marshal R.E. McBurney, had served most of the war in Ottawa and had few decorations to show for his service. The RCAF's legal staff sent Squadron Leader Alexander A. Cattanach to serve as judge advocate.

The prosecution was conducted by Squadron Leader Oliver 'Pat' Durdin, a lawyer from London, Ontario, whose investigations had already given him an intimate knowledge of the facts of the cases he was about to prosecute. In a strange twist of fate, Durdin had narrowly escaped death in an airplane crash just two weeks before the trials were to begin. His death would have deprived the RCAF of its most capable and well-informed prosecutor at a crucial moment. All of the German accused were either civilians or from army units. However, in violation of section 7(3) of the regulations[34] that entitled an accused to have at least one judge from his own service, no army representatives would sit on the court. The Canadian press paid little attention to the RCAF trials and the exercise was even dismissed as inconsequential in one newspaper report: 'With the trials limited to five, the war crimes action of the RCAF is regarded as a token effort following up the army's trial of SS Maj. Gen. Kurt Meyer last December.'[35] In truth, however, while they never attracted the attention of the Meyer trial, the RCAF trials were far from token efforts for the prosecution was conducted in deadly earnest and the defence with stolid desperation. For the men whose lives were at stake, and for the principles of fairness in military justice, the issues at hand in many ways overshadowed those of the Meyer trial.

The first defendant before the court, Johann Neitz, seemed the living opposite of Kurt Meyer. Formerly a cook for the searchlight batteries in northwest Germany, Neitz, 'wearing an ill-fitting old grey-black suit, faced the court with a hang-dog look, his shoulders slumping and his face deadly pale.'[36] During the investigation of his case, the war crimes unit had not been able to find him in a prisoner camp; eventually, however, Neitz's girlfriend was located and an envelope with a return address led investigator John Blain to Neitz's hideout in Hanover.[37] The charge against him claimed that, on 16 October 1944, he had attempted to murder a Canadian airman. Durdin's first witness was an elderly German lighthouse keeper, Paul Bornert. He recounted how, on the night of 15 October, a Canadian flyer had knocked on his lighthouse door and sought refuge from the incoming tide. After searching him to make sure that he had no weapons, Bornert and a friend took off the airman's clothes and gave him some food and drink. The following morning Bornert went to the shore to report their prisoner. He returned with the soldier Neitz. Along the way to the lighthouse Neitz remarked, 'I am not going to take him back ashore. I am going to bump him off on the way,'[38] and he showed Bornert the bomb crater where he would dump the body. After Bornert protested that the Canadian had given himself up, was unarmed, and had been hurt in his fall, Neitz brushed him aside with the comment, 'We are not going to fool around with him very long.' Under cross-examination by Neitz's lawyer, Squadron Leader Victor Collins, Bornert maintained that Neitz was entirely serious when he made the statement that he would kill the captive.

Next to testify was the victim himself, Flying Officer Rudolph Anthony Roman. A bomb aimer from 408 Squadron, Roman's plane had been attacking Wilhelmshaven when it was hit by flak just short of the target. Roman bailed out and landed heavily in a tidal flat near the Voorslapp lighthouse. The morning after being taken in by the lighthouse keeper, Roman was surrendered to Neitz. The soldier curtly ordered the Canadian to raise his hands, and at that moment his sinister intent almost dissolved into low comedy. The magazine fell out of Neitz's revolver and bullets went rolling about the lighthouse floor. Once Neitz had reloaded, he searched Roman again to make sure that he had no weapons and ordered him to walk towards the shore. Seeing a fighter flare, Neitz ordered the flyer to carry it even though the Canadian's injured hip made it difficult for him to walk at all.

Upon reaching the shore, Neitz ordered Roman to put down the flare and raise his hands. Roman did so. Neitz then raised his gun and shot him in the abdomen. As he pitched forward, Roman turned his body and partially deflected another shot into his stomach. Neitz then picked up the flare and walked away. Shortly thereafter, a group of soldiers came upon Roman and took him away for treatment. He eventually recovered in a prisoner camp. As it was likely that the court would accept Roman's testimony, Collins's only hope lay in trying to get Roman to admit that the ordeal might have blurred his memory:

Q.236   You were not in the best of shape, so that your recollection of everything that happened, you would not want to guarantee?
A.   My recollection of the whole incident is quite clear.
Q.237   Did this harrowing experience not affect you in any way so that you would not be in a position to remember?
A.   It did not.
Q.238   Even the shooting did not affect your memory?
A.   It did not.[39]

The defence had so little going for it that Collins had nothing to lose by calling the accused Neitz to testify. The latter stated that, prior to the incident, he had risked his own life to rescue two Allied airmen caught in the tides and, notwithstanding Bornert's testimony, his sole purpose in going to the lighthouse was to bring the prisoner into custody. However, Roman was an intractable sort who had to be goaded along the way and who, upon reaching the shore, had refused to go any farther. In desperation, Neitz fired a warning shot that inadvertently hit the prisoner. Reeling, the Canadian seemed to reach for a weapon and, in self defence, Neitz fired again. Under Durdin's cross-examination, Neitz's story unravelled for he was forced to concede that until they had arrived at the shore Roman had obeyed every order. Moreover, since he had been searched twice for weapons and none had been found, the idea of his reaching for a gun seemed far-fetched. If Neitz's story was true, then every other eyewitness, both Canadian and German, was a liar. Unfortunately for him, Neitz could not even lie consistently. During his re-examination by Collins, Neitz said that his first shot was intended only to injure Roman, whereas in his examination-in-chief he had said that he had meant to fire a warning shot. Collins then called as a witness a young boy, Willi Saueresigg, who had seen part of the incident from a dyke. However, this evidence backfired when the boy confirmed Roman's story that the cook had shouted, 'Hands up!', Roman had complied, and then the cook had shot him.

In summation, Collins argued that these events had occurred 'not in a civilian setting but in the midst of active warfare in a heavily bombed area'[40] and that a guard such as Neitz had reason to watch Roman closely and deal harshly with any refusal of orders. Durdin had only to point out the many contradictions in the defence's case. Not only had Neitz confessed his murderous intent to Bornert, the defence's own witness, Saueresigg, confirmed that the assault was unprovoked. judge advocate Cattanach left the evidence for the judges to consider, only asking them to put the recent war out of their minds. There was no doubt in the court's mind, and Neitz was convicted and sentenced to life imprisonment at hard labour. Everything considered, he had been exceedingly lucky, for two members had wanted the death penalty and three had been satisfied with life imprisonment.[41] Even so, Neitz would file an appeal against the conviction, proclaiming his innocence and asking for mercy: 'I had heard that Canadian justice was fair but having heard the finding and sentence I can only say it is too harsh and I cannot understand your justice.'[42] The appeal was denied.

As Neitz was taken from the courtroom, the next case, which would present considerably more challenging questions as to fact and law, was called to order. As in some other instances, the way in which it had come to trial was highly circuitous.

In the autumn of 1945, French prisoners reported to the British war crimes unit at Bad Oyenhausen that an Allied flyer had been murdered in the Bavarian town of Oberweier. Lieutenant-Colonel Leo Genn travelled there in September and his first stop was the mayor's house. Josef Lindenbolz, a local anti-Nazi who had been made burgomaster by the occupation forces, recalled that on the night of 29 July 1944 an airplane had crashed near the town. Shortly thereafter he saw an Allied airman confined at the local town hall, or *Rathaus*. Usually, the cells at the *Rathaus* were reserved for the twenty-five French prisoners who worked in

Oberweier as farm labourers. As a fireman, Lindenbolz possessed some authority and he proceeded to search the prisoner and discovered that he was a Canadian. Outside the cell, Lindenbolz was confronted by the local Nazi leader and burgomaster, Wilhelm Jung. 'Kill the pilot,' Jung ordered him. 'Beat him to death. The *Kreisleiter* [regional Nazi chief] doesn't want to see him alive.'[43] Stunned, Lindenbolz replied, 'I think you are mad. You must leave this pilot to the military authorities.' As far as Lindenbolz was aware, all local Nazis were instructed to kill captured airmen and the *Kreisleiter*, Tiefenbacher, was particularly fanatical on the issue. When it became apparent that no civilians would kill the prisoner, Jung sent for the town policeman, Johann Schumacher, and ordered him to do the deed. According to Lindenbolz, Schumacher resisted but Jung took him to his office to confirm the order from Tiefenbacher. After the call, Schumacher went straight to his house to fetch a rifle and then took the prisoner from the *Rathaus* and down the road out of town. Enraged at what he knew was about to happen, but helpless to prevent it, Lindenbolz went home. After about ten minutes he heard a rifle shot and, turning to a friend, sighed, 'Well, this poor chap has been killed now.' This was not the end of the incident, for eight days later he was arrested for having refused Jung's order and was held by the Gestapo for three months.

Another villager, Anton Kustner, was present and heard Jung order the policeman, 'We must kill the American,' to which Schumacher had replied, 'But where? We can't do it here in front of all the villagers.' Jung then told him to take the doomed man outside the village to avoid any disturbances.[44] Other residents added more details. An old soldier, Peter Scherer, brought the airman to the *Rathaus* and offered to go to the military authorities. To Scherer's surprise, Jung said, 'No, beat him to death, shoot him.' Another onlooker, August Mach, cradled a rifle and was ordered by Jung to shoot the prisoner. Mach simply refused. Jung's exhortations did encourage some others who began to beat and choke the Canadian. The French prisoners, whose sympathies lay with the Allied airman, rescued him from the beating.

The eventual murder of the captive created a sensation in the remote town. There was an ineffable sense of horror at such a cold-blooded killing of a defenceless man who had literally fallen from the sky. Even Hilda Jung, the burgomaster's wife, confronted him. 'I was excited and furious over the whole thing,' she testified, 'and I said that "such a thing should not happen,"' to which her husband sheepishly replied, 'The Kreisleiter gave this order,' and excused himself by saying that he had merely relayed the death sentence to Schumacher.[45] Everyone seemed eager to cover up the incident for the town gravedigger was ordered to disinter the body and remove all identification tags. He did so and placed a simple cross over the grave. However, the French prisoners knew the truth. They covered the grave with flowers and on the cross wrote 'Pilote Canadien.'[46]

Genn had the body disinterred again and examined by a military pathologist. Although it was badly decomposed, the pathologist detected a fatal bullet wound in the temple. Before the case was turned over to the Canadians, the British made one further discovery. They uncovered a letter from Jung to his wife indicating that the tables had been turned and that he was now a French prisoner in Strasbourg.

In October 1945 Macdonald wrote to Durdin that 'this appears to have the makings of a good case' and urged him to pursue it vigorously. Durdin established that the victim was an air gunner from 100 Squadron and that all other crew members, save one, had perished. Squadron Leader Beck was dispatched to Oberweier and located the town clerk, Wendelin Kappenberger, who confirmed Lindenbolz's story that Jung had telephoned Tiefenbacher for instructions and after hanging up had announced, 'the Kreisleiter does not want to see the airman alive.' Kappenberger reminded Jung that on another occasion they had simply called the military to come and pick up the airman. Why not do the same now? Jung, pale and agitated, only repeated that they must obey Tiefenbacher's order.[47]

By 26 February 1946 Jung had been sent to Bad Salzuflen and his version of the events departed radically from every other eyewitness. At no time that night had he talked with Lindenbolz, Mach, or Scherer or ordered them to kill the captive. Yes, he had talked with the *Kreisleiter*. But, when the latter had ordered him to kill the airman, Jung had replied, 'You can't just beat a prisoner to death.' Jung had then summoned the soldier Schumacher and relayed Tiefenbacher's order. Portraying himself as a reluctant intermediary, Jung said to Schumacher, 'I didn't approve of this,' and then Schumacher replied that it 'was a small matter; he would take care of it.' Jung told him to take the prisoner to the nearby city of Rastatt or to a police station. Later, he was surprised to hear people talking about the Canadian's murder. In contrast to all other witnesses, Jung maintained that he had not ordered the body disinterred to remove the identity tags, that Kappenberger had never reminded him that they could turn their prisoner over to a military post, or that he had commanded Lindenbolz and the others to beat the prisoner. He even denied his wife's comment that he had relayed the death sentence to Schumacher. 'I don't believe that, I only ordered the constable to take him away.' When directly confronted with his wife's statement, he gave way and admitted that it was possible that he had said such things.[48]

Neither Schumacher nor Tiefenbacher had appeared in any prison camp and so the unit dispatched Wady Lehmann to Oberweier to pick up their trail. On 27 February, only days before the scheduled opening of the RCAF trials, Lehmann arrived in Oberweier where he learned that Schumacher had belonged to the home guard, the 'Landes-Schuetzen,' and that before the war he had been a farmer in the Freiburg area. After contacting French investigators, Lehmann was eventually directed to Schumacher's farm near the town of Tiengen. There, in a ceremony that gave him no joy, Lehmann arrested him in the presence of his wife and six children. Resigned to his fate, Schumacher left without protest and even helped Lehmann change a flat tire on the trip back to Bad Salzuflen. As for Tiefenbacher, he had last been seen in a command bunker at Hilberthof and was rumoured to be in a French camp. He was never found. Before he left Oberweier, Lehmann noticed a fragment of doggerel on a latrine wall: 'The same old story / Captives shot like wild animals; / Like lions and tigers. / As happened in Oberweier, / That is German culture – / Vengeance is near!'[49]

In fact, vengeance was almost at hand for Schumacher was hurriedly interrogated by Durdin and an all-RCAF panel. Instead of denying the events, Schumacher was completely forthright. His function in Oberweier was to guard the French prisoners and, as the only Wehrmacht member in the town, he would get weekly orders from a control NCO. He recalled the incident of 29 July and remembered that, when he arrived at the *Rathaus*, civilians were beating the airman. Schumacher stopped this and locked the Canadian away with the French prisoners. Then Jung arrived. He explained to Schumacher that he had called Tiefenbacher, who had ordered that the airman be killed and that Schumacher was to carry it out. 'I refused at first,' he said, and added, 'I can't contradict my superiors. The kreisleiter had more rights than one from the Wehrmacht.' Schumacher noted that the burgomaster seemed uneasy, that he 'did not want it but that he just went on instructions from the kreisleiter.' Schumacher kept nothing back and even confirmed that, in company with a civilian, he had marched the Canadian out of town and then shot him twice, once through the heart and once through the head. 'There is no point to deny things. If I have to tell the truth there is no point that I deny things.' With his examination almost over, Schumacher made some further, damning admissions:

Q.215   What orders did you have from your captain and NCOs about shooting
         airmen who baled out of aircraft?
A.   If I could catch them, I should turn them into the company.
Q.216   Those were your orders from the captain and the NCOs, is that correct?
A.   Yes.

Acknowledging that the killing was improper and that it amounted to
murder, Schumacher could only sigh, 'I am sorry enough that I am here
today as the murderer. Today the whole burden is being put on my
shoulders.'[50]

Thirteen days after this interrogation, both Schumacher and Jung were
arraigned in Aurich for the murder of the Canadian airman. They were
given far less time than Meyer to consult a lawyer or prepare a defence, for
the Canadian army of occupation was being dissolved and the trials had to
be completed while there was still a venue in which to hold them.
Schumacher had less than two weeks to consult with his appointed lawyer,
Squadron Leader S.H. Hollies, while Jung had only slightly more time
with Neitz's former lawyer, Victor Collins. Once again, the prosecution
was led by Durdin, but now assisting him were Squadron Leader J.S.H.
Beck and an army officer, Captain George Drynan.

The two defendants were something of a contrast. Jung, fifty-three years
old, an ex-soldier and long-time Nazi was described by reporters as a
'hard-faced Bavarian who looks like a battered prize fighter.' Schumacher,
on the other hand, was forty-two, non-political, uneducated, and a man
who, until the war, had never left his farming district.[51] Appearing in court
with a 'cowed appearance and bent shoulders,' Schumacher surprised
everyone by blurting out in response to the charge sheet, 'I am partially
guilty.' That evening Hollies explained the seriousness of the situation to
him, and the following morning he changed his plea to not guilty.[52]

Even though the prosecution brought forward numerous villagers, their
direct knowledge of the plot to murder the airman was limited and Durdin
was compelled to ask them a series of questions that were clearly hearsay.
In the case of Reinhard Strohm, one of the locals who had captured the
airman, Durdin asked if it was common knowledge in the town that Jung
had ordered Schumacher to kill the prisoner. Collins protested, but
Cattanach, the judge advocate, advised the court that section 10(1) of the
regulations permitted hearsay evidence and that the court could 'attach
such weight as they deem it requires.' Another witness, Peter Scherer, was
reluctant to testify about rumours concerning the dead airman even when
pressed by Durdin. This time Hollies challenged the prosecution and

asked, 'Does the ruling of the court go so far as to allow [the prosecution] to press for hearsay evidence when the witness is obviously unwilling to give it?'[53] Nevertheless, Scherer was directed to answer and he replied that village gossip had it that Schumacher was the killer.

The following witness, August Mach, was far more incriminating. Mach had been in the group that had taken the Canadian to the *Rathaus* and, once there, Jung had approached him and another man, exhorting them, 'Beat him to death or shoot him dead.' When they refused, they heard Jung exclaim, 'Is there nobody here who will do it?'[54] When Collins tried to get Mach to explain an inconsistency between his previous statement and his current testimony, the court president, McBurney, interrupted and said that the court was not concerned and that 'I don't think you need to labour that point too long.' A frustrated Collins responded by reminding him that 'you are trying this man for charges that practically amount to murder and if we are going to admit hearsay which means that the thing can be passed along to five or ten different people and then come out of a witness here in court, the defence should be entitled to challenge the memory of the witness as to what was said.'[55]

The free-ranging admission of hearsay as permitted under the war crimes regulations was, in the defence's view, putting the notion of a fair trial in jeopardy. The reception of hearsay, or communications made by a person other than the one testifying, was a throwback to early Anglo-Norman law where jurors were permitted to rely on their personal knowledge, rumour, or gossip in determining a case. With the growth of the adversarial system, jurors were supposed to consider only direct evidence and ignore hearsay.[56] The RCAF trials were, in this sense, a recreation of earlier days when recollected conversations or rumour was accepted as evidence.

Next to testify was Lindenbolz. When he came to the part of his testimony concerning Jung's telephone call to Tiefenbacher, Durdin asked him his opinion of the conversation. This seemed to be asking the witness to conjecture on the contents of a conversation he had not heard, and Collins asked in exasperation: 'Mr. President, I believe I am appearing in a court of Law and if I am wrong in what I say I would like to withdraw. I think my friend should likewise appreciate that these men – and I presume Squadron Leader Hollies will agree with me on this – are here on trial for being concerned in a killing, which is tantamount to murder, and if these men are convicted on village gossip I would like to withdraw from the court.'[57] On the judge advocate's advice, the question was disallowed and Collins remained.

Lindenbolz described Tiefenbacher's speeches in which he had exhorted the public to kill the airmen – 'boiling water should be thrown over them and everything possible should be done to destroy them.' On cross-examination by Hollies, Lindenbolz admitted that even though he was only a civilian he had been sent to jail for so contemptuously refusing Jung's order to kill the captive. He also admitted that Schumacher had protested Jung's order and was reluctant to carry it out. On Jung's behalf it was brought out that his only function was that of Nazi party leader and that he held no military position. According to Lindenbolz, he had urged Jung to turn the prisoner over to military authorities. After he confirmed that Schumacher was the only soldier in Oberweier, Collins asked rhetorically, 'I want to get clear in my mind that Jung did follow your good advice.'[58]

In his defence, Jung declined to testify but instead was permitted by the court to give an unsworn statement. This enabled him to avoid what would undoubtedly have been a devastating cross- examination by Durdin but it also meant that the court was not obliged to put much reliance on what he said. In the statement, Jung maintained that when he called Tiefenbacher the latter had roared at him, 'What? This air gangster is still alive? Why hasn't he been beaten to death or shot?' Jung was commanded to kill the prisoner forthwith. In a panic, Jung returned to the men at the *Rathaus* and may well have repeated what Tiefenbacher had just told him. Still uncertain of what to do, he had summoned Schumacher, told him of Tiefenbacher's order, expressed his own uncertainty, and left it to Schumacher to take the captive to Rastatt or Muggensturm. As the statement was laboriously translated from German into English, it must have occurred to every listener that Jung's account differed from all the previous witnesses who had seen Jung as a dutiful, if not enthusiastic, facilitator of the airman's murder.

Perhaps recognizing the hopelessness of Schumacher's situation, Hollies called the self-effacing soldier to testify in his own defence. As he had done in his interrogation, Schumacher simply recounted his own reluctant part in the killing. By turns cruel and poignant, he described how he felt about the fact that his orders from Jung bound him to commit the deed and that he had carried it out as quickly and painlessly as possible. Schumacher was a ready target in cross-examination and Collins had only to point out that shooting the prisoner was a direct violation of his own orders to forward captured airmen to higher authorities. In a surprise, if not desperate, move, Hollies called Schumacher's guard, Flight Lieutenant G. Low, to testify on his mental state. All Low could add was that Schumacher was typical of a class of Germans 'who has to be told about everything and follow them blindly.'[59]

In summation, Durdin went to great lengths to paint both defendants as fanatical killers. He stressed that Schumacher would not carry out the execution alone and that he had asked for a fireman to accompany him. 'There is nothing brave or courageous about persons who are so easily procured to murder unarmed defenceless persons,' said Durdin, 'and it is not strange that we therefore find the accused asking that some other persons go with him.' Far from being a guileless simpleton, Schumacher, Durdin said, was a 'hateful coward obsessed with an ideology which he now has seen crumble about him.'[60] As for Jung, Schumacher's words, even if they were those of an accomplice, were sufficient to 'put his conviction beyond question.' The facts were entirely in the prosecution's favour; the law on the other hand was questionable. Durdin cited section 15 of the regulations: 'The fact that an accused acted pursuant to the order of a superior or of his government shall not constitute an absolute defence to any charge under these regulations: it may, however, be considered either as a defence or in mitigation of punishment if the military court before which the charge is tried determines that justice so requires.'

Historically, the defence of superior orders had rarely been successful. Axtell, the commander of the guards who had executed King Charles I in 1649, was tried for treason and had pleaded that he was merely following orders. 'That was no excuse,' the court ruled, 'for his superior was a traitor and all who joined with him in that act were traitors.'[61] Almost two centuries later, during the American Civil War, the Confederate Captain Henry Wirz claimed that he had only been following orders in his treatment of Union captives in the infamous prison at Andersonville. The court accepted the judge advocate's view that 'a superior officer cannot order a subordinate to do an illegal act, and if a subordinate obey such an order and disastrous consequences result, both the superior and the subordinate must answer for it.'[62] Wirz was executed. Yet it is the essence of a soldier's duty to obey and increasingly it became the accepted view that a well-drilled soldier was unlikely to make fine moral distinctions. A British court recognized this dilemma in *Reg.* v. *Smith* (1900), in which a soldier was tried for the murder of Boer internees. Justice of the Peace Solomon observed: 'Especially in time of war immediate obedience ... is required.' In a widely quoted comment that defined the accepted state of the law in Britain, Solomon held that obeying a superior's order could well be a valid defence: 'If a soldier honestly believes that he is doing his duty in obeying the commands of his superior, and if the orders are not so manifestly illegal that he must or ought to have known that they were unlawful, the private soldier would be protected by the order of his superior officer.'[63] By the turn of the century, texts on international law indicated that, while there might be bad officers, there were no bad men. In L.P. Oppenheim's *International Law* of 1906, superior orders were said to constitute a complete defence: 'If members of the armed forces commit violations by order of their Government, they are not war criminals and cannot be punished by the enemy ... In case members of forces commit violations ordered by their commanders, the members cannot be punished, for the commanders are alone responsible.'[64] The same view was set out in the British *Manual of Military Law*. However, this approach enabled lower ranking personnel to evade responsibility for heinous acts committed during wartime, and it was challenged after the First World War in a case concerning an atrocity committed by Germans against Canadians on high seas.

The *Llandovery Castle* was a hospital ship used to transport wounded from Europe back to Canada. It was properly marked and its name had been communicated to German naval authorities. Nevertheless, it was sunk by a U-boat off the Irish coast and most of the crew and medical staff perished. However, three lifeboats escaped, and one of them was taken in tow by the U-boat. The commander, Patzig, interrogated some of the survivors and appeared upset to learn that there were no combatants or munitions on board. The presence of the nurses and medical staff in the lifeboat convinced him that the *Llandovery Castle* was indeed a hospital ship and that he had violated his own strict orders by torpedoing it. Following their interrogation, the survivors were returned to their lifeboat (a U-boat was too small a vessel to take on prisoners). Then, after cruising indecisively on the surface for some time, the U-boat opened fire on the two lifeboats that had initially escaped, killing all their survivors. But the other lifeboat drifted away and its crew survived to testify at the Leipzig trials in 1921. While Patzig had disappeared, two other officers who had participated in the destruction of the lifeboats were tried by the German *Reichsgericht* (Superior court) for murder. The judges held that the killing of the survivors was undoubtedly a war crime and a disgrace to the German navy. However, the issue before the court was whether the officers were not guilty by reason of their obedience to Patzig's orders. The officers had correctly inculcated the necessity of obedience to their superiors, but Patzig's command to murder helpless, shipwrecked people, merely to cover up his previous criminal act, was so grossly criminal in nature that the officers should have realized this and refused to comply. Their conduct was 'in the highest degree contrary to ethical principles,' ruled the

Reichsgericht, and both officers were sentenced to four years' imprisonment.[65] Ironically, this German decision would become a leading precedent for British and Canadian lawyers.

In the inter-war years, though, the case was not regarded as a precedent and leading texts continued to hold that a soldier could not be punished for acting under orders. It was not until the 1940 edition of Hersch Lauterpacht's *International Law* that the principle in *Llandovery Castle* was cited as correct: 'members of the armed forces are bound to obey lawful orders only, and they cannot therefore escape liability if, in obedience to a command, they commit acts which both violate unchallenged rules of warfare and outrage the general sentiment of humanity.'[66] It was this last principle, only recently accepted by British jurists, that Durdin sought to enforce against the two German defendants. He referred extensively to the *Llandovery Castle* case as showing the limitations on the defence of obedience to superior orders.

Durdin quoted the above passages of *International Law* to the court, arguing that the accused's acts were so manifestly illegal that they could not claim the defence of superior orders. If the defence was applicable, the finger of blame would inevitably go up the ranks of the Nazi party until 'the late Adolph Hitler would be the world's sole war criminal.' As for the accused, their own testimony indicated that they recognized the act to be murder. In Durdin's view, Jung could have ignored the dictates of his Nazi superiors, but he rather 'chose to further his own ends to glorify and improve his own position in the Nazi Party.' As even he had admitted, Schumacher could have delivered the prisoner to his officer, but he rather 'chose to disregard the proper orders of his proper superior officer and followed [Jung's] direction.'[67]

Summing up on behalf of Schumacher, Hollies pointed out that section 15 of the regulations applied to a simple soldier such as his client and permitted the court to use superior orders 'as a defence or in mitigation of punishment.' According to Hollies, 'Jung was occupying a position of authority over Schumacher' or at the very least Schumacher thought that he did, and, given the pervasive power of the Nazi party, disobedience was unthinkable.[68] Schumacher was responsible to Jung for his ordinary duties and had had no choice but to carry out the latter's instructions: 'Can you wonder, bearing in mind the mentality of the accused, that he considered all orders of the Burgomeister had to be obeyed by him?' Schumacher may have been more than a simple soldier. His guards noted that he frequently derided Jung, making gestures that he expected the guards to hang him, and then thump his own chest and say, 'Me too, boom, boom –.'

According to the guards, this seemed to amuse Schumacher immensely. In light of such behaviour, his mental competence seems questionable.[69]

Collins's defence of Jung was brilliant considering that his client was no simpleton, that he had appeared eager to kill the prisoner, and that he had avoided the truth in all his previous examinations. The defence set the stage by repeating Durdin's quotations from *International Law* and stressing to the court that it was dealing exclusively with war crimes. This was not an extraordinary civilian tribunal such as Nuremberg but a military court trying breaches of the law of war. From this, Collins reached the remarkable conclusion that Wilhelm Jung had not committed any war crime.

As a civilian, Jung was not subject to the laws of war, and the prosecution had never proven that he had any authority to give orders to members of the Wehrmacht. Any soldier foolish enough to obey a civilian's command did so at his own peril. The simple, inescapable fact was that Jung was not subject to the laws of war, gave no military commands, and could not be convicted of breaching the laws of war. Collins illustrated the point: 'Surely to heavens if we had a Women's sewing bee and some woman rushes in and says 'The parson says so and so, what are we going to do about it?' And then some jackass, if I may use the term, in the crowd does something radical ... we can't suggest that the woman who came bursting in ... that she should be blamed for what the other radical did and that is exactly the position we are in this trial.'[70] Collins also suggested that there were gaps in the prosecution's evidence. There was no conclusive proof that the man buried at Oberweier was the murdered airman, and it was entirely possible that it was another Allied serviceman.

In his summation, the judge advocate dismissed Collins's argument as 'legal sophistry' and that the issue of whether the laws of war applied to Jung was 'so elementary' as to be beyond dispute. An incensed Collins sprang to his feet. He accused Cattanach of unfairness, claiming, that 'for him to state that the law is so elementary, I think is perhaps overstepping himself' and that there was no prosecution evidence that Jung had committed any violent act whatsoever against the prisoner.

The court adjourned at 3:15 on the afternoon of 25 March to consider its verdict and in twenty minutes the judges returned. In a few minutes they had reviewed a complex factual situation and resolved several novel points of law. Their decision was brief and without comment. Both Jung and Schumacher were found guilty and both were sentenced to death.

This speedy verdict and Cattanach's superficial charge left lingering questions as to whether the court had really taken into account the absolute nature of command that existed in Nazi Germany. Wartime Germany endured a rigorous military regime that made the stealing of army socks a capital offence. In one case, a mere comment from a soldier when shown a photograph of Hitler behind a barbed wire fence – 'Thank God they put that madman behind bars' – resulted in a death sentence. Military law had been extended to the entire nation by a series of decrees that 'virtually abolished any distinction between members of the armed forces and civilians.' As the Allied armies pushed deeper into Germany, the country witnessed the 'virtual disappearance of all difference between military and civilian criminal justice.'[71] In order to intimidate an exhausted people, the authorities made any defeatist talk or failure to obey orders instantly punishable by death. This unquestioning obedience was incomprehensible to Canadians. For example, in begging the court to invoke section 15 and mitigate Schumacher's sentence, Hollies asked the judges to note that Schumacher seemed unable to grasp the fact that obeying Jung's command had made him liable for a death sentence: 'I have been over that with him, sir, four or five times, and I don't think the accused realizes today that he is guilty in the eyes of the law. He has been so imbued with complying with orders and doing what he was told that he has no idea where he is.' Section 15 of the regulations was a safety valve that might have recognized these extreme conditions and allowed the court to impose sentences short of death. But there appeared a reluctance to apply the section, a reluctance that would become even more apparent in the following case.

8

Opladen: The Forgotten Case

After the attempted assassination of Adolf Hitler in July 1944, the Nazi regime, already ready to crush the slightest opposition, became fanatical in its suppression of any internal threat. Selected officers of absolute loyalty to Hitler became a special liaison between the Nazis and the army. These *standsgerichtsoffizier*, whatever their rank, had unlimited powers to order the execution of any suspects, including senior officers. One of these special officers was an Oberleutnant, Robert Schaefer. Near the end of March 1945, Schaefer was in charge of three Canadian airmen in the small town of Opladen north of Cologne. With the roar of American artillery plainly audible, and Hitler's Reich obviously collapsing, Schaefer seized the opportunity to commit one last sadistic act of revenge. He would enlist in his scheme a number of German soldiers who, in a way, would also become his victims.

The first indication of an atrocity in Opladen came by way of a letter to war crimes investigators of the 7th U.S. Army in June 1945 which reported that a Nazi leader, Brinkschulte, had murdered three airmen. The informant, Matthias Erff, had heard of the killings and he urged the Americans to investigate. While nothing came of the accusation against Brinkschulte, the Americans found one villager, Hubert Broichhaus, who confirmed that at least two Allied airmen had been murdered in the town. Broichhaus confessed that he had been forced to do one of the killings.[1]

The bodies of two victims were found and a U.S. army pathologist confirmed that, although they were so decomposed as to be unidentifiable, they wore uniforms with RAF badges. One had died from a shot to the head. The other had been badly wounded, the left leg all but shattered, but death had resulted from two shots at close range to the head.[2] Even though the Americans had interviewed witnesses, placed all suspects under arrest, and completed pathological reports by 4 October 1945, Canadian investigators were not told of the case until over three months later. One explanation for the delay may lie in the Americans classifying the victims as 'British aviators'. It was not until one of the Germans mentioned a 'Canada' flash on the uniforms that it was recognized as a Canadian case and forwarded to Bad Salzuflen.

On the face of it, the emerging story seemed straightforward and the guilt of the suspects manifest. However, the Opladen case became one of the most complex Canadian investigators would ever have to unravel, for it pitted Germans against Germans, a local clique of the Nazi party against outsiders. In its way, it revealed the inner history of the dying Nazi regime on a local level where some still upheld the brutal mystique of Nazi ideology while others realized the post-war implications of atrocities. Amid the conflicting stories and shades of difference, it would take time to sort out the truth, to check every story and assemble the relevant witnesses. But time was severely limited. The remaining occupation troops (including the staff of the war crimes unit) were about to be repatriated to Canada.

Investigations had to be done as quickly as possible. All the suspects (except two) were interrogated in Bad Salzuflen between 9 to 13 March by Oliver Durdin. It is a measure of the time pressure on the RCAF staff that these examinations were completed just as Durdin was about to present the case against Neitz. As soon as the Oberweier case was completed on 25 March, the case against the Opladen defendants was called to order. Robert Holzer, a sergeant in the military police, and Walter Weigel, a Volkssturm (militia) soldier, were charged with murder. Another Volkssturm, Wilhelm Ossenbach, was charged as an accessory. For the first time, Germans were defended by German lawyers. One reason for this change was that Canadian military lawyers would no longer defend accused German war criminals. Victor Collins was said to have protested 'against a situation where Canadian barristers were ordered to defend Germans.'[3] The German lawyers asked for an adjournment of at least ten days since they were unfamiliar with the court's procedures and none of them could speak or read English. McBurney granted them one week to prepare and ordered the judge advocate to explain the war crimes regulations to them.

In the short time available, Durdin, with substantial help from Squadron Leader J.L. Eustace, had put together a strong case for the prosecution. Their main source of information came from the men of the Opladen Volkssturm. This 'people's militia,' composed of previously deferred men aged sixteen to sixty, was mobilized in the last months of the war. While poorly armed, and of dubious military value, on occasion the Volkssturm fought ferociously.[4] Mobilization of the Volkssturm also erased the final distinction between military and civilian in Germany, for all men were effectively made subject to military control.[5]

The prosecution's principal witnesses would be drawn, ironically enough, from the hard-core Nazis who formed the *Politische Staffel*, the guard at the Nazi headquarters. Just weeks before this incident, these men had exchanged their brown party uniforms for the field grey of the Volkssturm. One Staffel member, Josef Caspers, was on guard at the headquarters on an afternoon in late March 1945 when three Canadian airmen were brought in. Although he saw none of the subsequent shootings, Caspers revealed a remarkable ability to testify about events he had not seen. The first airman was taken away in a car and later shot by Sergeant Holzer and Oberleutnant Schaefer. The second prisoner was taken away by Holzer and a fellow Volkssturm, Hubert Broicchaus, and executed as well. The third had been badly wounded and had to be carried to the car by a number of men, including the accused Ossenbach and Weigel. 'I heard that Holzer and Schaefer had shot him,' Caspers testified, 'although Weigel later on told me that he had also fired.'[6] According to Caspers, everyone at the HQ knew that the prisoners were doomed and that Holzer had said in a sneering aside that 'the three of them would be dealt with,' that is, murdered.

On the day after the incident, another guard, Matthias Erff, talked with a number of the participants. Erff, an ardent Nazi since 1932, was sure that the killings had taken place on 22 March. On the following day, he had noticed a hole being dug and some clothing and two pairs of boots about to be buried. Broicchaus explained that the previous day Brinkschulte had ordered two airmen to be shot and that he had 'umlegen' (bumped off) one of them himself. Erff was taken aback and asked if this was necessary, to which Broicchaus had replied that these 'dirty pigs' were not worth anything else.

As to the death of the third, the wounded airman, the prosecution had an invaluable eyewitness in Wilhelm Ossenbach. Unlike Caspers and Erff, Ossenbach had not been a career Nazi but a local farmer, described by a Canadian investigator as 'a friendly looking fellow, a little on the portly

side.'[7] Ossenbach gave a compelling account, sparing no details and implicating a number of his fellow Volkssturm. But some of his sworn evidence
was not only hearsay but double hearsay:

Q.108 When did you first learn what was to be done with these 'flyers.'
A.   I learned that in the afternoon from Caspers who said to me that Holzer
       had expressed himself in this way – 'these three "flyers" will not get away
       from under my hand.'[8]

Ossenbach left the impression that Volkssturm troops were mere pawns
and that Schaefer and Holzer had orchestrated the killings. At one point,
Holzer had said that 'they would take the flyers one by one and they
would disappear.' When Ossenbach and Weigel were ordered to carry the
wounded airman to Holzer's car, they had no illusions as to his fate.
Holzer took the lead and drove to a nearby woods; Schaefer followed in his
own car. Significantly, Ossenbach insisted that Holzer led the way to the
place of execution. Upon their arrival, Schaefer gave Holzer the order to
shoot and Ossenbach saw him put his revolver to the airman's temple and
pull the trigger. The weapon appeared to be jammed, but finally a shot
went off. Schaefer then administered a final shot to the head. No argument
had been raised, nor did Holzer object to the shooting. Acting as a devil's
advocate, Eustace pressed Ossenbach if he had seen Holzer threatened by
Schaefer but Ossenbach denied any suggestion of coercion. His examination also damned Broicchaus, who, he testified, had seemed most pleased
to have killed the second prisoner. Broicchaus had not been compelled to
kill for 'I am quite sure he would have told me,' Ossenbach concluded.
After the war, Broicchaus had approached him, begging him to conceal the
truth, but Ossenbach had refused.[9]

After Ossenbach had all but doomed two of his comrades, Durdin
interviewed him four days later regarding a third killer. Before the previous interrogation, Ossenbach had casually mentioned that another
Volkssturm, Walter Weigel, had also shot a prisoner. Durdin recalled him
for examination and asked him about this further incident. Ossenbach said
that, as they had driven away from the murder site, Weigel had leaned
over to him and whispered, 'I have shot him.'[10] This whisper would
become the full extent of the prosecution's case against Walter Weigel.

Ossenbach insisted that, he had neither seen nor heard Weigel shoot. He
assumed that after they had set the wounded airman down and before
Schaefer and Holzer had approached, Weigel must have fired a shot.
However, he heard nothing and never saw Weigel's pistol removed from

its holster. Other details from the supplementary examination revealed something of Wilhelm Ossenbach's addled state of mind and should have raised suspicions as to his value as a witness. He told Durdin that, at the time they set the flyer down, Holzer and Schaefer were about 15 metres behind them, so far away in the darkened woods that Ossenbach could not see them.[11] In these circumstances, how could Ossenbach possibly know (as he had previously insisted) whether or not Schaefer and Holzer were quarrelling, or whether Holzer had refused the order to shoot? Durdin tried to recover from this lapse and suggest to Ossenbach that the two groups were within a short distance. Ossenbach willingly agreed. Durdin then continued with a series of questions which should have cast doubt on Ossenbach's ability to answer intelligently any queries:

Q.81   Ossenbach, from the investigations that I have made and from the evidence I have obtained I am satisfied that all four of you who were there that night, Schaefer, Holzer, Weigel and you, shot the flyer; what do you say about that?

A.   Yes.

Q.82   There is no question of that is there that you, Schaefer, Holzer and Weigel, shot this third flyer about whom we have been talking?

A.   That is correct.

Q.83   I want to be sure that you understand what I am saying to you Ossenbach – I am saying to you that you shot the flyer, Weigel shot the flyer, Holzer shot the flyer and Schaefer shot the flyer – that is correct, isn't it?

A.   No.[12]

Twice he had confessed his own guilt before he correctly understood the meaning of the question and reversed himself. While eager to agree with any suggestion from the officers of the powerful army of occupation, Ossenbach did not seem to possess the mental capacity to recall accurately what had occurred. A simple, uneducated man, he was not being duplicitous but, as he saw it, helpful. Yet the purpose of the trial was to seek out the truth based upon reliable evidence. In the Opladen case, much of the prosecution case would rest on the confused words of Wilhelm Ossenbach.

After the week's adjournment, the trial began on 1 April. The German lawyers still felt it unfair that they had so little time to prepare, and they also raised objections as to the jurisdiction of the court. Holzer's lawyer, Wilhelm Schapp (who had assisted in preparing Meyer's petition), argued that the Geneva Convention did not permit extraordinary tribunals but rather required war criminals to be tried by regular courts martial. In addition, Schapp would eventually take exception to Holzer's trial by a panel composed entirely of Canadian airmen: 'To defend a man before a court of RAF officers who is in some way engaged in the killing of a wounded POW airman is indeed a task which cannot be imagined as more difficult.'[13] It was also contrary to section 7(3) of the regulations, which should have guaranteed the accused at least one army officer on the panel. All motions were denied. While the German lawyers may have been unfamiliar with the procedures, they were skilled at their profession. John Blain, who assisted Durdin and Eustace in the prosecution, recalled Schapp as 'an old gentleman, very quiet, no histrionics ... I thought he gave Holzer an effective defence.'[14]

In his opening statement, Durdin indicated that almost all of the prosecution's case would be based upon the previous interrogations. Instead of presenting witnesses to prove guilt, as would be standard in a criminal case, he would merely read into the court record selected questions and answers from the interrogations. Even though all three of the accused stood a good chance of being shot if convicted, the case against them would be founded on recorded evidence, none of which would be subject to the defence's cross-examination. Neither would the demeanour of the witnesses (such as the appallingly confused Ossenbach) be subject to scrutiny. In the Oberweier case, the prosecution had placed great reliance on hearsay evidence. Now in the Opladen case they went a step farther and called little evidence at all, instead relying completely on sworn statements. While subsection 10(1)(d) of the regulations permitted the receiving into evidence of 'any examination made by any officer detailed for the purpose by any military authority,' subsection 10(2) cautioned the court that such evidence was not always to be relied on and that 'it shall be the duty of the court to judge of the weight to be attached.' Macdonald had rationalized the admission of such extraordinary evidence (which would never have been admissible in a regular court martial) on the basis that the chaos of the war had created an unusual situation 'where such witnesses were dead, unable to attend the trial, or where it was impractical for them to do so.'[15] It is unlikely that he had in mind an entire prosecution based on sworn statements instead of witnesses.

Nevertheless, the first two days of the trial were taken up by the reading of the statements from Erff, Broicchaus, and Ossenbach and their translation into German. The only witness called by the prosecution was the guard Caspers, who had seen nothing but was able to repeat all the rumours that were floating about the HQ and to claim that it was 'common knowledge' that all the airmen were to be shot. Almost by the by, Caspers did observe that one of the accused, Weigel, had tried to refuse to go along to shoot one of the flyers.[16] This testimony, from the only prosecution witness, should have stood Weigel's case in good stead.

After Casper's testimony, Durdin closed the prosecution's case. Insubstantial as it may have been, it was essentially based on the claim that between them Schaefer and Holzer had conspired at the execution of the two airmen. The fate of the first airman was never determined. Increasingly, it seemed that the prosecution's case focused (in the absence of Schaefer, for as in so many cases the prime culprit had disappeared) on Robert Holzer. As the trial unfolded, the personality of this obscure member of the military police seemed to dominate the proceedings.

Thirty-six years old, thin, and so nondescript in appearance that his own lawyer referred to him as 'an unimportant and a modest office clerk,'[17] Holzer was not a convincing villain. After army service from 1929 to 1931, he had returned to his Opladen home as an office worker. Never a Nazi supporter, he ran afoul of the party in 1937 for not taking 'necessary measures' against his Jewish employers. Holzer was arrested for this and spent a year and nine months in Anrathe concentration camp.[18] Shortly after his release the war broke out and he was recalled to the army. Serving on the Eastern Front, he was wounded seven times and was awarded the Iron Cross second and first class, the Infantry Attack Badge in bronze and silver, and the Close Fighting Badge in bronze, silver, and gold. His last injury came from being buried alive by a shell, an experience that almost killed him and resulted in his medical discharge. In the desperate days of February 1945, he was recalled to service as a military policeman and made a driver on the staff of Field Marshal Walter Model. After the war the French had selected individuals of known anti-Nazi views to serve the occupation authorities and Holzer was assigned to the Allied government in Düsseldorf. He was working there when the Americans arrested him in September 1945.

His statement to the Americans was to prove highly contentious at trial. Holzer stated that one day in late March he was ordered to assist Oberleutnant Schaefer in transferring certain prisoners to the Nazi headquarters. An injured airman was taken to the orderly room while two other flyers were held under guard. Schaefer ordered Holzer to drive one of the uninjured flyers to the 'O.Q. Staff,' the nearby military interrogation centre. On the way, they encountered a sergeant Koenlich who had another prisoner, and Holzer drove them both to the O.Q. Staff. When they returned to the HQ, Schaefer ordered Holzer, the other uninjured flyer, and the Volkssturm soldier Broicchaus into the staff car. Holzer asked him where they were going, and Schaefer merely told him to 'ride along.' When they made a sudden turn into a forest, Broicchaus called out helpfully that they were going the wrong way. Schaefer snapped back that he should keep his mouth shut: 'We ride where I command.'

Once the road became impassable because of the number of bomb craters, Schaefer ordered everyone out. Broicchaus and the prisoner tarried in the car until Schaefer yelled at them to follow. As they walked into the woods, Schaefer drew his revolver and his intentions became obvious. Holzer protested: 'Must this be?' he asked, to which Schaefer replied, 'It is certain and my order is being carried out,' and, turning to the highly decorated veteran, he added, 'So Mr. Sgt. now you can show that you are a man.' He gestured for him to shoot the Canadian. Holzer refused. Schaefer unloosed a volley of insults against him and waved his pistol in the air. But Holzer merely turned on his heel with the curt reply, 'I got the order to drive,' and returned to the car. He then heard Schaefer turn his wrath on Broicchaus and a short time later they returned without the prisoner.

After their return to Opladen, Holzer was ordered to return to the O.Q. Staff and fetch the first prisoner. There he again encountered Koenlich and his prisoner, and he drove both of them to the military camp at Wermelskirchen. This camp had been closed and so he deposited both captives with the local police. As night was falling, the third prisoner, despite his grievous injuries, was loaded into Holzer's car. Following Schaefer's car, Holzer drove into a woods and stopped by a meadow. Holzer asked Schaefer if the airman could get medical attention, but the officer brushed the suggestion aside and instead rounded on Holzer: 'Go ahead, this time you don't get by with it.' As they approached the wounded Canadian, who by now had been laid out by the edge of the meadow, Schaefer pulled out his pistol and held it against Holzer. It was only then that Holzer drew his pistol and held it to the airman's temple. However, he had fixed the magazine so that the weapon appeared to be jammed. In exasperation Schaefer screamed, 'Man don't you want to?' and Holzer later admitted to investigators that 'if I, during this excitement and under the threat of the pistol, really shot, I do not deny it.' Holzer's pleas to bury the body were refused and Schaefer remarked to him as they returned to their vehicles, 'We two are not finished as yet.' Shortly thereafter, the Gestapo came searching for Holzer and it was only his luck that he was no longer in Opladen that saved him from summary execution.[19]

This was the statement given to the Americans. However, it was only a synopsis and Holzer was at pains to show that it was neither comprehensive nor accurate. For one thing, everything the Americans did not like had been deleted.²⁰ Before the trial, Squadron Leader Eustace had interrogated Holzer and obtained a far more detailed account. Holzer had secured the three prisoners in the HQ as ordered and later driven the first airman to the O.Q. Staff for interrogation. Still later, Schaefer had ordered him to drive the second airman and Broicchaus out to the woods by the cemetery. Coming to the end of a heavily cratered road, Schaefer left the car, drew his pistol, and said to Holzer, 'We will have a little fun with him now.' Schaefer added wistfully that it was a pity that the first airman was not yet back so that he, too, could be shot. Holzer implored him to reconsider: 'I have been a soldier for 14 years and I have never seen anything like this before.' Their argument became loud and furious, for Holzer was now convinced that Schaefer 'would have shot me without the slightest hesitation. He was a fanatical idiot.' Remembering police procedures, he asked to see Schaefer's authority, to which the officer snapped, 'I don't have to show you.' Eventually the sergeant stormed back to the car, saying that 'if the soldier [Broicchaus] wants to take the responsibility, that is alright.' A short time later he heard a shot and the two Germans returned without the prisoner. Once, Holzer had looked back and seen Schaefer pushing Broicchaus with a pistol. Why, Eustace asked him, had he not helped a raw soldier such as Broicchaus? Holzer replied: 'What could I do? I couldn't help him. There was nothing I could do. After all, Schaefer was a very important man. He was the liaison officer between the General Staff and the Party.'²¹ Eustace's following question betrayed a failure to appreciate the pervasiveness of Nazi authority in German society:

Q.96 Why didn't you shoot Schaefer if you knew he was doing the wrong thing?
A.   Just imagine if I would have done a thing like that. One could not do such a thing – shoot an officer.

Upon their return to the HQ, Holzer was ordered to bring back the first airman. Fully aware of what Schaefer had in mind for him, Holzer asked the staff to give him a work order to transport the flyer, as well as Sergeant Koenlich's prisoner, to a camp. To his disappointment, the camp was closed, but he did manage to leave the prisoners with the police. According to Holzer, the police gave him a receipt for the prisoners. Unit investigators followed up on this but could find no record to support Holzer. Schaefer was not pleased to be cheated of his prey, but the work ticket was proof that Holzer had acted under orders. However, the wounded prisoner was still in his power. Again he ordered Holzer to drive while Ossenbach and Weigel carried the wounded man. According to Holzer, he did leave Opladen first, but Schaefer passed him on the road and led the way. When Holzer made a turn in the direction of a hospital, Schaefer stopped his car and, waving a flashlight (night had fallen), signalled for him to stop. Schaefer ordered the prisoner to be taken out, and Holzer turned the car around in a farmyard. He then described what happened: 'I was sitting in my car and Schaefer said "get out you coward." He had a pistol in his hand. He told me to come along with him and I did. We went to the place where the flyer was lying on the ground and the two soldiers were standing next to him. Schaefer shouted at me "this time you are not going to get away with it, you are going to shoot this flyer."'

Q.122 Yes, then what happened?

A.   I said 'no, I am not going to do it this time either' and told him to take his pistol away. He got louder and louder all the time and I got my pistol out myself because I knew what he would be capable of. I said to him 'take your pistol away, after all I am no criminal.' He shoved his pistol into my face and I pointed my pistol in the direction of the flyer and did as if the pistol were jamming, which in actual fact, it was not. I did that three times ... He [Schaefer] shoved me aside and then I heard a shot go off. I did not see this as I had been turned around.

Q.123 Do you now say Holzer that you did not shoot this flyer?

A.   I did not shoot this man. During my first interrogation I was not sure whether a shot had gone out of my pistol or not. Everything and everybody was very excited at that time but I now am sure that I myself did not fire. I am doubly sure because when we were sitting in the car on the way back I asked these other two people, Ossenbach and Weigel what had happened and they said that Schaefer had fired the shot – that Schaefer had shot the flyer.

Q.124 When you made a statement to the Americans did you tell them that you had shot this flyer?

A.   I said to the Americans 'whether in this excitement a shot had gone off from my pistol I could neither deny nor confirm.'[22]

Eustace then confronted Holzer with the statement that he had given to the Americans to the effect that he had fired. But Holzer corrected him, pointing out that he had only said that 'a shot had gone off,' not that he had fired it. As for the Volkssturm statements that Holzer had fired the fatal shot, he reminded the investigator that 'all those soldiers belonged to the Politische Staffel and that Schaefer also had a lot to do with the Kreisleitung.' It was certainly convenient for the local Nazis to pin the guilt on outsiders.

At the trial, Schapp had Holzer testify about his trip to retrieve the first airman. Because of his position on the army staff, Holzer was able to see a senior officer, Colonel Jakob, and tell him about Schaefer's murderous conduct and threats of court martial. Jakob reminded him of the wilderness of fear prevailing in Germany and cautioned him to'"keep quiet." This Oberleutnant is a Liaison officer between the army Supreme Command and the Party, and those are the orders who were put in office after the 20th of July, and who had unlimited powers, and even against very high-ranking German officers. He then suggested to me not to report this matter.' Holzer insisted that he had not shot the wounded flyer. When his weapon jammed, Schaefer had grasped his arm to look at the pistol. As far as he knew, no shot had come from his weapon.

The prosecution seized on this last point to attack his story. All the other witnesses had seen Holzer fire at the Canadian's head. He riposted that there could well be a conspiracy against him: 'They certainly had time enough to prepare their story when they were hearty friends together.'[23] Durdin attacked another chink in his armour, that he had admitted to the Americans that he might have fired a shot. Holzer responded that the American interrogation had not been fair, that favourable material had been removed, and that he had made corrections that the Americans had not kept. Yet it was not entirely Holzer's word against the Opladen men. Broicchaus was also an outsider from the town of Schlebusch. In key areas, his testimony would substantiate Holzer's, but the two versions of events were not entirely consistent. This was not surprising, of course; a trial rarely presents a neat package of facts leading to an inexorable conclusion. The Opladen case was an instance of confusion and excitement, of civilians suddenly tossed into uniforms and confronted by a sadistic fanatic bent on murdering helpless men. The truth, if it could be established, remained an elusive goal.

In his first examination before Major John Blain, Broicchaus described how he had bandaged the wounded airman, given him a cigarette, and chatted about home. About 6:00 or 6:30 that evening he drove with Holzer and Schaefer into the woods outside Opladen. After the vehicle stopped, Schaefer and Holzer got out and walked away. Convivially, Broicchaus had offered the Canadian a cigarette. Suddenly, Schaefer called out with sneering impatience for Broicchaus to come along with the prisoner. After they had walked about fifty metres, Schaefer turned to Holzer and asked, 'Feldwebel, will you carry out what you are supposed to do?'[24] The two then got into a terrific argument over Holzer's refusal to kill the prisoner. As Broicchaus described the scene at trial, 'the way they were facing each other it appeared that they were about to fight each other.'[25] Eventually, Holzer stormed back to the car, saying that there was someone else who could do it. Schaefer then turned to Broicchaus and ordered him to kill the prisoner. He remonstrated that this was against his conscience, that he was not really a soldier anyway, until Schaefer put his own pistol under his shoulder and growled, 'Damn weaklings ... no more of your nonsense, come on, bump this fellow off.' Broicchaus then fired one shot into the back of the Canadian's head.

Why, Blain wondered, had Holzer been able to avoid killing while Broicchaus had submitted. 'I only had been a soldier for two months,' he replied, 'and I was very much afraid of Schaefer.'[26] On the trip back to Opladen, Schaefer freely used the term 'court martial' and castigated Holzer: 'You Feldwebel who are covered with decorations, you ought to be ashamed.' However, on one point, Broicchaus's story clashed with the others; he denied burying the airman's clothes, an incident that several others had witnessed. Broicchaus's examination lent credence to Holzer's defence that he had opposed Schaefer as much as he could. Holzer had dared to refuse an order from an officer and even argued with him until he was threatened with court martial. So crucial was Broicchaus's evidence that Durdin insisted on a second interrogation a month after Blain's.

Unlike Blain's initial examination, Durdin's examination was an impassioned frontal assault on Broicchaus's veracity. Both Caspers and Erff had talked with Broicchaus while he was present when the airman's clothes were being buried. But, on being questioned by Durdin, Broicchaus again denied being there or knowing anything about the burial. This denial remained a stark contradiction of the testimony offered by the other witnesses. Another such contradiction was Broicchaus's denial that he had ever bragged to Erff about shooting the prisoner. Carefully choosing his words, Broicchaus admitted that he had told Erff of the killing but not that he was the killer. Under intense questioning Broicchaus wavered, saying that he could no longer recall what he had said to Ossenbach or whether he had confessed to the Americans that he was one of the killers.[27]

Time and again Durdin confronted him, attempting to break this (in his view) carapace of lies. Durdin put it to him that when they drove away from the HQ they were determined to murder the airman. Broicchaus denied it and added a further twist to the story. The only reason he had gotten into the car at all was that he had asked Schaefer if he was driving past Broicchaus's home in Schlebusch. He had the next day off and wished to take advantage of a ride. Durdin was incredulous. 'When did you think up this story? I haven't heard this one before.' Broicchaus replied, 'That I have written myself at the interrogation with the Americans' but it was apparently a detail the Americans saw fit to discard. Broicchaus also doggedly maintained his version of the final scene. Holzer and Schaefer had a furious quarrel: 'They used insulting language at each other at the top of their voice' until Holzer had refused to shoot the prisoner and stomped off. Durdin then asked a series of questions that highlighted the confusion and excitement of the moment and perhaps some of the examiner's inner feelings:

Q.301 Now, when you say that Schaefer ordered you to shoot this pilot you knew it was murder. Why didn't you shoot Schaefer instead of the pilot?
A.   You must realize Schaefer was an officer of the permanent court-martial and I was only a very small man. He could have shot me right away.
Q.302 But he didn't shoot Holzer, did he?
A.   I was surprised myself that Holzer took such a cheeky attitude but he was a member of the field gendarmerie.
Q.303 What difference does that make? Why couldn't you have refused to do it as well as Holzer if you didn't want to do it?
A.   I assume I have done the same but only that I have done it in a more begging manner and asked him to spare me to do so, but when he pushed me I had to do it.
Q.304 Why did you have to do it? If he had shot you through the arm that wouldn't have killed you, would it?
A.   Under such circumstances, gentlemen – I don't know if you have witnessed it yourself – but it put me in such a state that I didn't know what I was doing.
Q.305 No, I have never witnessed it myself; I have never shot any prisoners of war like you have.[28]

Even under this rigorous cross-examination, Broicchaus's version seemed consistent. He had confirmed that he had killed, but only under great duress; and moreover, he had observed Holzer absolutely refuse to be a party to murder and Schaefer's dark threats that a court martial would be the reward for his refusal.

When he cross-examined Broicchaus at trial, Durdin again relied on the statement prepared by the Americans in which Broicchaus related how, in the midst of their argument, Holzer had said, 'There is also someone else,' implying that Broicchaus could do the killing. Dr Schapp interjected and asked if the witness could add to that answer. Durdin tried to cut him short: 'He has answered the question; he says it is the truth.' Court President McBurney was not going to restrict the answers and he told Broicchaus to add whatever he wished. Broicchaus continued: 'But when Schaefer said to Holzer "Will you do this? Will you accomplish this act this time?" it sounded more like a last demand on him.'[29]

In re-examination, Schapp wanted to go over the circumstances in which the original statement was made to the Americans. Durdin, who felt that he had a favourable answer already, was not about to let it slip away: 'This man was read a passage of the statement, and he said he had signed it and that it was true.' Judge advocate Cattanach reminded Durdin that he had raised the issue of the statement in cross-examination and Schapp was now entitled to go into it. McBurney agreed. Broicchaus then described how he had written his statement only to have the Americans return and tell him that it was 'wrong' and destroy it. Another statement was prepared, some of which he agreed with, and other parts of which had been made up by the interpreters. The court may have been left with the impression that the statement taken by the Americans was of dubious value. Dr Ernst Dietrich, the doctor who had attended to the wounded flyer, was called to the stand. Upon his arrival at the HQ he found that Broicchaus had bandaged the injured man. Unlike Caspers, Dietrich did not sense any hostile atmosphere to indicate that the prisoners were about to be killed. Neither did he recall any conversation with Holzer in which the latter had confirmed his intent to kill. Schapp closed the defence by calling some of Holzer's comrades who testified that he loathed the Nazis. His fiancée, Elizabeth Hartberg, said that after this incident the Gestapo had tried to find him. Schapp then asked for an adjournment in order to call Colonel Jakob. His evidence could obviously be the key, for if he confirmed Holzer's warning that Schaefer was a murderous fanatic, the remainder of Holzer's story became highly credible. The prosecution had known of this vital witness since September 1945, Schapp pointed out, but nothing had been done to locate him. Durdin protested at any notion of an adjournment for 'we could go on ad infinitum.' Jakob would never testify.

On the fourth day of the trial, Walter Weigel presented his defence. That Weigel was a reluctant participant was apparent even from the prosecution's witness, Caspers, who testified that he had heard Weigel refuse to go along to shoot the wounded flyer. Before Weigel helped carry the man to Holzer's car, Schaefer had approached him and told him that this time it was his duty to shoot the prisoner. Weigel said nothing but got in the car and sat in silence with the others, no doubt contemplating the pitiless amorality of shooting a crippled man. Upon arrival at the place of execution, Holzer ordered Weigel and Ossenbach to carry the wounded man from the car. It was almost dark when they set him down in the meadow and Weigel, determined to get his task done as soon as possible, drew his pistol and fired just wide of the pilot. Shortly thereafter, Schaefer and Holzer appeared, the former calling out, 'Have you finished yet?' Adamantly insisting to the court that he had fired wide, Weigel further testified that after the shot he had faded into the darkness. However, he was able to see Holzer put his pistol to the airman's temple and observe the gun jam several times before a shot went off. Durdin asked if he had seen Holzer protest the killing and he denied seeing anything. But he added, 'I had the impression that Holzer himself did not want to fire the shot either, but due to the threatening attitude of Schaefer ... there was nothing left for him to do.'[30]

Lastly, Ossenbach's lawyer, Dr Plenter, presented his defence. Ossenbach had taken no part in the killings and had been present only because he had been ordered to carry the airman. While he was a member of the Nazi party, he insisted that he had joined simply in order to get a job and had remained a devout Catholic. Throughout his case, the awkwardness of German lawyers handling a Canadian case was apparent. Plenter insisted on leading Ossenbach, despite Cattanach's reminders that only the witness could give evidence during the examination-in-chief. Nevertheless, there was no contradiction to the evidence that Ossenbach had been little more than a bystander. Under cross-examination by Weigel's lawyer, de Wall, Ossenbach admitted that they were both very excited and that he might have misunderstood Weigel's whispered comment that 'I shot the flyer':

Q.1221 Is it possible he said 'I shot at the flyer?'
A.1221 I don't want to deny it.[31]

The only piece of incriminating evidence against Weigel, the aside in the car, was now of dubious value since even the only witness to the remark conceded that it might have been a confession that he had fired wide of the injured man. De Wall highlighted this distinction by advising the court 'Mr. President ... I noticed that the witness [Ossenbach] expressed himself in two very different ways ... In the one case the witness said "I have shot" and once he said "I shot him." I only want this to be recorded to show how easily it is possible in this sentence to make a mistake.'[32] Before leaving the stand, Ossenbach also confirmed that, other than the shots to the head, he saw no fresh wounds on the airman's body.

In his summation on Ossenbach's behalf, Plenter stressed that even as a Volksstrum, Ossenbach was obliged to carry the wounded man as ordered. How could this possibly be a war crime? Weigel, on the other hand, lay accused of actually firing a fatal shot at the Canadian. His lawyer argued that the evidence that he had fired wide was far more credible. Durdin had suggested to the court that, under Schaefer's gaze, Weigel was unlikely to have violated an order and deliberately fired wide. But de Wall pointed out that even Ossenbach agreed that Schaefer was at least ten metres away at the time when Weigel could have fired. From that distance, at night, it was impossible for Schaefer to have seen the direction of Weigel's shot. However, he would have heard the report and thus assumed that Weigel had carried out orders. 'This way of action is quite logical,' de Wall argued. 'If he had shot a few moments later then he would not have been in a position to fire aside; then he would have been under the immediate control of Schaefer,' but as it was 'Schaefer noticed nothing and yet felt that Weigel had carried out his orders.'[33] Furthermore, there was no evidence of a bullet wound to the torso for the American autopsy had revealed only the two fatal shots in the skull. Even Ossenbach had testified, without contradiction, that the only visible wounds to the airman, other than his pre-existing injuries, were the two bullet wounds in the head. The most likely conclusion, he suggested, was that Weigel had deliberately shot wide.

Schapp had the most difficult case, but he carefully marshalled all favourable evidence. The first airman had not been shot at all but rather had been saved from Schaefer's fury by Holzer's audacity in transferring him to Wermelskirchen. Furthermore, he had tried to alert Colonel Jakob to the situation, only to be told that it was hopeless. According to Broicchaus, Holzer had also tried to save the second airman, but Schaefer had found another executioner. That left the third airman. Schapp reminded the court that the only evidence against Holzer came from his co-accused, Ossenbach and Weigel, and neither German nor Canadian law gave much weight to the statements of co-accused because it was obviously to their advantage to shift guilt to other persons to save themselves.

In any event, how reliable was Ossenbach? He presented himself as a religious man, but how honest or accurate were his observations? Schapp believed that Holzer had withstood Durdin's withering cross-examination, noting, 'After this interrogation of the Prosecutor, I thought Holzer was saved.' The defence had seemed to show that the killing force in Opladen was the fanatic Schaefer. Durdin, on the other hand, stressed in his summation that, to the prosecution, all the accused were part of a malign conspiracy, 'the murder to which all of these accused persons had agreed and subscribed.' Ossenbach's guilt lay in obeying orders to carry the wounded man, an action that made him 'a fully confessed accomplice to a bestial crime for which there must be few parallels.' As for Weigel, his story of shooting wide was implausible, and it was most likely that he had confessed his guilt to Ossenbach. Durdin also relied on Ossenbach's recollection of Holzer's leading role in the killing of the wounded airman, and of how Holzer had led the way to the execution site, ordered the airman from the car, and, 'as he lay upon the ground, his body racked with pain and anguish of wounds which he had sustained in the performance of his duty,' fired a shot into his head.

Far less passionate, but equally fatal to the Opladen men was the judge advocate's summation of the law. Cattanach referred to Oppenheim's *International Law* and the opinion that a violation committed in pursuance of a direct order did not 'deprive the act in question of its character as a war crime.' Even the threat of death was no defence in crimes of a heinous character. Referring to a number of English authorities, including Sir James Stephen's dictum that 'urgent necessity no matter how grave is no excuse for the killing of another,' he discounted duress as a defence.[34]

The court retired on the afternoon of 6 April 1946 to consider its verdict. Over and above all the conflicting testimony and learned argument, the one image that must have been before these senior officers was that of the injured Canadian airman. He had barely survived his bomber's crash, only to lie for hours in clenched agony in the HQ and then be taken to a secluded woods to be murdered. They were also aware that his case was only one of scores in which airmen had been executed. At 4:30 the court returned, and all three accused stood to attention to learn their fate. McBurney read the sentences: Holzer and Weigel were convicted of murder and sentenced to death, while Ossenbach was convicted of being an accessory to murder and sentenced to fifteen years. These men were not cut from the same cloth as the glorious warrior Kurt Meyer, and they collapsed at the translation of the verdict. Holzer had to be carried from the courtroom. Once outside the chamber, both he and Weigel broke down and wept.[35]

After the trial, several days passed while appeals were made to higher authorities. For most of the prisoners, their confinement in Aurich compared favourably to the privations of Nazi Germany. 'In fact it is like a holiday here,' Ossenbach wrote to his wife. 'The Herr Kommandant of this house [is] almost the best man of the world. He treats us just as if we were his own children.' Another prisoner awaiting trial wrote that 'the Canadian officers and soldiers have made an extraordinarily good impression on me, and I do not doubt that the case will be tried impartially and with due regard to the circumstances of the case.' But for those sentenced to death, their impending execution was foremost in their minds. In his last letter to his wife, Wilhelm Jung expressed his profound remorse: 'We fools believed in the swastika rather than the cross of Jesus.' While maintaining that he had only obeyed orders, he attributed his sentence to his part in the murder of a helpless man; he had 'crossed the path of God ... forgive me for what I did and now have to account for.'[36]

'I am convinced that the Canadian people intend to have war crimes prosecuted on principles of justice only. I am afraid that in the case in hand this has not been fully taken into consideration.' So began Schapp's appeal on Holzer's behalf.[37] In fact, since the Meyer case, the Canadian people had taken little interest in the war crimes trials. Nevertheless, Schapp presented a long and occasionally wandering appeal beginning with an interesting (if largely irrelevant) discussion of the Notstand (emergency) and Notigungsnotstand (duress) sections of the 1871 German Penal Code. Unknown in Canadian law, these provisions enabled an accused person to have punishment mitigated if he killed in order to save his own life. Schapp suggested that his client had two alternatives to obeying Schaefer; he could take his own life or that of Schaefer. In the event of the latter, 'he had to count on the most revolting manner of death.' It was this element of extreme duress that the court had either failed to consider or given insufficient weight to.

Schapp also argued that the entire process was suspect. Both German and Canadian law guaranteed an accused a right to hire a defence lawyer. Elizabeth Hartberg had hired a lawyer for Holzer in September 1945, but this individual was not admitted to the court. As a result of this denial of representation, two crucial facts had not been adequately explored. Holzer had told the Americans of Colonel Jakob in September 1945; however, no one had seriously tried to locate him. He had also told investigators of the two Allied airmen taken to Wermelskirchen. Holzer had asked to go to Wermelskirchen himself to look at the records, a request that was originally granted but never fulfilled. Amazingly enough, Schapp had recently discovered that the police records at Wermelskirchen did have an entry for two airmen for 5 April (Canadian investigators had looked only at the March records), and he speculated whether this evidence, which had not been available at trial, vindicated his client. Had a proper defence been available, he suggested, it would have shown Holzer 'protecting the prisoners of war as best he could.' Persuasive as this seemed, Schapp then launched into an argument that was not likely to gain him support from senior RCAF officers.

The air campaign had been a nightmare for Germany; and the entire nation had suffered 'a heavy mental burden and a torture for everyone's nerves.' He described the firestorm at Hamburg and Dresden where 'women, children, babies perished in the flames, that they ran into the asphalted streets which began to boil up ... and finally died like living torches in horrifying anguish and pain.' Was Schapp suggesting that these apocalyptic experiences legitimized the murder of captured airmen? He implied that this new form of warfare had 'weighed down the minds of the inhabitants of Germany to such a degree that acts of revenge against airmen who were taken prisoner might occur.' While an innovative argument, it hardly seemed to advance his client's cause when the appeal was to the officers who led these attacks.

There was no indication that the higher authorities of the RCAF had any intention of changing the result. In light of the uproar created by the Meyer commutation, they may have been afraid to touch pitch and be defiled by any reduction of sentence. Or a review of the case may have led them to conclude that there was no reason to alter the result. In a short note dated 6 May 1946, Air Marshall G.O. Johnson stated that he could 'see no valid reason for varying the finding and sentence of the Court.'[38] All petitions – on behalf of Jung, Schumacher, Weigel, Holzen, and Ossenbach – were dismissed.

The outcome of the Opladen case remains highly suspect. While it was of minimal interest to the press and the public, the issue of whether the Canadian military could fairly judge accused enemy war criminals received its harshest test at Opladen. Based on any standard, Canadian justice failed for there existed a wide abyss between the evidence and the result. The prosecution's case, even in the form of out-of-court interrogations, was not sufficiently persuasive or reliable to justify a death sentence. It is extremely unlikely that any criminal court would have concluded that Holzer and Weigel were guilty of a capital offence. Even Ossenbach's sentence of fifteen years for an act that could not be considered a war crime at all seems to be an indication of a court bent on retribution, not justice. While the court officers acted sincerely, conscious of their duty to give due process to the murderers of helpless airmen, the principle of applying even-handed justice seems to have been lost in Opladen. In this final war crimes trial conducted by the Canadian military, the legitimacy of law as an intractable and unswerving source of right was lost. The failure to represent fully the rights of the defeated enemy cast doubts on the validity of the enterprise and lent credence to later accusations of victor's justice.

Four days after Holzer and Weigel were dragged from the Aurich courtroom, measures were being taken to terminate the prosecution. To some, these measures were already overdue. Even during the Meyer trial, the deputy adjutant-general, Brigadier W.H.S. Macklin, had treated with derision Macdonald's request for adequate staff to carry on the prosecutions. He reported to the chief of staff that 'I am as anxious as anybody else to hang a few of the German perpetrators of outrages against Cdn troops, but am somewhat doubtful if much good is going to be done by allowing this investigating unit to go on working on its present lines. The fact is that after a year and a half of investigating, including six months by this large and expensive unit, we have so far succeeded in bringing one single German to trial, and we are not at all sure that we are going to be able to hang him.'[39]

On 10 April, CMHQ requested the adjutant-general for authority to 'wind up the War Crimes Unit at that headquarters and turn over to the British for trial any cases involving Canadian interest which remain as yet untried.' The regulations required that the accused had to be within the limits of command of a Canadian convening officer, and it was not practical to keep Canadian forces in Europe solely for that reason. Higher authority agreed, and Vincent Massey's office recommended on 11 April that the No. 1 Canadian War Crimes Investigation unit be disbanded by 1 May on the ground that 'no purpose of substance is likely to be served by its continuance.'[40] Never enthusiastic about the war crimes business, officialdom was eager to put it to an end. However, one Ottawa mandarin was dismayed by this precipitous withdrawal from international responsibilities. E.R. Hopkins of External Affairs wrote to Under-Secretary of State Norman Robertson of his concern that Canadian interests were being handed over to another government. At the very least, a Canadian representative should stay in Britain to review Canadian cases and advise the British.[41] Withdrawal would inevitably lead to some cases simply being abandoned, as Brigadier Orde reported with dismay to National Defence on 12 April 'There will be at least 30 cases untried when it will be necessary to discontinue the RCAF court on April 15th.'[42] In Ottawa, the cabinet considered and approved the disbandment of the unit effective 1 May.[43] The Canadian War Crimes Advisory Committee was dissolved as well, and Arthur Slaght was given a perfunctory note of thanks.[44] On 2 May 1946 Bruce Macdonald was posted to other duties. Major J.A. Macdonald took over what remained of the unit as the remaining staff were repatriated or assigned elsewhere. By 31 May it was over, and J.A. Macdonald noted in the war diary that 'the Unit ceased to function as a War Crimes Investigation Unit.'[45] Canada's first venture in war crimes prosecutions was over.

There was one piece of unfinished business. On 15 April both Wilhelm Jung and Johann Schumacher were shot by a Canadian Provost firing squad. Just before 6:00 A.M. on 11 May, Walter Weigel, a man against whom there was only the slimmest evidence of murder, and Robert Holzer, a brave man and patriot who insisted to the end that he had done everything in his power to rescue Allied prisoners, died before a Canadian firing squad.

9

Hong Kong: The Law of the Imperial Japanese Army

By September 1945 Canadian prisoners were returning from Asia and their emaciated bodies were a testament to the four years of suffering they had endured. Only 4 per cent of Allied prisoners died in German captivity; in contrast 25 per cent of Western prisoners perished in Japanese hands. Similarly, whereas only 4 per cent of the Canadians held by Germany had died, 20 per cent (290 men in total) of those captured by the Japanese did not return.[1] The survivors had endured in camps where they were almost worked to death, subjected to brutal punishment for minor infractions, and deprived of almost all medical attention. A group of returning prisoners stopped in Toronto and tried to explain what they had been through. As William Moles put it, 'they tried to freeze us to death, starve us to death, beat us to death, when they couldn't, they quit.' He had seen a comrade collapse on the parade square and be viciously punched and kicked by guards. 'The Japanese are just animals – they're not human,'[2] he concluded. A captured flyer recalled Yakama camp, where 'the diet was a starvation one, and beatings were the order of the day.' He had witnessed beheadings and the bayonetting into graves of live prisoners.[3]

The origin of the tragedy lay in Mackenzie King's decision to comply with a British request to supply garrison troops for Hong Kong. The defence of Hong Kong by the young men of the Winnipeg Grenadiers and the Royal Rifles of Canada (collectively known as 'C' Force) is an epic no Canadian should ever forget. While it was a brave sacrifice, its futility has been amply explored. When the two battalions arrived in November 1941, they were neither trained nor equipped for battle. They were 'deliberately sent into a position where there was absolutely no hope of victory, evacuation or relief.'[4] Less than three weeks after their arrival they were in combat and by Christmas Day they had surrendered. During the fighting, 227 men of the 2,000-strong force had died and a further 13 had been killed after the surrender.

At first, the Canadian survivors were kept at North Point, a former detention centre that had been badly damaged in the fighting. Not only was it a shambles, the Japanese had been using it for stables and the area was filled with horse carcasses and manure. Conditions were bound to be primitive in the wake of battle, but the meagre rations seemed almost a sure death sentence. For the first few months each man received less than 900 calories a day, and diseases caused by malnutrition prevailed. 'Weakened by disease and lack of food, many prisoners were simply unable to carry on the struggle; once they lost the will to live, they died in a matter of days.'[5] When diphtheria broke out, camp doctors were helpless to treat the disease even though antitoxins were readily available in Japanese medical stores.[6]

During the war Canadian authorities had little knowledge of these conditions. In one instance, a Canadian who dared tell a Red Cross officer that meat rations and sporting equipment had only been provided for show was later severely beaten.[7] In November 1943 Canada was requested to join an inter-Allied protest at Japanese treatment of prisoners and, true to form, when the issue came before the British war cabinet, Canada was the only one of eight governments to request more time to consider the matter.[8] Eventually, Ottawa decided to participate and in a statement to the House of Commons on 28 January 1944 King declared that 'the evidence of Japanese brutality and organized sadism is so horrible and overwhelming as to be almost incredible.'[9] By this time, the prime minister had learned of the sinking of the Lisbon Maru, in which the Japanese crew had deliberately held the prisoners below decks and fired on those who were trying to escape. In his speech, King noted that many prisoners had been moved to Japan where, it was to be hoped, conditions were better. He did not know that, as he spoke, prisoners were suffering through a bitter Japanese winter with only grass capes for warmth and rush mats for beds.

Public opinion was inflamed by the early stories from Hong Kong. The Globe and Mail condemned the Japanese as even more bestial than the Germans: 'In the light of their terrible deeds, ignorant and unbridled cannibals beyond the fringe of civilization are revealed.'[10] The stories from the returned men went even farther in generating profound rage. 'Thousands have died and thousands will never enjoy the health they did before imprisonment at the hands of the vicious Japs,' editorialized the service-men's newspaper, the *Maple Leaf*: 'The big-time operators of crime in the German fold are coming under the hammer soon. Officialdom will do well to track down every bandy-legged son of Nippon who had a part in looking after Allied prisoners of war and let 'em have it – but good!'[11] Hysteria seemed to be the reaction of many to the Japanese record of mistreatment. 'We have to forget,' stated one newspaper, 'quite a few of our traditional principles. We need, for instance, to forget our ideas of chivalry towards a beaten foe ... We need not fear being too cruel.'[12]

Despite this ominous rhetoric, the Asian war crimes trials would still adhere to principles of law. Trials would be based on the examination of evidence, and the collection of evidence became the prime concern. War crimes investigation sections were established in Ottawa and London to interview returned men.[13] Before he left Britain, Bruce Macdonald located William Stewart, the senior medical officer at the Niigata camp in Japan, who told him of two soldiers who were tied to a post in freezing weather until they died of frostbite. Stewart recalled that at Niigata ill and mal-nourished men were regularly beaten for minor or no offences.[14] British investigators shared with Canadians the affidavit of Major S.R. Kerr, who had observed that 'great suffering was caused to sick prisoners of war during the whole of our captivity by the neglect and ill-treatment of Dr. Saito.' As for the camp commandant, Colonel Isao Tokunaga, 'he did nothing to improve matters or to stop the cruelties of his subordinates. His attitude was one of treating us like dogs.'[15] Both Saito and Tokunaga would be marked for special consideration. Evidence of Japanese war crimes were so widespread that the army was anxious to take part in the trial of any suspects.

While many of the prisoners were still on their way back to Canada, a conference was held at the British War Office on 16 October 1945 to determine commonwealth policy. Attending for Britain were three major-generals, the chief army legal officer, Brigadier Henry Shapcott, and the attorney general, Sir Hartley Shawcross. The best Canada could do was send the CWCIU's administrative officer, Major G.K.M. Johnston. A pro-posed organization for southeast Asia was discussed and it was agreed that all cases would be tried under the British royal warrant.[16] The greatest obstacle to Canadian participation was the absence of any occupation force in Asia, for, as the high commissioner's office observed, 'military courts can only be convened by senior officers in command of forces and as Canada has no occupation forces in the Far East, no Canadian courts can therefore be convened in that area.'[17] This difficulty was overcome with surprising ease through the cooperation of Britain and the United States. As early as November 1945, Americans had suggested that the Canadians join them in joint prosecutions as an 'inter-Allied investigating and prosecuting agency.'[18] External Affairs agreed and, on 16 January 1946, the cabinet instructed the department to make arrangements with the two major powers.[19] On 6 February 1946 the British commander in southeast Asia was advised that, while all those accused of crimes committed against Canadians would be tried by British courts, there would be 'Canadian participation in prosecution when so requested.' As well, he was forewarned that a legal team, headed by a lieutenant-colonel, was on its way to assist in prosecuting Canadian cases.[20] A similar arrangement was made with the Americans in Japan. E.R. Hopkins (now a civilian and, under Read's tutelage, a rising star in External Affairs) wrote to the deputy minister of national defence on 22 February that cabinet's instructions of 16 January had been carried out and that arrangements were in place with both the United States and Britain. As an added bonus, the Americans had asked Canada to send a senior officer to preside over the Canadian trials.[21] It only remained to get the men.

The legal team would be headed by Lieutenant-Colonel Oscar Orr and his second-in-command, Major George B. Puddicombe. The two had remarkably similar careers. Both had served in the First World War and Orr still proudly displayed the piece of shell extracted from his skull. After the war, both had successful legal careers, Puddicombe with a Montreal firm and Orr as a crown attorney in Vancouver. Both had volunteered for active service in 1939; Puddicombe became paymaster of the Victoria Rifles, while Orr served as adjutant-general in the Pacific Command. Neither had spent a particularly noteworthy war when the request came from Ottawa for experienced legal staff to represent the Canadian military in the Far East. Orr was not enthusiastic. Almost fifty-four and looking forward to returning to civilian life, he tried to decline. However, he finally accepted the task and, in November 1945, was promoted to lieutenant-colonel and appointed to head the Directorate of Administration that would investigate war crimes in Japan. Puddicombe would monitor and prosecute cases of concern to Canada in Hong Kong.[22]

According to his instructions, Orr was to deal only with cases of death or permanent injury. However, he had talked with enough survivors to know that this was unrealistic. The torture practised by the Japanese could have an insidious, invisible impact on its victims. The constant beatings and brutality had destroyed many men, and 'while in the case of the living who have stood this treatment, the true results will be hard to analyze for many years, the mental result is painfully apparent to the laymen in many cases.'[23] It was this maltreatment that would be the focus of the prosecution. Assisting Orr with these cases would be two former prisoners, warrant officers Robert Manchester and H.B. Sheppard, and two legal officers, Captains J.H. Dickey and John Boland. Colonel Thomas Moss was also dispatched to Tokyo to act as a judge in the American military courts.[24]

Puddicombe's team arrived in Hong Kong to find that the British already had a number of defendants in custody with trials imminent. The chief investigator, Lieutenant-Colonel F.C. Munshall-Ford, reported that a number of strong cases were ready for trial.[25] The British military would prosecute 920 Japanese at 23 locations – one-fifth of all Japanese to be prosecuted by the Allies. These prosecutions never attracted the attention of comparable European cases, and, perhaps for this reason, the courts could dispense justice without political second-guessing.[26] While Japanese responsibility for the deaths of millions of Chinese was as heinous as the Nazis record of mass murder, and their starvation and torture of prisoners as savage as SS conduct, the war crimes trials would deal with comparatively minor episodes. They also would examine 'specific experiences from the points of view of the victim and the malefactor in a manner which is all but impossible to discern in the swirling horrors of mass atrocities.'[27] By May, the four officers and NCOs of Canada's war crimes detail were in Hong Kong. As well, Major J.T. Loranger was made available to sit on the British courts.

In a trial that in many ways mirrored that of Kurt Meyer (except that it was totally ignored in Canada), Puddicombe prosecuted Major-General Ryosaburo Tanaka, the former commander of the 229th Infantry Regiment. Soldiers of his regiment had stormed ashore on Hong Kong island on the night of 18 December 1941 with their objective being the hills north of Victoria City. Almost hidden in these hills, the Salesian Mission was a medical depot staffed by ten men of the Royal Army Medical Corps, eight Canadian medical orderlies, and several nurses and orderlies, all under the command of a Canadian medical officer, Captain S.M. Banfill. The mission was draped with Red Crosses and all the staff carried identification as medical personnel. In the early morning of 19 December the Japanese surrounded the mission before the orderlies even knew that they were in the area. Banfill ordered his staff to surrender and the Japanese proceeded to separate the nurses from the male orderlies. An English-speaking officer, a Lieutenant Honda, asked Banfill what kind of command he led. He responded that they were an aid station. Banfill was identified as an officer and tied up as the men from the mission were marched past him to a gully.[28] A British nurse, Lois Fearon, had a better view of subsequent events: 'While the men were halted the Japanese soldiers who were in the rear began bayonetting men from the back. Some of our men fought back with bare hands, while others ran away only to be shot.'[29] From his position Banfill could see the carnage and, turning in horror to Lieutenant Honda, asked why his men were being butchered. Honda shrugged and replied, 'Order is all captives must die,' and he added that after Banfill had guided them through a minefield he would be killed as well.

As the Japanese advance proceeded across the slope of Mount Parker, Honda chatted away, describing the Anglican school he had attended in Tokyo and the morality of the current war. When the troops rested, Honda sighed that it was too bad that Banfill had to die and he then took it upon himself to speak to their commander to see if the prisoner could be spared. Honda came back and reported, 'I am so sorry, all captives must die,' but he added hopefully that they would take him to headquarters.[30] On the way there they came across a wounded soldier. The Japanese asked Banfill to identify his regiment. After he did so they 'lifted him up on their bayonets and threw him on to the path and then shot him to make sure that he was dead.' Twice more the Japanese would bayonet wounded men in their path. Despite this savagery, Banfill would survive capture.

There was little that Tanaka's lawyer, Yusuke Sakai, could do with this evidence. He did uncover one detail, that the killers had worn long boots and might have been marines instead of Tanaka's infantry. But the slaughter appeared to have been systematically carried out by the invading regiment. As one of the survivors, Captain Osler Thomas of the Hong Kong Volunteers, observed, the guards had carefully lined up the victims and then 'suddenly three Japanese soldiers started to bayonet our unsuspecting men from the road amidst cheers from the enemy onlookers.' Thomas survived only by pretending to be shot and lying among the dead until nightfall.[31]

Nor was this the only incident concerning the 229th. A Chinese volunteer described an incident (eerily similar to the Abbaye Ardenne) where twenty-six Chinese prisoners were held in a magazine. After a Japanese officer had spoken with the prisoners, they were forced to come to the door and, one by one, bayonetted to death.[32] Speaking in his own defence, Tanaka insisted that he had cautioned his subordinates to treat prisoners correctly. He reminded them that they were trying to break down the fighting spirit of the enemy and that a wounded or surrounded man was no longer an enemy. In the fighting in southern China, he had addressed his troops on the Geneva Convention and specifically on the prohibition against attacking Red Cross facilities.[33] He positively denied Banfill's story that there were standing orders to kill prisoners. Disclaimers were one thing, the actions of the 229th quite another. Puddicombe had convincingly shown that men under Tanaka's command had killed scores of prisoners on several occasions, and the guilt lay upon him as regimental commander. In his summation Puddicombe considered it unlikely that Tanaka had ever told his men about the laws of war; instead, he probably told them of the Bushido code, which held that it was a profound disgrace to be captured. Moreover, in the face of all the evidence, Tanaka still maintained that 'no prisoners were bayonetted at Sai Wan, no civilians or soldiers executed at the Salesian Mission.' Considering the extent of the atrocities, Tanaka was fortunate to receive a sentence of only twenty years' imprisonment. A Japanese-Canadian interpreter, Roy Ito, found Tanaka to be (like many senior officers) a gentle and courteous man. During the trial Tanaka confided to Ito that he never knew that his soldiers had butchered prisoners and 'if he had been aware of it he would have dealt with the offenders severely.'[34] Nevertheless, Ito was left wondering what Tanaka was like in the days when he commanded these ferocious troops.

Each accused was judged, not as a defeated enemy, but on the circumstances of his case. The commander of the 230th Regiment, Toshishige Shoji, had led the soldiers on Tanaka's right flank. In his after-battle report he wrote of fierce fighting with the Canadians at Jardine's Point and the capture of the Canadian HQ at the Wongneichong Gap. As Shoji proudly recorded, 'the only prisoners captured in Wongneichong Gap were taken by Shoji Butai.'[35] Puddicombe submitted evidence that Canadians at the top of Jardine's Lookout were massacred after capture, as were the staff of the quartermaster store in the Gap. No sooner had the prosecutor finished than Shoji's lawyer, Junijiro Takano, made a detailed motion of 'no case to answer' or 'non-suit.' He dissected Puddicombe's evidence and said that at crucial points the prosecution could not demonstrate that Shoji's men had actually committed atrocities. Takano referred to Shoji's 1942 drawing of the battle that showed his troops capturing pillboxes on the side of the Lookout but not passing through the scene of the crime. One of the Canadians who survived the mass bayonetting described the attackers as carrying light artillery on pack horses, obviously not a part of Shoji's infantry. The Canadian HQ was captured by Shoji's men, but the only mistreatment was to bind the prisoners, and as a Captain Philips stated, 'the combatant Japanese troops to whom we surrendered treated us very reasonably in the circumstances.' The defence was not required to present evidence, and Shoji was acquitted on all charges. His acquittal was an indication that 'almost without exception, courts scrupulously adhered to the principle that an accused must be freed unless he could prove beyond reasonable doubt to be guilty of a specific, individual [as opposed to collective] offence.'[36]

The overall Japanese commander, Takeo Ito, was charged with war crimes in January 1948. His case summarized the graphic stories of prisoners being systematically bayonetted by Japanese troops. One witness observed seven British soldiers marched out of the Repulse Bay Hotel and made to sit at the edge of a cliff. 'He saw a Japanese soldier shoot them one by one from behind.' Yet there was an odd contrast between these brutalities and Ito's courtly, military bearing. He calmly testified that 'the first time I learned of the acts of war crimes was when I was accused of them. It was more than my regret that such things were committed by Japanese forces.' Moreover, he was full of praise for his enemies. 'The Canadian forces might have been better than the Japanese and I thought our soldiers should in some way emulate their example.' When he learned that 'C' Force's commanding officer, Brigadier Lawson, had died at the head of his troops, he felt that 'the Canadian officer must indeed have been a valiant man in sacrificing himself in action.' He gave orders for Lawson's burial and himself prayed at his grave. While he was convicted, Ito's demeanour seemed to impress the court and he was sentenced to only twelve years. After sentencing, he thanked the court, wished its members the best, and shook hands with all concerned.[37]

While the killings detailed in the Shoji, Tanaka, and Ito cases had occurred in the heat of battle, the deaths that were a normal feature of the Hong Kong prisoner-of-war camps seemed part of a systematic policy of maltreatment. One of the most notorious offenders, Genichiro Niimori, was the interpreter at the Shamshuipo camp. At the Bowen Road hospital, two Canadian orderlies, J.T.F. Murray and James Archibald, were accused of theft and interrogated by Niimori. He had their hands tied behind their backs and hung from a hook so that they could not touch the floor. They were left like this for three hours. Later, they were beaten and told to change their pleas of innocence. After two more days they were whipped again and hung as before. The beatings continued until Archibald was told that 'in Japan when criminal acts were committed someone was punished for them and was asked if there were anyone in the camp I did not like and told to name him as the person who had taken the satchel.'[38] This remark exemplified the cultural chasm that separated the Japanese from their captives. One authority has noted the 'Japanese soldier's abiding need for self-justification: once having made an accusation, to save face he would continue to attempt to extract a confession even if it became obvious that he had made a mistake in identification.'[39] The two unfortunate Canadians were victims of this attitude. At the trial, the prisoners' medical officer, Dr James William Anderson, identified Niimori as 'easily the most frightening and worst interpreter we ever met.'[40] In his defence, Niimori called Dr Shunicki Saito (himself awaiting trial), who had led some of the interrogations. Saito's disclaimers of undue pressure, that 'I did not force any answers. Just asked,' convinced no one. Moreover, Niimori was a proper martinet who had overworked the labour parties and compelled sick men to work. When one man collapsed of exhaustion at the 'Happy Valley Race Course,' Niimori sneered, 'That will teach you,' and kicked the man. One beating he gave to a prisoner probably brought on the man's death.[41] In light of all this, Niimori might have considered himself fortunate to have received a sentence of only fifteen years' imprisonment.

Not all the victims were soldiers. T.C. Monoghan, an official of the Canadian Pacific Railway, was among a group of civilians accused of espionage and tortured. Oscar Orr reported to Ottawa that he was monitoring the case, which was being prosecuted by an Australian officer. Orr forwarded the evidence of a Jesuit priest that all suspects were crammed into one cell where eight men died of beriberi. Monoghan was subjected to the 'water cure' in which a wet towel was fastened over the victim's face to simulate drowning.[42] Despite having learned nothing about the alleged spying, the Japanese executed Monoghan in 1943. One of his torturers, Riki Yakabuki, was sentenced to ten years and the conviction was lauded in Canada under the headline 'Oscar Orr secures Jap conviction.'[43]

Not only were some Japanese charged with direct abuse of prisoners, sheer neglect could also cause deaths. The medical officer at Stanley Gaol, Choichi Sato, was convicted of war crimes by refusing to tend to the sick and forbidding a prisoner-doctor to render assistance.[44] The extent of Japanese abuse of their captives surprised many who were aware that, during the Russo-Japanese war of 1905 and the First World War, Japan had scrupulously observed its international obligations.[45] Despite Japanese assurances in 1942 that it would observe the 1929 Geneva Convention, its record was one of indifference if not disdain for the convention's terms. What appears to have changed Japanese attitudes was the militarist philosophy that consumed the country in the 1930s and brutalized all aspects of society. Because the Japanese soldier was beaten from his first days as a recruit, he accepted beatings as commonplace and inflicted them on others. And because the soldier was continually told that it was the supreme disgrace to surrender, he treated the surrendered enemy with utmost contempt. 'There is little evidence to document any official pressure to adhere to the Geneva Convention,' Charles Roland has observed, and while humane individuals occasionally helped the prisoners, 'nevertheless, major contraventions of at least some specific clauses of the Geneva Convention of 1929 were routine throughout the war years.'[46]

Two men, Colonel Isao Tokunaga and Dr Shunkichi Saito, embodied the Japanese indifference to the prisoners' lives. Tokunaga, Saito, and three lesser figures were arraigned on 17 October 1946 and would endure Puddicombe's relentless parade of witnesses until February of the following year. The case against Saito lay in his lack of interest in the prisoners' suffering, an apathy far deadlier than Japanese bayonets. The prosecution's leading witness, Dr J.N.B. Crawford, was a highly experienced physician who had graduated from the University of Manitoba and done post-graduate work in New York. In his view, the daily ration of less than 2,000 calories a day could barely sustain a man doing hard labour. Crawford had seen fifteen Canadians die of simple malnutrition.[47] Unfit men were regularly forced to join work crews, and even Saito went out on these details where he was 'brutal in his behaviour. He quite refused to accept the manifest exhaustion of many of the prisoners.'[48] The hospital conditions at North Point were beyond primitive, with open latrine buckets in the halls and men stacked on the floors of the overcrowded rooms.

All this was nothing compared to the horrors that ensued when a diphtheria epidemic broke out in August 1942. Crawford advised Saito that serum was needed desperately or the infection could spread. No serum was forthcoming and the disease spread rapidly among the closely packed prisoners. Saito did not react until diphtheria was raging in October. Crawford read through the dead list:'Fifty four men died of diphtheria – they should not have died. Twenty one men died of dysentery – they should not have died.' In all, 101 Canadians had died from easily preventable diseases.[49] Captain E.L. Hurd of the Royal Rifles kept a diary of the epidemic between October 1942 and February 1943. In it he recorded that death became a regular visitor to Shamshuipo camp. A typical entry, for 23 October 1942, read: 'Working parties are very heavy. Men being forced to work that are not fit to be out of bed. No amount of pleading will alter the Japs brutal treatment.'[50] A British doctor, James Gray, knew that diphtheria serum was available and obtained it for the British compound. However, the Canadians could not get access to this supply and eventually

460 of them would contract the disease. This neglect was all the more unforgivable in that Hong Kong had huge stockpiles of medicine; one supplier testified that he had enough serum to last for two years.[51]

In contrast to Crawford, Saito had barely graduated from medical school when he was drafted into the medical corps. Crawford was amazed that he seemed unable to identify the diphtheria germ when it was placed before him on a microscope. Dr Gray was 'disposed to wonder whether he had ever received any medical training far less held a medical qualification.' At the height of the diphtheria outbreak, in October 1942, a month in which forty-one Canadians died, Saito ordered the medical orderlies (combat soldiers who had volunteered for hospital duties) on parade. Men were dying, he declared angrily, because of their indolence, and he ordered any man who felt that he was doing his duty to step forward. They all did so. Saito walked up and down the row slapping the men and flogging them with his stethoscope. Feeding his rage, he drew his sword and called on any man who still felt that he was doing his duty to step forward and be punished. One orderly, Lance Corporal Varley, did so. Saito paused and slapped Dr Crawford but turned to Varley and said that he was indeed a brave man and dismissed the parade.[52] Knowing that the camp's medical record was a disgrace, Saito ordered Crawford not to mention diphtheria on medical certificates. Just before Hong Kong surrendered to the Allies, Saito seized all medical records and none of them was ever seen again.

In his defence, Saito said that as soon as he realized the seriousness of the diphtheria outbreak he tried to get the authorities to send help. He failed, for the Japanese medical staff were busy fighting a cholera outbreak in their own camp. Moreover, the Canadians proved intractable, for they spread the disease by not using the mouthwash provided or observing the segregation of the sick ward.[53] Saito had no control over food supplies or medicine, and in the words of his defence lawyer, he did his best 'in the face of difficulties.' Canadians were malnourished, he alleged, because their metabolism could not adjust to a diet with far more carbohydrates than fat and consequently they drew less nourishment from the food. As for the slapping of the orderlies and officer, he could only say that 'it is customary in Japanese army, and it has been always carried out for instructional purposes. It could not be considered either punishment or ill treatment.' The court did not accept his shifting of the blame and he was convicted and sentenced to death.

'Fat Pig' was probably the commonest sobriquet the Canadians applied to the camp commandant, Colonel Tokunaga. In other circumstances he might have been comical, for one prisoner recalled that his portly frame 'cut a ridiculous figure as he waddled around in his high leather boots, sword almost dragging on the ground, sweat pouring down his neck.'[54] But there was nothing amusing about forcing 80 men into a 36-by-5 metre hut originally designed for 32 men. There was also bitter rage at his known theft of Red Cross parcels for sale on the black market and forcing ill men to work on the extension of the Kai Tak airfield. It was Tokunaga's idea to have the Canadians hand dig the Happy Valley Race Course for cultivation. For thirty days and nights all men, including the ill, were forced to work. 'Colonel Tokunaga, the "Beast of Hong Kong," came every day to view our progress ... Many a night during our thirty day ordeal we had to work until midnight. On rainy days and nights, it was real hell. Our sick men getting soaked on the ground, our workers wading up to their knees in mud and water.'[55]

All these infractions were overshadowed by one incident in August 1942. Soldiers die in battle, but the deaths of four Canadian soldiers violated both the laws of war and humanity. Sergeant John Payne, Lance Corporal George Berzenski, and privates John Adams and Percy Ellis had escaped from North Point and tried to sail out of the harbour. However, their boat floundered and they were recaptured. Another prisoner later learned from a Chinese that the escapees were taken to the commandant's HQ and severely beaten; 'each of them had barb wire run through their hands and ... he was strung up suspended by the hands in front of the Peninsular Hotel.' A Chinese boy witnessed Tokunaga supervise the torture session and, according to one Japanese who was present, the colonel took part in striking the captives.[56] Afterwards, the four were taken to the King's Park football field where they were executed. The torture and death of the Canadians was made a public spectacle to discourage other escapees. Tokunaga was admonished by Hong Kong's governor for laxness in guarding the prisoners and one solution he devised was for each prisoner to swear that they would not attempt to escape. Those who refused were sent to prison and put on a starvation diet until they complied. Captain J.A.G. Reid remembered that, when prisoners protested that this was against international law, Tokunaga informed the assembled prisoners that they 'should think of no appeal to international law as that no longer existed for them. He stated that there was only one law in the world, that being the Imperial Japanese Army Law.'[57]

Tetsuo Fujita, Tokunaga's defender, tried to present his client as an unfortunate middleman. When he assumed command there was no provision for so many prisoners and the available buildings were badly damaged. He obtained some repair materials and organized the camps as best he could. While the huts seemed overcrowded to the Canadians, by Japanese standards they were acceptable. Tokunaga recalled a delegation of prisoners protesting that their work on the military airfield at Kai Tak violated the Geneva Convention, but he could only shrug and tell them that the orders came directly from the governor general of Hong Kong. The camp commandant portrayed himself as the helpless executor of the governor's commands. Even so, on many occasions he championed the prisoners' welfare to the extent that 'he was asked by the Governor General whether he expected to receive a medal from the British.'[58] Fujita conceded that there was great indifference to the prisoners' fate, but that this came from higher authority. 'Another person in Colonel Tokunaga's place could not have made a better job of his role of Camp Commandant. The accused must not be held guilty for matters outside his scope of responsibility.'

None of this excused Tokunaga's part in the execution of the four Canadians or of five British soldiers who were planning an escape tunnel. While these executions violated international law, his nuanced defence to the accusations was that he was bound by superior orders. 'There is order and system of command in the Japanese Army,' said Fujita, and the chief of staff, Colonel Arisue, had masterminded the crimes. 'I say that Arisue is responsible for ordering the execution, not the man who conveyed his order [Tokunaga].'[59] But how much of a bystander was he? Tokunaga's guards were known to bayonet Chinese civilians for sport and prisoner Ken Cambon would later remember that 'the guards took perverse pleasure, for no apparent reason, in stopping some coolie, tying him to a pole and bayonetting him, all done with shrieks of laughter from the onlooking guards. I still painfully remember them killing a Chinese woman and her baby when she went down to the seawall beside the camp.'[60] These guards were responsible to Tokunaga, but Fujita argued that he could not be held responsible for their crimes: 'If an individual took it upon himself to assault a Chinese – on whose head should it be but his own.' Following this logic, Tokunaga's acts were caused by his superiors' orders while the brutality of his own men was strictly their fault. Perhaps it was the only defence available, but it was not persuasive. Tokunaga was also sentenced to death.

Next to Kurt Meyer, the most intriguing character ever prosecuted for war crimes against Canadians was a native of Kamloops, British Columbia, and an interpreter for the Japanese army, Kanao Inouye. Described in the Canadian press as the 'most sadistic of all camp officials,' Inouye, in revenge for all the insults he had endured during his youth in British

Columbia, was alleged to have been especially cruel to the Canadians.[61] According to Sergeant Arthur Rance of the Hong Kong Volunteers, 'Inouye went out of his way to be offensive to the Canadian prisoners. He continually directed very foul and abusive language at them.'[62] Another prisoner remembered him as 'bigger than his colleagues, quite handsome, bright and terribly mean. He made it known that he had been called a yellow bastard in Canada, and that now he was top dog.'[63] According to Rifleman William Allister, 'the Kamloops Kid, as he was dubbed, was a monster, driven mad somehow, somewhere. Mad with hate for all things white and Canadian. His craving for vengeance was awesome.' But even while he taunted the prisoners with predictions of the Rising Sun flag flying over Ottawa and their sisters being raped by the victorious Imperial Japanese army, part of him seemed almost friendly. The impression he often gave was of a man torn between his foreignness in Japan and nostalgia for his former land.[64]

Physically, Inouye was 'fairly tall for a Japanese, better appearance than most,' and he regularly used Canadian slang in conversation.[65] According to his birth certificate, he was born in Kamloops in 1916. The RCMP investigated his background and discovered that both his parents had been born in Japan and that his father had served in the 131st Overseas Battalion of the Canadian Expeditionary Force in the First World War and been awarded the Military Medal. After his father's death in 1926, Inouye's mother had moved to Slocan, British Columbia. His sisters still lived in Canada but all had applied to return to Japan.[66]

The unique circumstances of a Canadian torturing Canadian prisoners caused the army to enquire if Inouye could be returned to Canada for trial. But the evidence of war crimes was not substantial. Although he had beaten two prisoners, he had not caused any permanent injuries and the deputy minister of defence conceded that 'conduct of this sort by a British subject is treason; the same conduct by an alien is a minor war crime.'[67] The Justice Department added that, while his deeds may have been treasonous, they had been committed outside Canada and could be tried only under the Treason Act of 1351. It is a measure of the timelessness of the law that only a few months after the first use of atomic weapons, recourse had to be made to a statute from the days of King Edward III and the Black Death. By March 1946 External Affairs recommended that Inouye be brought back to Canada and the question was referred to cabinet for a decision.[68] The politicians, by contrast, had no eagerness to take over the case and it was agreed to let the British handle it.[69] This was just as well for, by May 1946, preparations for Inouye's trial were well advanced.

The first two charges against Inouye dealt with his assault on Captain J.A. Norris and Major F.T. Atkinson on 21 December 1942. That morning two Canadians were missing from parade and the camp commander angrily accused Norris and Atkinson of helping them escape. The two men were discovered an hour later asleep in their huts. Still raging, the commandant ordered Inouye to slap Norris. He proceeded to slap both Norris and Atkinson and, even after they collapsed, he continued to kick them. Atkinson was so badly beaten in the face that he almost lost an eye. A few days later, Norris reported, Inouye told him that 'he was sorry that he had lost his temper. I did not accept his apology.'[70] At trial Inouye explained that he had to administer the beatings: 'I had to carry out the orders or get into trouble myself. If I had not done that I would have gone to Stanley [prison] for six months, that would mean death.' However, the third charge, relating to his conduct as a Kempeitai (secret police) interpreter from 1944–5, was far more damning. In many cases involving Hong Kong civilians he had actively participated in their torture by way of burning with cigarettes or administering the water torture.

Lam Sik, a wireless operator, stood accused of communicating with the Nationalist Chinese and received the water torture from Inouye. After several sessions, Inouye beat him with a dog whip to extract information about a transmitter. As army interpreter Roy Ito observed, 'one by one witnesses came into the court to tell their stories and with vehement hatred in their eyes pointed to Inouye as the man who had tortured them.'[71] Among these witnesses was Ramphal Ghilote, a civil servant, who described Inouye as the 'chief torturer of my body and soul.' After being given the water torture by Inouye, he was taken before an officer and Inouye asked that he be shot without trial. The officer refused and Ghilote was left chained in a cell without food or water for days. Inouye demanded that he confess that he was a spy and, when he refused, Inouye continued the torture sessions, burning him on the face and tongue with a lighted cigarette.[72]

By far the most powerful witness against Inouye was a fifty-five-year-old British woman, Mary Violet Power. Her husband had been arrested in June 1944 and died in Japanese custody that November. Mrs Power was also arrested and Inouye took part in her water torture. Laying her flat on the floor with a towel over her face, the Japanese then poured water over her face to simulate drowning. This went on until she vomited. Water was forced into her again until the guards slapped and kicked her to expel the water, and the session ended by hanging her by her hands with her feet barely touching the ground. She was left like this for six and a half hours.

Inouye then asked her if she was ready to speak. When she said she had nothing to say, he took a cigarette and burned her hands, face, and cheek until 'I fainted and wet myself and they let me down.' On following days she was beaten and burned again.[73] Many civilians were arrested on suspicion of spying and given the same treatment and a number of them did not survive. While Inouye actively participated in these sessions, the evidence showed that he was primarily the interpreter and that the chief guard, Moriyama, was in command.

Interpreter Roy Ito's first reaction to Inouye was one of intense dislike for the man who had tortured prisoners and created ill feelings towards Japanese Canadians. Puddicombe, for his part, was concerned that Inouye's defence might be based on a reaction to his mistreatment in Canada and he therefore asked Ito to be prepared to rebut any such allegations from the witness stand. Ito, who had experienced discrimination in his youth, was left wondering just how he was expected to respond.[74] However, the issue never arose for Inouye described his early life in British Columbia in glowing terms. He had done well in school and had many friends among his white schoolmates. In 1936, at the age of twenty, he travelled to Japan to further his education. Though well connected in Japanese society – his grandfather, Chotahara, was president of Keio Electric Trainways, and a member of the Diet and the House of Peers – Inouye was struck by the extreme chauvinism of Japanese life. Because he had lived in the West so long, he was treated with suspicion and contempt. For merely befriending a Nisei reporter, Inouye was arrested and given the water torture. Afterwards, he had to go to a sanatorium to recover his health. He was so ashamed of having been tortured by the police that he was unable to tell his revered grandfather why he was ill. In May 1942 he was conscripted as a civilian interpreter for the prisoner camps in Hong Kong. Even though they were civilians, Inouye and his fellow translators were roughly treated by the NCOs and ordered to give unquestioned obedience to military authority.[75]

In an unexpected romantic twist to his story, Inouye then testified that he had fallen in love with a Mrs W.R. Parker (formerly Ho Wai Ming), who was recently divorced from a British police official from Shanghai. Parker had been running a popular tearoom. But when the authorities closed down all such establishments for security reasons, she became completely dependent upon Inouye's support. This liaison continued until September 1943, when he was transferred to Singapore. It was a move Inouye attributed to Tokunaga's fear of someone revealing his scheme to steal the prisoners' Red Cross parcels for resale on the black market. Unable to marry Parker without his family's consent, Inouye had to wait until his discharge and return to Japan in March 1944 to get their approval. In the meantime, he obtained a job as a clerk with an import-export company and in this capacity he returned to Hong Kong in June 1944. While he now was able to marry, he was also subject to the military who again drafted him, this time as an interpreter for the Kempeitai. However, Inouye did not seem particularly devoted to the imperial cause, for in February 1945 he again obtained a discharge and returned to work in a commercial firm.[76]

While he had been present for many torture sessions, Inouye maintained that he had taken no part in them but only done the translations. As well, he accused Ghilote of being a double agent and testifying against him to cover up his own treason. In an evocative summation, Puddicombe asked the court to consider the effects of the water torture; what it must have been like for the victims as they struggled against a never-ending drowning. The defending officer, Lieutenant J.R. Haggan, unable to erase this horrific picture, gave a calm, mannerly defence. He began by complimenting Puddicombe for his 'superb coolness of manner and common sense for which most of his nation are famous.' Haggan argued that there was no convincing proof that Inouye participated in any torture that led to death, and while he may have abused prisoners, 'slapping a person is second nature to the Japanese.' As a mere civilian interpreter, Inouye was a secondary figure at best, and 'such orders [to hang suspects] are not given by civilians, and if given by civilians would not be obeyed. These hangings up must have been authorized by persons in authority.'[77] The court president, Lieutenant-Colonel J.C. Stewart, was unimpressed and was especially influenced by Inouye's background. In sentencing him, he felt that: 'Some of these acts involved such wanton and barbarous cruelty that it was a mere accident of fate whether the victims survived or not. Your culpability is greatly aggravated by the fact that you were the guest of the Dominion of Canada in your youth and there you received kindness and free education which should have impressed on your mind the decent ways of civilized people and made it impossible for you to be concerned, directly or indirectly, in such an outrage against humanity.'[78] Inouye was convicted of the mistreatment of civilians but exonerated of direct responsibility for any deaths. Ironically, the guards who had carried out the tortures but who had not been exposed to the 'decent ways of civilized people' received prison terms. Inouye was sentenced to death. Disparities in sentences were becoming a concern. In Singapore, three Japanese were sentenced to death even though none of them were convicted of murder. A death sentence in the absence of a finding of murder seemed unduly harsh. However, instead of appealing the sentence, Inouye's lawyers attacked the validity of the trial itself. They succeeded.

On 19 November 1946, the confirming authority (the area military commander with responsibility for the trial) ruled that the court had no jurisdiction to try a British subject under the Royal warrant.[79] This unanticipated result generated a spurt of telegrams from Ottawa asking if Inouye was still being held and if he was going to be tried for treason.[80] Even Canada's diplomatic representative conceded that 'Inouye's behaviour towards Canadian prisoners of war is a comparatively minor aspect of the charges against him'[81] and it would be for the best if he were tried in Hong Kong. From a distance, Orr was trying to sort out the muddle of Inouye's nationality and he admonished Puddicombe that this should have been done long ago 'and not have been the subject of any snap judgment based on incomplete evidence.'[82] But, if anything, Orr merely added to the confusion. Sargeant Rance recalled Inouye saying that he had been born in Tokyo and later had obtained a false Canadian birth certificate. Orr confirmed that this was possible for the provincial Vital Statistics Act 'was used as a vehicle for frauds.'[83] Hong Kong's victims were not prepared to wait while this issue was settled, and in December 1946 the colony's administration charged Inouye with treason on the basis of his Canadian birth. The mystery was greatly dispelled by the discovery of an abstract of census from Japan's Kanagawa Prefecture. These meticulous family records confirmed that Inouye had been born in Kamloops in 1916 and notice of his birth was accepted by the Japanese consul in Vancouver in 1918.[84]

At his civilian criminal trial, Inouye stood directly implicated in the deaths of men who had not survived his torture sessions. Evidence was submitted that he was a British subject by birth and that he had violated the 1351 Treason Act by 'adhering to the King's enemies.' During this second trial, Inouye displayed a chameleon-like ability to alter his testimony to suit the situation. Now he swore that he had been proud to enlist in the Imperial army in 1937 and swear allegiance to the emperor. His sole allegiance was to Japan for he had never been accepted in Canada, had been denied job prospects, and was thus 'very embittered against the Canadian people.'[85] He was pleased to serve in the Kempeitai since it was his duty to root out espionage against his nation. At one point in his testimony he suddenly burst out, 'My body is the Japanese Emperor's body – my mind and my body belong to the Japanese Emperor!' When the prosecutor pressed him on the inconsistencies between his current story and his previous testimony, Inouye snapped to attention and called out, 'Long live the Emperor!' The presiding judge, Sir Henry Blackall, looked over at Inouye and calmly told him that there was no need for theatrics.

Inouye's lawyer, Charles Loseby, argued that none of the evidence submitted constituted proof of treason for Inouye's allegiance was to Japan not Britain. He argued that *Calvin's Case* (1609)[86] applied and that the essence of treason is the breaking of the bonds between king and subject. If these bonds do not exist, they cannot be broken. Sir Henry Blackall carefully summed up the law of treason. By birth, Inouye was a British subject and he could change his nationality only by a 'declaration of alienage.' There was no evidence that he had done this and, moreover, a subject could not change his allegiance to the king's enemies during the course of a war. According to the judge, it was for the jury to determine 'whether accused was merely actuated by pure patriotic motives' or was rather 'nursing a grievance against the Anglo-Saxon race and their allies.' The jury had no doubt. After deliberating a mere ten minutes it unanimously found Inouye guilty. According to observers, he shuddered slightly and stiffened as the judge donned the black cap. For the second time Kanao Inouye heard the sentence of death pronounced over him.

This conviction was also appealed, and the heart of Inouye's plea was that he was not a British subject and that 'the Chief Justice had been wrong just as Judge Tucker had been in the William Joyce trial.'[87] This reference to the trial of 'Lord Haw Haw' – the American-born fascist who had made wartime propaganda broadcasts from Germany – would be crucial in determining Inouye's fate. In Joyce's case, the British courts gave an exceptionally wide interpretation of allegiance to conclude that, even though Joyce had not been born in Britain, was not a naturalized British subject, and was not on British soil when the offences were committed, he nevertheless owed fealty to the king. This seemed to stretch the law of treason to an absurdity for, as Glanville Williams has observed, a 'conviction seemed undesirable when it could be gained only by what was regarded as a legal device.'[88] In the face of the torture and beatings he had administered, Inouye's culpability was proven and his breach of allegiance was shown by his own previous sworn testimony that he was a British subject. The only avenue of escape lay in showing that he had denied his allegiance. But, once again, his previous testimony damned him for there was no indication that he had formally renounced his citizenship. His merry chase of trials and appeals came to an end when the Hong Kong

Supreme court rejected his final appeal. The interpreter from Kamloops was executed on 25 August 1947.

In that same month, the news arrived in Canada that two condemned Japanese had had their sentences commuted. Dr Saito's death sentence was reduced to twenty years and Tokunaga's to life imprisonment. Canadian authorities had been aware of the commutations since July, even though the military commander of Hong Kong chose not to communicate directly with Ottawa. Saito and Tokunaga's clemency plea had been sent to a case reviewer in Singapore who seemed especially swayed by the comments of Hong Kong's director of medical services, Dr Selwyn-Clarke. He confirmed that, while Saito was not officially allowed to supply the prisoner camps with medicine, he had permitted medical supplies to get through by irregular channels. As for Tokunaga, he permitted food parcels to get into the camp and they 'contributed very largely to the welfare of the inmates.' As camp administrator, Tokunaga was 'lazy and greedy rather than deliberately sadistic,' and, as for Saito, it was Selwyn-Clarke's view that 'he is not altogether normal mentally.'[89] However reasonable the commutation appeared in this light, in Canada it appeared to be just another case of misplaced sympathy for war criminals.

'Both men,' declared the Montreal *Star*, 'obeyed and exceeded their instructions in animalistic cruelty to Canadian prisoners.'[90] The survivors also protested. Lieutenant-Colonel Trist of the Winnipeg Grenadiers recalled Tokunaga's part in the agonizing death of four of his men and described him and his underlings as 'savages with a thin veneer of civilization.'[91] The departments of defence and external affairs discussed the commutations and speculated on how best to contain the protests. External Affairs Minister Louis St Laurent sent a message to Britain seeking further details but reminded the press that the decision was solely in the hands of a British general.[92] At least this enabled Ottawa to remain at a distance from an unpopular decision.

At the same time as Canadian sensibilities were being inflamed by another commutation, the Commonwealth Conference on Pacific Problems was being held in Canberra, Australia. Canada's representative, Brooke Claxton, was calling for a 'positive and dynamic' peace between all nations in the region.[93] The realities of the post-war world seemed to override any residual concern for punishing war crimes. There was a bitter irony that, as Canadians learned of Saito's and Tokunaga's commutation, a deputation from the Winnipeg Grenadiers and Royal Rifles was in Hong

Kong supervising the burial of some 300 of their dead. As correspondent Dick Sanborn reported, this ceremony occurred 'almost at the same time as British officers were wiping out the death sentences on two enemy officers who were largely responsible for the deaths of many of these Canadians.'[94] To the survivors, the enemy had had the benefit of scrupulously fair trials and it was the height of injustice that after their condemnation they should be reprieved. Such mercy seemed intended only to appease a bloodless diplomacy and left unrealized the promise of condign punishment.

The Japanese Trials: Camp Guards
and the Architects of War

Although it was never expressly stated, one of the objectives of the war crimes trials seems to have been the systematic description of just what happened to Canadian prisoners. Much as the Meyer trial had uncovered and detailed the crimes in Normandy, the Asian courts martial would give life to the horror of the prison camps. In all, 1,183 Canadians were sent from Hong Kong to Japan as forced labour and harnessed to the imperial war machine. From the accounts of those who survived, the conditions there were worse than those in Hong Kong. As one sergeant recalled, sick men were forced to work for 'if you could stand up you had to go. And in those circumstances, the food was barely enough to keep one alive.'[1] Not all prisoners were Hong Kong survivors. RCAF officer Wing Commander Leonard Birchall had radioed a warning to the British fleet in Ceylon of an imminent Japanese attack. After being shot down, his surviving crewmen were strafed in the water and only six out of nine men survived. Taken for intensive questioning at Ofuna, Japan, Birchall and his men were repeatedly tortured to extract information. 'You were beaten from the moment you got up till the time you went back to bed,' Birchall reported. Food was at the starvation level and 'if you didn't get out in six months you weren't going to get out – you'd die in that place.'[2] Even if they lived long enough to go to the labour camps, life was always precarious. And yet even Birchall recalled rare instances of humanity, such as the occasion when their British Columbia-born translator, Tomeji Onami, brought his family to the camp to have tea with the men. For this act of courtesy Onami was fired.[3] William Allister fondly remembered the translator Koyanagi, who had lived in Windsor, Ontario, for eleven years and who greeted the prisoners with friendly, sardonic humour. At his own expense and risk he also smuggled drugs into the camp.[4] These were the exceptions. The rule was the local hospital where Birchall saw attendants experiment on sick men – 'operations without any anaesthetics, lumbar punctures, putting in spinal injections of urine and so on.'

Before any legal officers were sent to Asia, one set of trials, oddly enough held in Winnipeg, would give Canadians a vivid picture of how Japan treated its captives.

In March 1946 Winnipegers were anticipating a prosperous new world. The celebrations had been held, the rationing ended, and for most people the war was memory. However, in one building in Fort Osborne Barracks it was another time and place. Hut 78, originally the Canadian Women's Army Corps recreation room, had been stripped of its refrigerator, chesterfield, and all signs of gaiety. Instead it had been turned into a bleak courtroom, the only splash of colour coming from a large Union Jack displayed behind the judge's podium. As the court convened and grim faced witnesses trooped in, it was once again February 1944 and the scene was a prisoner-of-war camp in Oeyama, Japan.

The first accused, Sergeant J.H. Harvey, Royal Army Medical Corps, saluted smartly and pleaded not guilty to manslaughter. Facing him was court President Major-General J.W.A. Haugh and four other British officers. Although Harvey faced British military justice, almost all the witnesses against him would be Winnipeg Grenadiers. The victim, Private John Friesen, was a Grenadier who allegedly died as a result of a beating by Harvey. Overwork and malnourishment had put Friesen in the camp hospital, and once there he started to rave about Red Cross parcels; according to one witness, 'he was delirious. He was raving about food.' Everyone in the ward was screaming until Harvey, the head orderly, came in and struck Friesen until he stopped. Several minutes later, Friesen began to crawl about the ward and Harvey struck him several more times. Friesen died shortly thereafter. In Harvey's defence, Winnipeg lawyer J.J. Kelly gave the court a different perspective. The hospital had no sedatives and the only way to control a hysterical man was to subdue him physically. When Harvey had expressed remorse over Friesen's death, he was in turn admonished by the camp doctor: 'You were not to blame. If you carry on like this, we will be losing you.' Harvey was acquitted of manslaughter but faced twenty-nine additional charges of collaboration.[5]

The prosecution's evidence gave a glimpse of what life was like in a typical Japanese camp. To mitigate the brutality of Japanese punishment the prisoners, at the suggestion of Lieutenant-Commander Stenning, had formed a 'Big Four' of senior NCOs (one of them being Harvey) who controlled camp life. When one Canadian was caught stealing food, he was taken to the Japanese for questioning. However, after a number of blows by Harvey, he was released. Another Canadian, J.J. Tandy, was twice caught raiding stores for Red Cross parcels. Harvey struck him several times and knocked him out. Questioning Tandy on the consequences of stealing Red Cross parcels, Kelly asked, 'Did you ever think that, if you did something to displease the Japanese, you might not get that parcel?' To this Tandy replied, 'I didn't think about that, Mr. Kelly.' Tandy also admitted that, while they were in Shamshuipo camp, Hong Kong, Harvey had shared Red Cross parcels with him and had once smuggled medicine into the camp to save a soldier's life. Months later, Tandy felt so run down that he was close to death, but Harvey gave him some extra food to revive him. Kelly asked:

Q. So that, if it wasn't for this conduct on the part of Harvey at this time, you might have died?
A. I thought that myself sir.[6]

An example of 'Big Four' justice was the trial of Private Podolsky for stealing fish. Witnesses were called and arguments made before the Big Four. Podolsky was convicted and caned by Harvey. But prisoners did not have to accept punishment. Private Percy Thompson, caught buying rice with cigarettes, refused Harvey's punishment of a slap. Instead, a Japanese guard ran him around the parade square 'about a 1,000 times,' made him sing 'God Save the King' for an hour and a half, and finally struck him on the side of the head with the flat of his sword. When asked why he would not accept Harvey's punishment, Thompson replied, 'I didn't think it was right ... I told him I was a white man.'[7] However laudable Harvey's motives, many prisoners found him excessively assiduous, marching about the camp in his Sam Browne belt and glorying in his position. When Harvey led the prisoners in singing for the camp commandant, several felt that they were being put on display for the enemy's amusement.

Harvey testified that, when he arrived at Oeyama in September 1943, conditions were deplorable. Sick men simply lay on the hospital floor and each was covered by a single blanket. The food was meagre and the guards 'seemed to take a delight in disciplining the prisoners ... everyone of them joined in.' During the winter of 1943–4, thrity-eight men died and Japanese discipline had reached the stage where 'mass punishment was always imminent.' To regain control, the Big Four assured the Japanese that troublemakers would be punished. The commandant reluctantly agreed but forbade the use of a guardhouse and instructed Harvey that *binta*, or slapping, would be the only acceptable punishment. As for serenading the commandant, Harvey recounted that he had been ordered to take a rest party for a walk outside the camp. During one of these walks the commandant ordered them to sing. Harvey's testimony, usually firm and unruffled, rose in an emotional pitch as he described how he led the pathetic band of Canadian, British, and American prisoners through the village of Oeyama singing 'Land of Hope and Glory.'

By far the most important witness on Harvey's behalf was an American medical officer, Major L.C. Bleich. He confirmed Harvey's account of how he saved a American prisoner who had literally lost the will to live. Harvey talked to the man daily and told him that he would get a Red Cross parcel when he could walk. 'The man walked and I kept my promise. That was the only man I gave a full parcel.' Unpleasant as he may have seemed, Harvey had used many tricks (including a thermometer set a degree above normal) to keep sick men in camp. While many men were starving and rightfully felt that the Red Cross parcels (kept under Japanese guard) belonged to them, the attempted thefts 'might have resulted in mass punishment and a deprivation of privileges for the whole camp.' In Bleich's view, extreme conditions justified the use of force.[8] Harvey was exonerated on collaboration charges but held partially responsible for striking prisoners.

When the Canadian member of the Big Four, Company Sergeant-Major Marcus Tugby, was tried (ironically, before a court headed by Harry Foster), much the same evidence was produced. Tugby had beaten prisoners who stole food from Japanese gardens, and it was alleged that he was diverting Red Cross parcels to his own use. His lawyer, David Golden of Winnipeg, was formerly a captain in the Grenadiers and had promoted Tugby to company sergeant-major just before the Japanese attack on Hong Kong. Conditions at Oeyama in the winter of 1944 were near-disastrous. The men were filthy, dying of disease, and losing discipline and self-respect. The camp's only officer, Lieutenant-Commander Stenning, asked Tugby to be the Canadian representative on the NCO committee. A strong factor in Tugby's defence was Bleich's recollection that firm direction from the NCOs was essential to combat the numbness that was breaking down discipline: 'The attitude of the men in the camp and their reactions are almost impossible for me to describe and almost impossible for the court to understand, not having been there. It might be best described as numbness. I remember seeing myself and the men with me assuming this attitude. The Japs were constantly present, constantly in, and out of the huts, harassing the men ... The men got in a state of mind in which they weren't soldiers any more. They ceased to know what discipline was.'9

Foster's court seemed sympathetic to Tugby and he was acquitted on eleven out of twelve charges.

The court's sympathies became even more evident in the last trial, that of Regimental Sergeant-Major Deane of the British army. On one occasion, a sentry had ordered Deane to *dinta* (punish) to a man who had broken camp rules. Deane felt that he had no choice but to slap the man or they both faced worse consequences. Several times Deane had absorbed punishment that was intended for others. He was cleared on all charges.

For six weeks the trials had described the conduct of three of the non-commissioned officers at Oeyama (the fourth, Sergeant E. Rogers, was tried at Montreal and honourably acquitted) and the verdicts, if not complete exonerations, had recognized the extraordinary conditions in the camps. While the judge advocate insisted that the non-commissioned officers were bound by military law, how relevant was this law to the privation and brutality of the camps? If *binta* was the only method to avoid mass punishments, the non-commissioned officers seemed justified in using it. Military justice had developed in peacetime conditions or in situations where the laws of war were understood. How could officers in Winnipeg who had never endured the bitter hell of Oeyama sit in judgment on these men? The predicament of the court mirrored the situation in the RCAF trials. How appropriate was it to apply accepted laws to the extreme duress prevailing in Nazi Germany? In both cases, it was difficult for the judges to appreciate the turmoil in the minds of those involved. The difference was that, while there was some sympathy for the plight of Allied non-commissioned officers in Oeyama, there was none for the Volkssturm of Opladen.

Canadian involvement in the Japanese war crimes trials was limited by the absence of an occupying force and the pervasive American control of postwar Japan. Shortly after V-J Day, John Read wrote to the Canadian ambassador in Washington asking what plans the United States had for Japanese war criminals.10 He learned that the Americans contemplated an inter-Allied panel to try all grades (based on the serious of the offence) of war crimes. External Affairs responded that 'there being no Canadian Commander in Far East, Canadian Government would prefer to associate in joint plan such as that embodied in United States proposal.'[11] On 16 January 1946 the cabinet approved this plan and agreed that a liaison team should go to Japan to ensure the trial of persons who had killed or tortured Canadians.[12] Not only did the Americans concur, they also asked that Canada send a senior officer to sit on the military court. The Department of National Defence selected Colonel Thomas Moss and hoped that his appointment 'will be satisfactory to United States authorities.' E.R. Hopkins of External Affairs tartly reminded National Defence that Canada was a sovereign country and that United States approval was unnecessary.[13]

After establishing Puddicombe's team in Hong Kong, Oscar Orr consulted with the British high commissioner in Singapore and then travelled on to Tokyo. When the Canadians arrived in May 1946, the trials were already well under way. The War Crimes branch had been organized in March 1945, and by December of that year the commanding officer of the 8th army, Lieutenant-General Robert L. Eichelberger, had appointed military commissioners to conduct trials. The legal division of SCAP (Supreme Commander for the Allied Powers) had 36 prosecution officers and anticipated 300 trials involving 500 accused. The final figures would be double that. Two hundred suspects were in custody, many of them having voluntarily surrendered when their names appeared on wanted posters.[14] 'We had to use American rules of evidence,' Orr recalled, 'which was somewhat disconcerting to me because I was trained in the different English common law.'[15] One of his first tasks would have nothing to do with war criminals.

Hundreds of Japanese Canadians were being forced back to Japan and Orr was dispatched, as a feeble humanitarian gesture, to assist them upon arrival. Another Canadian soldier had also volunteered to help the repatriates. Tadashi Ode, a Nisei interpreter attached to the International Military Tribunal, tried to help the dazed newcomers. Most seemed overcome by their own misfortune and were oblivious to the two Canadian soldiers who met them in Yokohama.[16]

The Canadians accustomed themselves to American ways and fitted themselves into the ongoing war crimes process. Because the victims were a mixture of British, Dutch, Canadians, and Americans, it was never possible for the Canadians to monitor a case exclusively of national concern. For example, when Kozaku Hazama was charged for failure to discharge properly his duty as commandant of Oeyama camp, the charge sheet included a variety of Canadian and American victims. For that reason, Oscar Orr was delegated as assistant prosecutor. In one charge, Joseph Delorme of the Winnipeg Grenadiers deposed that an American named 'Swede' was viciously beaten by a guard and the beating stopped only when Delorme stepped in to argue that Swede was ill. However, the American was barely conscious and died later that afternoon.[17] While severe beatings were common at Oeyama, occasionally prisoners were subjected to the 'bamboo treatment,' which forced a man to squat for long periods on a bamboo pole while holding a weighted pole behind his back. The prisoner had to remain in this excruciatingly painful position until he collapsed unconscious.

The commandant seemed to be an unlikely war criminal. Kosaku Hazama was a thirty-eight-year-old university-educated economist who had worked for the municipality of Osaka until drafted in 1942. Hazama's crime, the prosecutors argued, was not that Oeyama had little food or medicine but that the commandant stole portions of the pitiful rations that were supplied. While he may not have personally beat the prisoners, his crime was permitting the guards to do as they pleased, in the 'utter and sheer neglect of the duties as camp commander.'[18] In a strange twist, Hazama's trial was almost a mirror image of the Winnipeg court martial of Harvey and Tugby. By early 1944 camp discipline was under the control of the Big Four, or the 'White Nips,' and this left the prosecution in a quandary, for in effect they were charging a Japanese for war crimes committed by Allied troops. Compounding their dilemma was the result of the Winnipeg court martial, which, the prosecution conceded, 'might be said to be disappointing.' Nevertheless, the prosecution was determined to hold Hazama guilty for the crimes of British and Canadian collaborators. For his part, Hazama maintained that self-government was the prisoners' idea and, if anything, he had tried to restrain the more violent NCOs such as Harvey.[19]

Hunger, cruelty, and degradation had been the standard for the prisoners at Oeyama and the other camps. William Allister recalled the lot of the prisoner, or *furyo*: 'The despised *furyo*, the lowest of the low ... Sweating in the unrelenting summer sun or shivering through bleak winter days with all our worldly clothing on our backs and nothing inside to heat us ... Sneaking into garbage cans, diving for discoloured butts, chewing savagely on a much trodden orange peel.'[20] The men of Oeyama were to work till they died. Despite a bad heart, Pvt. Latvala was forced to carry wood. When he was unable to carry a full load uphill he was beaten until he could not get up. He died later that night.[21] Oeyama had the highest sickness rate and the thinnest workers in the Osaka area.

While Hazama was a monster in Allied eyes, his superior, Colonel

Sataro Murata, had assigned him to his post because he appeared 'mild and kind ... I consider him very fit for the job.'[22] An officer of Japan's War Information Bureau inspected Oeyama and thought that it was properly run.[23] Hazama testified that, when the prisoners had first arrived in Japan, he had allowed them to rest and tried to get them adequate food. Indeed, he had so improved their quarters that local residents complained that he was coddling the *furyos*. It was Hazama who reminded the factory guards that they were supervising prisoners of war and that under international law they had no right to strike them. Aghast at the numerous affidavits detailing the regular beatings at his camp, Hazama exclaimed, 'These incidents were not reported to me at all.' He denied ever seeing the bamboo treatment and testified that he had even disguised himself as a civilian to spy on his guards.[24]

The commission accepted none of it. The guards had a manic obsession with beatings that Hazama did nothing to control. Red Cross parcels had been withheld from the men and the prosecution even located civilians who had helped carry parcels to Hazama's house. He was sentenced to fifteen years of hard labour. As a safeguard against improper convictions or sentences, the Americans had provided that every case be forwarded to a review branch. There, the evidence would be gone through again and any suggested changes sent back to the judge advocate. In Hazama's case, the civilian reviewer concluded: 'By comparison with sentences imposed by other commissions on other accused war criminals, the sentence is extremely lenient. It is considered that the sentence imposed for his contribution to the death of prisoner Latvala, for beatings, abuses and mistreatments of other prisoners of war is inadequate.' The judge advocate also thought that 'such a low sentence as was returned under the facts in evidence bespeaks a serious miscarriage of justice,' but he grudgingly confirmed the fifteen-year sentence.[25]

Indelibly military in origin, the commissions increasingly came to reflect civilian standards of justice. By September 1947 the prosecution division had fifty lawyers, only two of whom were military officers. The defence division provided approximately forty lawyers, five of whom were military personnel. So conscientious were the defence counsel that the accused regularly sent their families to the defence offices to express their thanks.[26] The importance of displaying even-handed justice was apparent in the case of Itchisaku Kojima.

The Rinko Coal Company, a primitive transfer station for Manchurian coal, was directed by Kojima and staffed by foremen known as *honchos*, most of whom 'were just ornery and mean while still others were plainly psychotic.'[27] Canadians filed affidavits that they worked all day at the coal docks on two small cups of rice and a cup of stew. Warrant Officer Victor Myatt observed that the camp commandant, Masato Yoshida, seemed to fear Kojima and that 'both of these officers drove sick, and dying men out to work to satisfy the demands of the civil authorities.'[28] Rest days were infrequent, not more than one a month and sometimes less. Hellish as these conditions were, Kojima's defence pointed out that he directed only the coal operations and had no direct control over the men. The charge that he mistreated Canadian Sergeant James Martin by making him work barefoot while ill and thereby contributed to his death was without proof for Martin had died many months after he stopped working at Rinko.[29] 'There is no doubt about it – this was a horror camp,' argued Kojima's lawyer. 'But, is there one shred of evidence that this was due to failure of the accused or that he had something to do with housing? Of course not.' Without his counsel having to present any evidence, Kojima was acquitted on all counts. While this may have been proof of the commission's objectivity, to the survivors it was poor justice. They remembered Kojima as a merciless taskmaster, directly in control of the Rinko works and indirectly responsible for many deaths. For them, his acquittal was an unforgivable error.[30]

Occasionally, the Americans thought that Orr took impartiality to extremes. For example, there was the case of Ed Shepherd of the Royal Rifles who had been jabbed by a bayonet after he had attacked a guard. While the Americans insisted on a prosecution, Orr responded, 'What do you expect. Here's a prisoner of war, hits a guard, gives him a good poke in the nose, and the guard pushes his bayonet. What would you expect?'[31] Shepherd agreed to drop the charges.

Perhaps even more than the German trials, the Japanese trials showed the cultural chasm between the triers and the accused. In Europe, it had been difficult to understand the pervasive Nazi control of German life. In Japan, the commissions were faced with accused motivated since early youth by the Bushido code of absolute obedience and disdain for everything that was not Japanese. Occasionally, the commissions got a glimpse of the harsh reality that motivated every Japanese soldier.

Of all the brutal guards at Niigata camp, Kanemasu Uchida, 'Pete the Tramp,' was foremost in Canadian minds. 'He was a very strict disciplinarian,' a prisoner recalled. 'Right from the start and without delay he commenced beating the Prisoners of War for the least infringement of Camp regulations.' When some men were discovered with stolen beans in their pockets, Uchida took a bamboo sword and struck each man over the head. After work, men were forced to drill on the parade square and if anyone made a mistake 'Uchida would beat him with his fist, sword or stick, or anything he could get his hands on.'[32] The propensity of Japanese guards to beat prisoners, with little or no provocation, was the cause of scores of deaths. As R. John Pritchard has observed, 'beatings were more prejudicial to a victim's survival than any other means which the Japanese employed to punish or torture people. Quite simply, far more individuals died from being beaten than from any other technique.'[33] And Uchida was one of the worst. The prosecutor described him as 'a cruel, constant and brutal beater.'[34]

Near the end of the trial, the defence raised the accused's obligation under the Japanese military code, the 'Imperial Precepts to the Soldiers and Sailors of Japan,' to obey all orders. However, the prosecution turned this to its advantage by pointing out the code's admonition to all soldiers: 'To be incited by mere impetuosity to violent action cannot be called true valor. The soldier and sailor should have sound discrimination of right and wrong, cultivate self-possession, and form their plans with deliberation. Never to despise an inferior enemy or fear a superior, but to do one's duty as a soldier or a sailor – this is true valor.'[35] It was a duty, the prosecutor argued, that Uchida had failed to perform and he deserved the death sentence as a result.

Uchida benefited from a vigorous defence in which his counsel pointed out that 'the mistreatments were only the result of age old Japanese customs. It is my regret that they are not occidental, but, in Japan, it is regarded as a method of education and discipline. In the matter of discipline, the mistreatments and severity in the Japanese army was an established custom.'[36] And if laws are sand, such customs are rock. There was evidence that Uchida had warned prisoners against breaking the rules and that one beating resulted from a prisoner attempting to punch him. Even a Canadian medical officer felt that Uchida's conduct was 'just according to his training and army experience.'[37] Uchida was not executed; the reprieve was sanctioned by the case reviewer who felt that 'there is much in the record to show provocation by the prisoners of war.' In reflecting on these cases, Orr recognized the lack of common reference points. 'Beating a prisoner was common in the Japanese Army ... They thought nothing at all of cracking a private soldier over the head with a club, or the flat of a sword ... But of course, we didn't.'[38]

As a public display of justice for war criminals, the Japanese trials were a dismal failure for they passed almost without comment in Canada. This indifference was all the more unfortunate given that Canadians took a significant part in one of the major trials. Niigata camp, on Japan's west coast, had received its first 300 prisoners (276 of them Canadians) in September 1943. In a time of acute hunger and brutality, Niigata was especially horrific and men were expected to do hard labour with little food or rest. One of the survivors, Ken Cambon, remembered that men were constantly ill with diarrhoea: 'Many were so weak they could hardly stand. Some fell and were carried away. Slowly they filed by, that is if they were allowed to because many were intercepted by a Japanese guard or Honcho who slugged them with a stick.'[39] The commandant, Lieutenant Masato Yoshida, was described as a 'small, squat, ugly man' who welcomed the new arrivals by screaming at them that they would stay at the camp forever and work or die. Most considered him quite mad.[40] Guards Katsuyasu Sato and Hyoichi Okuda and medical orderly Takeo Takahashi were all accused of mistreating prisoners. Their trial began on 25 September 1946 and would be prosecuted by a Canadian, Captain John Boland. Another Canadian, Colonel Thomas Moss, sat on the commission as the 'Law Maker' (the senior legal-judicial officer).

Boland's opening address to the commission was not auspicious. 'A very considerable number of deaths' had been caused, he noted, 'by failing to provide adequate and proper food.' This was far too general for the commission president, who interrupted him: 'I have never heard of a commission on which I have sat has there been a finding that there was contribution to the death of an unnamed and unspecified number of prisoners of war.' When further pressed on the point, Boland insisted that it was impossible to be specific. Sato's beatings had been continuous, a 'daily occurrence,' and severe; 'and by these beatings and by threats of beatings,' he forced men 'who were in a debilitated condition to work.'[41] Unlike the prosecution in other trials, Boland had a number of witnesses at hand, including a Niigata survivor, Warrant Officer Robert Manchester. He testified that before every work detail Sato would see each sick man and, if he could detect nothing wrong with him, pull him from his bed: the prisoner 'would be kicked in the parts of the body he had indicated as being ailing him; mainly in the stomach' and then forced to go to work.[42] At the Rinko coal yard, men would be paraded and counted and then would work barefoot until the end of the day. Before leaving they would be given a speech by the yard manager, but since none of them understood Japanese the inspiring words were lost. Manchester also described how an American prisoner, Gerald Titman, was punished for stealing a rice box. Although temperatures were below freezing, he was tied up to a post outside the guardhouse and left there overnight. On the second day he escaped, but he was recaptured and again tied to the post until he died of exposure.[43] Similar treatment was given to a Canadian soldier, Private Mortimer of the Royal Rifles, for stealing a tin of bully beef. For ten days he 'remained attached to the post all the time. The Japanese used to beat him regularly every day with their rifle butts.' After ten days his feet and hands were frozen and turning black. He was brought to the camp hospital where he died of his injuries.[44]

Another Royal Rifle, Lloyd Doull, filed an affidavit identifying Yoshida as a sadist 'responsible for the deaths of many of our boys,' and he recalled the prolonged deaths of Titman and Mortimer as being carried out right outside Yoshida's window.[45] The bulk of the prosecution was made up of affidavits such as Sergeant Doull's, and this prompted the defence to object. In the early days of the trials, the use of affidavits might have been justified, they argued, but 'the hostilities have ceased for well over a year and the need for the use of affidavits has passed.' The commission disagreed. 'This is a waste of time,' the commission president interjected. 'You only want to get it on the record. You certainly don't expect it to be taken seriously.' Colonel Moss added to the colloquy that, if the defence did not like the rules, they could complain to SCAP or General Douglas MacArthur but until then 'we are able to take anything we think of probative value.'[46] SCAP regulations for war crimes trials were remarkably similar to the Canadian regulations; affidavits were admissible notwithstanding the defence's inability to cross-examine on them.

One difficulty in trying so many defendants was that their defences were liable to conflict. Mid-way through the trial the lawyers for the guards asked that their case be separated from Yoshida's. They intended to erect a defence based on obedience to superior orders, but the linking of the guards' case to that of Yoshida prejudiced this approach. However, before the end of the trial, it was determined that Yoshida was insane and his part of the case was discontinued.

The guard Sato's defence was handicapped by the mass of material proving his wanton brutality. Sato was remembered as a 'sadist who was only happy if he was beating or shouting at some unfortunate ... On the slightest suspicion he would unmercifully beat some poor soul into semiconsciousness. Even his fellow *honchos* were afraid of him.'[47] His conviction was one of the few certainties of these trials, for even the case reviewer concluded that 'obedience to orders is not in itself a justification for criminal acts ... The beatings and torture inflicted by the accused upon the prisoners of war were of such a nature that any man of ordinary understanding should have seen that they were illegal.'[48] Sato was sentenced to forty years hard labour. Other cases were more problematic. While the Niigata prisoners held a hearty dislike for the medical orderly Takahashi,[49] he pleaded that he had dispensed the few medical supplies available to him. He begged the commission to consider that he had no control over which prisoners were excused from work or which ones received medicine.[50] Nevertheless, he was also convicted and sentenced to fifteen years. The other guard, Okuda, was given thirty-three years in prison. The *Yoshida* trial had been a long, exhausting process lasting almost six months. Even though it had been given no publicity in Canada, some measure of justice had been administered to the officers and guards who had so egregiously broken standards of basic humanity.

As a measure of National Defence's concern about the prosecutions, Wing Commander Birchall was flown back to Japan in late 1947 to testify at the trial of Ushioda Hiroshi. Birchall confirmed that he had been responsible for the beatings that had been common at Sendai camp No. 4. Hiroshi was convicted and sentenced to ten years' imprisonment.[51] While he was present to see that justice was done, it was difficult for Birchall to make the distinction between justice and revenge: 'All I could think about was what would it be like if they had won the war, and the treatment we would have received.'[52] It was Birchall's observation that MacArthur was set on appeasing the Japanese by releasing as many of the accused as possible. 'What he did do was he brought in all the sharpest Chicago lawyers he could get. They were there on the defence. They had all the facilities, everything.' In contrast, Birchall protested, 'the people on the prosecution team had *nothing*. We couldn't even get a doctor to testify on our behalf.' After a successful prosecution of an entire set of camp guards, Birchall was ordered deported from the American zone. 'The rest of the prosecution team, they were out within a week. They fired the whole God damn bunch of them – old MacArthur did ... he did not want to ruffle the feathers of the Japanese.'[53]

MacArthur did appear to view the trials as matters of policy and not of justice. In his *Reminiscences*, he reported being pleased that the Japanese seemed impressed by the fairness of the proceedings and this advanced the policy of rendering Japan a democratic, law-abiding state.[54] Ultimately, the punishment of the minor war criminals would be extremely lenient and more indicative of an anodyne spirit of generosity than of the promised exemplary justice. Those who had carried out medical experiments on unsedated prisoners or who had cut off the heads of prisoners for sport received short prison terms. Of the 5,700 'B' and 'C' class criminals, only 920 were executed, a paltry figure compared to the hundreds of thousands who had died while in captivity.[55]

As the trials wore on, cooperation between the Allied powers seemed to flag for there were chronic problems of overlapping jurisdiction. Orr advised Ottawa that General Renusuke Isogai, then in a Tokyo prison, was wanted in Hong Kong 'as the Canadian interest in the case was very strong' because of his responsibility in the operation of prison camps. However, the Chinese also wanted him and the British seemed unwilling to press a counter-claim. Orr urged Ottawa to direct the Americans to send Isogai to Hong Kong.[56] An External Affairs memorandum noted that Isogai, one of the leading militarists, had planned the annexation of northern China and had undoubtedly directed the mistreatment of Canadian prisoners. On the other hand, British interest in a man who had struck 'a blow against British prestige in the Far East' outweighed Canadian concerns, and it was considered inadvisable 'for the Canadian government to run the risk of pinching its fingers in the tension which exists between the British and Chinese governments over the status of Hong Kong.' In the margins, External Affairs secretary E.R. Hopkins simply directed that the Isogai correspondence be filed.[57]

By the spring of 1947 Orr was becoming infuriated that so many suspects in Canadian cases were being sent to Singapore, where they were out of reach of Canadian influence. Takeo Kambiyashi, for instance, had killed three RCAF men, but he had been transported to Singapore and so Puddicombe's detachment could not supervise his trial. 'There is apparently some very poor co-ordination throughout the whole of the British war crimes administration,' Orr complained.[58] Despite these frustrations, Japanese were put on trial throughout Asia for the murder of Canadians and both British and Dutch authorities would execute the killers of RCAF prisoners.[59]

While these trials were taking place, the Canadian public was uninformed and possibly indifferent to the fact that justice was slowly being handed down in the Far East. However, the trial of the major war criminals, the architects of the Pacific War, would take place in the full light of the world's press, and because Canada had the foresight to send men of considerable ability to this trial, it would play a larger role than its power might have warranted.

Perhaps even more than Nuremberg, the Tokyo war crimes trial was an international phenomenon. Eleven countries, some only on the cusp of nationhood and most of the rest (including Canada) not being numbered among the great powers, had come together to judge the leaders of an aggressor state. Though Japan's instrument of surrender had vested all authority in Douglas MacArthur as the supreme commander for the Allied powers, he indicated as early as November 1945 that he wished to convene 'military courts from an inter allied panel to try Far Eastern war criminals of all grades.'[60] MacArthur's special proclamation of 19 January 1946 creating the International Military Tribunal for the Far East (IMTFE) ensured the multilateral nature of the court. It would include not only the countries who were party to Japan's surrender but India and the Philippines as well.[61]

Class 'A' suspects, those who had planned the war and broken treaties, would be tried by the IMTFE. On 8 January 1946 the Canadian cabinet considered whom to appoint to the Tokyo tribunal and, at first, Justice J.A. Hope of the Ontario Supreme court seemed the likely candidate. However, Chief Justice Robertson of Ontario objected, and Hope (much to his displeasure) was bypassed in favour of a Quebec judge, E. Stuart McDougall.[62] McDougall had served with the Princess Patricia's Canadian Light Infantry in the First World War. Wounded in that conflict, he had risen to the rank of major by 1918. During the 1920s and 1930s he had an exceptional legal career in Montreal, and for a short time he served as treasurer in the provincial Liberal government of Joseph-Adélard Godbout. He had been a judge only since 1942 and, as one American observed, 'his complete lack of background' for the Tokyo tribunal initially 'raised eyebrows in both Japan and Canada.' However, if he was appointed because of his links with the Liberal Party, McDougall was a jurist of rare ability and Americans would later fondly recall him as 'one of the better judges at Tokyo.'[63]

In addition to a judge, Canada was also entitled to send an assistant prosecutor to the International Prosecution Staff (IPS). Brigadier Henry Nolan, the vice-judge advocate general, would be Canada's contribution. As later events would show, this capable officer was to be a valuable asset to the prosecution. The IPS may have needed all the help it could get, for the chief prosecutor, Joseph B. Keenan, had no background for the task at hand. 'Joe the Key' was a flamboyant figure in Franklin D. Roosevelt's inner circle, but he had few pretensions as a trial lawyer. Many of those from both the prosecution and the defence did not feel that he measured up to the job.[64] Perhaps as a result of Keenan's unfamiliarity with international affairs, individuals from smaller powers such as Canada came to the fore. Nolan, for example, was respected for his knowledge of international law and even among Americans he was 'widely considered among the top legal minds in the IPS.'[65]

The most pressing task facing the prosecutors was the preparation of the indictment. The circumstances in which Japan had entered the war varied widely from those in Germany and almost defied unravelling. As A.S. Comyns Carr, the British assistant prosecutor noted, 'the whole Japanese situation is infinitely more complicated than the German for the purposes of a prosecution, as all the politicians, soldiers and sailors were all squabbling and double-crossing one another all the time.'[66] By 14 March, Nolan had reported back to External Affairs on the state of the indictment. 'I have been engaged in making a study of Treaty Violations which I find not interesting,' he wrote, adding that the job was a forbidding one. 'You can understand that with the mass of evidence and documents complete with the language difficulty the preparation of an indictment is a tremendous task.'[67] Not only did Nolan have to make sense of a mass of treaties, he also had to understand how the Japanese government operated. This last objective was rendered almost impossible by the destruction of all Japanese administrative documents just before the occupation. It was another Canadian who, perhaps unintentionally, provided the key evidence. Herbert Norman, the civilian chief of research and analysis in SCAP's counterintelligence corps, was reviewing the dossiers of likely class 'A' war criminals. He strongly urged the arrest of Marquis Koichi Kido, a principal confidant of Emperor Hirohito. Shortly after Kido's arrest, prosecutors were amazed to find that he had kept a detailed diary from 1930 to 1945 which was almost a complete blueprint of Japan's plans for conquest. Here at last was an authoritative record on which to build a case for the imperial war conspiracy.[68]

While the prosecutors, most of whom were Americans, may have originally focused on the Japanese attack on Pearl Harbor, it became clear that the plans for aggression extended back to 1928. The various counts detailed Japan's victims, including count 11, where it was alleged that since 1928 all the defendants had 'planned and prepared a war of aggression and a war in violation of international law, treaties, agreements and assurances, against Canada.'[69] Appendix B of the indictment, probably the work of Nolan, was a detailed compilation of broken treaties. Since 1899 Japan had been party to agreements to settle disputes without force, and the Nine-Power Treaty of 1922 had obliged it to respect the sovereignty of China. All of these guarantees were broken while Japan gave continual assurances that it had no warlike ambitions. The indictment became a landmark of international law for the twenty-eight defendants (including fourteen generals and Hidecki Tojo, the wartime prime minister) were charged with the murder of combatants and civilians through the initiation of 'unlawful hostilities.' Aggressive war ceased to be a matter of policy and became a criminal act.

Stressing the international aspect of Tokyo (as opposed to the restricted four-power tribunal at Nuremberg), the Associated Press featured a photograph of the American judge, John P. Higgins, the Dutch judge, B.V.A. Röling, and Canada's McDougall leaving California for Japan.[70] When he arrived in Tokyo, McDougall was disappointed to learn that the indictment was far from ready. The seniority of the judges had also proven to be something of a problem, for IMTFE's president, Sir William Webb of Australia, decided to depart from the instrument of surrender and assign priority of place 'to suit his own convenience.' As a result, Canada was demoted below France and the Netherlands. It was a small point but hardly reassuring, and McDougall thought 'the President [Webb] is a little bit shaky.'[71]

It is not the intention here to detail the events of the Tokyo trial. Canada's role was a small one and its influence limited to a few key individuals. In the early going, Webb seemed more than a little 'shaky' as he petulantly refused to listen to a defence lawyer and was upset when an interpreter asked him to slow down. The significance of the issues finally came into focus when defence lawyer Ichiro Kiyose objected to the indictment and the creation of 'crimes against peace.' None of the leading texts in international law considered the planning of a war to be a crime, and when Japan accepted the Potsdam terms for surrender there had been no mention of new law being applied to the vanquished.[72] Keenan's bombastic response was to ask if the Allies were to be stopped from bringing to justice those who had shed 'incalculable quantities of blood.' All preliminary motions were dismissed and the trial proceeded.

In his opening address, Keenan argued that there was no justice when 'transgressors in the high place of a nation, who bring about these international tragedies, remain unpunished.' The shambling men in the dock had initiated wars, wars they knew would result in massive loss of life. It was left to Brigadier Nolan to outline how the Japanese had come to this state. He described the development of the imperial tradition and its subordination to the military. After the Meiji Restoration in 1868 Japan developed a rudimentary Parliament but, even under this constitution, the government was heavily influenced by the military. The cabinet itself consisted of concentric power rings, being really a double cabinet with the premier nominating most ministers except for the ministers of war and navy who were appointed by their respective services. For two days, Nolan outlined this convoluted system of government and concluded that after the restoration there was 'in Japan an absence of an effective system of responsibility of Government to the people' and that the constitution served the purpose of stilling popular clamour for democratic rule while 'power was retained in the hands of a small group of personal advisers around the Throne.'[73] Even beyond the constitution was another world of military cliques who jostled each other for power. While at Nuremberg the lines of Nazi responsibility were relatively clear, in Tokyo blame could be as wide or as narrow as the observer wanted it to be.

Evidence at the trial revealed that the 1931 war with China was the result of a plot among the officers of the Manchurian army. Despite protests from the civilian government, the conflict widened until military cliques were effectively directing Japan's war of aggression.[74] Any civilian politician who dared to oppose them risked assassination. By the fall of 1946, the trial had moved on to examine the Japanese slaughter of prisoners and civilians in conquered territories. Even though Japan had not ratified the 1929 Geneva Convention, the Japanese government had communicated through neutral powers that it would apply the convention's terms.[75] Nevertheless, witnesses established that after the fall of Singapore 5,000 civilians were massacred. Japanese troops broke into the Alexanadra Hospital and bayonetted a soldier undergoing surgery and then killed the surgeon and his staff. The 200 wounded in the hospital were all taken out and shot. The Japanese then embarked on one of their cruelest atrocities, the construction of the Siam-Burma Railway. Approximately 50,000 Allied prisoners and 250,000 Asian slave labourers were driven unmercifully with little food or medicine. It was estimated that 27 per cent of the prisoners and half of the Asians died building the railway. By December 1946 the prosecution's case had advanced as far as the battle of Hong Kong. It was a tale of such numbing brutality that it differed only in detail from those that had preceded it.

Nolan took over the prosecution's case and proceeded to call one witness, Captain James Barnett, the chaplain of the Royal Rifles. On Christmas morning 1941 he was working at St Stephen's College Hospital in Hong Kong. At about 6:00 A.M. he saw five Japanese soldiers storm in and immediately bayonet 15 or 20 men as they lay in their beds. The remaining staff and patients, the latter numbering about 160, were herded into a storeroom. On two occasions a soldier was taken out and his screams were later audible. Barnett was released later that day and toured the hospital: 'I found the two men who had been taken out of our room, their bodies were badly mutilated, their ears, tongues, noses and eyes cut away from their faces; about 70 men, wounded men, killed by bayonet in their beds; many more men seriously wounded than they were ... I found the commanding officer of the hospital, together with his adjutant, down on the ground floor, their bodies were very badly mutilated.'[76]

Concerned about seven missing nurses, Barnett scoured the hospital and found four of them. All had been repeatedly raped and one had been forced to lie on two dead bodies as Japanese soldiers raped her. The other three nurses had been bayonetted to death after being raped. After his arrival at the North Point camp, Barnett was given an insight into Japanese orders. Lieutenant Honda drove him to the hospital and on the way they talked over the battle. Honda recalled a Canadian medical officer, a Captain Banfill, and that he was the one man spared when the order was given to kill all the prisoners at an aid station. Unknown to Barnett, Honda had just described the massacre at the Salesian Mission.[77] At North Point conditions deteriorated, especially when Colonel Tokunaga demanded that the prisoners sign oaths not to escape. Those who refused (such as Barnett) were sent to Stanley jail where they were tortured until they complied. Because the Japanese demanded large work parties to extend the Kai Tak airport, ill, malnourished men, some carried on stretchers, were sent off to work. The men were called out at 4:00 A.M. and returned about 7:00 P.M. When a diphtheria epidemic broke out in October 1942, three or four Canadians were dying every day. The medical officer, Dr Saito, said that there was no serum, even though a Japanese interpreter managed to smuggle serum into the camp. For this humane act, the interpreter was sent to prison.[78]

Nolan's examination of Barnett was the only time that Canadians have presented a case before an international military tribunal. However, the event was ignored in Canada. There was no press coverage, and no concern about the horror of the St Stephen's College massacre. The survivors coped as best they could with their traumatic memories, and the public put these unpleasant, faraway events out of mind. For all its impact on Canada, the Tokyo trial was truly a waste of effort. But for its impact on Japan, the trial did seem to impart a significant benefit. Barnett's evidence was described in detail in the Nippon *Times* as this 'damaging testimony under direct interrogation by Canadian prosecutor Brigadier Henry Nolan.'[79] Journalist Arnold Brackman noticed that the daily accounts of the trial were being avidly read and that sordid details of military coups hatched at drinking parties or at bordellos were revelations to the Japanese public.[80] It was essential, the Tokyo *Shimbun* explained, to 'dispel militarism from the minds of the people.'[81] Now the average Japanese was finding out how badly their leaders had misled them. If nothing else, the Tokyo trial had recorded historical events and illustrated to the Japanese the folly of their wartime leadership.

Yet the trial was not without its absurdities. Pursuant to the court's charter, the proceedings had been conducted exclusively in English and Japanese until, at Soviet insistence (and with the availability of an unused channel on the interpreters' intercom), simultaneous translation into Russian was also allowed. When the French prosecutor, Robert Oneto, began his case, he made it clear that he would speak in French. On 28 September 1946 McDougall learned of this and warned Webb that it would be contrary to the charter. When Oneto next rose in court, the defence objected to the irregularity of his speaking in French and Webb commanded him to proceed in English. When Oneto pressed his argument in French, an outraged Webb exclaimed, 'He is speaking French again!' With wounded Gallic pride, Oneto responded that 'if I am not allowed to speak here in French in the name of the French Republic, I shall withdraw!' Instead, it was the judges who withdrew as Oneto, still shouting and waving his arms, held the podium. The following day tempers cooled. Oneto apologized, Webb withdrew his threat of contempt of court, and the trial proceeded in French.[82] The Soviets, however, could not resist a chance to disrupt a western ally. *Pravda* reported the Oneto incident under the headline 'Scandal in international incident in Tokyo' and reported that Canada's McDougall had opposed the use of French. This was confirmation, *Pravda* hinted, of the French language being persecuted in Canada.[83]

By January 1947, after almost 150 days, 4,000,000 words, and 2,000 exhibits, the prosecution rested. A vigorous defence would consume the rest of the year. Attempts were made to paint Japanese expansionism as merely the creation of a benevolent 'Co-Prosperity Sphere.' Cross-examiners would ask if the looting and enslaving of populations was a necessary part of their liberation. With one exception, the accused defended their role in the war and justified it as a struggle for national survival. Only the emperor's close adviser, Marquis Kido, agreed with the prosecutors that an army clique had sparked the war to the detriment of all Asia. Kido even conceded that the atomic bombing of Hiroshima and Nagasaki was a blessing, for without this display of overwhelming force the militarists would have insisted (as they had at Okinawa, where one-third of the civilian population perished) that the war go on until the Japanese race faced extinction. Speaking in defence of the militarists, ex-premier Hideki Tojo cited the American embargo against Japan as justification for war and expansion. To ensure Tojo's thorough cross-examination, Keenan had arranged for an American expert in the field, John W. Fihelly, to attend. But unable to step aside when the world press was watching, Keenan asked the IMTFE's indulgence to permit his participation. Webb angrily reminded him of the rule that, in order to keep the trial moving, only one lawyer could cross-examine. Keenan then decided to proceed on his own, and Fihelly, who had worked for months and come to Tokyo for nothing, stormed from the courtroom. According to the U.S. press, a cabal of stodgy judges had prevented Fihelly from doing his job.[84]

In a letter to Canada, McDougall gave a glimpse of what had really happened.'Keenan with his usual effrontery and vanity had to be on the Tojo case & he therefore asked us to permit him a few preliminary questions.' Since this was clearly not permitted, 'I insisted that he give a reason for thus breaking our rules.' Keenan responded that he was a 'busy man' and could do only a portion of the cross-examination. McDougall considered that 'his most pressing business and duty was to see that Tojo was properly examined.' The judges conferred and decided that only one lawyer could ask questions. Then, in a reference to Webb's ham-fisted control of the court, McDougall reported that, instead of merely stating this, 'our President with his usual facility for putting things the wrong way' told Keenan that he would have to do without Fihelly. The truth was that it was either Keenan or Fihelly and Keenan strode to centre stage.[85] As even one of his colleagues admitted, on this occasion 'Keenan was not up to it' but Tojo's assertions that the war had been forced on Japan were such an easy target that even Keenan could score points. That is, until he asked Tojo to agree that aggressive war was a war crime, a question that sparked defence objections and Webb's exasperated comment that 'we are getting no help from this type of cross-examination.'[86]

Shortly after Keenan's theatrics, Brigadier Nolan cross-examined Suzuki Teiichi, one of the young officers who had planned the invasion of China. Nolan's questions displayed a thorough understanding of the historical record and quickly rooted out attempts on Teiichi's part to minimize the guilt of his commander. The head of the Canadian mission in Tokyo reported back to Ottawa that 'I was much impressed by the skill and knowledge displayed by our prosecutor in cross-examining such a slippery witness.' Later, he was advised by McDougall that 'Brigadier Nolan's performance on this occasion was one of the high spots of the whole trial' and that his 'mastery of his brief' was in favourable contrast to that of the chief prosecutor.[87]

With all its absurdities and hyperbole, IMTFE had shown in painstaking detail how a war of aggression had been planned and put into operation. The exercise was particularly important to demonstrate to the Japanese how an international body could both record and illuminate the past and apply impartial justice to the guilty. But the trial was not an abstract process: seven of the leading militarists (including Tojo) were hanged in

December 1948, and all others were given lengthy prison terms. 'They [the Japanese leadership] brought ruin to their own people, and brought atomic energy into action as an instrument of war. If ever men were guilty, these are,' ran one of the few Canadian editorial comments on the Tokyo trial.[88] This pat understanding was probably common among those few who thought about the trial's significance.

While the birth of a son to Princess Elizabeth was widely reported in Canada, the fate of the men who had condemned millions of innocent people to death received little note. This massive indifference may be explained by the distance in time and place of the Pacific war; or perhaps Canadians had reason to be circumspect. In a thoughtful editorial the Ottawa *Citizen* saw Japan's war conspiracy as so vast and sinister as to make any punishment unsatisfactory. But Canada had no reason to be smug. For years it had ignored China's agony and profited from the sale of war material to Japan. The Tokyo trial was no proof that Canada had learned the lesson that aggressive war against one state threatens all.[89]

For revisionists, the Tokyo trial is an easy target because it is alleged that the Japanese were being condemned for defending themselves. It has even been suggested that the United States was at fault for the attack on Pearl Harbor; as one writer puts it, 'Japan was moved in significant measure by considerations of self-defence, and the attack was not without provocation.'[90] The real misfortune of the trial may have been that it did not go far enough and that many responsible individuals avoided prosecution. For all their significance, the Tokyo and Nuremberg trials were half-way revolutions that were more concerned with immediate justice to a few key individuals than in establishing new norms of international conduct. Indeed, the criminalization of aggressive war was soon subsumed by the diplomatic considerations of the Cold War. It seemed that there were compelling reasons to forget the past. Commenting on the 1947 Commonwealth Conference on Pacific Relations, the Winnipeg *Free Press* stated that it was impossible, 'in the home of the Winnipeg Grenadiers, [to] forget the savagery and contemptuous disregard of the rules of war with which Japan conducted her campaigns.' But the paper then added that 'revenge is an evil counsellor, and no one suggests that the settlement with Japan should be marred by feelings of hatred. That way lies madness.'[91]

Perhaps in the end there was a superabundance of pragmatism and too little justice. The meagre lessons of these trials were put away for half a century until the world again tried to deal in an objective way with criminals who plotted war and inflicted barbarism on the helpless.

11

'Siegergericht'

By 1948 the war crimes staff had returned to a prosperous country and stepped back into or began successful careers. George Puddicombe rejoined his Montreal law firm and in 1960 became a judge of Quebec's Queen's Bench. Judge McDougall returned to Canada in mid-1948 (two years later than he had planned) with an appreciation for Oriental art and an impressive collection of Japanese woodcuts. Of the European staff, Victor Collins, John Blain, and Maurice Andrew became outstanding lawyers in their communities. One of the translators, the urbane Raymond Robichaud, became the chief translator for the House of Commons. While the war crimes trials were soon only a memory for the men involved, the unfinished business left by the untimely winding up of their unit occasionally imposed itself on Ottawa.

In 1948 Johann Schumacher's widow, Emma, wrote to Ottawa stating that 'the approaching Christmas gives me the courage after nearly three years of waiting, to approach the Canadian Ministry of War with the prayer that it may at least let me know the place of burial of my husband.' The first reaction to this plaintive request was an overly cautious fear that the disclosure of war criminals' graves would create Nazi shrines. External Affairs overrode this inflated concern, located the grave, and advised Emma Schumacher.[1] The incident illustrated how sensitive the administration was to the manner in which Germans perceived war criminals. With accusations that the trials were not fairly conducted, that they were merely 'victor's justice' or *siegergericht*, the occupying powers were being put on the defensive by their former enemies. Allegations were raised that the war crimes trials were hopelessly biased and that the Allies' conduct had been no better than that of the men they had put on trial. And, of course, the Allies had never put their own war criminals on trial.

Before he left Europe, one of Bruce Macdonald's final tasks was to arrange for the transfer of Canadian war crimes files to the British. With cases such as Mouen and the Chateau d'Audrieu, Macdonald had little hope of charges ever being laid.[2] However, the British vigorously pursued the remaining cases. In June 1944 two Canadian airmen had been murdered after their capture near Hongue-Mare, France. In 1948 two Germans were convicted of murder and one, Harold Heyns, was sentenced to death *in absentia*; the other convict, Herbert Koch, was given eight years' imprisonment.[3] Another trial resulted in a death sentence for Hans Wilhelm Boesenberg for the killing of an RCAF flight-sergeant. Boesenberg's accomplice, Max Sommer, received a fifteen-year sentence.[4] On 30 May 1947 three Germans were convicted of the massacre of one British and three Canadian airmen at the town hall in Lüttringhausen. The crew had been held for three days until a Luftwaffe officer tried to take them to a prisoner-of-war camp. Before he could do so, a Nazi clique headed by Erich Wilinski and Hans Kühn shot the airmen on the town hall steps. Wilinski was hanged and Kühn was sentenced to twenty years' imprisonment. Four days later, the same court convicted Johann Lueftering of murdering an RCAF flying officer and condemned him to death. In July 1947 Rottenfuhrer Josef Frank was sentenced to eighteen years' imprisonment for his part in the killing of four unidentified Canadian prisoners.[5] British courts had proceeded with ruthless efficiency in dealing justice to those who had killed prisoners.

A special RAF investigative branch tracked down those responsible for the execution of fifty escaped flyers, including six Canadians, who had been part of the 'Great Escape' from Stalag Luft III. Sixty suspects were arrested and thirty-two were either executed or committed suicide. As in so many cases, the soldiers at the bottom of the command structure seemed to suffer the most severe penalties. One of the prime suspects, Gestapo chief Oskar Schafer, escaped punishment while the men who had carried out his orders were hanged.[6] Another fortunate beneficiary of the confusion at the end of the war was Graf von Reitzenstein. This officer, either alone or with Gerhard Bremer, had planned the first mass execution at the Chateau d'Audrieu. While von Reitzenstein had been seized by the

French after the war, he was released for lack of evidence. On 19 March 1952 the French military tribunal at Rennes issued a ruling discontinuing any investigation.[7]

When they left Europe, the Canadians were troubled that many of the Waffen SS's most despised killers had evaded prosecution. One of the most tragic consequences of Canada's hurried repatriation of the war crimes unit was that these cases would go unresolved. Macdonald was outraged to learn that two key witnesses, Jan Jesionek and Withold Stangenberg, had been sent back to Poland in early 1946.[8] The latter had been the only surviving eyewitness to Wilhelm Mohnke's deliberate execution of the three Canadian prisoners at Haut du Bosq, and his loss was a severe setback. In the meantime, Bernhard Siebken, the commander of Mohnke's 2nd battalion, was still in custody. August Henne, an army officer who had cooperated with the Canadians, recalled Siebken as a humane and popular officer: 'I liked him very much. He was a sympathetic type. He was very calm.'[9] Strangely enough, little attention was being paid to this quiet SS officer.

At one of the last interrogations, Macdonald talked at length with Siebken. An early and ardent Nazi, Siebken had joined the SS in 1931 and transferred to the Waffen SS in 1933. Siebken's battalion led the attack on Putoten-Bessin on 8 June and captured scores of prisoners. Macdonald confronted Siebken with evidence that on the morning of 9 June, at his own battalion's aid post, an officer had ordered the execution of all wounded Canadians. Siebken refused to believe it and thought that only ten or eleven prisoners had come in and that these had been sent along to division HQ. This was in accordance with instructions from Mohnke to send prisoners back for interrogation. When confronted with the fact that thirty-five prisoners captured by his troops had been massacred at Fontenay-le-Pesnel, Siebken appeared astonished: 'It was known that I would never allow such a thing to go on. I would like to say, however, that it became known that the contents of an order from General Eisenhower gave the impression that the Allies were not interested in taking prisoners.'[10] At one point in the battle Mohnke had stormed into Siebken's HQ, told him of Eisenhower's order that no prisoners be taken, and shouted to the officers present that 'we should adopt a similar policy. But I, myself, remained of the opinion that prisoners of war should be dealt with correctly.' Mohnke was an impulsive man who shortly thereafter telephoned Siebken ordering him not to send back so many prisoners. Siebken understood this to mean that Mohnke wanted the prisoners killed. Siebken replied that prisoners would be treated according to the laws of war and sent back to regimental HQ.

This telephone conversation might explain the mystery surrounding the massacre at Fontenay-le-Pesnel. Siebken had refused to kill prisoners at his command post and instead sent them along to headquarters as per the normal procedure. This may explain why the surviving prisoners recalled being held at various command posts until their column was marched to the German rear. They then saw an officer halt the column and berate the guards. This led to the herding of the prisoners into a field, the arrival of the execution squad, and the resulting massacre. Did Mohnke react to Siebken's refusal to kill captives at his battalion HQ by intercepting the column and personally seeing to their execution? Did he have another officer carry out this task for him? There would never be sufficient evidence to resolve responsibility for the massacre at Fontenay-le-Pesnel, the 'Canadian Malmédy,' but the fact remains that the Canadians had left Siebken's command unharmed and only later had become victims of a war crime.[11]

British investigations were increasingly focused on the killing of three wounded Canadians at Le Mesnil-Patry. The other incident at the aid post which was witnessed by Henri St Martin was never resolved. However, two orderlies who took part in the first incident, Heinrich Albers and Fritz Bundschuh, had survived the war and were in custody. Albers, who had acquired an English fiancée, seemed particularly cooperative. He even passed on an intimate conversation he had with Siebken in which the latter had instructed Albers to tell the orderly officer Dietrich Schnabel to put all the blame on Mohnke. After getting depositions from all accused, the Le Mesnil-Patry case came on for trial at the Curio Haus, Hamburg, on 21 October 1948.

The prosecution had one compelling witness in SS man Michael Wimplinger. On the stand he recounted how he and the other orderlies had brought in the wounded Canadians. The medical officer, Major Shütt, talked with the prisoners and learned that one was from Ottawa and had four children. The prisoners slept that night at the aid post and in the morning washed up and were given milk for breakfast. Later that morning, Dietrich Schnabel arrived in his staff car and Wimplinger heard him announce to Dr Shütt: 'The prisoners must be shot. Because of a lack of transport we can't transport them to the rear, and as the Battalion has already suffered heavy losses, we can't spare men from the front line to escort the prisoners back.'[12] Shütt protested that the prisoners were helpless wounded, but Schnabel replied that these were the orders from 'the commander.'

Bundschuh testified that the firing squad, composed of the three medical orderlies, had sprayed the Canadians with submachine-gun fire. Schnabel gave a *coup de grâce* to each victim. The fact of the execution was beyond question; the only issue was on whose command it took place. In his pre-trial deposition, Wimplinger stated that Dr Shütt told him that Schnabel had said that the order had been issued from Siebken: 'I remember for certain that he mentioned the name Siebken and did not use the expression "commander."' But not only was this double hearsay, the other witnesses to the damning statement were not so sure who the 'commander' was.

Their lawyer, Anna Oehlert, faced multiple difficulties of operating in English before a British military court. Adding to these problems were depositions given by her clients. On 12 August 1948, Siebken stated that Mohnke had never given any orders to shoot prisoners. He recalled their telephone conversation in which Mohnke had told him not to send back so many prisoners and had interpreted this as meaning that 'I should not send back prisoners individually or in small numbers but wait until I had collected a large number and then send them back.'[13] This completely contradicted the statement given to Macdonald in March 1946. While the statement exonerated Mohnke, Siebken must have understood that it left him completely liable for the subsequent crimes. This was reinforced by Schnabel's deposition. He recalled Mohnke's visit to the battalion HQ shortly after the D-Day landing when he had condemned the Allies for murdering German prisoners and ordered his officers to retaliate. He also recalled that 'a few hours after Mohnke had driven off again, Siebken repeated these remarks in the same manner. One could already take this as an order.'

Schnabel declined to testify at trial and instead defended himself through the evidence of an SS man, Willi Poehne, who swore that Mohnke had threatened Schnabel with a pistol to force him to conduct the executions. This was so patently in conflict with Schnabel's previous statement that it was not credible and Schnabel's fate was sealed. Siebken, on the other hand, presented a formidable defence. His lawyer, Oehlert, did not dispute that the executions had occurred, but she maintained that it was a valid reprisal for the murder of German prisoners. She presented an array of senior officers who swore that the Allies had already committed similar crimes. An intelligence officer, Colonel Meyer-Detring, claimed that he had twice received information that Canadian troops had not taken prisoners and that an order to that effect had been found in the pocket of a dead officer. On this note, Meyer-Detring had found the sentence 'no prisoners to be taken.'[14] Apparently, these notes were widespread for the

12th SS's chief operations officer, Hubert Meyer, also claimed to have discovered a similar note on a Canadian captain. But perhaps the most direct evidence of Allied war crimes came from a German victim. Count Clary-Aldrigen, an adjutant in the 130th Armoured Artillery Regiment, was captured on the morning of 8 June by a reconnaissance patrol of the British Inns of Court Regiment. Eight other soldiers, including the regiment's commander, Colonel Luxenburger, were also captured. The British tried to use the Germans as human shields to protect them on their drive back to their lines. However, when the Germans refused Luxenburger was beaten unconscious and tied to one of the armoured cars. All the others were machine-gunned and only Clary-Aldrigen escaped. He made his way to the aid post at Le Mesnil-Patry.[15] There he was treated by the battalion clerk Klödden and gave a complete report of the atrocity which was forwarded to Mohnke's HQ. These facts enabled Oehlert to argue that the shooting of the three Canadians was a reprisal permitted by military law.[16]

Siebken's defence then moved on to a more compelling argument – that he had never given the execution order at all. As he explained the sequence of events, Mohnke had come to his HQ after midnight on 9 June and his appearance had coincided with Dr Shütt's report of the three wounded Canadians. The enemy was not taking prisoners, Mohnke roared, and neither should we. He ordered all prisoners to be shot. Siebken refused and an angry confrontation erupted between the two. In Siebken's view, Mohnke was 'beyond all measures excited' and, turning his wrath on the more malleable orderly officer Schnabel, he ordered him to carry out the executions forthwith. Quietly observing this commotion at his desk, the battalion clerk Klödden confirmed that Siebken had refused the order to kill prisoners and said, 'I shall send back the prisoners in the proper fashion and I refuse to treat them in an unfair manner.' After this confrontation, Siebken decided to bypass Mohnke and complained directly to the operations officer, Hubert Meyer, that Mohnke was issuing illegal orders to kill prisoners. Meyer immediately tried to find out what was going on and issued instructions that all prisoners were to be sent to division HQ. Klödden further noted that over 400 prisoners passed through their HQ in the first days of the invasion. On the face of it, there seemed considerable doubt that Siebken was in any way responsible for ordering the executions. Nevertheless, both he and Schnabel were convicted and sentenced to hang. In deference to their youth and vulnerability to senior orders, the medical orderlies were acquitted.

While there was little doubt as to Schnabel's role, Siebken's guilt was more problematic. Ordering these executions would have been out of character and inconsistent with policies he regularly followed. His assertion that it was Mohnke who issued the fatal order was confirmed by several witnesses. Nonetheless, in one of the last military executions to result from the Second World War, both Schnabel and Siebken were hanged on 20 January 1949.

This trial, only the second one concerning the Canadians murdered after capture in Normandy and the only one in which SS men paid with their lives, met with profound indifference in Canada; there was neither official nor press coverage of the case. With stunning speed, Canadians had not only withdrawn from Europe but become coldly disinterested in the militarist evil that they had paid such a price in lives and sorrow to crush. They also seemed callously oblivious to the tragedy that had befallen European civilians. Three Canadian prisoners had been sent to the Auschwitz death camp on a work detail, and although they had been correctly treated, they reported the horrors they had seen.[17] In 1947 Poland conducted a trial detailing the slaughter of over 60,000 Polish civilians at Auschwitz and a Canadian representative was asked to attend. However, the Canadian chargé d'affaires in Warsaw confessed that he had no interest in seeing Auschwitz, for 'the special train provided was dirty, was delayed for hours, lacked comforts, sanitary conveniences, and decent accommodation for ladies.' In any event, he wrote, 'the Polish interest in this major Polish camp of cruelty and extermination is almost morbid; and bolsters up their rabid anti-German feelings,' but he added that 'an examination of the descriptions given at the trial is enough to justify that feeling.'[18] Had 60,000 Canadian civilians been slaughtered in similar circumstances, one wonders whether this official would have considered a prosecution to be 'morbid.' It was an inability to understand the depths of feeling created by the war crimes that seemed to steer Canadian policy into a benign forgetfulness.

One beneficiary of this forgetfulness was former brigadeführer Kurt Meyer. During his first weeks of confinement at Dorchester Penitentiary, Meyer had demanded to be treated as a prisoner of war until the warden, George Goad, impressed on him that he would get no preferential treatment. Meyer grumbled but soon came to accept the prison regime and his assigned tasks of cleaning cells and floors. Although he lived apart from the other prisoners in a hospital cell, he got along surprisingly well with other inmates. To Goad's astonishment, they asked if Meyer could lead them in daily exercises. Always a fanatic about conditioning, Meyer was exercising daily, and those prisoners who could keep up with his pace wished to take part.[19] During his almost monastic existence, Meyer steadily read books on military history and theory. He completed a review of the Caen-Falaise battles and contrasted the plodding tactics of the Canadian general Guy Simonds with the brutal but more effective Soviet plan of attack. On one remarkable occasion, Meyer was surreptitiously removed from Dorchester, issued a Canadian army uniform and taken to critique army manoeuvres.[20] His perceptive appraisals gained him the respect of Canadian officers.

Shortly after his arrival at Dorchester, unlikely guardians came to Meyer's aid. A German building contractor in Moncton, Fritz Lichtenberg, and his wife Ina, befriended him. The Lichtenbergs had no children and their concern for a countryman imprisoned in a foreign land impelled them to seek him out. In addition to providing moral support, Lichtenberg hired H.P. MacKeen, one of the finest lawyers in the Atlantic provinces, to represent Meyer. While there were no ready avenues of appeal, MacKeen waged a limited war in the press by encouraging writers to comment on the 'injustice' of Meyer's conviction.[21]

Not everyone was sympathetic. Clarence Campbell, now the commissioner of the National Hockey League, spoke in Montreal a year after the commutation of Meyer's sentence criticizing the 'maudlin sentiment' that had led to the reprieve. Reaching down to touch the two bulky volumes of testimony taken at Meyer's trial, Campbell concluded that there was no basis for a change in the sentence.[22] Two years later, reports were leaking to the press that sympathetic officers were working towards Meyer's release.[23] This sparked an impassioned letter from Campbell to Defence Minister Brooke Claxton decrying any additional leniency towards Meyer. The commutation itself was an 'unsatisfactory end [and] must be a Canadian responsibility, and I do not believe that it should be necessary to advertise our shortcomings.'[24] Some writers (perhaps at MacKeen's instigation) were eager to broadcast Canada's shortcomings. Foremost among them was Ralph Allen, a reporter who had covered the Meyer trial at Aurich. In a leading article in *Maclean's* in February 1950, Allen purported to review the trial and concluded that it fell short of the 'most precious principles of Canadian law.'[25]

Emotional and superficially compelling, Allen's account went over his reaction to the trial, how he had returned to Canada convinced that Meyer, this brilliant leader and warm family man, was innocent. However, when it came to specifics of the injustice, Allen was vague. He condemned the admission of sworn depositions and hearsay evidence and asserted that 'Meyer was tried according to rules which contradict some of the first and most precious principles of Canadian law.' Of course, had the rules of evidence not been altered, it is unlikely that any concentration camp personnel or war criminals would ever have been convicted. Atrocities do not occur within easy reach of the police but within enemy territory, and news of the crimes does not surface until long after the event. While evidence of Meyer's role had been obscured (at his own orders), that did not make his guilt any less compelling. Allen also tried to dismiss the one direct link between Meyer and the execution of the prisoners. In his view, Jesionek was a witness 'weakened to the verge of debility' who had acted with a death threat over his head. Moreover, he had 'frequently contradicted himself on both minor and major points of evidence.' Allen cited no examples. Omitted from his analysis was the fact that the death threat had occurred after Jesionek had given his statement condemning Meyer. Also left out was any reference to Jesionek's vigorous cross-examination, in which he had given a clear and consistent account of Meyer's role in the murder of prisoners. Despite the ingenuity of the article, it was remarkably void of substance or objectivity.

On 12 December 1950 Meyer formally petitioned the Justice Department for clemency. For the first time, he conceded that he had lied to his interrogators. But he was justified, Meyer argued, since the war was still in progress and 'if I had admitted that prisoners had been killed, such a statement by me would be used for propaganda purposes by the enemy.' Yet he still held to his own innocence. On Meyer's behalf, MacKeen argued that the regulations were void because they had no effect outside Canada and that in any event the penalties exceeded those contained in the War Measures Act. He also excoriated Parliament's 1946 passage of a statute to re-enact the War Crimes Regulations as an act of Parliament and to deem the act to have come into force in 1945.[26] To MacKeen, this enactment was preposterous, 'legalizing as it did 'an illegal criminal proceeding by an act of Parliament,' and was 'without precedent in English or Canadian history.' It seemed especially unfair that, unlike all other war criminals, and even common criminals, Meyer was imprisoned in a foreign land far removed from his family. Strangely enough, the petition closed with an offer by Meyer to serve in a Canadian or United Nations force so long as this did not conflict with his loyalty to Germany.[27] MacKeen and an associate, R.A. Ritchie, added a memorandum of law in which they argued that it was never the government's intention to permit the wide latitude in the admission of evidence to be 'used and abused to the extent which the record indicates.' Also, while the doctrine of command responsibility had been applied against Meyer, thus making him guilty for the acts of his soldiers, 'the procedure was of course not applied to Canadian commanders.'[28]

The petition and memorandum were referred to the cabinet's defence committee. By this time, there remained only a vestigial interest in war criminals but there was a confluence of concern between the departments of Defence and External Affairs about the need to build a strong West Germany. In early 1948 the British government announced that it had completed all investigations and that there would be no new trials after September.[29] By 1950 the Korean War had stirred Ottawa to reconsider its own priorities and resurrect its armed forces. The fear of Communist expansion spurred the St Laurent government to send Canadian troops to West Germany. Now regarded as an ally to be defended instead of a conquered country to be occupied, West Germany figured prominently in geopolitical considerations. As Lester Pearson recalled, 'the Korean War had increased our fears of Soviet military aggression; a contribution by West Germany to NATO forces and its acceptance of NATO responsibilities was held to be essential.'[30] In that light, the prisoner in Dorchester Penitentiary could be viewed as a potential asset instead of a war criminal.

At the cabinet defence committee meeting to review Meyer's case, the chief of the general staff, Lieutenant-General Guy Simonds, felt that 'Meyer had been convicted on the basis of evidence that he had known what his men were doing. This evidence, he thought, was far from conclusive.' Simonds knew the battlefield and believed that Meyer would have been far too occupied to bother about a few prisoners. 'Meyer would not have known that his men were killing prisoners,' Simonds said, then adding that 'he had always felt that the basis of Meyer's conviction ran counter to Canadian concepts of justice.'[31] To the generals, the mass of evidence that existed against Meyer seemed never to have existed. Prime Minister St Laurent agreed that Meyer should be returned to Germany but balked at an outright release. The cabinet also considered Ossenbach's case and St Laurent was the first to agree that he had 'merely been in a position of a bystander, might have been court-martialled if he had disobeyed and was therefore in a different category.' The under-secretary of State for External Affairs, Lester Pearson, also felt that Ossenbach should be released. Indirectly, these views seemed to cast considerable doubt on the validity of his initial conviction and sentence. In September 1951 the committee recommended that Meyer be transferred to the British military prison for war criminals at Werl, West Germany, and that Ossenbach be released. There were no mitigating circumstances affecting Johann Neitz's case.[32]

Given the public sensitivity to Meyer and the feeling that a mass murderer had barely escaped a firing squad, any surreptitious action should have been rejected outright. It was not. On 19 October, in the best cloak-

and-dagger tradition, Meyer was secretly removed from Dorchester. Two army officers arrived at the prison during the dead of night and dressed Meyer in a Canadian uniform. Using a window for an exit, the trio left in a getaway car.[33] The army and air force staff involved in the transfer (described by the *Globe and Mail* as a 'tintype melodrama') were sworn to secrecy and given immediate leave upon their return.

Repatriating Meyer reopened a wound that had not closed since the commutation of his death sentence. Mere hints of Meyer's release in February 1951 prompted Toronto MP David Croll to wonder whether the government was so eager to appease West Germany that 'ex-German generals, former Nazi leaders and war criminals are starting to roll off the allied amnesty lines like Fords in Windsor.'[34] Even the manner of Meyer's repatriation was cause for concern. Defence Minister Claxton moved to reassure the House of Commons that Werl prison had been designated a Canadian service prison and Meyer therefore remained technically under Canadian control. When asked if Meyer could be released without Canadian approval, Claxton emphatically responded 'No.'[35]

A chance event undid all these reassurances. Reporter Douglas How and a group of Canadian officers had travelled to Offleben to visit Kate Meyer. They were amazed to find the brigadeführer himself in the parlour playing with his children. Only a few days after his arrival at Werl, he had been granted an unescorted leave to visit his family. How was given a remarkably candid interview in which Meyer confessed that he was a fanatical nationalist when first sent to Canada but that now he realized that nationalism was dead. 'A united Europe is the only answer,' he told How. Chatting amiably amidst his children, and under a portrait of himself wearing the Knight's Cross, Meyer diplomatically gave a terse response to a query concerning Canadian generalship, merely noting that it was 'overly cautious.'[36]

The How interview had an explosive impact in Ottawa. The Opposition demanded answers from the government on how, only a few days after he had been mysteriously smuggled from the country, the nation's foremost war criminal was at home with his family. Obviously, Claxton had misled the people by stating that Meyer was still under Canadian control when prison authorities could, without consulting Canada, release him whenever they wished. A parliamentary assistant lamely explained that the government was trying to ascertain the rules of Werl prison and 'as soon as we have that information we will give it.'[37] One Liberal MP, George Cruickshank, expressed the profound rage felt by many Canadians that 'this rat' was allowed to go home 'when at least 18 Canadian mothers are regretting the deaths of their sons who were murdered.' The government's glaring ineptness caused the *Globe and Mail* to declare that 'they [cabinet] have never been honest about the Kurt Meyer case. They have never told Parliament what their policy was towards him.' Neither could the newspaper resist an opening to attack the Liberal administration: 'It is significant but not surprising that this latest controversy involves the Defence Department. Everything Mr. Claxton touches turns to trouble.'[38] The Meyer case suddenly loomed as dangerous as it had been during the days of the commutation. Once again, Ottawa was deluged by petitions of protest. Unions, legions, the families of the dead, all demanded that Meyer be returned to Canada to serve his full sentence.[39] To most Canadians, Kurt Meyer was the embodiment of Nazi evil and the least deserving of any leniency.

The fires were further stoked when the lawyers MacKeen and Ritchie issued a statement that the order-in-council authorizing the War Crimes Regulations 'mutilated the time honoured rules of evidence' and had to be legalized a year after the events.[40] Even the *Globe*, the newspaper that had bayed the loudest for Meyer's blood in 1946, now argued that the case should be reconsidered by the courts: 'As for the Germans with whom Canada is now trying to establish harmonious relations, they must be shown that justice is our only guide.'[41] 'What needs to be discovered now,' declared a Montreal newspaper, 'is whether or not our national hands are clean in this matter of Meyer ... what we need to do is to right a wrong, if wrong had been committed.'[42]

One person had no qualms about the validity of Meyer's conviction. After his discharge, Bruce Macdonald had resumed his profession in Windsor, Ontario. By 1950 that border city had become notorious for organized crime carried out openly on the city's streets. The police were considered corrupt or inefficient and the attorney general, Dana Porter, wanted a strong new man to bring order. Macdonald was appointed crown attorney and for the next several years he restored strict law enforcement in Windsor. Convictions, not plea bargains, became the objective of Macdonald's prosecution office.[43] On 3 December 1951 Macdonald and Clarence Campbell issued a statement that should have reassured the government. Despite all the misinformed comment, Meyer's conviction was perfectly legal; most of the evidence came from his own soldiers and 'was amply sufficient to justify conviction in any court,' and, moreover, the trial had been certified as correct by the army's chief legal officer. However, if Ottawa deemed it appropriate to release Meyer so that he could serve in a NATO army, then so be it. 'Nothing can be done for the 18

Canadian victims,' Macdonald said, 'but much can be done to spare the lives of other young Canadians which may be lost in another war ... I would gladly support his [Meyer's] complete release in these dangerous times for that reason alone.'[44]

In all the turmoil, the remaining prisoners seemed all but forgotten. The German embassy had also asked for remission of sentence for Neitz and Ossenbach. While Neitz would remain in prison, Ossenbach was released on 17 October 1951 pursuant to an order-in-council. It was not until the following February that reporter Douglas How uncovered this order-in-council among 500 others that had been tabled at that time and publicly disclosed the news that Canada had released a war criminal.[45] This latest revelation and the stealthy removal of Meyer added to public suspicion. 'Without reference to the reasons involved in the removal of Meyer from Canada to Germany, the complete release of Ossenbach ... the Government has not acted in a manner to inspire confidence,' editorialized the Montreal *Gazette*. 'All this secrecy in such matters seems inexcusable.'[46] Over and above the government's fumbling was the question of whether Meyer was guilty or not. 'This confusion of policy and interest in the Meyer case has created a great deal of confusion in Canadian minds,'[47] stated the Montreal *Herald*. But, in the end, it was pragmatism, not justice, that would guide Canadian policy.

The treatment of war criminals in a sovereign West Germany was a growing problem. Kühn, the soldier who had killed an RCAF prisoner, escaped from Werl in late 1952. While he was captured by German police and returned, the German Interior Ministry questioned the legality of arresting Allied war criminals who had never been convicted under German law.[48] By the 1950s all prosecutions of war criminals had been turned over to Germans. In one case that had the unpleasant odour of the Leipzig trials, Walter Schnautz was tried by a German court in 1953 for murdering a Canadian airman. Witnesses testified that he had boasted of killing the prisoner in revenge for the death of his girlfriend in an air raid. He denied this and asserted that another man had killed the prisoner. Acquitted owing to the lack of convincing evidence, Schnautz was set free. 'The handling of the case appears to have been unsatisfactory,' reported the Canadian embassy, but in fairness to the Germans it noted that Schnautz had been arrested twice by the Americans and once by the British and released on each occasion for lack of evidence.[49]

The delicate balance between resurgent German interests and residual Canadian rage over war crimes seemed to intersect when German Chancellor Konrad Adenauer visited Werl in June 1953. He talked with a number of generals, including Meyer, and told them that he was doing everything to secure their release. The previous April, Adenauer had visited Washington and Ottawa and asked for the creation of a tribunal to review the sentences. A memorandum from External Affairs noted that a statement by the German chief of protocol mentioning the 'importance of war criminals' was designed for 'German public opinion.' But Adenauer did not directly raise the issue since the German government had at last recognized that 'there was considerable feeling in Canada about these cases.'[50] Nevertheless, the idea of using an independent tribunal offered an intriguing way to create a buffer between the intractable Meyer problem and the Canadian government. This would be especially true if Canada's representative on the tribunal was an individual beyond political reproach.

Brigadier Sherwood Lett had served honourably in the First World War, and thereafter had a rising career in the British Columbia bar. Rejoining the army in 1939, he led the 4th Infantry Brigade at Dieppe. Despite being wounded, he continued to give orders as he lay on the stretcher of the landing craft. At Normandy, he commanded the same brigade until he was again wounded. Lett was not only a man of great courage and leadership, he possessed sound diplomatic skills. After the war he served on a government mission to Asia and in October 1953 he was asked to attend meetings of the Mixed Consultative Board (British Zone) in Bonn. Neither the press nor his friends knew the purpose of his mission. The board, consisting of five members, two German, two British, and a chairman appointed by Britain's high commissioner, could make recommendations for the termination or reduction of sentences. While Lett sat in on cases of concern to Canada, he was only an observer and did not express an opinion. He noted the board's recommendation to reduce Meyer's and Neitz's sentence to fourteen years and, in his report to the minister of national defence, he concluded that this was consistent with similar cases. Furthermore, one-third of the sentence would be remitted for good behaviour. The recommendation was accepted by Defence Minister Claxton, who wrote to the governor general on 15 January 1954 to implement the reduction.[51] In response to a question from John Diefenbaker, Claxton stated that this clemency was similar to that granted in other cases. However, the fumble-prone minister went on to observe that other war criminals had been sentenced to life imprisonment 'for much more serious crimes than this.' What was a more serious crime, the Opposition roared, than slaughtering scores of Canadian prisoners?[52]

Finally, on 7 September 1954, almost ten years to the day after his capture, Meyer was released and given a hero's reception in the town of

Niederkrüchten. Hundreds of Waffen SS veterans and sympathizers flooded the town to see him. Young people holding flares formed a triumphal laneway for his homecoming. Almost overcome with emotion, Meyer was reunited with his family and comrades. It was therefore something of an anti-climax when a few weeks later he took up employment as a beer distributor for the Andreas brewery of Hagen. As a final irony, one of his major clients was the mess of the Canadian army in Soest, Germany, and it was there that the former SS brigadeführer could be found 'as a sort of resident military genius. "Panzer" [the Canadians' nickname for Meyer] used to lounge around the Soest mess, lecturing the Canadians on armored tactics.'[53]

After his release, Meyer rapidly became a leading figure in the Waffen SS's veterans organization, HIAG. When the West German government refused to recognize SS men as eligible for war pensions, Meyer championed their cause, arguing that they had served as honourably as any of the Reich's soldiers. His stature was augmented by his 1957 memoirs, *Grenadiere*, which glorified his own and the SS's part in the war. Meyer's leadership of HIAG made him a major figure in West Germany and his rallies became political events. One Canadian reporter felt that 'if Nazism ever returns to Germany, its vehicle will be the Meyer machine "Hiag."'[54] At a massive HIAG rally in 1957, Meyer was the principal speaker. There were no flags on the rostrum since the SS veterans, though disdaining the Bonn government, dared not use any Nazi regalia. Meyer was tumultuously cheered when he declared that 'we stand behind our old commanders, come what may.' Later, and much to the dismay of the crowd, he became quite conciliatory, telling the veterans that Hitler's Germany had made many mistakes but that, in any event, those days were past and it was time to look to the future.[55] However, Meyer never seriously pursued a political career and in fact the war years had left him drained. Although only in his forties, he needed a cane to walk and suffered from kidney and heart disease. He died on his fifty-first birthday, 23 December 1961, and was given a lavish military funeral.

Many Canadians remained bitter over his release. 'Considering that he was convicted of inciting cold-blooded murder of eighteen Canadian prisoners of war during the Normandy campaign, Meyer has escaped remarkably lightly,' editorialized the Edmonton *Journal*. The same newspaper also questioned why Neitz, who had never killed anyone, was Canada's longest serving war criminal. 'The sergeant's mistake,' the *Journal* said, 'presumably lay in not being a general.'[56] In a thoughtful comment on Meyer's release, the Montreal *Star* wondered if the ideals of the trials had been forever lost in 'some curious emergence of a professional spirit, a kinship between officer corps, between men who, as professionals in war, do not like the development of a trend which means that orders given in the heat of battle can be held against them.' The hope given to the world by the Nuremberg and the lesser trials was being thrown away in a cynical determination to appease a new ally: 'Better not to have tried Meyer at all, or, having found him guilty, to have shot him, than to stumble through to the point where a few years' good behaviour in jail entitles such a man to freedom. The war trials have been, in other words, a farce.'[57]

As for the man who bore responsibility for the murder of far more Canadian prisoners than Meyer, Wilhelm Mohnke passed the post-war years in the bleak Lubyanka prison outside Moscow. He knew enough about Hitler's inner circle to give his paranoid keepers bits of information they hoped would be of use against the West. In 1955 he returned to West Germany and dropped from public view. It was not until the mid-1970s, when British clergyman Leslie Aitken was investigating the murder of eighty British soldiers at Wormhout, France, that attention was again turned towards Mohnke. After learning that Mohnke was living near Hamburg, Aitken wrote to the authorities enquiring about a prosecution. Citing insufficient evidence, they declined to act. Next, he contacted the Canadian Judge Advocate General's Department, and despite some typical misgivings that 'there may be reasons why Canada may not wish at this point in time to be involved directly in the prosecution of war crimes,' the investigative documents were forwarded to the West German prosecutor's office.[58] Nothing was done.

In April 1985 an eighty-two-year-old Bruce Macdonald testified before the federal Commission of Inquiry on War Criminals (Deschênes Commission) and Mohnke's unresolved case was foremost in his mind. Macdonald remained convinced of his guilt: 'Here we have a case which, if found, ought to be prosecuted,' he told the commission.[59] Macdonald was unaware that Mohnke was alive and living quietly near Hamburg. It took a reporter from the Ottawa Citizen to find Mohnke and interview him. Stolidly insisting that 'none, repeat none [prisoners] were shot on my order,' Mohnke denied all charges.[60] Again, nothing was done. Mohnke's name flared up in 1988 when British writer Ian Sayer published an extensive account showing that, in May 1940, Mohnke had commanded SS troops who had killed several prisoners of the rear guard at Dunkirk.[61] Finally, on 28 June 1988, the British Ministry of Defence revealed that there had been an investigation of Mohnke's case and that two SS men had given hearsay evidence on his leading part in the atrocity.[62] Under intense pressure from Britain, West Germany reopened the Mohnke file and at last demanded that he submit to an examination by a criminal prosecutor. In 1990 Canada's External Affairs Department tried to push the process along and urged the Germans to complete the investigation.[63] It was a futile attempt. German authorities declared that there was no reliable evidence in existence (Stangenberg had died in 1985) and the case was closed in 1994. That summer, as Canadian veterans flooded into Normandy to commemorate the fiftieth anniversary of the invasion, there was great bitterness that one of the most notorious war criminals of the Second World War remained unprosecuted and indeed was living comfortably on a generous SS veteran's pension. To the dwindling number who remembered, Mohnke seemed an undeserving recipient of a desire to forget the past so as not to renew old animosities.[64]

Over the years, Clarence Campbell had studiously followed both the Meyer and Mohnke cases and dolefully observed the mounting pressure for clemency. Several weeks after Meyer's release, Campbell spoke to a veterans' group in Sudbury and contrasted Meyer's tumultous reception in Germany with the quiet resolve of those Canadians who knew they were about to be shot at the Abbaye. With tears glistening in his eyes, he asked the audience to consider those young men shaking hands with each other before they were lead out to execution. 'I ask you, which was the greater courage?'

12

Canadian War Crimes
and the Consequences

If the courtroom is the appropriate laboratory to test the consequences of international law, one of the tragedies of the Second World War was the Allies' unwillingness to subject the conduct of their soldiers and generals to investigation. In this lapse lay a cautionary tale about one-sided justice that did not bode well for the future. Despite this lapse, however, Canadian soldiers were regularly subject to the rigours of military discipline.

The spoils of war were sweet indeed for the Canadian army in 1945. In the view of the Netherlands commander, Lieutenant General Guy Simonds, they were a bit too sweet for some. On 9 January 1946 he accused his chief of staff, Brigadier J.F.A. Lister, of having improperly requisitioned a house in Amsterdam and seized coal and food for his own use. The prosecutor, Bruce Macdonald, considered this assignment a punishment of sorts for his protest of the Meyer commutation. It was not a case he could win, for, as he wrote to his wife, 'everyone will be watching this case and many will be hoping he gets off. If he is not convicted when he should be Ottawa will be displeased, as they have evidently ordered the prosecution.'[1] At the trial, Lister's lawyer, Lieutenant-Colonel C.H. Gage, went on the attack and showed that his client's actions were no different from those of other generals. Gage effectively turned the tables by putting Simonds on trial for his lifestyle. The court perused photographs of Simonds's 'very large and luxuriously furnished house,' which was staffed by three chefs and four gardeners.[2] Macdonald called Simonds to testify and he conceded that Lister had been charged on less than compelling evidence. After a short deliberation, Lister was acquitted and, appropriately enough, he ordered fifteen bottles of champagne for a celebration that was attended by the court officers and even by prosecutor Macdonald.

If Lister's trial contained elements of comedy, another series of prosecutions in August 1945 were a grim reminder of the pressures facing prisoners. Three Essex Scottish soldiers taken at Dieppe were charged with high treason. The first accused, Private J.G. Galaher, had his trial held in secret because CMHQ did not wish to reveal how information had been transmitted from prison camps to the Allies. Despite a defence presented by Maurice Andrew, Galaher was convicted.[3] So was the next defendant, who protested that his favoured position in the camp arose simply because he was a friend of a German NCO. But the most controversial case was that of Private Edwin Martin, who had volunteered to serve in the 'Legion of St. George' in 1943. Not only had he joined an armed formation of the Wehrmacht, Martin had divulged information on armaments and British factories. Transferred to the British Free corps, he had designed the corps' flag, a Union Jack on a black background with three leopards in the fly. However, several prisoners testified that Martin was an idealist who attempted to undermine the corps by convincing its members to desert or by discrediting the fanatics before their Nazi superiors. None of this convinced the court, which convicted Martin. Along with the other two convicts, he served a short prison term.[4]

Violations of service discipline, usually less notable than the Lister case or the treason trials, were a regular feature of military life. The ordinary fare for the courts martial was desertion, disorderly conduct, and insubordination. And as the pressures of the war increased, so did the incidence of crime among the troops. Especially during the grinding Italian campaign, men who had spent years overseas and who seemed to face inevitable death or mutilation became prone to desert in increasing numbers.[5] During the Canadian army's occupation of northern Germany, many offences that could be considered war crimes were handled by the Canadian Provost corps. Accusations of rape brought by German women not only discredited the Allied forces but indicated a serious decline in discipline. One particularly brutal case occurred at Faikenburg, where a sixteen-year-old German girl was seized and raped by a Canadian soldier. After displaying her as a trophy to a number of his pals he raped her several more times. The provost squad needed the intervention of company officers before the girl could be rescued and the soldier taken away. Eventually, he was convicted and sentenced to fifteen years' imprisonment and dismissal.[6] In contrast to the Soviet sector, where rape seemed all but encouraged, Canadian military police dealt severely with all reported cases. At Oldenberg, by 10 May 1945, eight accused rapists were being held by military police and in Aurich there were over twenty arrests for rape.

As for violations of the law of war, Bruce Macdonald had always intended that war crimes investigations would be extended to Canadians. The Canadian regulations applied to 'any accused' and were of equal application to Canadians and their enemies. Macdonald sincerely believed that all rumours of Canadian atrocities were followed up.[7] Significantly, one of the questions Macdonald posed at Meyer's initial interrogation was whether he was aware of any Canadian infractions. No such reports were made in his sector, he assured Macdonald, and anyway 'there were many cases in which prisoners came back and the fact that they came back alive was the best proof that there was no fooling of this sort.'[8] Certainly during the Italian campaign both sides seemed to fight by the rules and most Canadians recalled being under strict orders to bring in prisoners unharmed.[9] Many battle memoirs are filled with situations where humanity was shown to the enemy. Strome Galloway recalled an incident in Italy where Germans and Canadians traded wounded and during the process both sides stopped for a drink. When a German paratrooper mistakenly wandered into Canadian lines he was allowed to return since any more prisoners would only create an 'administrative nuisance.'[10] When told of the 12th SS's conduct in Normandy, one Canadian commented, 'They must have been different Germans.'[11] He could not recall any atrocity committed against captives during the Italian campaign. Exceptions seemed to arise near the end of the fighting when the stubborn and costly German defence resulted in Canadians denying quarter when they at last overran German positions.

British writer Alexander McKee exposed a livid scar in his 1964 book *Caen: Anvil of Victory*. In his account of the battle for Caen (based largely on anecdotes) McKee expressed his conviction that on many occasions Canadians had killed prisoners.[12] He cited instances of Canadians slitting the throats of wounded Germans and reported the comment of one private of the South Saskatchewan Regiment that 'the Germans weren't too eager to surrender. We Canadians never took any SS prisoners now, and sometimes dealt with Wehrmacht formations in the same way.'[13] Controversy followed McKee's claims, as did a disclaimer from one of his sources, who stated that he did not witness Canadian atrocities as McKee had alleged.[14] These claims were not new, for, even at the time of Meyer's trial, some veterans freely discussed instances of German prisoners being killed at Normandy. As we have seen, writers to the *Maple Leaf* wrote of the 'secret huddles "off the record"' where prisoners were murdered. 'Are we such innocent little angels with regard to the same charges?' three officers asked.[15]

Unlike the well-researched German cases, the accusations against Canadian servicemen remain strictly anecdotal. Yet it seems certain that on many occasions Canadian troops did murder prisoners of war. Furthermore, these violations of the laws of war were largely ignored. Many were ignored because (unlike the large-scale executions conducted by the 12th SS) they were mostly spontaneous acts of revenge committed near the fighting. In one instance, a Canadian shot down two Germans who had approached his position with hands raised. His officer was outraged at this cold-blooded killing; however, the culprit, 'a lousy human being, but a good soldier,' was merely given a dressing down and told that if it ever happened again he would be shot.[16] Veterans recalled instances where prisoners were sent to the rear but disappeared en route. On other occasions, Germans trying to surrender would be cut apart by an artillery barrage deliberately aimed at them.

One incident is perhaps typical. Near the end of the war, a Canadian patrol suddenly came under German fire and one man was killed. Without any further resistance, the three ambushing Germans surrendered. The patrol's sergeant had been a close friend of the dead man, and with no hesitation he took the three Germans down the road and shot each one through the head. Even though a junior officer was present, nothing was said. Later, the men in the patrol speculated that the Germans had intended to surrender and had been surprised by the one man and fired at him. They knew that their sergeant was not inclined to mistreat prisoners and the killings were dismissed as just part of the give and take of battle.

Were there some atrocities committed under orders? In January 1945 Robert Sanderson of the Essex Scottish brought back a German prisoner for interrogation. When this was completed, an officer turned to Sanderson and another soldier and ordered them to kill the prisoner. Unable to kill in cold blood, Sanderson and his comrade simply let the man go free.[17] Soldiers take their cue from their commanders, and when Major-General Chris Vokes decorated a soldier who killed three prisoners he could not bring back to his own lines[18] all his comrades understood the official value of prisoners' lives.

Despite our inclination to feel that war crimes could only have been committed by the enemy, the facts are clearly otherwise. Yet, since alleged violations of the laws of war by Canadians were never investigated, the number of crimes will never be known. While none of them rivalled the extent or the pre-meditation of the 12th SS's crimes, nothing excused Canada's failure to investigate those crimes that should have come to the attention of officers and to see that the accused were put before courts martial.

Some understanding of why prisoners were shot after capture can only arise from an exploration of the universal urges that consume men in combat. Revenge is probably the most potent motivator. A medical orderly on Normandy beach heard the wounded talking about the discovery of bodies at the Chateau d'Audrieu and voicing their resolve, if they ever returned to combat, to seek revenge: 'O.K. no more prisoners' was their attitude.[19] Late in the war, Canadians in northern Germany faced a counter-attack at the town of Sogel. Civilians were said to have ambushed a field ambulance, and one Canadian officer grimly reported, 'We levelled their town for them and there has been less trouble since.' But investigators found no evidence of civilian participation in the attack, and the revenge was for a purely imaginary offence.[20] Especially among the close-knit SS, revenge was always a factor. The one American prisoner shot in Normandy was killed in retaliation for SS losses. When the killer was reproached by the French family with whom he was billeted, he shrugged and replied 'Égal, égal.'[21] Revenge seems justifiable when troops are regularly told that their enemy will not take them captive. A French girl tending to a wounded SS man in Normandy recalled his terror at being captured and shot by the Allies. He begged her to hide his SS uniform and warned her that all French who helped the SS would also be shot.[22] A Canadian intelligence officer reported that captured Germans understood that they would be executed and their first question was usually, 'Will we be shot?'[23] Because so many thought that the other side obeyed no rules, it seemed appropriate to reciprocate.

The purpose of combat is to kill. As Richard Holmes has observed, 'no soldier who fights until his enemy is at close small-arms range, in any war, has no more than perhaps a fifty-fifty chance of being granted quarter. If he stands up to surrender he risks being shot with the time honoured comment "Too late chum."'[24] Sydney Frost, a Canadian officer in the Netherlands, described the flushing out of German snipers: 'The Wehrmacht either gave up or dashed for the open where Bill Stutt was waiting with his flamethrowers and MMGs [mounted machine-guns]. Altogether it was a lot of fun.' But those Germans who did not resist were taken alive, for Frost also boasted of his unit's tally of prisoners.[25] Often, however, soldiers in the heat of battle are likely to kill and keep on killing even if the enemy wishes to stop. The slaughter can become almost a hysteria, especially for unseasoned troops. As Major Learment observed at Authie and Buron, the 12th SS seemed like berserk adolescents 'continually yelling and screeching to one another ... I thought they must have been on drugs.'[26] The first experience of combat certainly seems to have had an almost narcotic effect on the Hitler Youth, for another Canadian felt that 'the SS troops were acting in a very queer inhuman way and certainly in battle like madmen, not shirking to advance into direct fire. I thought many times that they may have been doped as their eyes were always dilated.'[27] A similar hysteria possessed the Japanese at Hong Kong. One defence lawyer described them as 'a conquering army intoxicated with victory, and with the picture of dying brothers and friends still with it, is not all-together a sane body of men.'[28] Undoubtedly many Canadian soldiers must have experienced the surge of adrenalin at their first combat, at seeing the enemy repulsed and surviving where others had died. 'It was exciting as hell,' young Farley Mowat wrote to a friend after his first battle, but he added ominously that 'I didn't lose a single man, though I guess that kind of luck can't last forever.'[29]

Combat is a strange country to those who have never visited it, a country of emotions rather than rules. As Bruce Macdonald admitted, reports came in of Canadians killing prisoners shortly after battle. While these acts were violations of the laws of war, they were not taken seriously for 'in action there is bound to be zeal and passion involved and it is very likely that prisoners surrendering at the last minute wouldn't be given any quarter at all. After all, if they have just killed a number of your buddies, and they just at the last minute think they are going to escape by holding up their arms, that somebody is going to say "to hell with you."'[30]

While revenge for enemy misdeeds and the passions of battle make killing prisoners possible, what makes it palatable is the perception that the enemy is foreign, 'not one of us,' and that killing him does not incur the consequences of killing one of us. One group of North Novas were on the point of being executed when their officer called out to their captors in German. Recognition that the prisoners spoke their language immediately stopped the imminent killing.[31] When the shared humanity of the captive is perceived, the drive to kill him abates. As Major Banfill, the only man spared from the Salesian Mission massacre, marched with his captors, he talked with Lieutenant Honda about his personal and spiritual life. Honda grew so concerned about Banfill that, in his eyes, the Canadian became human and he succeeded in saving him from being murdered.[32] Conversely, when the enemy's humanity is denied, killing becomes as easy as getting rid of a household nuisance. This was especially true for SS units where the racial inferiority of Germany's enemies was a constant theme. The 3rd SS Division, 'Totenkopf,' for example, had indoctrinated its men (most of whom were former concentration camp guards) to despise all 'enemies behind the wire.' The 3rd SS was responsible for numerous atrocities, including the slaughter of 100 British prisoners at Le Paradis in 1940 and countless atrocities in the Soviet Union.[33] Canadian regiments could never match this level of fanaticism. 'How do you kill a young man with his hands in the air and trembling uncontrollably?'[34] asked one Canadian veteran of Normandy. However much they may have despised their enemies, there was no driving ideology on the Canadian side that denied the opposition's humanity.

Yet generals, in their eagerness to secure victory, could encourage their men to the worst excesses. As we observed earlier, Theodore Roosevelt warned in 1902 that 'Loose and violent talk by an officer of high rank is always likely to excite to wrongdoing those among his subordinates.'[35] When a leader accepts command, they also assume a responsibility to uphold the laws of war. Meyer's exhortation to his troops (interpreted by so many of them to mean 'take no prisoners') bore its evil fruit at Authie and Buron where Canadian prisoners were systematically slaughtered. It is unlikely these massacres would have occurred had not the Hitler Youth thought they were doing exactly what was expected of them. Nor was Meyer an exception. In Sicily two American soldiers were tried for the killing of scores of prisoners. Both raised as a defence the fact that their commander, Lieutenant-General George S. Patton, had ordered them to behave this way. One defendant recalled Patton's speech almost verbatim: 'When you get within two hundred yards of him [the enemy] and he wishes to surrender, oh no! That bastard will die! You will kill him. Stick him between the third and fourth rib.' These sanguinary thoughts percolated down the ranks until, as one officer recalled, Patton's orders were interpreted as 'the more prisoners we took, the more we'd have to feed, and not to fool with prisoners.' Such words bore an eerie resemblance to those of Kurt Meyer at the Abbaye Ardenne.[36]

Canadian generals as well seemed to invite their men to commit atrocities. When Canadians first landed in France in 1940, General A.G.L. McNaughton told his officers that 'you must be absolutely ruthless ... tell the men we are not particularly interested in prisoners.'[37] In Italy, General Chris Vokes was reported to have given a 'no prisoners' order to his men, an order that was quickly revoked by the 8th army commander, General Sir Oliver Leese.[38] This was the same Chris Vokes who was prepared to equate Meyer's conviction of exhorting his men to commit murder to 'a .

motorist who kills a pedestrian with his car through negligence.' Men such as Vokes and Meyer failed to grasp that it is the very essence of evil to encourage a large group of excited and heavily armed young men to kill prisoners. They did not comprehend that it is their words, the climate they create, that determine whether or not their men will behave correctly or not. 'A positive set of rules,' it has been said, 'if they are judicious, serves the interests of belligerents and is far from hindering them, since by preventing the unchaining of passion and savage instincts – which battle always awakens, as much as it awakens courage and manly virtues, – it strengthens the discipline which is the strength of armies.'[39] To attain this end, soldiers must understand that their leaders expect them to respect the basic laws of humanity.

The degree of responsibility of commanders such as Meyer, Patton, or Vokes remains difficult to gauge. Yet when irresponsible statements lead to killings, it seems unconscionable that the common soldier bears the burden for the actual deed while the commander escapes punishment because of his distance from the criminal act. Those who have the power also seem to have the immunity from punishment. One Japanese general seemed to grasp the significance of command responsibility. In his successful defence, General Shoji stated that he had reminded his soldiers that the Hong Kong attack would be a 'historical campaign' and 'carried out with the eyes of the world looking on and most likely many prisoners of war will be captured ... the laws and customs of war must not be violated.'[40] While this may have fallen on deaf ears, Shoji at least attempted to remind his men of the grave character of their task.

None of this should detract from the remarkable extent to which the laws of war sheltered the defenceless. During the Second World War, the vast majority of prisoners taken on the Western Front were not harmed and hospital ships and medical staff were not usually attacked. As a result, 'the number of those who owed their lives to the fact that the law of war was observed probably ran into several millions.'[41] This may well have been because of the similarities in race and religion among the western armies. Even Meyer's comment to a Canadian officer, 'Why do we smash each other's skulls?' betrays a fellow feeling.[42] One cannot imagine him making such a comment to a Soviet officer. Many German soldiers, including SS, were shocked to learn of the extent of the atrocities at Normandy. As one junior officer explained: 'If I can be of any help and use I will place the burden where it belongs regardless of whether officers are involved or not. Had I been given any such order I would not have executed it. I firmly believe that as a human being, a prisoner once taken should have his life and if I can be of any assistance I will give it.'[43] He went on to recount that during the battle for Falaise 'I lugged him [a wounded Canadian] with me for three days, and such food as we had he also got. When the N.C.O. from the Wehrmacht took a wristwatch off this prisoner it was I who saw that the watch was returned.' On many occasions, Germans obeyed the laws of war and tried to stop other Germans who flouted them. Bruce Macdonald was impressed by the fact that in each German soldier's paybook was a 'Ten Commandments,' one of which read: 'While fighting for victory the German soldier will observe the rules of chivalrous warfare. No enemy who has surrendered will be killed. Prisoners of war will not be ill-treated or insulted.'[44] There was no similar exhortation to Canadian soldiers.

After the British army's victory over the Mahdist forces at Omdurman in 1898, one subaltern wrote to his mother that the victorious commander, General H.H. Kitchener, had tolerated the murder of wounded enemy prisoners. In his view, these 'acts of barbarity' had sullied the great victory.[45] While at the time no one else was greatly concerned, the same subaltern, Winston Churchill, would persevere to see acts of inhumanity punished in the formal setting of the Nuremberg trials.

Shortly after Omdurman, the first Hague Convention of 1899 made remarkable advances in codifying the law of war. This conference, as well as its 1907 successor, provided rules of humane conduct which were incorporated into military manuals. In the age of total war, it seems questionable whether these documents made any real difference. Yet, after the Second World War, many German observers accepted the Nuremberg trials as valid and thought they had been conducted with 'the utmost impartiality, loyalty and sense of justice.' The only caveat to this was that the victorious nations had not looked within themselves to apply the Nuremberg principles to their own troops.[46] Should it be an animating principle of international law that acts of murder committed against prisoners (whether our own or the enemy's) should be fairly prosecuted? The social order that must exist in every army should be directed to control the tendency to violate the laws of war. If this law is to be effective, it must be applied, and to that extent the trials at Aurich were a first step in proving that enforcement is possible.

The 1949 International Law Commission of the United Nations recodified the laws of war and this resulted in a further Geneva Convention that extended protection to civilians.[47] Yet the lack of any judicial machinery to enforce these laws severely limited their use. American commitment to international enforcement of the laws of war was put to the test during the Vietnam War. It failed. In late 1969 it was revealed that a company of troops from the Americal division had butchered at least 400 Vietnamese civilians at the hamlet known as My Lai. The only officer convicted in the atrocity, William Calley, was confined for a mere three years and nine months, and most of that time was spent in detention on a military base. This was a ludicrous result for a crime as serious as the German massacre of civilians at Oradour or Lidice. But, much as the German public could not accept the guilt of their men, Americans rallied to Calley.[48] Later, the world passively watched genocide occur in Cambodia during the 1970s and the use of poison gas by Iraq against Kurdish civilians in the 1980s. Notwithstanding these failures, however, humanity seems slowly to be coming to the conclusion that the promise of Nuremberg and Tokyo should be kept alive. During the Gulf War of 1990–1, American forces scrupulously observed the rules to the extent that they sometimes sought direction where civilians might be endangered. This revealed a remarkable concern for international law from the same army that only twenty-two years previously had been responsible for My Lai.[49]

It has taken the stark horror of the Yugoslavian civil war to bring the need for international judicial systems to the fore. Between 1992 and 1995, Serb militias in the former Yugoslavia carried out a policy of extermination to the extent that it has been estimated that one out of every ten Muslims in Bosnia were killed.[50] Canadian diplomats pressed for the creation of an international criminal court to try accused war criminals,[51] and in 1993, the United Nations created the International Tribunal for Yugoslavia. One of the most respected international jurists, Canada's Jules Deschênes, was selected to preside as one of the judges. The following year, in response to the slaughter of 750,000 ethnic Tutsis in Rwanda, a further tribunal was created.[52] In February 1994 an unassuming Serb living in Germany, Dusan Tadic, was arrested and charged with war crimes, including the torture and murder of inmates of a concentration camp. For the first time since the Tokyo trial, an accused war criminal sat in the dock. Attempting to apply justice in the middle of a war brought formidable obstacles. 'We're not in a Nuremberg situation here,' said William Fenrick, Canadian adviser to the prosecution. 'We don't have a conquering army, and we don't have the mass of captured documents or people which they had at Nuremberg.'[53] What they did have, however, was a determination to see that war crimes were fairly punished.

The absence of an international court has resulted in an absence of enforcement, for domestic laws cannot readily adapt to the circumstances of international conflicts. This lacuna in the law became painfully apparent as a result of the prosecutions resulting from the Deschênes Commission. In 1985–6, this commission investigated the extent to which war criminals had entered Canada since 1945 and established a program to prosecute war criminals still in Canada. But, despite enormous expense, only a handful of prosecutions resulted. There were no convictions.[54] The futility of the exercise was glaringly apparent in the *R. v. Finta* case (1994), where the trial judge left convoluted issues of intent to commit war crimes and obedience to superior orders to a jury to interpret. After the accused's acquittal, the Supreme Court of Canada upheld this approach, which, for all practical purposes, made it impossible to prosecute war crimes in Canada. The dissenting judges pointed out that Canada had abandoned its international obligations by calling on lay juries to determine the contents of treaties and leaving the door open to 'manipulative lawyers.' Justice Gérard LaForest sadly concluded that in Canada 'war crimes and crimes against humanity were viewed as so heinous as to require a procedure so unmanageable as to make successful prosecution unlikely.'[55] To that extent, we have failed to incorporate the lessons from our own past; the drafters of the 1945 Canadian War Crimes regulations recognized that the circumstances of war required special rules and that there had to be a wide latitude in the admission of evidence that went far beyond the usual rules of domestic law. This was far from the most significant Canadian failure in international law.

That Canadian soldiers in Somalia would slowly torture a teenager to death is a tragedy that still haunts Canadians' image of themselves. Dispelling any assumptions of moral superiority, it led to a re-examination of our willingness to control the military. Like many other troops in similar circumstances, Canadian soldiers were 'surrounded by a civilian population which has every reason for detesting them, whose language they do not understand, and whose every movement they suspect – it is then there occurs the kind of atrocities committed by the Germans at Oradour or, I am afraid it must be said, by the Americans at My Lai,'[56] or, it may be added, the Canadians in Somalia. The atrocity itself was an isolated sadistic act but perhaps the most notable feature of the Somalia tragedy was that it was not glossed over. Canadians did perceive criminals in their own country's uniform, even though some politicians (in eerie similarity to the Leipzig trials where 'our' troops can never be considered guilty) attempted to exonerate the convicted.[57] The Somalia affair also demonstrated a marked failure in command. A major (later convicted of negligence) told his soldiers that they could 'abuse' Somali civilians. Prior to the mission, when a legal officer had attempted to brief an officer on the law of war, his comments were shrugged off: 'All that doesn't matter,' the officer said, 'you just throw down some loose rounds,' implying that spent ammunition could be thrown on the ground to make it appear that an unarmed intruder had been armed.[58] It was this cavalier attitude towards the law that appeared all too common among Canadian officers and led to valid questions about failure in command during the Somalia mission.

Applying the law to war criminals has not been easy. As Canadians learned in 1945–6, the rules of domestic law are not easily applicable to times of military conflict. In recent years, their successors have attempted to apply civil standards of evidence to the battlefield, and these attempts have (perhaps predictably) failed. There is, nevertheless, a growing consensus that war crimes are offences, not only against the state or individual victims, but against humanity. The struggle to ensure proper treatment in times of war is a part of the wider struggle to incorporate humanitarian principles into the consciousness of mankind. If there is meticulous regulation of the comity of nations on the high seas, in air-traffic control, health and commerce, and other areas, why not in war? An ad hoc system that lies dormant until triggered by war is unlikely to be effective. Therefore, if war is a disagreeable but likely instrument of policy, should not the international instruments to regulate war be permanent? A standing military tribunal, experienced in the administration of military law, may finally fulfil the 'Nuremberg promise.'

The Canadian government's ambivalence to the war crimes prosecutions is not a memorable episode in the history of Canada's emergence as a nation. This restraint did not arise from any legal limitations but rather from 'a sense of the limited influence that a nation of Canada's capacities could exert on world politics.'[59] That it took a lieutenant-colonel to cajole Ottawa into setting up a structure for the trial of crimes against Canadian prisoners was a gauge of official unwillingness to foster Canadian interests. In the end, Bruce Macdonald's relentless pursuit of justice gave some measure of dignity to the sacrifice of the murdered prisoners. Moreover, as he said in his final address, he was conscious that these trials were serving a purpose beyond the needs of immediate justice: 'If this trial is to serve its purpose as a deterrent for the future, so that if, despite our best efforts, war again should come to our nation and its forces, then it must serve as an object lesson of inexorable justice, effectively to restrain under battle conditions, all, no matter what their rank may be, who, even momentarily, consider the murder of prisoners of war.'[60]

The story of the Canadian victims of war crimes has passed into history. The Vico family preserved the story of the murdered Canadians at the Abbaye Ardenne, but there was no official recognition. It was only through the private efforts of Lieutenant-Colonel I.J. Campbell that a plaque commemorating the victims was erected in the garden of their execution.[61] The Chateau d'Audrieu is now a luxury hotel, a little gem in the lush Norman countryside. Near a swimming pool stands the wall where eleven Canadian prisoners spent their last moments. In many other Norman crossroads where prisoners died, no memorials exist.

If we owe anything to the young Canadians who met their deaths in the garden of the Abbaye Ardenne, it should be to remember the promise that international law has the potential to restrain human conduct in the worst situations. If war cannot be abolished, it can at least be controlled. A system of enforceable international justice should exist to punish those who wantonly murder prisoners or the helpless. These laws can be effective only if people of courage and perseverance see that they are enforced. It is perhaps the most fitting memorial to our host of young men lost in the first half of this century that Canada has taken a role, in the war crimes trials and afterwards, in punishing lawlessness by soldiers. To tolerate unrestrained conduct, either murder by soldiers or reckless invitations to violence by officers, would be to sanction the unrestrained barbarity that murdered the prisoners at the Abbaye. It is our duty to see that such behaviour does not prevail.

Appendix

Charge Sheet of Kurt Meyer

The accused, Brigadeführer Kurt Meyer, an officer in the former Waffen S.S., then a part of the Armed Forces of the German Reich, now in the charge of the 4th Battalion, Royal Winnipeg Rifles, Canadian Army Occupation Force, Canadian Army Overseas, is charged with:

First Charge: Committing a war crime in that he in the Kingdom of Belgium and in the Republic of France, during the year 1943 and prior to the 7th day of June 1944, when Commander of the 25th S.S. Panzer Grenadier Regiment, in violation of the laws and usages of war incited and counselled troops serving under his command to deny quarter to Allied troops.

Second Charge: Committing a war crime in that he in the Province of Normandy and Republic of France, on or about the 7th day of June 1944, as Commander of the 25th S.S. Panzer Grenadier Regiment, was responsible for the killing of prisoners of war, in violation of the laws and usages of war, when troops under his command killed twenty-three Canadian prisoners of war at or near the villages of Buron and Authie.

Third Charge: Committing a war crime in that he at his Headquarters at L'Ancienne Abbaye Ardenne, in the Province of Normandy and Republic of France on or about the 8th day of June 1944, when Commander of the 25th S.S. Panzer Grenadier Regiment, in violation of the laws and usages of war, gave orders to troops under his command to kill seven prisoners of war, and as a result of such orders the said prisoners of war were thereupon shot and killed.

Fourth Charge: (Alternative to the Third Charge) Committing a war crime in that he in the Province of Normandy and Republic of France on or about the 8th day of June 1944, as Commander of the 25th S.S. Panzer Grenadier Regiment, was responsible for the killing of prisoners of war in violation of the laws and usages of war, when troops under his command shot and killed seven Canadian prisoners of war at his Headquarters at the L'Ancienne Abbaye Ardenne.

Fifth Charge: Committing a war crime in that he in the Province of Normandy and Republic of France on or about the 7th day of June 1944, as Commander of the 25th Panzer Grenadier Regiment was responsible for the killing of prisoners of war in violation of the laws and usages of war, when troops under his command killed eleven Canadian prisoners of war (other than those referred to in the Third and Fourth Charge) at his Headquarters at L'Ancienne Abbaye Ardenne.

R.J. Orde, Brigadier,
Judge Advocate-General

Source: Windsor Municipal Archives, box 1, file 1/5 Macdonald Papers.

Notes

Abbreviations

DHist   Directorate of History, Canadian Defence Headquarters (Ottawa, Ont.)
NAC   National Archives of Canada
     RG 2   Privy Council Papers
     RG 24   Department of National Defence Records
     RG 25   Department of External Affairs Records
     MG 26L   Louis St Laurent Papers
NARA   National Archives of the United States (College Park, Md.)
     RG 153   Records of the Office of the Judge Advocate General (Army)
PRO   Public Records Office (Kew Gardens, England)
     WO   War Office Records
WMA   Windsor Municipal Archives (Windsor, Ont.)
     MP   Bruce Macdonald Papers
     CP   Clarence Campbell Papers

Preface

1 DHist, 81/146, Lakehead and District Peace Council to Justice Deptartment, 4 Feb. 1951.

Introduction

1 Karl von Clausewitz, *On War*, ed. and trans. Michael Howard and Peter Paret (Princeton University Press: 1976), 76.

2 Peter Karsten, *Law, Soldiers, and Combat* (Greenwood: 1978), ch. 1.
3 M.H. Keen, *The Laws of War in the Late Middle Ages* (University of Toronto Press: 1965), ch. 10. Keen says (245) that the medieval laws of war were 'formulated and applied with a view to the protection of the rights of individual soldiers, not to regulating the conduct of troops of warring nations.'
4 Julius Stone, *Legal Controls of International Conflict* (Holte, Rinehart, Winston: 1959), 13–14.
5 Hugo Grotius, *The Law of War and Peace*, ch. 4, as quoted in Leon Friedman, ed., *The Law of War: A Documentary History*, 2 vols. (Random House: 1972), 1:35.
6 Gerhard von Glahn, *Law among Nations* (Macmillan: 1981), 4:660.
7 Geoffrey Best, 'Restraints on War by Land before 1945,' in Michael Howard, ed., *Restraints on War: Studies in the Limitation of Armed Conflict* (Oxford University Press: 1979), 20.
8 R.S. Hartigan, *Lieber's Code and the Law of War* (University of Chicago Press: 1983).
9 Geneva (Red Cross) Convention of 1864, St Petersburg Declaration of 1868, and Declaration of Brussels of 1874, as reprinted in *American Journal of International Law*, 1907, supplement, 90.
10 'Convention concerning the Laws and Customs of War on Land and Regulations,' signed 18 Oct., 1907 at the Hague, as reprinted in *American Journal of International Law*, 1908, supplement, 1. On Fisher's comment, see Friedman, *Law of War*, 153.
11 Claud Mullins, *The Leipzig Trials* (Witherby: 1921).
12 Alfred M. de Zayas, *The Wehrmacht War Crimes Bureau, 1939–1945* (University of Nebraska Press: 1989), 6–8.
13 Geneva Convention Relative to the Treatment of Prisoners of War, signed 27 July 1929, vol. 108, *League of Nations Treaty Series*, 343.
14 I.D. DeLupis, *The Law of War* (Cambridge University Press: 1987), 280–1.
15 de Zayas, *Wehrmacht War Crimes*, 91.
16 William Parks, 'Command Responsibility for War Crimes,' *Military Law Review* (fall 1973), 1 at 6.
17 United States Congress, House of Representatives, *Barbarities of the Enemy Exposed in a Report ...* (Adancourt: 1813).
18 E.A. Cruikshank, 'John Beverley Robinson and the Trials for Treason in 1814,' *Ontario Historical Society Papers and Records*, vol. 25 (1929), 191 at 213.
19 Charles R. Sanderson, ed, *The Arthur Papers ...* (Ontario Historical Society: 1947), 3 vols., (pt. 2): 431, Arthur to Airey, 10 Dec., 1838. See also R. Alan Douglas, *John Prince, 1796–1870: A Collection of Documents* (Champlain Society University of Toronto Press: 1980) 26–36.

20 Max Aitken, *Canada in Flanders* (Houghton: 1916), 101.
21 Paul Fussell, *The Great War and Modern Memory* (Oxford University Press: 1975), 117–18.
22 John Mellor, *Forgotten Heroes: The Canadians at Dieppe* (Methuen: 1975), 111–15.
23 Claude Bissell, *The Imperial Canadian: Vincent Massey in Office* (University of Toronto Press: 1986), 145. See also S.P. Mackenzie, 'The Shackling Crisis: A Case Study in the Dynamics of Prisoner-of-War Diplomacy in the Second World War,' *International History Review*, vol. 17 (Feb. 1995), 78–97.

1: Rumours of Murder

1 House of Commons *Debates*, 23 June 1944, 4,098.
2 Ibid., 4,099
3 *Globe and Mail*, 24 June 1944.
4 Ibid.
5 House of Commons *Debates*, 13 July 1944, 4,804.
6 *Globe and Mail*, 13 July 1944.
7 Nicholas Tolstoy, *Victims of Yalta* (Hodder and Stoughton: 1977), 33–5. See also Mathew Cooper, *The German Army, 1933–1945: Its Political and Military Failure* (Stein and Day: 1978), 549; and Alexander Dallin, *German Rule in Russia, 1941–1945: A Study of Occupation Policies*, 2nd ed. (Stein and Day: 1981), 419–20. Dallin suggests that over four million Russians died in German captivity.
8 NAC, RG 24, vol. 12,837, file 392–9, Dieppe, Elwes to High Commissioner Vincent Massey, 11 May 1944.
9 *Punishment for War Crimes: The Inter-Allied Declaration Signed at St. James' Palace, London, 13 Jan. 1942*, in *Punishment for War Criminals* (His Majesty's Stationary Office: 1944).
10 Ibid.
11 *History of the United Nations War Crimes Commission: And the Development of the Laws of War* (United Nations War Crimes Commission: 1948), 'Thus, through the work of the Commission and other agencies, the United Nations had already to their hands when the time came, a more or less practical scheme for the prosecution and punishment of war criminals' (at 3).
12 Comment in *Canadian Bar Review*, vol. 23 (1945), 352. See also Cordell Hull, *The Memoirs of Cordell Hull*, 3 vols. (Macmillan: 1948), 2:1,289.
13 Sheldon Glueck, *War Criminals: Their Prosecution and Punishment* (Knopf: 1944), 5.
14 Reginald H. Roy, *1944: The Canadians in Normandy* (Macmillan: 1984), 26–30.
15 Will R. Bird, *No Retreating Footsteps: The Story of the North Nova Scotia Highlanders* (privately published, Kentville, N.S.: n.d.), 90–2.

16 C.P. Stacey, *The Victory Campaign: The Operations in North-West Europe, 1944–1945*, 4 vols. (Queen's Printer: 1966), 3:128–33.
17 *Globe and Mail*, 21 June 1944.
18 NAC, RG 24, vol. 12,842, file 393–53, memo of Capt. J.F. Neil in the field, 14 June 1944, sent to SHAEF 25 June 1944.
19 Ibid., memorandum to CMHQ, 5 July 1944.
20 Ibid., memorandum of telephone conversation, Brig. Beament, 8 July 1944.
21 Ibid., memorandum of Lt. Gen. P.J. Montague, 13 July 1944.
22 S.R. Elliot, *Scarlet to Green: A History of Intelligence in the Canadian Army, 1903–1963* (Canadian Intelligence and Security Association: 1981). John Page was 'the man who, more than any other, put Intelligence in a firm administrative footing' (at 95). In appointing Page, CMHQ noted that 'Major Page possesses special qualifications for this task, being an experienced Intelligence Officer.' See NAC, RG 24, vol. 12,842, file 393–53, memorandum of 5 July 1944.
23 Author's interview with John Page, 30 Dec. 1993.
24 WMA, MP, box 2, 'Report of the Court of Inquiry Re: Shooting of Prisoners of War by German Armed Forces at Chateau d'Audrieu, Normandy, 8 June 1944' (hereinafter 'Chateau d'Audrieu') file I 2/1, ex. no. 12, Monique Level, 4.
25 Ibid., ex. no. 10, Beatrice Delafon, 5.
26 Ibid., ex. no. 14, Raymond Lanoue, 4.
27 Ibid., pt. 2, 'Findings of the Court.'
28 NAC, RG 24, vol. 12,842, file 393–53, Crerar to CMHQ, 10 July 1944. Crerar urged that the investigators be discreet: 'Civilian witnesses have been most cooperative up to the present but they are greatly concerned lest their testimony should involve retaliation on their relatives who are still living in Occupied France or who are detained in Germany.'
29 WMA, MP, box 2, 'Report of the Court of Inquiry Re: Shooting of Prisoners of War by German Armed Forces at Mouen, Calvados, Normandy, 17 June 1944' (hereinafter 'Mouen'), file I 2/2, ex. no. 4, Antoni Budowski, 2.
30 Ibid., ex. no. 10, R. Pele, 2.
31 NAC, RG 24, vol. 12,842, memorandum for secretary of state, July 1944.
32 Ibid., CMHQ memorandum of Brig. M.H.S. Penhale, 25 July 1944.
33 Ibid., Crerar telegram to all Canadian troops serving with 21st Army Group, 1 Aug. 1944.
34 *Globe and Mail*, 3 Aug. 1944.
35 House of Commons *Debates*, 2 Aug. 1944, 5,771–2.
36 *Globe and Mail*, 3 Aug. 1944.
37 NAC, RG 24, vol. 12,842, file 353–53, SHAEF to Barker, 7 Aug. 1944.
38 Ibid., memorandum to chief of staff, Bedell Smith, from Barker, n.d.
39 Roy, *1944*, 88–95; and Stacey, *The Victory Campaign*, 174–6.

40 WMA, MP, Macdonald to Norma Macdonald, 20 Aug. 1944.

41 Raymond Robichaud memorandum to the author, February 1994, 2.

42 Ibid., 6; and WMA, MP, box 1, file 1/2, 'Investigation of Atrocities and Trial of War Criminals Administrative Instruction No. 104.'

43 Ibid., 7

44 WMA, MP, box 2, 'Report of the Court of Inquiry Re: Shooting of Allied Prisoners-of-War by German Armed Forces in the Vicinity of Le Mesnil-Patry, Les Saullets, Buron and Authie, Normandy, 7–11 June, 1944' (hereinafter 'Buron and Authie'), file I 2/3, ex. no. 3A, Maj. F.E. White.

45 WMA, MP, Macdonald to Norma Macdonald, 8 Sept. 1944.

46 Author's interview with John Page, 30 Dec. 1993.

47 WMA, MP, Macdonald to Norma Macdonald, 3 Nov. 1944.

48 'Buron and Authie,' Les Saullets, 7.

49 Ibid., ex. no. 3E, Maurice Guilbert, 15.

50 Ibid., ex. no. 20, Clément Faucon.

51 Ibid., ex. no. 34, L/Cpl. W.L. MacKay, 3.

52 Ibid., ex. no. 33, Major John D. Learment, 4.

53 Ibid., ex. no. 50, L/Sgt Dudka, 4.

54 Ibid., 6.

55 Ibid., pt. 2, 'Findings of the Court.'

56 Ibid., 13.

57 'Buron and Authie,' ex. no. 51, Raymond Robichaud.

58 Contemporary Canadian military staff referred to the Ancienne Abbaye d'Ardenne as the 'Abbaye Ardenne' or simply the 'Abbaye.' In this book, I use the two latter terms.

59 WMA, MP, box 3, 'Supplementary Report of the SHAEF Court of Inquiry Re: Shooting of Allied Prisoners by the 12th SS Panzer Division (Hitler-Jugend) in Normandy, France, 7–21 June 1944' (hereinafter 'SHAEF Supplementary Report'), file I 2/5, ex. 11, Rfm. W.R. Lebar, 9.

60 Ibid., pt. 5, 'Additional New Reports and Evidence,' 30.

2: Murder Division

1 Craig Luther, *Blood and Honor: The History of the 12th SS Panzer Division 'Hitler Youth,' 1943–1945* (Bender: 1987), 13.

2 George H. Stein, *The Waffen SS: Hitler's Elite Guard at War, 1939–1945* (Cornell University Press: 1966), 27–34; James J. Weingartner, *Hitler's Guard: The Story of the Leibstandarte SS Adolf Hitler, 1933–1945* (Carbondale: 1974); Berndt Wegner, *The Waffen SS: Organization, Ideology and Function* (Basil Blackwell: 1990).

3 On *Härte*, see James J. Weingartner, *Crossroads of Death: The Story of the Malmedy Massacre and Trial* (University of California Press: 1979), 10–11.

4 Stein, *The Waffen SS*, 13.

5 Luther, *Blood and Honor*, 57–63.

6 Ibid., 74.

7 On Meyer's early life see Tony Foster, *Meeting of Generals* (Methuen: 1986) chs. 1–4; on Meyer's campaign in Poland, France, and the Balkans, see, Kurt Meyer, *Grenadiere* (Fedorowitz: 1994) 3–37.

8 Weingartner, *Crossroads of Death*, 66–73. SHAEF first learned of the Malmédy massacre from tape recodings made by survivors to reporters. A Canadian officer, Lt. R. Robichaud, took the tapes to the Canadian mission in Paris for transcribing.

9 Charles B. MacDonald, *A Time for Trumpets: The Untold Story of the Battle of the Bulge* (Morrow: 1985) 216–30.

10 WMA, MP, Macdonald to Norma Macdonald 10 Feb. 1945.

11 'SHAEF Supplementary Report,' ex. no. 5, Friedrich Torbanisch.

12 Ibid., ex. no. 6, Georg Mertens.

13 Ibid., ex. no. 18, Walter Nimmerfroh, recounting an address given by their company officer in which he warned the men never to be captured because 'the English and the Americans are said to be taking no prisoners.' Later, 'the men discussed among themselves the matter of taking prisoners and thought that they likewise, should not take any.'

14 See Best, 'Restraints on War,' 24: 'The legal and official literature, understandably enough, takes no notice of the possibility that within armed forces a kind of sub- culture or "private" culture may exist, the norms and tendencies which may conflict with those prescribed in the manuals of military conduct.'

15 'SHAEF Supplementary Report,' pt. 6, 'Arcques Case,' 35. On Les Hogues, see NAC, RG 24, vol. 12,842, file 393–53, affidavit of L.H., 12 Sept., 1944.

16 'SHAEF Supplementary Report,' pt. 6, 36.

17 Ibid., pt. 5, '26 Regiment Headquarters Case,' 32–3; and affidavit of Withold Stangenberg, 7 Nov. 1944.

18 On the conduct of the 25th PGR and its first battles with the Canadians, see Stacey, *The Victory Campaign*, ch. 2. On the battles for Falaise and Caen, see Luther, *Blood and Honor*, ch. 10, and Stacey, *The Victory Campaign*, 221.

19 As quoted in the report of Sepp Dietrich awarding the Swords to Meyer's Knight's Cross with Oak Leaves. See Foster, *Meeting of Generals*, 365. Also, see Meyer's debriefing by Canadian intelligence of 24 Aug. 1945 in which the rallying of the 89th Division is described. As the interrogator said, 'he [Meyer] must certainly have looked an impressive figure, this 35 year old Div. Cmd. wearing the highest decorations ... quietly but confidently facing

this disorderly mob and by his example and sheer determination influencing the whole Div. to turn back into line and take up the fight once more.' WMA, MP, box 5, file I 3/2.

20 WMA, MP, Macdonald to Norma Macdonald, 25 March 1945.
21 A.P. Scotland, *The London Cage* (Random House: 1957).
22 'SHAEF Supplementary Report,' ex. no. 8, Kurt Meyer, 8.
23 Ibid., 39
24 de Zayas, *Wehrmacht War Crimes*, 116: The British forwarded a note to the German Foreign Office through the Swiss legation in Berlin indicating that 'after capture by German armed forces certain Canadian officers and men had been shot ... On or about June 8th one Canadian officer and 18 other ranks met their death in the vicinity of Pavie in the Department of Calvados, Normandy, at or near Chateau Audrieux.' The Wehrmacht War Crimes Bureau was informed of but did not participate in the case, which was left with army intelligence. It accepted Meyer's explanation at face value (ibid., 117).
25 'SHAEF Supplementary Report,' ex. no. 8, Kurt Meyer, 41.
26 'SHAEF Supplementary Report,' ex. no. 8, Kurt Meyer, 46.
27 Allen Andrews, *Exemplary Justice* (Harrap: 1976), 112.
28 Scotland, *London Cage*, 90–1.
29 'SHAEF Supplementary Report,' ex. no. 9, Kurt Meyer, 33.
30 Ibid., 26.
31 WMA, MP, Macdonald to Norma Macdonald 1 April 1945.
32 'SHAEF Supplementary Report,' pt. 1, 2.
33 Ibid., pt. 3, 8.
34 WMA, MP, box 1, file 1/2, Macdonald to Barker 7 April 1945.
35 NAC, RG 24, vol. 12,839, file 372–53, H.A. Hanson to JAG, 5 June 1945. The Canadian echelon with 21 Army Group had been forwarding war crimes reports to CMHQ, which did not acknowledge receiving them. It urged CMHQ to create a war crimes staff: 'If Cdn. investigating teams are coming to this theatre in the immediate future we would feel that much easier. As you will appreciate, the evidence is getting stale and Cdn. formations are leaving areas in which reports originated.' NAC, RG 24, vol. 12,837, file 392–11, Morden to First Canadian Army, JAG, 13 June 1945.
36 WMA, MP, Macdonald to Norma Macdonald, 28 April 1945: 'Maj. Gen. Barker decided it was more important for me to remain in the Canadian cases on which I was working and phoned CMHQ who then cancelled the I Corps job.'
37 WMA, MP, box 1, file 1/2, Col. H.H. Newman of SHAEF to CMHQ, 14 April 1945.

38 Ibid., file 1/2, examination of Jan Jesionek by T/Sgt. Sigmund Stern, 22 April 1945.

39 Ibid., examination of Jan Jesionek 3 Oct. 1945. Further details of Jesionek's story are given in Bruce J.S. Macdonald, *The Trial of Kurt Meyer* (Clarke Irwin: 1954), 58–63.

40 Ibid., 63–4.

41 WMA, MP, box 1, file 1/2, Macdonald to Brig. B. Matthews, 8 May 1945.

42 NAC, RG 25, vol. 3,28, file 5,908–40,pt. 3, minutes of meting held in High Commissioner Vincent Massey's office, 24 April 1945.

43 NAC, RG 24, vol. 16,408, 'No. 1 Canadian War Crimes Unit War Diary, (hereinafter 'No. 1 CWCIU War Diary'), 4 June 1945, administrative order no. 71/45.

44 WMA, MP, box 1, file 1/2, Massey to External Affairs, 8 June 1945.

45 Ibid., External Affairs to Dominion, 23 July 1945.

46 A.P.V. Rogers, 'War Crimes Trials Under the Royal Warrant: British Practice 1945–1949,' *International and Comparative Law Quarterly*, vol. 39 (1990), 780 at 786–7: 'This royal prerogative was, in Dicey's words "nothing else than the residue of arbitrary authority which at any given time is legally left in the hands of the Crown."'

47 Despite observations from British jurists that the royal warrant was 'a procedure unprecedented in our own criminal courts, civil or military,' the British military courts were highly effective: eventually 1,703 accused would be tried, 1,403 convicted, and 372 executed. See 'The British Court for War Criminals,' *The Law Journal*, vol. 95 (15 Sept. 1945), 300.

48 WMA, MP, Macdonald to Norma Macdonald, 11 June 1945.

3: Indifference to the 'War Crimes Business'

1 NAC, RG 25, vol. 2,108, file 2,626–40C, memo of Marcel Cadieux, 'Punishment of War Crimes,' based on a memorandum from Paul Tremblay, 15 April 1943.

2 Ibid., 30.

3 NAC, RG 25, vol. 3,247, file 5,908–40C, King to Slaght, 3 Nov. 1943. John Read indicated that reasons of economy lay behind the appointment for 'as an MP he [Slaght] could not take fees.' But on the other hand, he added, 'there would be a very large element of prestige in being selected.' Ibid., Read to deputy, 14 Sept. 1943.

4 Ibid., Read to deputy, 14 Sept. 1943.

5 Ibid., minutes of CWCAC meeting, 29 Dec. 1943.

6 Alti Rodal, 'Nazi War Criminals in Canada: The Historical and Policy Setting from the 1940s to the Present,' unpublished report prepared for the Canada Commission on War Criminals, Jules Deschênes, commissioner (Sept. 1986), 19.

7 NAC, RG 25, vol. 3,247, file 5,908–40C, affidavit of J. Riley.

8 *Globe and Mail*, 3 March 1944.

9 NAC, RG 25, vol. 3,247, file 5,908–40C, Capt. L. Impey to Curran, 5 March 1944. On the massacre of Canadian Jesuits at Suchow, China, see Ibid., USSEA [under-secretary of state for external affairs] to Curran, 17 March 1944. The head of the Jesuits had noted, 'Quand la pleine lumiere sera faite sur tous les événements ne pourrons-nous parler de martyre?'

10 *Globe and Mail*, 11 Jan. 1944.

11 NAC, RG 25, vol. 3,247, file 5,908–40C, minutes of CWCAC meeting, 15 May 1944.

12 NAC, RG 25, vol. 2,108 A-12, file AR 405/4, pt 2, Massey to External Affairs, 28 Jan. 1944.

13 Ibid., memorandum of P.A.B. to John Read, 6 March 1944. See also Rodal, *Nazi War Criminals*, 20.

14 NAC, RG 25, vol. 3,728, file 5,908–40, pt. 3, High Commissioner Vincent Massey to External Affairs, 23 Dec. 1944.

15 Before Arthur Slaght travelled to Washington to discuss joint war crimes policy, he wrote to the prime minister that 'I have been somewhat concerned with the lack of progress and lack of practical results in the work of the Commission with its varied racial and international membership. I doubt very much whether the presence of a Canadian member at the Sittings of the Commission for many months past would have been able to make much difference in the result.' NAC, RG 25, vol. 2,108 A-12, file AR 405/4 pt. 2, Slaght to King 8 Nov. 1944.

16 Ibid., memorandum, External Affairs to Dominion, 26 Sept. 1943. In response to Soviet objections, Canada replied, 'We will be primarily interested in cases affecting Canadians or members of the Canadian forces.'

17 NAC, RG 25, vol. 3,728, file 5,908–40C, pt. 3, Read to Slaght, 27 Dec. 1944.

18 NAC, RG 25, vol. 2,108 A-12, file AR 405/4, pt. 2, note to USSEA, 26 July 1943.

19 Ibid., High Commissioner Vincent Massey to External Affairs, 2 Nov. 1944.

20 Ibid., Slaght to King, 8 Nov. 1944.

21 NAC, RG 25, vol. 3,728, file 5,908–40C, pt. 3, Read to Robertson, 16 Jan. 1945.

22 R.D. Cuff and J.L. Granatstein, *Canadian-American Relations in Wartime: From the Great War to the Cold War* (University of Toronto Press: 1975), 104: 'From being a vital link in the defence of the hemisphere in 1940–41, Canada had

become a mere appendage of limited importance.' See also C.C. Lingard and R.G. Trotter, *Canada in World Affairs: Sept. 1941 to May 1944* (Oxford University Press: 1950), 131.

23 J.L. Granatstein, *A Man of Influence: Norman A. Robertson and Canadian Statecraft, 1929–1968* (Deneau: 1981), 203.

24 de Zayas, *Wehrmacht War Crimes*, 99.

25 NAC, MR 26L, Louis St Laurent Papers, vol. 4, file 'International Justice and War Crimes,' Massey to External Affairs, 8 June 1945.

26 Ibid., Read, note for the prime minister, 12 June 1945.

27 NAC, RG 25, vol. 3,728, file 5,908–40C, pt. 3, memorandum of discussions between E.R. Hopkins and A. Slaght, 12 March 1945.

28 WMA, MP, box 1, file 1/2, Hopkins to heads of division, 5 June 1945.

29 Ibid., minutes of CWCAC meeting of 20 June 1945. The War Measures Act provided only that the government could promulgate regulations for the 'speedier and most effective prosecution of the war.'

30 Ibid., minutes of CWCAC meeting of 3 July 1945.

31 'No.1 CWCIU War Diary – NWE Detachment,' 2 July 1944.

32 Robichaud memorandum, 11. Robichaud had been transferred to the British Army's No. 1 War Crimes Investigation Team and had begun work on the Bergen-Belsen concentration camp case.

33 Author's interview with John Blain, 4 Feb. 1994.

34 'No. 1 CWCIU War Diary – NWE Detachment,' 10 Oct. 1945.

35 Other RCAF officers serving at Bad Salzuflen included S/L Staff Beck, S/L Gus Eustace, and F/L D. McTaggart.

36 Service history of Capt. Harold Hunter, provided to the author by Glenn Wright of the RCMP staff historical section.

37 Robichaud memorandum, 13.

38 See Macdonald's opening statement at the Meyer trial: 'Each investigating team is composed of a Lt. Col. and Major (both with legal training and experience) to carry out the interrogation. The main interrogation is conducted by the Lt. Col., while the Major acts as his assistant, but has the particular duty of cross-examining the witness on behalf of any prospective accused.' WMA, MP, file 3/7, 16.

39 'No. 1 CWCIU War Diary – NWE Detachment,' Aug. 1945: Major Neil Fraser did not intend that the system of three-man teams be inflexible. As was stated in the NWE Detachment's War Diary, 'the legal officer in each team will be either the examining officer or cross-examining officer in cases alloted to his team ... The organization outlined above is not intended to be rigid or to preclude one team using the services of someone on the other team for geographical or other reasons.'

40 Robichaud memorandum, 16.
41 John Blain to G. Hussey, author's collection, 10 Jan. 1989.
42 Wady Lehmann memorandum to the author, Dec. 1993, 3.
43 Ibid., 3.
44 Ibid., 4.
45 WMA, MP, box 4, file 2/10, 'Final Report of the No. 1 Canadian War Crimes Investigation Unit on Miscellaneous War Crimes, against members of the Canadian Armed Forces in the European Theatre of Operations 9 Sept. 1939 – 8 May 1945' (hereinafter 'Final Report') pt. 1, file Buchenwald/1. See also NAC, RG 24, vol. 12,837, file Buchenwald, report of Capt. J.W. Blain, 19 Aug. 1945; J.E. Read to High Commissioner Vincent Massey, 14 June 1945; and B.J.S. Macdonald to Massey, 8 Sept. 1945. Another Canadian agent, John McAlister of the (Special Operations Executive) was also executed in September 1944. See Roy MacLaren, *Canadians Behind Enemy Lines, 1939–1945* (University of British Columbia Press: 1981), 72–3.
46 Ibid., file 98, Verneuil/1.
47 Robichaud memorandum, 16.
48 'Final Report,' file 14, Calcar/1.
49 Ibid., file 25, Dunkirk/1. See also NAC, RG 24, vol. 12,838, Dunkirk case, B.J.S. Macdonald to O. Durdin, n.d.
50 Oppenheim, *International Law* (Longmans: 6th ed.).
51 'Final Report,' file 15, Calcar/2.
52 On the Dresden case, see NAC, RG 24, vol. 12,842, file 393–41. On the shooting of a Canadian prisoner on the order of Lt. Gen. Erdmann, see 'Final Report,' file 36, Gristede/1, and NAC, RG 25, vol. 3,728, file 5,908– 40. It is noted in the file: 'Should it develop that the accused [Erdmann] did in fact conduct a hearing it is to be doubted if a charge of murder against him could be maintained.'
53 'Final Report,' file 86, Stalag VIIIB/3.
54 Ibid., file 76, Stalag IID/3.
55 Ibid., file 70, Santec/1.
56 Ibid., file 71, Senio/1.
57 WMA, MP, box 3, 'Report of the No. 1 CWCIU Re Shooting of Canadian Prisoners of War by the German Armed Forces at Mouen, France, 11 June 1944,' file I 2/6, ex. no. 2, interrogation of Paul Kuret, 6 Aug. 1945.
58 Ibid., ex. no. 3, interrogation of W. Nimmerfroh, 7 Aug. 1945.
59 WMA, MP, box 4, 'Supplementary Report of the No. 1 Canadian War Crimes Unit, Re Shooting of Prisoners of War by the German Armed Forces in the Vicinity of Galmanche, Chateau d'Audrieu, Le Mesnil-Patry, Les Saullets, Normandy, France 7–11 June, 1944' (hereinafter 'CWCIU Supplementary

Report'), file I 2/9, Chateau d'Audrieu, ex. no. 10, interrogation of Karl Walter Becker 13 Aug. 1945, 8.

60 Ibid., 'Facts Disclosed by 21 Army Group,' 1.

61 'Final Report,' pt. 3 Chateau d'Audrieu.

62 Ian Sayer and Douglas Botting, *Hitler's Last General: The Case Against Wilhelm Moltke* (Bantam: 1989), 183.

63 *No. 1 CWCIU War Diary – UK Detachment*, 16 July 1945.

64 Ibid., 7 Aug. 1945.

65 John Blain to G. Hussey, author's collection, 10 Jan. 1989.

66 'CWCIU Supplementary Report,' Galmanche. See also Macdonald, *Trial of Kurt Meyer*, 34–6.

67 'CWCIU Supplementary Report,' Le Mesnil-Patry, ex. no. 12, interrogation of Germaine St Martin, 26 Oct. 1945.

68 Ibid., Le Mesnil-Patry, ex. no. 17, interrogation of Henri St Martin 26 Oct. 1945.

69 Ibid., report, 25 Nov., 2.

70 Ibid., Le Mesnil-Patry, ex. no. 16, interrogation of Wilhelm Stremme, 22–3 July 1945.

71 'SHAEF Supplementary Report,' file I 2/5, ex. no. 10, interrogation of Lt. D.A. James.

72 WMA, MP, box 3, 'Report of the No. 1 Canadian War Crimes Investigation Unit Re Shooting of Canadian Prisoners of War by the German Armed Forces Near Fontenay-le-Pesnel, Normandy, France, 8 June 1944' (hereinafter 'Fontenay-le-Pesnel'), file I 2/8. Accounts of the massacre are given in the interrogations of Cpl. Hector McLean, 15 June 1945; Gun. Weldon F. Clarke, 31 July 1945; Rfm. G.J. Ferris, 15 June 1945; and Pvt. Arthur Desjardins, 8 Aug. 1945. All these men survived the atrocity. On Lt. William Ferguson, the author has drawn on a letter generously supplied to him by Ferguson's daughter J'Anne. It is a letter from Sala Ferguson to Mabel Cosgrave, 1941, enclosing a note from William Ferguson.

73 'Fontenay-le-Pesnel,' interrogation of Weldon Clarke, 15.

74 Sayer and Botting, *Hitler's Last General*, 164–5.

75 'Final Report,' pt. II, Macdonald note.

76 'CWCIU Supplementary Report,' ex. no. 15, Paul Kuret.

77 Macdonald, *Trial of Kurt Meyer*, 94–5.

78 Ibid., 47–8.

79 Ibid., 48.

80 'Fontenay-le-Pesnel,' ex. no. 17, Georg Isecke. Macdonald gave this explanation to Isecke prior to his examination by Maj. H.H. Griffin.

81 Weingartner, *Crossroads of Death*, 74.

82 'The British Court for War Criminals,' *Law Journal*, vol. 95 (15 Sept. 1945), 300. See also, *Royal Warrant: Regulations for the Trial of War Criminals*, issued by special army order, War Office, June 1945.

83 Ibid.

84 WMA, MP, box 1, file 1/2, memorandum on the first draft of the War Crimes Regulations, 3 July 1945.

85 War Crimes Regulations (Canada), order-in-council, 30 Aug. 1945, section 10(1).

86 Ibid., Macdonald's comments on the second draft submission, 16 July 1945.

87 Ibid.

88 See subsections 10(4) and 10(5) of the Canadian regulations.

89 Meyer, *Grenadiere*, 201.

90 Foster, *Meeting of Generals*, 453.

91 Macdonald, *Trial of Kurt Meyer*, 51.

92 WMA, MP, box 1, file 1/2, extracts from a lecture given by Col. von der Heydte and Wildermuth, 'The Legal Aspects of War Crimes,' 3 April 1945.

93 de Zayas, *Wehrmacht War Crimes*, 92–4.

94 Ingo Müller, *Hitler's Justice: The Courts of the Third Reich*, trans. Deborah Lucas Schneider (Harvard University Press: 1991), Ch. 20. Within a single month in 1945, the German military passed as many death sentences as it had during all of the First World War. On discipline in the German army, see Martin van Creveld, *Fighting Power: German and US Army Performance, 1939–1945* (Greenwood: 1982).

95 de Zayas, *Wehrmacht War Crimes*, 108. The Wehrmacht War Crimes Bureau had no authority to investigate the Waffen SS, and even with respect to the Wehrmacht, it could deal only with official protests from foreign governments.

96 Ibid., 117.

97 WMA, MP, box 1, file 1/3, Macdonald to CWCAC and External Affairs, 10 Aug. 1945.

98 Ibid., Macdonald to DAG (deputy adjutant-general), 4 Sept. 1945, 3.

99 Ibid., Macdonald to DAG, 8 Sept. 1945.

100 House of Commons *Debates*, 13 Sept. 1945, 134–5.

101 WMA, MP, box 1, file 1/3, Macdonald to Orde, 23 Aug. 1945.

102 WMA, MP, Macdonald to Norma Macdonald, 2 Oct. 1945.

4: Questions of Partiality

1 WMA, MP, box 1, file 1/3, Macdonald to Orde, 27 Sept. 1945.

2 WMA, MP, Macdonald to Norma Macdonald, 9 Dec. 1946.

3 See G.W.L. Nicholson, *The Canadians in Italy, 1943–1945: Volume II of the Official History of the Canadian Army in the Second World War* (Queen's Printer: 1956).

4 Foster, *Meeting of Generals*, 350.

5 WMA, MP, Macdonald to Norma Macdonald, 9 Dec. 1945.

6 On the layout of the courtroom, see Macdonald, *Trial of Kurt Meyer*, 87. Just before the Meyer trial, Macdonald had gone to Luneberg to see British preparations for the Bergen-Belsen trial. He was most impressed: 'Microphones, floodlights, guards drilling in front of the court ... whoever is doing the stage managing for the Canadian trials might take a look at this.' NAC, RG 24, vol. 12,839, file 392–51, Macdonald to JAG, 10 Sept. 1945.

7 WMA, MP, box 5, file 3/2, 'Debriefing of Kurt Meyer,' 24 Aug. 1945.

8 *Re Mackay and the Queen* (1977), 78 D.L.R. (3d) 655 at 657 (FCTD).

9 *Re Mackay* (1980), 114 D.L.R. (3d) 393 at 414 (SCC).

10 Macdonald, *Trial of Kurt Meyer*, 39.

11 WMA, MP, box 6, 'Record of Proceedings: Trial by Canadian Military Court of S.S. Brigadefuhrer Kurt Meyer, Aurich, Germany 10–28 Dec. 1945' (hereinafter 'Meyer Trial'), file I 3/7, 676.

12 Ibid., 681.

13 Macdonald, *Trial of Kurt Meyer*, 74.

14 WMA, MP, Macdonald to Norma Macdonald, 15 Oct. 1945.

15 WMA, MP, box 1, file 1/5, Macdonald to Orde, 21 Oct. 1945.

16 Ibid., Macdonald noted 'delete' next to the charge of mutilation of bodies.

17 NAC, RG 24, vol. 12,839. file 392–51, Memorandum of Clarence Campbell, 26 Oct. 1945.

18 'Meyer Trial,' 688.

19 Ibid., 695. Meyer was not prepared to concede that men from his regiment had committed the killings until confronted with this evidence at trial.

20 WMA, MP, box 1, file 1/4, Macdonald to Page, 6 Nov. 1945.

21 On Meyer's return to Germany and arraignment, see Canadian Press report of William Ross, 1 Nov. 1945, Windsor *Star*, 31 Oct. 1945, and Ross Munro's report of the same date in *Globe and Mail*. See also Meyer, *Grenadiere*, 197–8.

22 Meyer, *Grenadiere*, 198.

23 New York *Times* 13 Oct. 1945.

24 *Toronto Globe and Mail*, 2 Nov. 1945.

25 Ibid., 1 Nov. 1945. The charge sheet was described as 'The first official disclosure of atrocities against Canadian prisoners in Normandy other than one announcement in August, 1944.'

26 Ibid., 3 Nov. 1945.

27 Osgoode Society interview with B.J.S. Macdonald, Sept. 1984, 43.

28 NAC, RG 24, vol. 12,839, file 392–51, Macdonald to ADAG (assistant deputy adjutent-general), 18 Oct. 1945.

29 WMA, MP, box 1, file 1/5, memorandum of Macdonald to DAG and CMHQ, 6 Nov. 1945.

30 NAC, RG 24, vol. 12,839, file 392–51, Griffin to ADAG, 25 Oct. 1945.

31 As recounted in the Macdonald video for JAG officers, 1985. This incident is not described in his 1954 book, *The Trial of Kurt Meyer*.

32 WMA, MP, box 1, file 1/5, Macdonald to CMHQ and DAG, 6 Nov. 1945. The press was suspicious about the abrupt change in lawyers. See *Globe and Mail*, 3 Nov. 1945: 'The defence job might have interfered with Col. Wright's early repatriation and, although the same reason already had been given for Col. Andrews, it apparently no longer applies and he is taking over the job.'

33 Foster, *Meeting of Generals*, 459. Although no citation is given, this apparently is taken from the author's interview with Maurice Andrew.

34 Ibid., 460.

35 NAC, RG 24, vol. 12,839, file 392–51, Macdonald to Vokes, 19 Nov. 1945.

36 Ibid., certificate of Col. G. Elms (U.S. Army), 26 Nov. 1945, indicating that both Milius and Geyr von Schweppenburg were unavailable.

37 Ibid., file 392–52, Campbell to OC (officer commanding) 3rd Cdn. Graves Reg. Unit, 17 Nov. 1945.

38 Macdonald, *Trial of Kurt Meyer*, 84.

39 WMA, MP, box 1, file 1/5, Macdonald to CMHQ and DAG, 6 Nov. 1945.

40 NAC, RG 24, vol. 12,839, file 392–52, memo of 16 Nov. 1945.

41 Ibid., file 392–51, memo to the file, 14 Nov. 1945.

42 WMA, MP, box 1, file 1/5, G/C Strathy to F.P. Varcoe, deputy minister of justice, 17 Nov. 1945.

43 NAC, RG 24, vol. 12,839, file 392–51, memo to secretary of state for external affairs from J. Read, 10 Nov. 1945.

44 WMA, MP, box 1, file 1/3, Read to Orde 17 Nov. 1945.

45 Ibid., telegram, Defensor (National Defence) to Canmilitary (CHMQ), 19 Nov. 1945: 'By well established Canadian constitutional practice Governor General acting on advice of His Majesty's Privy Council for Canada has powers under British North America Act, War Measures Act, Militia Act and otherwise to establish procedures for trial and punishment by Canadian military courts of violations of the laws and usages of war not less extensive than those exercised under the Royal Warrant.'

46 WMA, MP, file 1/5, note from Louis St Laurent to governor general, Nov. 1945.

47 Ibid., file 1/3, Orde to Bredin, 21 Nov. 1945.

48 Ibid., file 1/5, Macdonald to Orde, 29 Nov. 1945.

49 Ibid., file 1/5, Macdonald to CMHQ and DAG, 6 Nov. 1945.
50 WMA, MP, Macdonald to Norma Macdonald, 15 Oct. 1945.

5: Brigadeführer on Trial

1 Meyer, *Grenadiere*, 20.
2 Toronto *Globe and Mail*, 11 Dec. 1945.
3 'Meyer Trial,' 20.
4 Ibid., 42.
5 *Globe and Mail*,11 Dec. 1945.
6 'Meyer Trial,' 50.
7 Macdonald, *Trial of Kurt Meyer*, 95–6.
8 'Meyer Trial,' 102, 106.
9 *Globe and Mail*, 13 Dec. 1945.
10 'Meyer Trial,' 192.
11 *Globe and Mail*, 13 Dec. 1945.
12 'Meyer Trial,' 134.
13 Ibid., 166.
14 Ibid., 297.
15 Ibid., 301.
16 Ibid., 309.
17 Ibid., 320.
18 Ibid., 347.
19 Ibid., 349–50.
20 *Globe and Mail*, 15 Dec. 1945.
21 Foster, *Meeting of Generals*, 467.
22 Halifax *Herald*, 15 Dec. 1945.
23 Toronto *Globe and Mail*, 17 Dec. 1945.
24 As quoted in Foster, *Meeting of Generals*, 469.
25 Ibid., 465.
26 In his account of the trial, Bruce Macdonald inferred that Lieutenant Windsor's declaration that he would answer only the three questions prescribed by the Geneva Convention 'accounted for the fact that he and others in their party never got beyond the Abbaye Ardenne, but there paid the price with their lives for their loyalty to their comrades and devotion to duty' (*Trial of Kurt Meyer*, 130). While for Macdonald this is only an inference, Cliff Chadderton states categorically in the video *Take No Prisoners!* (War Amps: 1995) that Canadians were shot because they refused to divulge information. He presumes that, if the Germans had been aware of the weakness of the Allied beachhead, they would have driven the Allies off. This ignores the fact

that German counter-attacks (such as Meyer's) were as determined as their resources allowed. Furthermore, Chadderton states that Windsor was subjected to 'frightening interrogation.' But there were no witness statements as to Windsor's interrogation. As well, the Abbaye was not an intelligence-gathering point; this was done at the 12th SS's divisional HQ. The only eyewitness to the executions, Jesionek, cited Meyer's words to get rid of the prisoners as a nuisance. Of the murdered prisoners, the vast majority were privates and unlikely to have much useful information. Of the thirty-five men shot at Fontenay-le-Pesnel, none was interrogated. To state that the prisoners died nobly while refusing to turn traitor romanticizes the events and detracts from the reality that the killings were unnecessary and purely criminal acts.

27 'Meyer Trial,' 463.
27 Ibid., 490. The prosecution did not make any charges with regard to the death of L/Cpl. Pollard because his body was not found and he was officially listed as 'missing.'
28 Ibid., 542.
29 Ibid., 558.
30 Ibid., 574.
31 *Globe and Mail*, 19 Dec. 1945.
32 'Meyer Trial,' 602.
33 Ibid., 604.
34 Ibid., 632.
35 Macdonald, *Trial of Kurt Meyer*, 141.
36 *Globe and Mail*, 20 Dec. 1945.
37 'Meyer Trial,' 679–80.
38 Ibid., 681.
39 *Globe and Mail*, 21 Dec. 1945.
40 'Meyer Trial,' 695–6.
41 Macdonald, *Trial of Kurt Meyer*, 145.
42 'Meyer Trial,' 699.
43 *Globe and Mail* 21 Dec. 1945.
44 Meyer, *Grenadiere*, 206–7.
45 NAC, RG 24, vol. 12,839, file 392–52, Stonborough to Crawford, 8 Jan. 1946.
46 'Meyer Trial,' 726.
47 *Maple Leaf*, 27 Dec. 1945. In Foster, *Meeting of Generals*, an extremely pro-Meyer account of the trial, it is incorrectly stated that Macdonald chose to 'drop the matter [La Villeneuve incident] as a side issue' and that 'the question still remained on how the German soldiers riding in their reconnaissance vehicles had met their deaths' (473). As the trial transcript clearly shows, Macdonald was eager to explain to the court what had occurred at La

Villeneuve. Ultimately, the 'question' was answered by the affidavits filed by the officers of the Regina Rifles.

48 Robichaud memorandum. Robichaud questioned the wisdom of his becoming actively involved in the trial: 'I have no qualms of conscience about what I had done, though as a servant of the Court – which I was temporarily – I suppose I had no business working for the prosecution' (21).

49 Macdonald, *Trial of Kurt Meyer*, 153.

50 *Globe and Mail* 24 Dec. 1945.

51 Macdonald, *Trial of Kurt Meyer*, 155.

52 WMA, MP, Macdonald to Norma Macdonald, 22 Dec. 1945.

53 Toronto *Daily Star*, 20 Dec. 1945.

54 Meyer, *Grenadiere*, 210.

55 'Meyer Trial,' 808.

56 Ibid., 825.

57 Royal warrant, subsection 8(ii): 'Where there is evidence that a war crime has been the result of concerted action upon the part of a unit or group of men, then evidence given upon any charge relating to that crime against any member of such unit or group may be received as *prima facie* evidence of the responsibility of each member of that unit or group for that crime.' The comparable section in the Canadian War Crimes Regulations was subsection 10(3).

58 Parks, 'Command Responsibility for War Crimes,' 9.

59 K. Steiner, 'War Crimes and Command Responsibility,' *Pacific Affairs*, vol. 58 (summer 1985), 293–8.

60 Roland L. Lael, *The Yamashita Precedent: War Crimes and Command Responsibility* (Scholarly Resources: 1982), 32–7.

61 Parks, 'Command Responsibility for War Crimes,' quoting the written opinion of the commission, 7 Dec. 1945, 30.

62 Lael, *The Yamashita Precedent*, 123: 'In exercising their powers, the five military officers in Manila imposed an awesome standard on commanding officers. By accepting the prosecutor's argument that Yamashita either must have known or should have known of the widespread violations of the law of war, the court firmly rejected the defence argument that exemplary circumstances should mitigate, at the very least, any sentence on a commanding officer who faced adverse battle conditions.' For another view of the *Yamashita* case, see (no author), 'Command Responsibility for War Crimes,' *Yale Law Journal*, vol. 82 (May 1973), 1,274: 'By imposing duties of supervision and control, even where a commander is aware of no particular facts indicating that his subordinates are engaging in crimes, *Yamashita* accomplishes a greater expansion of command responsibility than would a mere recognition of 'constructive knowledge' (at 1,283).

63 'Meyer Trial,' 20–1.

64 Ibid., 842.

65 Ibid., 843.

66 Foster, *Meeting of Generals*, 480–1. Foster discussed the Court's deliberations with both his father, Harry Foster, and Bell-Irving. In an effort to put Meyer in the best possible light, Foster gives a truncated version of the evidence at trial. Meyer's numerous fabrications, including his denial, until the last possible minute, that any prisoners had been killed at his HQ are given little attention or weight. The crucial evidence of Daniel Lachèvre that there were no bodies in the garden from 8 to 10 June is totally ignored in Foster's account.

67 Ibid., 481.

68 Ibid.

69 Ibid., 484.

70 WMA, MP, Macdonald to Norma Macdonald, 28 Dec. 1945.

71 *Abbaye Ardenne Case* (1945) 4 UNWCC Law Reports of Trials of War Criminals 97.

72 L.C. Green, *Essays on the Modern Law of War* (Transnational Publishers: 1985). The author quotes extensively from Bredin's summation 'as regards the accusation of ordering the denial of quarter.' However, he includes in the quotation's final two paragraphs a portion of Bredin's instructions that do not deal with the denial of quarter charge but rather with the charge that Meyer directly ordered the killings at the Abbaye. Bredin's instructions on this point deal with the actual giving of orders to kill prisoners and are not related to the issue of command responsibility. Therefore, one of Bredin's comments in the final two paragraphs (as quoted by Green), that 'you must be satisfied before you convict, that some words were uttered or some clear indication was given by the accused that prisoners were to be put to death,' do not relate to command responsibility. It may be questionable to conclude, as Green has done, that the *Meyer* case required a closer link to the killing than the U.S. commission did in *Yamashita*, since Bredin's comments on command responsibility are not extensive and do not indicate any real variance from *Yamashita*.

73 *U.S. v. Wilhelm von Leeb (High Command Case)*, (1947–8) 10 TWC 1 and 11 TWC at 543–4. See also Parks, 'Command Responsibility for War Crimes.' Parks concludes after reviewing the command responsibility decisions of the Second World War that 'acceptance of command clearly imposes upon the commander a duty to supervise and control the conduct of his subordinates in accordance with existing principles of the law of war' (at 77).

74 *U.S. v. Wilhelm List (Hostages Case)*, (1947–8) 11 TWC 759.

75 See *Yale Law Journal*, 'Command Responsibility for War Crimes.' The author notes the trial of Gen. Kurt Student for crimes committed on Crete: 'The crimes did not constitute a policy or an established pattern, and there was no way – given his elevated rank and distance from the many battlefields – that the accused could have been aware of the occurence, or the imminence of any of the specific crimes; thus conviction depended on adoption of risks of crime as a mental object' (at 1,287f).

76 'Meyer Trial,', 849.

77 Ottawa *Evening Citizen*, 28 Dec. 1945.

78 'Meyer Trial,' 855–6.

79 Meyer, *Grenadiere*, 211.

80 Foster, *Meeting of Generals*, 484.

81 WMA, MP, Macdonald to Norma Macdonald, 28 Dec. 1945.

6: But for the Grace of God

1 Lehmann memorandum to the author, December, 1993, 13.

2 Meyer, *Grenadiere*, 212.

3 WMA, CP, Series I-5, endorsement on the Meyer appeal.

4 Foster, *Meeting of Generals*, 487.

5 WMA, MP, Macdonald to Norma Macdonald, 28 Dec. 1945.

6 NAC, RG 24, vol. 12,839, file 392–52, Macdonald to A.P. Scotland, 24 Jan. 1946.

7 Weingartner, *Crossroads of Death*, ch. 7.

8 London *Evening Free Press*, 29 Dec. 1945.

9 *Maple Leaf*, 11 Jan. 1946.

10 Ibid., 29 Dec. 1945 and 19 Jan. 1946.

11 Osgoode Society interview with B.J.S. Macdonald, Sept. 1984, 41.

12 Ibid.

13 Daniel G. Dancocks, *The D-Day Dodgers: The Canadians in Italy, 1943–1945* (McClelland and Stewart: 1991), 69.

14 Ibid., 50. See also Chris Vokes, *My Story* (Gallery Publishing: 1985). Describing the Ragusa incident in his autobiography, Vokes confessed that he had urged the battalion commander to shoot the snipers out of hand. When he did not and instead sent them back to brigade HQ, Vokes's first reaction was to 'shoot them on the spot' (at 97).

15 See Brereton Greenhous, 'Would it not have been better to bypass Ortona completely ...? A Canadian Christmas, 1943,' *Canadian Defence Quarterly*, vol. 19 (April 1989), 51.

16 Vokes, *My Story*, 206.

17 Ibid., 204.
18 WMA, MP, box 1, file 1/5, HQ, 3 Canadian Infantry Division to CMHQ, 5 Jan. 1946.
19 Ibid., memorandum of a conference held in the office of the high commissioner, 9 Jan. 1946: 'The unanimous opinion was that ... the extreme penalty of death would only be justified in a case where the offence was conclusively shown to have resulted either from the direct act of the commander or by his ommission to act when he knew that if he did not act a war crime would be committed.'
20 Vokes, *My Story*, 205.
21 WMA, MP, box 1, file 1/5, undated telegram in sequence for 12 Jan. 1946, *Canmilitary to Defensor*.
22 Ibid., Vokes to Murchie, 21 Jan. 1946.
23 Meyer, *Grenadiere*, 216.
24 As noted in the Calgary *Herald*, 17 Jan. 1946.
25 Meyer, *Grenadiere*, 218.
26 WMA, MP, box 1, file 1/4, Macdonald to Dean, 18 Jan. 1946.
27 NAC, RG 24, vol. 12,837, file 392–52, Macdonald to Scotland, 24 Jan. 1946.
28 WMA, MP, box 1, file 1/3, Macdonald to CMHQ, 17 Jan. 1946.
29 Peterborough *Examiner*, 15 Jan. 1946.
30 Toronto *Telegram*, 15 Jan. 1946.
31 Ibid.
32 *Globe and Mail*, 18 Jan. 1946.
33 Ibid., 15 Jan. 1946.
34 NAC, MG–J1, W.L.M. King Papers, vol. 399, S. Boyko, South Spadina Club Labour-Progressive Party, 17 Jan. 1946, 361,033.
35 WMA, MP, box 1, file 1/5, Vokes to chief of staff, 13 Jan. 1946.
36 Calgary *Herald*, 15 Jan. 1946.
37 The minister of national defence, Douglas Abbott, was unsure of who was responsible for the commutation. He commented that the government was 'quite satisfied to accept the judgment of our senior officers at Canadian Military Headquarters in London.' Toronto *Telegram*, 15 Jan. 1946.
38 *Globe and Mail*, 18 Jan. 1946.
39 Ibid., 23 Jan. 1946.
40 Ibid., 24 Jan. 1946.
41 NAC, MG 26, J–4 (Privy Council), vol. 419, cabinet conclusions, 16 Jan. 1946.
42 Press release from Department of National Defence, 17 Jan. 1946. It was stated in the release that Vokes was the sole officer empowered to commute the sentence and that he had done so because Meyer's degree of complicity did

not warrant a death sentence: 'What is not generally appreciated is that in fact the court had expressly found him [Meyer] not guilty of issuing any orders for such shooting.' Quoted in Windsor *Star*, 17 Jan. 1946.

43 House of Commons *Debates*, 1 April 1946, 432.
44 WMA, MP, box 1, file 1/5, Massey to External Affairs, 21 Jan. 1946.
45 Ibid., Vokes to Murchie, 21 Jan. 1946.
46 Ibid., National Defence to CMHQ, 23 Jan. 1946.
47 Canadian Press story. See Calgary *Herald*, 16 Jan. 1946.
48 *Globe and Mail*, 18 Jan. 1946.
49 Peterborough *Examiner*, 17 Jan. 1946.
50 Maurice Pope, *Soldiers and Politicians: The Memoirs of Lt. Gen. Maurice A. Pope* (University of Toronto Press: 1962), 291.
51 Peterborough *Examiner*, 19 Jan. 1946.
52 Vancouver *Sun*, 17 Jan. 1946.
53 Hamilton *Spectator*, 15 Jan. 1946.
54 *Globe and Mail*, 22 Jan. 1946.
55 Windsor *Daily Star*, 17 Jan. 1946.
56 Calgary *Herald*, 16 Jan. 1946.
57 Toronto *Telegram*, 15 Jan. 1946.
58 WMA, MP, box 1, file 1/4, Macdonald to I Davidson, liaison of the British army, 26 Feb. 1946. Although requested by Britain to adhere to the Four Power Agreement creating the International Military Tribunal at Nuremberg, Canada declined to do so. At the 88th meeting of the UNWCC on 29 Nov. 1945, Sir Robert Craigie noted that only China and Canada had not accepted the agreement. This prompted Vincent Massey to advise Ottawa that Macdonald's planned visit to Nuremberg in November 1945 had to be postponed until such time as Canada adhered to the agreement. See NAC, RG 24, vol. 12,843, file 393–58, UNWCC, Morden to high commissioner, 29 Nov. 1945; and high commissioner to External Affairs, 21 Nov. 1945. Canadian reluctance to sanction the Nuremberg process might be traced back to John Read's advice to USSEA that 'we should not adhere to an agreement in the negotiation of which we had no part and in the carrying out of which we were to have no voice.' NAC, RG 25, file 5,908–40C, pt. 4, Read note for USSEA, 29 Aug. 1945.
59 James P. O'Donnell, *The Bunker: The History of the Reich Chancellory Group* (Houghton Mifflin: 1978), 329–37.
60 Macdonald, *Trial of Kurt Meyer*, 29.
61 WMA, MP, box 5, file 2/7, Gatternig interrogation 5 March 1946.
62 Macdonald, *Trial of Kurt Meyer*, 69–70.
63 WMA, MP, box 5, file 2/7, Stift interrogation, 17 May 1946.

64 Macdonald, *Trial of Kurt Meyer*, 70. In Foster's *Meeting of Generals*, there is no mention of Gatternig or Stift or their refutation of Meyer's story at trial.
65 Meyer, *Grenadiere*, 200.
66 Hamilton *Spectator*, 11 Jan. 1946

7: Shot like Wild Animals

1 NAC, RG 24, vol. 12,837, file 391–39, Brackel, affidavit of Maria Hirsch, 10 Jan. 1946; and affidavit of Fritz Waescher, 6 Jan. 1946.
2 William L. Shirer, *Berlin Diary* (Knopf: 1941), 491.
3 John Terraine, *The Right of the Line: The Royal Air Force in the European War, 1939–1945* (Hodder and Stoughton: 1985), 292–3.
4 Ibid., 504–5.
5 Martin Middlebrook, *The Battle of Hamburg: Allied Bomber Forces against a German City in 1943* (Scribner: 1980), 75.
6 Terraine, *Right of the Line*, 507.
7 Middlebrook, *Battle of Hamburg*, 360.
8 W. Hays Parks, 'Air War and the Laws of War,' in Horst Boog, ed., *The Conduct of the Air War in the Second World War: An International Comparison* (Berg: 1992). Parks quotes international lawyer J.W. Garner in 1936: 'As to air warfare I think we can say there is practically no conventional International Law dealing with it' (at 351). However, one German commentator, Manfred Messerschmidt, did suggest that the belligerents of the Second World War 'assumed that there was a binding code for the conduct of the air war.' He does not cite any specific code. As well, the Hague Rules of Air Warfare of 1923, which would have significantly restricted bombing, were never ratified. See M. Messerschmidt, 'Strategic Air War and International Law,' 298–307.
9 Geoffrey Best, *War and Society in Revolutionary Europe, 1770– 1870* (St Martin's: 1982), 144–6.
10 As quoted in Lord Russell of Liverpool, *The Scourge of the Swastika: A Short History of Nazi War Crimes*, 11th ed. (1959), 39.
11 Hugh Trevor-Roper, ed., *Final Entries 1945: The Diaries of Joseph Goebbels*, trans. Richard Barry (G.P. Putman's: 1978). xxviii and 78, entry for 8 March 1945.
12 Middlebrook, *Battle of Hamburg*, 374–5.
13 'Final Report,' pt. 1, no. 18, Bremen/1.
14 Arthur A. Durand, *Stalag Luft III: The Secret Story* (Touchstone: 1988), 52–3.
15 Brereton Greenhous, S.J. Harris, W.C. Johnston, and W.G.P. Rawlings, *The Crucible of War, 1939–1945: The Official History of the Royal Canadian Air Force*, 3 vols. (University of Toronto Press: 1994), 3:802.

16 Maximilian Koessler, 'Borkum Island Tragedy and Trial,' *Journal of Criminal Law, Criminology and Political Science*, vol. 47 (1956–7), 183.

17 *Globe and Mail*, 3 June 1944.

18 NAC, RG 24, vol. 12,837, Diest/1. See also 'Final Report,' pt. 2, 67 Dienst/1: 'The German doctor in charge of the hospital, named Mahr, is known to have given strict orders that S. be not touched in any way and that the door to his room be at all times locked.'

19 Ibid., pt. 2, 67 Woltersdorf/1.

20 Ibid., pt. 2, 67/ Poggio/1 and Mireteto/1.

21 NAC, RG 24, vol. 12,843, file 393–69, Wassertrudingen.

22 Ibid., pt. 1, 67/ Frankfurt/1.

23 Ibid., pt. 2, 67/ Kassel/1.

24 Ibid., pt. 2, 67/ Hamborn/1.

25 Ibid., pt. 2, 67/ Frankenberg/1.

26 Ibid., pt. 2, 67/ Luttringhausen/1.

27 WMA, MP, box 1, file 1/2, memorandum of Brig. B. Matthews to CMHQ, 8 May 1945.

28 'No. 1 CWCIU War Diary – NWE Detachment,' 10 Jan. 1946.

29 Ibid., 4 March 1946.

30 Osgoode Society interview with B.J.S. Macdonald, Sept. 1984, 45.

31 NAC, RG 25, vol. 3,728, file 5,908–40C pt. 5, memorandum of minister of defence for air, 14 Feb. 1946.

32 Arthur Bishop, *Courage in the Air: Canada's Military Heritage*, 3 vols. (McGraw-Hill: 1992) 1: 241–2, 271–2.

33 Author's interview with John Blain, 4 Feb. 1994.

34 Subsection 7(3) states: 'If the accused belongs to the naval, military or air forces of an enemy or ex-enemy power, or if Canadian naval, military or air force personnel are in any way affected by the alleged war crime, the convening officer should appoint or detail, if available, at least one naval, military or air force officer as a member of the court, as the case may be.'

35 Windsor *Daily Star*, 1 April 1946.

36 Ottawa *Citizen*, 20 March 1946.

37 John Blain letter to the author, 12 Sept. 1994.

38 DHist., file 159,95023 (Do), Transcript of the Trial of Johann Neitz, 15–20 March 1946, Aurich, Germany (hereinafter 'Neitz Trial'), 16.

39 Ibid., 48.

40 Ibid., 173.

41 Alexander Cattanach letter to the author, 4 June 1994.

42 'Neitz Trial,' Neitz to Air Marshal G.O. Johnson, 23 March 1946.

43 WMA, MP, box 5, file I 2/12, 'Record of the Proceedings for the Trial of

Wilhelm Jung for Killing an RCAF Serviceman at Oberweier, Germany'
(hereinafter 'Oberweier Record'), examination of Joseph Lindenbolz, 4.

44 Ibid., examination of Anton Kustner, 4.
45 Ibid., examination of Hilda Jung, 3–4.
46 Ibid., examination of Karl Dehmer, 2.
47 Ibid., examination of Wendelin Kappenberg.
48 Ibid., examination of Wilhelm Jung, 19–20.
49 Lehmann memorandum to the author, December 1993, diary extract for Feb.
   1946. 'When I reached Tiengen and located Schumacher, he was living in a
   typical, modest German farm house. Neither he nor his wife and family
   seemed particularly emotional in our presence – as though they had been
   forewarned. As I recall he was of medium height and build, brown hair, gray-
   blue eyes, plain country features ... He had no air of arrogance, nor of
   subservience.'
50 'Oberweier Record,' examination of Johann Schumacher, 5.
51 *Globe and Mail*, 21 March 1946.
52 NAC, RG 25–F3, vol. 2,609, 'Trial of Wilhelm Jung and Johann Schumacher,
   15–20 March 1945, Aurich, Germany, vol. 1' (hereinafter 'Oberweier Trial').
53 Ibid., 50.
54 Ibid., 57.
55 Ibid., 62.
56 R.W. Baker, *The Hearsay Rule* (Pitman: 1950), 7–12; and R.J. Delisle, 'Hearsay
   Evidence,' *Law Society of Upper Canada Special Lectures* (1984), 59–64.
57 'Oberweier Trial,' 89.
58 Ibid., 111.
59 Ibid., 177.
60 Ibid., 184.
61 *Axtell's Case* (1661), Kelying 13, 84 *E.R.* 1055 at 1060.
62 H.R. (House of Representatives) Exec. Document No. 23, 40th Congress, 2nd
   Session 704.
63 (1900), 17 S.C. (Cape of Good Hope) 561 at 567–8.
64 Oppenheim, *International Law* (1906), 33. See also L.C. Green, 'Superior Orders
   and Command Responsibility,' *Canadian Yearrbook of International Law*, vol. 27
   (1989), 167 at 174–6; and L.C. Green, 'The Defence of Superior Orders in the
   Modern Law of Armed Conflict,' *Alberta Law Review*, vol. 31 (1993), 320 at
   323–5. Green details the reluctance of the text writers to consider atrocities
   committed under orders of a superior officer to be war crimes, even after the
   Llandovery Castle decision.
65 The facts of the *Llandovery Castle* case are taken from Friedman, *The Law of
   War*, 1:869–82. The German court noted the ingrained obedience of the naval

officer, which 'would have required a specially high degree of resolution' and mitigated any punishment. Nevertheless, 'the killing of defenceless, shipwrecked people is an act in the highest degree contrary to ethical principles' (at 882).

66 Oppenheim, *International Law,* (1940) s. 253 at 452. See also Green, *Essays on the Modern Law of War,* 57.
67 'Oberweier Trial,' 195.
68 Ibid., 197.
69 'No. 1 CWCIU War Diary – NWE Detachment,' 20 March 1946.
70 'Oberweier Trial,' 210.
71 Muller, *Hitler's Justice.*

8: Opladen: The Forgotten Case

1 WMA, MP, box 5, file I 2/16, 'Record of the Evidence for the Trial of Robert Holzer' (hereinafter 'Holzer Record'), affidavit of Tec. S. (Technical Sergeant) Eugene C. Ernst.
2 Ibid., pathological report in the affidavit of Max Berg.
3 *Globe and Mail,* 26 March 1946.
4 Opinions vary among German historians as to the Volkssturm's effectiveness. Martin Sorge, *The Other Price of Hitler's War* (Greenwood: 1986), recounts how it fought several pitched battles and sustained heavy casualties (at 48–50). On the other hand, M.G. Steinert, *Hitler's War and the Germans* (University of Ohio Press: 1977), dismisses the formation of the Volkssturm as a futile gesture (at 281).
5 See R.G. Reuth, *Goebbels,* 341: 'Party functionaries were put in charge of forming the units. These militia-like groups, completely meaningless in any military sense, were led not by soldiers but by Gauleiters in their capacity as Reich defence commissars.'
6 'Holzer Record,' affidavit of Josef Caspers.
7 Author's interview with John Blain, 4 Feb. 1994.
8 'Holzer Record,' affidavit of Wilhelm Ossenbach, 9 March 1946.
9 Ibid., 10.
10 Ibid., affidavit of Wilhelm Ossenbach, 13 March 1946 2.
11 Ibid., 'They were so far away that we couldn't see them yet – perhaps 15 meters' (4).
12 Ibid., 9.
13 NAC, RG 25, F-3, vol. 2,609, 'Trial of Robert Holzer, Walter Weigel, and Wilhelm Ossenbach at Aurich, Germany, 25 March–6 April 1946' (hereinafter 'Opladen Trial'), Schapp to W/C O'Brien, 15 April 1946.

14 Author's interview with John Blain, 4 Feb. 1994.
15 Macdonald, *Trial of Kurt Meyer*, 50.
16 'Opladen Trial,' 90.
17 Ibid., 281.
18 Ibid., 94.
19 Ibid., 25–9.
20 Ibid., 121.
21 'Holzer Record,' examination of Robert Holzer, 11 March 1946, 6–8.
22 Ibid., 12.
23 'Opladen Trial,' 141.
24 WMA, MP, box 5, file I 2/16, examination of Hubert Broicchaus, 18 Feb. 1946
   10.
25 'Opladen Trial,' 178.
26 Ibid., 183.
27 WMA, MP, box 5, file I 2/16, supplementary examination of Hubert
   Broicchaus, 5.
28 Ibid., 26.
29 'Opladen Trial,' 191.
30 Ibid., 251–7.
31 Ibid., 262.
32 Ibid., 273.
33 Ibid., 306.
34 Ibid., 344–6.
35 *Globe and Mail*, 8 April 1946.
36 DHist., file 181,003 (D5,405), A–11, translation of prisoners' letters.
37 'Opladen Trial,' Schapp to W/C O'Brien, 15 April 1946.
38 Ibid., postscript of A/M G.O. Johnson's Letter 6 May 1946.
39 NAC, RG 24, vol. 12,843, file 393–67, memorandum of Macklin to chief of
   staff, CMHQ, 13 Dec. 1945. Also: Rodal, *Nazi War Criminals in Canada*, 52; and
   NAC, RG 25, vol. 3,728, file 5,908–40C, pt.5, s. 8,959–9 (acting judge advocate
   general).
40 NAC, RG 25, vol. 3,728, file 5,908–40C, pt.5, High Commissioner Vincent
   Massey to External Affairs, 11 April 1946: 'The withdrawal of occupation
   forces, the claims of personnel to repatriation and the time now required
   owing to the nature of remaining work, point to handing over to British
   counterpart.'.
41 Ibid., Hopkins to Robertson, 17 April 1946. Hopkins did suggest that 'before
   any United Kingdom trials are held in respect of Germans accused of
   atrocities against Canadians only, a transcript of the evidence and any other
   necessary details should be transmitted to Ottawa for approval by the

Canadian Government' The high commissioner's office transmitted this request to the British military, adding that 'but once a Canadian case had been approved for trial, the trial itself would be entirely a United Kingdom trial.' Ibid., High Commissioner Massey to External Affairs, 8 May 1946.' Norman Robertson noted that these niceties were not always being observed. But in the end 'this jurisdictional tangle has not, in fact, upset the administration of the cases which were handed over to the United Kingdom Judge Advocate General. Only a few instances arose when any approval was necessary and the desired procedure was observed by both parties while the matter was still in the process of settlement.' Ibid., Robertson to External Affairs, 23 Dec. 1946.

42 Ibid., JAG to Ministry of National Defence for Air, 12 April 1946.
43 NAC, MG 26–J4 (Privy Council), vol. 419, cabinet conclusions 6 May 1946. The minister of national defence for air reported that 'with the withdrawl of Canadian forces from Europe the maintenance of the War Crimes Investigation Unit did not seem justified.'
44 NAC, RG 25, vol. 3,728, file 5,908–40C, pt 5, acting prime minister (Louis St Laurent) to Slaght, 14 May 1946.
45 'No. 1 CWCIU War Diary – UK Detachment,' 2, 31 May 1946

9: Hong Kong: The Law of the Imperial Japanese Army

1 On the comparison of death rates in European and Japanese POW camps, see R.J. Pritchard and Sonia Zaide, ed., *The Tokyo War Crimes Trials*, 22 vols. (Garland Publishing: 1981), vol. 6:14,902. On Canadian deaths, see 'Hong Kong vets raise an awkward question,' *Globe and Mail* 15 Aug. 1987.
2 *Globe and Mail*, 12 Oct. 1945.
3 Vancouver *Sun*, 1 Oct. 1945.
4 Carl Vincent, *No Reason Why: The Canadian Hong Kong Tragedy – An Explanation* (Canada's Wings: 1981), 35.
5 Jonathan F. Vance, *Objects of Concern: Canadian Prisoners of War through the Twentieth Century* (University of British Columbia Press: 1994), 192.
6 Daniel Dancocks, *In Enemy Hands: Canadian Prisoners of War, 1939–1945* (Hurtig: 1983), 236.
7 Vance, *Objects of Concern*, 188.
8 Ibid., 292n31.
9 House of Commons *Debates*, 28 Jan. 1944, 3.
10 *Globe and Mail*, 11 March 1942.
11 *Maple Leaf*, 7 Sept. 1945.
12 Windsor *Daily Star*, 15 Sept. 1945.

13 NAC, RG 24, vol. 12,839, Maj. Gen. E.G. Weeks to No. 1 CWCIU, 25 Jan. 1946. 'Men are being discharged and dispersed and it will be difficult in most cases and impossible in some, to even obtain additional copies of their depositions.'

14 Ibid., vol. 12,837, examination of W. Stewart, 18 May 1946.

15 Ibid., vol. 12,839, affidavit of Maj. S.R. Kerr, 15 Feb. 1946.

16 Ibid., vol. 12,839, report of meeting held 16 Oct. 1945, G.K.M. Johnston to Macdonald.

17 Ibid., High Commissioner Vincent Massey's office to Sir Eric Machtig, 30 Jan. 1946.

18 NAC, RG 25, vol. 3,641, file 4,060–13–40C, acting secretary of state for external affairs to high commissioner, 6 Nov. 1945.

19 NAC, MG 26, J–4, vol. 419, cabinet conclusions, 16 Jan. 1946.

20 NAC, RG 24, vol. 12,839, War Office to Alfsea, 6 Feb. 1946.

21 NAC, RG 25, vol. 3,641, file 4,060–13–40C, under-secretary of state external affairs to Department of national defence, 22 Feb. 1946.

22 On Orr, see Charles Roland interview with Oscar Orr, 23 April 1985, McMaster University Oral History Archives; and Vancouver *Sun*, 17 Nov. 1945. On Puddicombe, see, 'George Beverley Puddicombe,' 69–70.

23 NAC, RG 25, vol. 3,641, file 4,060–C–40, pt 1, memorandum by Oscar Orr, 22 Dec. 1945.

24 House of Commons *Debates*, 12 April 1946, 809–10.

25 *Globe and Mail*, 22 March 1946.

26 R. John Pritchard, 'Lessons from British Proceedings against Japanese War Criminals,' *Human Rights Review*, vol. 3 (1978), 104 at 105.

27 R. John Pritchard, 'The Historical Experience of British War Crimes Courts in the Far East, 1946–1948,' *International Relations*, vol. 6 (1978), 311 at 313.

28 PRO, WO file 235/1030, 'Trial of Ryosaburo Tanaka' (hereinafter 'Tanaka Trial').

29 NAC, RG 25, file 2,670–D–40C, statement of Lois Fearon.

30 'Tanaka Trial,' 20.

31 Ibid., affidavit of Capt. Osler Thomas.

32 Ibid., 62.

33 Ibid., 155–6.

34 Roy Ito, *We Went to War* (Canada's Wings: 1984), 267.

35 PRO, WO file 235/1015, 'Trial of Toshishige Shoji,' summation, 3.

36 Pritchard, 'The Historical Experience,' 318.

37 Hong Kong *China Mail*, 23, 30 Jan. 1948.

38 PRO, WO file 235/0892, 'Trial of Genichiro Niimori' (hereinafter 'Niimori Trial'), affidavit of J.W. Archibald.

39 Pritchard, 'Lessons from British Proceedings,' 109.

40 'Niimori Trial,' 89.
41 Ibid., 99–101.
42 NAC, RG 25, vol. 3,641, file 4,060–C–40, pt. 2, Orr to Secretary, National Defence HQ, 1 Aug. 1946.
43 Vancouver *Sun*, 21 Aug. 1946.
44 PRO, WO file 235/1027, 'Trial of Choichi Sato.'
45 Charles Burdick and Ursula Moessner, *The German Prisoners of War in Japan, 1914–1920* (Lanham: 1984).
46 Charles Roland, 'Allied POWs, Japanese Captors and the Geneva Convention,' *War and Society*, vol. 9 (Oct. 1991), 83 at 95–6. On Japanese assurances that they would uphold the Geneva Convention, see *Memorandum of Foreign Minister Togo to Swiss Minister*, 29 Jan. 1942, in IMTFE 'Record of Proceedings,' ex. no. 1, 490.
47 PRO, WO file 235/1012, 'Trial of Isao Tokunaga, Shunkichi Saito, *et al.*' (hereinafter 'Tokunaga-Saito Trial'), 23.
48 Ibid., affidavit of Maj. James Gray, ex. 'Y.'
49 Ibid., 28.
50 *The Royal Rifles of Canada in Hong Kong, 1941–1945* (Hong Kong Veterans Association: 1980), 190.
51 'Tokunaga-Saito Trial,' 191.
52 Ibid., 30.
53 Ibid., 603.
54 Ken Cambon, *Guest of Hirohito* (PW Press: 1990), 49.
55 *Royal Rifles*, 308.
56 'Tokunaga-Saito Trial,' affidavit of Mak Kee Sing, ex. 'H–4.'
57 Ibid., affidavit of Capt. J.A.G. Reid, ex. 'X.'
58 Ibid., defence summation, 8.
59 Ibid., 11.
60 Cambon, *Guest of Hirohito*, 43.
61 *Globe and Mail*, 11, 25 Sept. 1945.
62 NAC, RG 25, vol. 3,824, file 4,060–C–40C, affidavit of Sgt. Arthur Rance. See also *Royal Rifles*, where one Canadian recalls Inouye cursing, taunting, and beating Canadians whenever he had the chance. 'He was the cruelest – or one of the cruelest Japanese I ever saw. And he was a Canadian' (at 288). Another infamous war criminal, Kenneth Yunone (also known as Kenneth Muranake), who once boasted that he had 'magnificently beheaded' an Australian prisoner, had studied at St John's College, Winnipeg. see Montreal *Gazette*, 15 Oct. 1945.
63 Cambon, *Guest of Hirohito*, 49.

64 William Allister, *Where Life and Death Hold Hands* (Stoddart: 1989), 80.

65 PRO, WO file 235/0927, 'Trial of Kanao Inouye' (hereinafter 'Inouye Trial'), affidavit of Capt. J.A. Norris.

66 NAC, RG 25, vol. 3,824, file 4,060–C–40C, F.J. Mead, RCMP, to USSEA, 27 Sept. 1945.

67 Ibid., deputy minister of defence to USSEA, 18 Feb. 1946.

68 Ibid., N. Robertson to deputy minister of justice, 1 April 1946.

69 NAC, RG 25, vol. 3,728, file 5,908–40, pt. 5 cabinet conclusions, 22 May 1946.

70 'Inouye Trial,' 1st and 2nd charge; and affidavit of J.A. Norris.

71 Ito, *We Went to War*, 269. See also Roy Ito, *Stories of My People* (Nisei Veterans Association: 1994). In Ito's view, Inouye had merely 'assisted with the torturing and barbaric questioning of prisoners' and so death was not an appropriate sentence (354–67).

72 Hong Kong *South China Morning Post*, 23 May 1946.

73 'Inouye Trial,' 9–10.

74 Ito, *We Went to War*, 270.

75 'Inouye Trial,' 81–6, 102–4.

76 NAC, RG 25, vol. 3,824, file 4,060–C–40C, report from the Special Branch of Hong Kong Police.

77 'Inouye Trial,' 146.

78 Ibid., 149.

79 NAC, RG 3,824, file 4,060–C–40C, report of Maj. G.B. Puddicombe, 24 June 1947.

80 Ibid., USSEA to National Defence, 8 Nov. 1946.

81 Ibid., E.H. Norman to A.D.F. Gascoigne, 13 Nov. 1946.

82 Ibid., Orr to Puddicombe, 5 Dec. 1946.

83 Ibid., Orr to National Defence, 16 Dec. 1946.

84 Ibid., Register of the Kanagawa Prefecture, in Puddicombe to Land Forces, SEAC (South East Asia Command), 5 Sept. 1946.

85 Hong Kong *China Mail*, 19 April 1947.

86 *Calvin's Case* (1609) 7 Rep. 1, 77 E.R. 377.

87 Hong Kong *South China Morning Post*, 28 May 1947.

88 *Joyce* v. *D.P.P.* (1946) A.C. 347; 1 All E.R. 186. See also Glanville Williams, 'The Correlation of Allegiance and Protection,' *Cambridge Law Journal*, vol. 10 (1948), 54 at 55.

89 'Tokunaga-Saito Trial,' report of Dr Selwyn-Clark to Maj. Gen. G.W.E.J. Erskine, 17 Feb. 1947.

90 Montreal *Star*, 26 Nov. 1947.

91 Ottawa *Citizen*, 26 Aug. 1947.

92 Montreal *Star*, 25 Aug. 1947.
93 Vancouver *Sun*, 27 Aug. 1947.
94 Calgary *Herald*, 26 Aug. 1947

10: The Japanese Trials: Camp Guards and the Architects of War

1 Patricia Roy, J.L. Granatstein, Masako Iino, and Hiroko Takamura, *Mutual Hostages: Canadians and Japanese during the Second World War* (University of Toronto Press: 1990), 209.
2 Charles Roland interview with Leonard Birchall, 22 Feb. 1986, Oral History Archives, McMaster University, 14–16, 29.
3 NAC, RG 24, vol. 5,203, affidavit of Leonard Birchall, 3 Jan. 1946.
4 Allister, *Where Life and Death Hold Hands*, 160–1.
5 Winnipeg *Free Press*, 11, 12 March 1946.
6 Ibid., 15 March 1946.
7 Ibid., 19 March 1946.
8 Ibid., 27 March 1946.
9 Ibid., 5 April 1946.
10 NAC, RG 25, vol. 3,641, file 4,060–13–40C, Read to Canadian embassy, Washington, 15 Sept. 1945.
11 Ibid., acting secretary of state for external affairs to high commissioner, 6 Nov. 1945.
12 NAC, MG 26 J–4, vol. 419, cabinet conclusions, 16 Jan. 1946.
13 NAC, RG 25, vol. 3,641, file 4,060–C–40, pt. 2, National Defence to External Affairs, 30 March 1946; and External Affairs to National Defence 2 April 1946.
14 Paul E. Spurlock, 'The Yokohama War Crimes Trials: The Truth About a Misunderstood Subject,' *American Bar Association Journal* vol. 36 (May 1950), 387 at 388.
15 Charles Roland interview with Oscar Orr, 4.
16 Ito, *We Went to War*, 259–60.
17 NARA, RG 153, file 35–483, *US* v. *Hazama*.
18 Ibid., 14.
19 Ibid., 735.
20 Allister, *Where Life and Death Hold Hands*, 3.
21 *US* v. *Hazama* 19.
22 Ibid., 352.
23 Ibid., 466.
24 Ibid., 734.
25 Ibid., Case Review, 26.
26 Spurlock, 'The Yokohama War Crimes Trials,' 388, 436.

27 Cambon, *Guest of Hirohito*, 59.
28 NARA, RG 123, file 35–1097, *US* v. *Kojima*, affidavits of John Sellers, J.R. Stroud, and Victor Myatt.
29 Ibid., 357.
30 Cambon, *Guest of Hirohito*, 57.
31 Charles Roland interview with Oscar Orr, 8.
32 NARA, RG 123, file 35–867, *US* v. *Ushida*, affidavit of Sgt. Ernest Neal.
33 Pritchard, 'The Historical Experience.' Pritchard points out that beaters such as Uchida were unaware of how fatal their attacks were likely to be. 'The plain truth is that ordinary people are quite unaware of the fragility of the human frame' (at 109).
34 *US* v. *Uchida*, 408.
35 Ibid., attached as appendix, ex. 'G.'
36 Ibid., 411.
37 Ibid., affidavit of Maj. Anthony Reid.
38 Charles Roland interview with Oscar Orr, 9.
39 Cambon, *Guest of Hirohito*, 68.
40 Ibid., 56.
41 NARA, RG 153, file 35–84, *US* v. *Yoshida et al.*, 7, 15.
42 Ibid., 178.
43 Ibid., 205–7.
44 Ibid., affidavit of Ken Cambon.
45 Ibid., affidavit of Lloyd Doull.
46 Ibid., 406.
47 Cambon, *Guest of Hirohito*, 59.
48 *US* v. *Yoshida*, case review 29.
49 Cambon, *Guest of Hirohito*: 'In the two years or so he was in control of the health care of camp, I never once saw him show any compassion for a sick or injured man' (at 63).
50 *US* v. *Yoshida*, 715–20.
51 NAC, RG 24, vol. 5,203, G/C Carscallen to Canadian Joint Staff, 6 Feb. 1948.
52 Leonard Birchall letter to the author, 8 March 1996.
53 Charles Roland interview with Leonard Birchall, 24.
54 Douglas MacArthur, *Reminiscences* (McGraw-Hill: 1964), 319.
55 Gavan Daws, *Prisoners of the Japanese: POWs of World War II in the Pacific* (Morrow: 1994), 370.
56 NAC, RG 25, vol. 3,641, Orr to National Defence HQ, 15 July 1946.
57 Ibid., memorandum to E.R. Hopkins, 29 July 1946.
58 NAC, RG 24, vol. 5,203, Orr to National Defence, 10 April 1947.
59 Ibid., Orr to National Defence, 30 Sept. 1946, reporting on three Japanese of

concern to Canada being tried by the British and Dutch military. See also W.P. McClermont, 'War Crimes Trials,' *Canadian Army Journal* (1 July 1947), which reported that an Australian war crimes investigation team was ambushed and killed by natives while investigating the case of two RCAF men murdered by the Japanese in Java.

60 NAC, RG 25, vol. 3,641, file 4,060–13–40C, External Affairs to High Commissioner Vincent Massey, 6 Nov. 1945.

61 R. John Pritchard and Sonia Zaide, ed., *The Tokyo War Crimes Trial*, 1: Pre-Trial Documents ... (hereinafter 'Tokyo Trial') SCAP, (Supreme Commander for the Allied Powers) special proclamation, 19 Jan. 1946.

62 NAC, MG 26 J–4, vol. 419, cabinet conclusions, 8, 16 Jan. 1946.

63 See 'E. Stuart McDougall,' *Rapport du Barreau de Québec* (March 1957), 214–16. On American views of McDougall, see Arnold C. Brackman, *The Other Nuremberg: The Untold Story of the Tokyo War Crimes Trials* (Morrow: 1987), 66.

64 A.S. Comyns Carr, the British assistant prosecutor, arrived in Tokyo in March 1946 to find great disorder in the prosecutor's office and no direction as to how the indictment should be organized.

65 Brackman, *The Other Nuremberg*, 62.

66 'Tokyo Trial,' letter of Comnys Carr, 19 March 1946, xvii.

67 NAC, RG 25, vol. 3,641, file 4,060–C–40, pt. 2, Nolan to E.R. Hopkins, 14 March 1946.

68 In *The Other Nuremberg* Arnold Brackman suggests that Norman was a KGB agent and was only doing the work of his Soviet masters in trying to bring Emperor Hirohito to trial by implicating his close aide, Marquis Kido (at 49–50). While Brackman was convinced that Norman was a Soviet agent, evidence is far from conclusive. See J.L. Granatstein and David Stafford, *Spy Wars: Espionage and Canada from Gouzenko to Glasnost* (Key Porter: 1990), 88–103.

69 'Tokyo Trial,' indictment.

70 New York *Times*, 25 Feb. 1946.

71 NAC, RG 25, vol. 3,641, file 4,060–C–40, pt. 2, E. McDougall to N. Robertson, 23 April 1946.

72 'Tokyo Trial,' 125.

73 Ibid., 637–8.

74 Ibid., 1,553–8. See also J.H. Boyle, *China and Japan at War, 1937–1945: The Politics of Collaboration* (Stanford University Press: 1972). Gen. Kenji Ishiwara, for example, masterminded the Mukden incident but had opposed an expanded war with China (at 49–51).

75 'Tokyo Trial,' vol. 6: 12,856–82.

76 Ibid., 13,116.

77 Ibid., 13,122.
78 Ibid., 13,145–6.
79 Nippon *Times*, 19 Dec. 1946.
80 Brackman, *The Other Nuremberg*, 143–4.
81 As quoted in Philip R. Piccigallo, *The Japanese on Trial: Allied War Crimes Operations in the East, 1945–1951* (University of Texas Press: 1979), 15.
82 'Tokyo Trial,' vol. 3: 6,692–6,789.
83 NAC, RG 25, vol. 3,641, file 4,060–C–40, pt. 2, W.L. Magrand to External Affairs, 19 Oct. 1946, containing a clipping from *Pravda* of 16 Oct. 1946. Canada's chargé d'affaires in Moscow reported that 'my foreign colleagues as well as Russian friends have asked me whether this was not a confirmation of Ehrenberg's article on Canada in which he contended that the French language was being prosecuted.'
84 *Life*, 26 Jan. 1948, 48.
85 E. McDougall to wife, Margaret, 14 Feb. 1948, author's collection.
86 Brackman, *The Other Nuremberg*, 353.
87 NAC, RG 24, vol. 5,203, E. Norman to External Affairs, 10 Jan. 1948.
88 Windsor *Star*, 13 Nov. 1948.
89 Ottawa *Citizen*, 13 Nov. 1948.
90 Richard H. Minear, *Victor's Justice: The Tokyo War Crimes Trial* (Princeton University Press: 1971), 158.
91 Winnipeg *Free Press*, 28 Aug. 1947

11: 'Siegergericht'

1 NAC, RG 24, vol. 5,203, Emma Schumacher to Canadian War Ministry, 21 Dec. 1948; Hopkins to Schumacher, 3 May 1949; deputy minister of National Defence to Hopkins, 13 Jan. 1949.
2 DHist., 7/166, Macdonald to JAG, 22 May 1946.
3 NAC, RG 24, vol. 5,203, file 15–2,447, H. Mulligan, for chief of air staff, to J.R. Willis, 2 Feb. 1948; High Commissioner Vincent Massey to External Affairs, 11 Oct. 1948.
4 Ibid., High Commissioner Massey to External Affairs, 18 Nov. 1948.
5 NAC, RG 25, vol. 3,641, file 4,060–40, High Commissioner Massey to External Affairs, 4 Sept. 1947.
6 Allen Andrews, *Exemplary Justice* (Harrap: 1976), 200–1.
7 Letter to the author from the Depôt Central d'Archives de la Justice Militaire, 19 Sept. 1995.
8 NAC, RG 24, vol. 12,839, file 392–52, Macdonald to DAAG (deputy assistant adjutant-general), 27 Feb. 1946.

9 WMA, MP, box 3, file 1/8, ex. no. 16.

10 WMA, MP, box 5 (no file number), examination of Bernhard Siebkin, 15 March 1946 25.

11 The issue of responsibility for the Fontenay-le-Pesnel massacre is thoroughly canvassed in Ian Sayer and Douglas Botting, *Hitler's Last General: The Case against Wilhelm Mohnke* (Bantam: 1989). 'If the prisoners were massacred somewhere between Battalion HQ and Regimental HQ, and it was not the Battalion Commander who gave the order, there is logically only one other candidate for this infamy ... and this was Siebkin's superior officer, his Regimental Commander, Mohnke' (at 231).

12 Ibid., 198.

13 Ibid., 191.

14 Ibid., 202.

15 Ibid., 203–4. see also Luther, *Blood and Honor*, 188.

16 *Geneva Convention*, 27 July 1929, article 2, paragraph 3. See also Georg Schwartzenberger, *International Law: The Law of Armed Conflict* (Stevens: 1968), 453.

17 NAC, RG 24, vol. 12,837, file 391–33, Auschwitz.

18 NAC, RG 25, vol. 3,641, K.P. Kirkwood to External Affairs, 8 Dec. 1947.

19 George Goad, 'Kurt Meyer Was My Prisoner' *Weekend Magazine* vol. 9, no. 16 (1959), 32.

20 Foster, *Meeting of Generals*, 507–8.

21 Ibid., 505–6.

22 Montreal *Gazette*, 10 Jan. 1947.

23 Montreal *Standard*, 15 Jan. 1949: 'It is all very hush hush, but several army and air force officers are working for the release of Kurt Meyer, Canada's no. 1 War Criminal.'

24 WMA, Campbell Papers, file I 5/2, Campbell to Claxton, 18 Jan. 1949.

25 Ralph Allen, 'Was Kurt Meyer Guilty?' *Maclean's*, 1 Feb. 1950, 9.

26 *War Crimes Act* S.C. 1946, c. 73.

27 NAC, RG 2–18, vol. 209, file W–41, petition of Kurt Meyer, 12 Dec. 1950.

28 Ibid., memorandum of law, H.D. MacKeen and R.A. Ritchie, 12 Dec. 1950.

29 Sayer and Botting, *Hitler's Last General*, 102.

30 John Munro and Alex Inglis, ed., *Mike: The Memoirs of the Right Honourable Lester B. Pearson, 1948–1957*, 2 vols. (University of Toronto Press: 1973), 2: 85. See also, R. Bothwell and W. Kilbourn, *C.D. Howe* (McClelland and Stewart: 1979), 255.

31 NAC, RG 2, vol. 2,749, cabinet defence committee meetings, minutes of meeting, 12 Sept. 1951. On the official antipathy towards the war crimes prosecutions, see Charles Ritchie, *Diplomatic Passport: More Undiplomatic*

Diaries, 1946–1962 (Macmillan: 1981). In a discussion with senior generals in Europe on 23 Aug. 1946, Charles Ritchie of External Affairs expressed the view that those German officers who ordered the massacre of civilians deserved to be shot. Gen. Maurice Pope disagreed and even felt that 'The fact is that the Nurnberg [sic] Trials are scandalously unjust and should never have taken place' (at 8).

32 NAC, RG 2, vol. 2,751, cabinet defence committee documents, vol. 10, doc. D–304, 11 Sept. 1951.

33 Goad, 'Kurt Meyer Was My Prisoner.' See also *Globe and Mail*, 26 Oct. 1951, 'Meyer plan is veiled by curtain of secrecy': 'The mystery of Mission Meyer deepened today. It became the subject of iron-handed security regulations which shrouded the whole operation in the trappings of a tintype melodrama.'

34 House of Commons *Debates*, 6 Feb. 1951, 117.

35 Ibid., 22 Oct. 1951, 245.

36 Toronto *Globe and Mail*, 26 Nov. 1951.

37 House of Commons *Debates*, 26 Nov. 1951.

38 Toronto *Globe and Mail*, 27 Nov. 1951.

39 DHist., 81/146, file of representations to National Defence.

40 Ibid., 6 Dec. 1951.

41 *Globe and Mail*, 11 Dec. 1951.

42 Montreal *Star*, 19 Jan. 1952.

43 Windsor *Star*, 3 Dec. 1977.

44 Windsor *Daily Star*, 3 Dec. 1951.

45 Montreal *Gazette*, 6 Feb. 1952.

46 Ibid.

47 Montreal *Herald*, 4 Dec. 1951.

48 NAC, RG 24, vol. 5,203, file 5,908–40, pt. 6, memorandum from the USSEA, 27 Nov. 1952.

49 Ibid., Canadian ambassador in Bonn to External Affairs, 18 March 1953.

50 Ibid., memorandum, legal division of External Affairs, 27 April 1953.

51 Reginald Roy, *Sherwood Lett: His Life and Times*, 128–9.

52 House of Commons *Debates*, 25 Jan. 1954, 1,404.

53 *Weekend Magazine* vol. 7, no. 5 (1957). During an extended interview with Canadian reporter Omer Anderson, Meyer discussed his abiding fascination with military theory: 'The Bundeswehr, [German Army] must be completely armored – from quartermaster to signal vehicles, Meyer said. He envisions troops and their equipment being shuttled by air about the battlefield' (2).

54 Montreal *Star*, 12 Sept. 1957.

55 Ibid., 30 July 1957.

56 Edmonton *Journal*, 8 Sept. 1954.
57 Montreal *Star*, 8 Sept. 1954.
58 Sayer and Botting, *Hitler's Last General*, 330.
59 Windsor *Star*, 12 April 1985.
60 Ottawa *Citizen*, 12 May 1985.
61 Ian Sayer, 'Exposed the Mohnke Case,' *World War II Investigator*, vol. 1, no. 3 (June 1988).
62 United Kingdom, *Parliamentary Debates*, 28 June 1988, 337–42. See also London *Daily Telegraph*, 30 June 1988.
63 Montreal *Gazette*, 13 April 1990.
64 *Globe and Mail*, 6 June 1994.

12: Canadian War Crimes and the Consequences

1 WMA, MP, Macdonald to Norma Macdonald, 6 April 1946. See also Dominick Graham, *The Price of Command: A Biography of General Guy Simonds* (Stoddart: 1993), 226–7.
2 *Globe and Mail*, 9 May 1946.
3 Ibid., 1 Sept. 1945.
4 Ibid., 6, 7 Sept. 1945.
5 Robert Tooley, 'Appearance or Reality? Variations in Infantry Courts Martial: 1st Canadian Division: 1940–1945,' *Canadian Defence Quarterly*, vol. 22 (October 1992), 33, and ibid. (December 1992), 40.
6 H.C. Forbes, 'Military Police at War: The No. 2 Company Canadian Provost Corps in England and France 1942–1945,' *R.C.M.P. Quarterly*, vol. 2 (winter 1986), 8 at 22–3. The author thanks RCMP historian Glenn Wright for his guidance.
7 Osgoode Society interview with B.J.S. Macdonald: 'There were rumours that Canadians had shot prisoners, we investigated any that we got, and we were never able to find any evidence or proof of it at all' (at 39).
8 WMA, MP, box 3, 'Supplementary Report,' ex. no. 9, interrogation of Kurt Meyer, 26.
9 Author's interview with Jim Keck, PLDG (Princess Louise Dragoon Guards), 9 June 1993.
10 Strome Galloway, *Bravely into Battle* (Stoddart: 1988), 228; and Farley Mowat, *The Regiment* (McClelland and Stewart: 1973), 208–9.
11 Author's interview with Stan Szislowski, Perth Regiment, 12 July 1993.
12 Alexander McKee, *Caen: Anvil of Victory* (Souvenir: 1964). This book, in addition to having several inaccuracies (including references to Montgomery as a field marshal long before his promotion), contains large sections that are

made up of personal recollections with no reference to any official records. McKee also insists that Meyer's death sentence was commuted by Crerar instead of Vokes.

13 Ibid., 199–201.
14 Montreal *Gazette*, 23 Sept. 1964, headlined 'Did Allies murder prisoners?'
15 *Maple Leaf*, 11, 19 Jan. 1946.
16 The author wishes to thank Dr Robert Fraser for his help. Most of the following incidents were told to the author in confidence.
17 Robert M. and Marie Sanderson, *Letters from a Soldier: The Wartime Experiences of a Canadian Infantryman, 1943–1945* (Press Escort: 1993), 148.
18 Vokes, *My Story*, 148.
19 Author's interview with Jim Elliot, 22nd Field Ambulance, 28 Oct. 1994.
20 NAC, RG 24, vol. 12,841, file 393–28, Sogel.
21 NAC, RG 24, vol. 10,426, file 205 S.1 023 (D.6), St Sulpice Sur Risle, 10 June 1944.
22 WMA, MP, box 2, file I 2/1, 'Chateau d'Audrieu,' ex. no. 10, Beatrice Delafon.
23 Ibid., file I 2/3, 'Buron and Authie,' ex. no. 41, J.K. Motzfelt.
24 Richard Holmes, *Acts of War: The Behaviour of Men in Battle* (Freilieu: 1985), 382.
25 C.S. Frost, *Once a Patricia* (Vanwell: 1988), 440–1.
26 WMA, MP, file I 2/3, 'Buron and Authie,' ex. no. 33, affidavit of Maj. J.D. Learment.
27 WMA, MP, box 3, 'Supplementary Report,' ex. no. 11A, statement by Cpl. W.R. Lebar.
28 PRO, WO file 235/1012, 'Tokunaga-Saito Trial,' summation of Tetsuo Fujita, 14.
29 Farley Mowat, *And No Birds Sang* (McClelland and Stewart: 1979), 103.
30 Osgoode Society interview with B.J.S. Macdonald, 39.
31 Will Bird, *No Retreating Footsteps*, 96–100.
32 PRO, WO file 235/1030 'Tanaka Trial,' affidavit of S. Martin Banfill, 22 Dec. 1945.
33 The degree of fanaticism in the Waffen SS is an issue that will be endlessly debated. Former Waffen SS officer Paul Hausser has argued in books such as *Soldaten Wie Anderin Auch* (Soldiers Like Any Others) that the SS were simply well trained and motivated soldiers and no more inclined to commit war crimes than any other troops. On the other hand, histories of SS divisions reveal a darker side. From the first fighting on the Polish front, Waffen SS units were noted for their killing of Jews, intellectuals, and any opponents of Nazi ideology. See C.W. Sydnor, *Soldiers of Destruction: The SS Death's Head Division, 1933–1945* (Princeton University Press: 1977). 'The urge to massacre

272   Notes to pages 223-6

defenceless prisoners seems to have been a natural and logical by-product of the poisonous climate of fanaticism that had existed in the SS Totenkopf division since its creation' (at 107).

34 Author's interview with Capt. Alf Hodges, Essex Scottish Regiment, 9 June 1994.
35 Parks, 'Command Responsibility,' 9.
36 James J. Weingartner, 'Massacre at Biscari: Patton and an American War Crime,' *The Historian*, vol. 52 (November 1989), 24 at 30.
37 Vance, *Objects of Concern*, 102. Harry Foster diary entry for 23 May 1940.
38 Foster, *Meeting of Generals*, 350.
39 L.C. Green, *Essays on the Modern Law of War* (Transnational: 1985), 252.
40 PRO, WO file 235/1015, 'Shoji Trial.'
41 Martin van Creveld, *The Transformation of War* (Free Press: 1991), 89.
42 Geoffrey Best, *Humanity in Warfare: The Modern History of the International Law of Armed Conflicts* (Weidenfeld and Nicholson: 1980), 217.
43 WMA, MP, 'Supplementary Report,' interrogation of Wilhelm Stremme, 18.
44 As quoted in Lord Russell, *The Scourge of the Swastika*, 39.
45 Martin Gilbert, *In Search of Churchill* (HarperCollins: 1995), 84.
46 R.A. Klefisch, 'Thoughts about Purporse and Effect of the Nuremberg Judgment,' in W.E. Benton and Georg Grimm, ed., *Nuremberg: The German Views of the War Trials* (SMU Press: 1955), 201–11.
47 1949 Geneva Convention, signed 12 Aug. 1949, 6 *U.S.T.* (United States Treaties) 3516, 75 *U.N.T.S.* (United Nations Treaty Series) 287.
48 The U.S. military tried Calley pursuant to the uniform code of military justice whereas he might well have been tried as a war criminal. See J. Holmes Armstead, 'The United States vs. William Calley: An Opportunity Missed!' *Southern University Law Review*, vol. 10 (1984), 205. Also: Bolton and Sim, *Four Hours in My Lai* (Viking: 1991).
49 J.F. Addicott and W.A. Hudson, 'The Twenty-Fifth Anniversary of My Lai: A Time to Inculcate the Lessons,' *Military Law Review*, vol. 139 (winter 1993), 153.
50 Theodor Meron, 'War Crimes in Yugoslavia and the Development of International Law,' *American Journal of International Law*, vol. 88 (1994), 78: 'Its [international tribunal for Yugoslavia] creation portends at least some deterrence to future violations and gives a new lease on life to that part of international criminal law which applies to violations of humanitarian law. These are major, though obvious, achievements.' See also J. Webb, 'Genocide Treaty – Ethnic Cleansing – Substantive and Procedural Hurdles in the Application of the Genocide Convention to Alleged Crimes in the Former Yugoslavia,' *Georgia Journal of International and Comparative Law*, vol. 23

(summer 1993), 377.

51 Toronto *Star*, 7 Oct. 1992.

52 U.N. Doc. S/Res/955, 1994. See Theodor Meron, 'International Criminalization of International Atrocities,' *American Journal of International Law*, vol. 89 (1995). The author also points out the importance of national courts in the enforcement of humanitarian law. In Ethiopia, sixty-seven former members of the military dictatorship are being tried for murder and torture; see New York *Times*, 15 Dec. 1994. In Rwanda, six men were charged by national courts with genocide in the spring of 1995; see *Globe and Mail*, 7 April 1995.

53 Toronto *Star*, 21 May 1995.

54 *Canada Commission of Inquiry on War Criminals Report, Jules Deschênes, commissioner (1986), order-in-council P.C. 1985–348*. See also Michael Lewis, 'Justice Defied,' *Canadian Lawyer*, vol. 16, no. 4 (May 1992).

55 *R. v. Finta* (1994), 88 C.C.C. (3d) 417 at 467–8. See also Irwin Cotler, 'War Crimes Law and the Finta Case,' *Supreme Court Law Review*, vol. 6 (2d) 576.

56 Michael Howard, George J. Andreopoulos, and Mark R. Shulman, ed., *The Laws of War: Constraints on Warfare in the Western World* (Yale University Press: 1994), 10.

57 See comments by Reform MP John Cummins in *Alberta Report*, 31 Oct. 1994. On the one convicted soldier, Elvin Brown, Cummins commented, 'They've picked a scapegoat.'

58 Hamilton *Spectator*, 4 June 1994.

59 Edgar McInnis, 'A Middle Power in the Cold War,' in Hugh L. Keenleyside, ed., *The Growth of Canadian Policy in External Affairs* (Duke University Press: 1960), 143–4.

60 WMA, MP, file 3/7, 'Meyer Trial,' vol. 1:30.

61 Halifax *Chronicle Herald*, 6 June 1984.

Photo Credits

Wady Lehmann Collection: U.S. Army pathologist (photograph by Raymond Robichaud); Canadian War Crimes Investigation Vehicle; Meyer's assigned defence lawyers.

Municipal Archives, Windsor Public Library, B.J.S. Collection: Official portait of Lt. Col. Bruce J.S. Macdonald; Exhibit T-31 to the trial of Kurt Meyer; L'Ancienne Abbaye d'Ardenne; Commencement of the trial of Kurt Meyer; Prosecution team assembled; A reluctant Meyer.

National Archives of Canada: Brigadeführer Kurt Meyer, PA 174293; Lt. Kosaku Hazama, PA 197471. Canadian Army photographs by Lt. Cooper: Accused Japanese war criminals, PA 197472; Major G.B. Puddicombe, PA 197473. Canadian Army phtograph by Lt. Dare: Col. Isao Tokunaga in custody, PA 197470.

Index

Abbott, Douglas 108–9

Adams, Pte. John 168–9

Adenauer, Konrad: and German prisoners 212–13

Aitken, Leslie 215

Aitken, Max xviii

Albers, Heinrich 203

Allen, Ralph: covers Meyer trial 68, 77, 81, 87, 89; and Meyer article 207–8

Allister, Rfm. William 170, 178–9; describes prison camp life 184

American Civil War xvi, 131

Ancienne Abbaye d'Ardenne (Abbaye Ardenne) 15–16, 21, 26, 58–82 *passim*, 223, 229; described 27; atrocities at 73–5

Anderson, James William 165

Andrew, Maurice 65, 70–1, 77, 88, 98, 200, 218; appointed to defend Meyer 62; cross-examines Jesionek 74–6; examines Meyer 79–82; summation of 91–2

Archibald, James 164

Arisue, Col. 169

Athabaskan, HMCS 41

Atkinson, F.T. 171

atrocities. *See* war crimes

Aurich, Germany 25, 120; courtroom described 55

Auschwitz 206

Authie 23–4, 57, 70–1, 77, 81, 91, 99, 222; battle of 5–6, 21; atrocities in 13–15, 70–2

Bad Oyenhausen 37

Bad Salzuflen 120, 126; described 36–7

Banfill, S.M. 161–2, 222

Barker, Maj.-Gen. Raymond W. 9, 22, 24; appointed to lead court of inquiry 7, 8; encourages Canadian investigations 25

Barker, R.D.: at Fontenay-le-Pesnel 45

Barnes, Sir Thomas 28

Barnett, James: and St Stephen's massacre 194–5

Bataan death march 94

Beck S/L J.S.H. 126; at Oberweier
    trial 128–35
Becker, Karl Walter: describes
    Chateau d'Audrieu killings 41–2
Bell-Irving, Brig. H.P.: background
    of 55; deliberations of 96–7, 100
Bergen-Belsen camp 103
Berzenski, George 168–9
Beverloo, Belgium 18, 70
Birchall, Leonard: captured 178–9;
    describes the Japanese prosecu-
    tions 190
Blackall, Sir Henry 175
Blackhurst, Lt.-Col. W. 7, 8
Blain, John 36, 42, 122, 141, 200;
    describes investigations 38; and
    Opladen trial 146–7
Bleich, Maj. L.C. 181
Boland, John 161; conducts Niigata
    trial 188–90
bombing campaign against
    Germany 116–18, 154
Boraston, Lt.-Col. J.H. 11, 13, 19, 27, 36
Borkum Island incident 119
Boss, William 111
Brackman, Arnold 196
Bredin, Lt.-Col. W.B. 70, 105; ap-
    pointed judge advocate 54;
    questions proceedings 64–5;
    summation of 93–5
Bremer, Gerhard: at Chateau
    d'Audrieu 41–2, 201–2
Bretteville, battle of 74, 81
British Army of the Rhine 42
British Free Corps: Canadians in 218
Broicchaus, Hubert 136, 138–9; and
    Opladen trial 142–9
Brown Chaplain W.L. 42–3
Buchenwald camp: execution of
    Canadians 39

Buettner, Obsturm von: urges men to
    kill prisoners 46, 69–70, 73, 91;
    killed 81
Bundschuh, Fritz 203
Buron: atrocities in 13–15, 24
Bushido code 163, 186

Cadieux, Marcel 30
Caen 5, 6, 15, 21
Caen: Anvil of Victory 219
Calgary Herald 108
Calley, William 226
Calvin's Case (1609) 175
Cambon, Ken 169
Campbell, Clarence 46, 54, 61, 89, 216;
    transferred to No 1 CWCIU 36; and
    Meyer's pre-trial statement 58–9;
    objects to clemency for Meyer 207,
    211
Campbell, Lt.-Col. I.J. 229
Canada: experience with war crimes
    xviii; indifference to European
    investigations 30–5; diminished
    role in wartime alliance 33; impact
    of Meyer trial on 61, 71–2; uproar
    at Meyer commutation 108–12; lack
    of interest in RCAF trials 153;
    outrage at Japanese war crimes
    158–9; diplomatic reconciliation
    with Japan 176–7; indifference to
    Japanese war crimes trials 190–1,
    196–9; reconciliation with West
    Germany 209–11. See also Defence,
    Department of; External Affairs,
    Department of; and Justice,
    Department of
Canadian army 4, 15, 25; D-Day
    landings 5–6; reaction to atrocity
    report 10; reaction to Meyer's
    sentence 104; termination of No. 1

CWCIU 154–5; at Hong Kong 157–64; and post-war trials 217–19; war crimes allegations against 63–4, 82, 88–9, 219–23, 227–8. See also individual units and No. 1 Canadian War Crimes Investigation Unit

Canadian Military Headquarters (London) 7, 10, 34, 38, 61, 63, 64, 104, 105, 110, 218; requested to investigate war crimes 25–6; establishes No. 1 CWCIU 28; winds up war crimes investigations 155

Canadian Provost Corps 218

Canadian Scottish Regiment 6, 40

Canadian War Crimes Advisory Committee (CWCAC) 47, 64; formation of 31–2; lack of urgency of 35; and war crimes regulations 49; dissolved 155

Canadian War Crimes Regulations 35, 93–4, 104, 122; drafting of 47–9; criticism of 50; conflicts with War Measures Act 64–5; and defence of superior orders 131–5; and Opladen case 141; validity of questioned 207–9, 211; Canadians subject to 219

Carmichael, S/L M. 37

Caspers, Josef 138; and Opladen trial 147, 149

Cattanach, S/L Alexander 56, 124, 137; named RCAF judge advocate 121; and Oberweier trial 128–30, 134; and Opladen trial 149–50, 152

Central Registry of War Criminals and Security Suspects (CROWCASS) 33, 119; Canadians consult 46

Chartres 26–7

Chateau d'Audrieu 41–2, 46, 87;

Canadian prisoners murdered at 6–9; crimes left unpunished 201–2

China 32, 195, 199; prisoners murdered 162–3; civilians murdered 161, 169

Churchill, Winston 4, 225

Clark, Weldon: at Fontenay-le-Pesnel 45

Clary-Aldrigen, Count 205

Claxton, Brooke 176, 207, 213; bungles Meyer's repatriation 210–11

Collins, S/L Victor 200; defends Neitz 122–4; defends Jung 128–35; attitude towards Germans 137

command responsibility 58, 68, 105–6; defined 93–6, 250n.62, 251nn.72 and 73; Meyer case as defining 98; not applied to Canadians 208; discussed 223–4

commissar order 98

Commonwealth Conference on Pacific Problems 176, 199

Comyns Carr, A.S.: and Tokyo trial 193

court of inquiry (SHAEF): conducts war crimes investigations 11–14; report on Authie-Buron 15; interrogation of Meyer 22–4; supplementary report of 24–5; disbanded 25

Crawford, Dr J.N.B. 166–7

Crerar, Lt.-Gen. H.D.G. 9, 10; displeasure at SHAEF control of war crimes investigations 7

Croll, David 210

'Crucified Canadian' xviii

Cruickshank, George 210–11

Curran, Lt.-Cdr. R.E.: as secretary to CWCAC 31–2

Dagenais, Marcel 78
Dean, Dalton 78; assigned to Meyer
  trial 54
Deane, Sgt.-Maj. 182
defence committee (Canada): consid-
  ers Meyer petition 209
Defence, Department of
  (Canada) 108, 170, 176, 183, 190,
  207, 209; regrets discontinuance of
  investigations 155
Delafon, Beatrice 6–7; witnesses
  atrocities 8–9
'denazification' 60–1
Deschênes Commission 215, 227
Deutsche Volkszeitung 107
Dickey, J.H. 161
Diefenbaker, John 109, 213
Dieppe raid xviii, 4, 218
Dietrich, Dr Ernst 149
diphtheria epidemic: in Hong Kong
  camps 166–7, 196
Dorchester penitentiary 107, 112, 206,
  209–10
Doull, Lloyd 189
Dresden firestorm 118
Drynan, George 36, 128
Dudka, Stanley: describes atrocities
  14–15; testifies at Meyer trial 71
Durdin, W/C Oliver (Pat) 61, 121;
  heads NWE detachment 37; and
  Neitz trial 123–5; and Oberweier
  trial 126–35; and Opladen
  trial 137–40, 141–2
duress, defence of: in Opladen trial
  153–4; in Winnipeg trial 182

Eberbach, Heinrich 61, 99
Eden, Anthony 3
Edmonton Journal 214
Eichelberger, Lt.-Gen. Robert L. 183

Einhorn, Mike 37
Eisenhower, Gen. Dwight D. 11,
  59; appoints court of inquiry 7;
  allegations of order to kill prisoners
  202
Ellis, Percy 168
Erdmann, Wolfgang 40
Erff, Matthais 136, 138, 147
Essex Scottish Regiment 11, 218, 220
Eustace, S/L J.L.: and Opladen case
  138–9, 144
evidence 12; how gathered in war
  crimes cases 38–9; rules relaxed for
  trials 47–50, 128–9, 141–2; validity of
  questioned in Meyer case 208, 211
External Affairs, Department of
  (Canada) 29, 31, 65, 155, 193, 200,
  209; reluctance to participate in
  UNWCC 30–2; and Japanese trials
  160, 182–3; and jurisdictional
  disputes in Asia 191

Faucon, Clément 14
Fearon, Lois: at Salesian mission 162
Fenrick, William 226
Ferguson, Lt. William: at Fontenay-le-
  Pesnel 44–5
Fihelly, John W. 197–8
First Canadian Army 7, 10
1st Hussars 6
1st SS Division Leibstandarte Adolf
  Hitler 17–18
First World War xvii
Fisher, Adm. Sir John xvi
Fontenay-le-Pesnel 87, 202; descrip-
  tion of massacre 44–5; possible
  explanation of 203, 268n.11
Fort Osborne barracks 179
Foster, Maj.-Gen. Harry 63–4, 67, 77,
  86, 88, 90, 99, 105 181–2; appointed

court president 54; and deliberations 96–7; and death sentence 100–1; and commutation controversy 110
408 Bomber Squadron 121, 122
France 194, 202; and Tokyo trial 197
Franco-Prussian War xvi
Fraser, Neil: heads NWE detachment 36–7
Friesen, John: at Oeyama Japan 179
Frost, Sydney 221
Fujita, Tetsuo 168–9

Gage, C.H. 217–18
Galaher, J.G. 218
Galloway, Strome 219
Gatternig, Dr Erich 81; interrogated 112–14
Geneva Convention, 1929 xvii, 39; and Japanese trials 163, 165–6, 168–9; and Tokyo trial 195; extended in 1949 225. See also laws of war
Geneva (Red Cross) Convention, 1864 xvi
Genn, Lt.-Col. Leo 124, 126
German army 17, 18, 24; views of 12th SS 20; treatment of Canadian prisoners 32; and laws of war 50–1. See also individual units and Waffen SS
Germany 3–4, 17–18, 32, 38 90; concern for laws of war xviii–xix; Meyer trial to be held in 52; post-war situation 60–1; and bombing campaign 116–19; obedience to orders 135, 136–8; post-war importance of 209–13; reaction to Nuremberg trial 225
Geyr von Schweppenburg, Lt.-Gen. 62, 81

Ghilote, Ramphal: and Inouye trial 171–3
Glueck, Sheldon 5
Goad, George 206
Goebbels, Joseph; and airmen 117–18
Golden, David 181–2
Gouzenko spy case 112
Gray, James 166–7
Graydon, Gordon 4
Great Britain 30, 33, 54, 60, 107; develops plans for war crimes trials 4–5; urges Canada to join UNWCC 32; and Japanese cases 160, 161; takes over Canadian cases 201–2; presses for Mohnke's prosecution 215–16
'Great Escape' 3, 201
Greece xv, 19
Green, L.C. 98
Grenadiere 214
Griffin, Maj. H.H. 36, 46; role in interrogations 47
Gripsholm (exchange ship) 31
Grotius, Hugo xv–xvi
Guilbert, Constance: at Meyer trial 70–1

Haggan, Lt. J.R. 173
Hague Conventions, 1899 and 1907 xvi, 50
Hamburg firestorm 118, 154, 215
Hamilton Spectator 111
Hanson, Maj. H.A. 25
Happy Valley Race Course 168
Harris, Sir Arthur 117
Hartberg, Elizabeth 149, 153
Harvey, Sgt. J.H.: trial of 179–81
Haut du Bosq massacre 87, 202; described 20–1
Hazama, Kozaku: at Oeyama 183–4

Helzel, Alfred: implicates Meyer 46; at trial 69–70
Heydte, Col. von der: view of war crimes 50; advises Meyer 59–61
Heyer, Horst: at Meyer trial 70
HIAG (Waffen SS veterans) 214
Higgins, John P. 194
Himmler, Heinrich 5, 17, 18, 117
Hiroshi, Ushioda 190
Hirsch, Maria 116
Hitler, Adolf 5, 18, 98, 112, 136
Hitler Youth 17
Hogues: atrocity at 20
Hollies, S.H.: defends Schumacher 128–35
Holmes, Richard 221
Holness, F.W. 112
Holzer, Robert 137–41; described 142; on trial 142–54; executed 156
Homma Masaharu 94
Honda, Lt.: at Salesian Mission 161–2, 196, 222
Hong Kong: battle of 31, 157–8, 161–4; prisoners in 164–9; and Tokyo trial 195–6
Hong Kong Volunteer Regiment 162
Hope, Justice J.A. 192
Hopkins, E.R. 47, 160, 183, 191; visits London 34–5; protests abandonment of investigations 155, 259–60n.41
'Hostage case' 98
House of Commons (Canada) 3–4, 158; King announces war crimes trials 52–3; and Meyer commutation 109; debates Meyer's release 210–11
How, Douglas: and Meyer's release 210–11

Hull, Cordell 5
Hunter, Harold 37
Hurd, Capt. E.L. 166
Hurst, Sir Cecil: chairs UNWCC 32

Inns of Court Regiment 205
Inouye, Kanao: described 169–70; war crimes trial 171–3; treason trial 174–5; execution of 176
International Law (Oppenheim text) 40
International Military Tribunal. See Nuremberg trial
International Military Tribunal for the Far East. See Tokyo trial
International Prosecution Staff (Tokyo Trial) 192–3
Isogai, Renusuke 191
Ito, Roy 163; and Kanao Inouye 171–2
Ito, Takeo: trial of 164

Jacob, Col. 146, 153
James, D.A. 16, 44, 72
Japan: and militarist philosophy 165–6; and mistreatment of prisoners 178–91; and Tokyo trial 191–9
Japanese army: first reports of atrocities by 31–2, 158–9; treatment of prisoners 160–6; and absolute obedience 186–7. See also Bushido code
Japanese-Canadians: and Inouye trial 172; return to Japan 183
Jardine's Point 163
Jesionek, Jan 56, 68, 87–101 passim, 202, 208; first interrogations 26–8; described by Macdonald 58; testimony at Meyer trial 72–4; cross-examined 74–6; reply evidence 89–90

Jesuits: massacre of at Suchow 32
Jews 34, 142; atrocities against not
considered war crimes 31
Johnson A/M G.O. 154
Johnson, Tom 6
Johnston, G.K.M. 36, 159
Johnston, Ian S.: background of 55;
Meyer deliberations 96–7, 100
Joyce, William: and 'Lord Haw Haw'
trial 175
Judge Advocate General (Canada) 28,
31, 47, 192, 215; consents to Meyer's
prosecution 52; assigns Bredin and
Dean to Meyer case 54
Jung, Wilhelm: trial of 125–35
Justice, Department of (Canada) 31,
52, 65, 170; and Meyer petition
208–9

Kappenberger, Wendelin 126
Keefler, Maj.-Gen. R.H. 55
Keenan, Joseph B.: and Tokyo trial
192, 197–8
Kelly, J.J.: and Winnipeg trial 179–80
Kempeitai 171–4
Kharkov trial 33
Kido, Marquis Koichi 193
King, Mackenzie 3, 52, 30, 157–8;
announces reports of atrocities 10;
appoints Macdonald prosecutor 53;
implicated in Meyer commutation
109–10
Klödden, SS Mann 205
Kojima, Itchisaku: trial of 186
Korean War xii, 209
Kuret, Paul 41
Kustner, Anton 125

Lachèvre, Daniel: at Meyer trial 89,
91–2, 93

Latvala, Pvt. 184–5
Lauterpacht, Hersch 133
La Villeneuve incident 63, 82;
described 88–9
laws of war xv–xix, 4–5, 39, 154; and
Canadian regulations 48–9;
German views of 50; discussed in
Meyer summation 93–6; and
bombing campaign 116–18, 255n.8;
expanded by Tokyo trial 193–4,
198–9; and reprisals 205. See also
superior orders, command respon-
sibility, and Llandovery Castle case
Lawson, Brig. J.K. 164
Leach, Maj. D.J. 55
Learment, John D.: at Authie 14, 222;
and Meyer trial 72
Lebar, W.R. 16
Leeb, Wilhelm von 98
Lehmann, Wady 68, 77, 80, 102, 127;
background of 36; describes
investigations 38–9; assigned to
Meyer's case 63
Leipzig trials xvii, 132–3
Le Mesnil-Patry 9, 13, 87; battle for 6;
atrocity at 43, 202; and Siebken trial
203–6
Le Paradis 223
Lett, Brig. Sherwood 213
Level, Monique 8
Lichtenberg, Fritz and Ina 207
Lieber, Francis xvi
Lindenbolz, Joseph 124–6; and
Oberweier trial 129–30
Lisbon Maru 158
Lister, Brig. J.F.A.: trial of 217
Llandovery Castle case 132–3
London Daily Mail 9–10
London Free Press 103
Londonderry, siege of 94

Loranger, J.T. 161
Luxenberger, Col. 205

MacArthur, Gen. Douglas 192;
   Japanese trials as policy 190
McBurney, AVM R.E.: and RCAF
   trials 121, 129, 137, 152
McClain, Col. J.W. 7
Macdonald, Bruce J.S. 12, 13, 19–56
   passim, 103, 155, 159, 228–9;
   interrogates Meyer 22–4; interrogates Jesionek 27–8; commands No.
   1 CWCIU 28–9; tours U.S. camps
   46–7; drafts war crimes regulations
   47–52; named chief prosecutor 53;
   and Meyer's defence 61–2; and La
   Villeneuve incident 63–4; conducts
   Meyer prosecution 68–79, 88–90;
   summation of 92–3; reaction to
   verdict 98–101; reaction to commutation 107–8; interrogates Stift and
   Gatternig 112–15; and RCAF trials
   120–1, 126; and later events 211–12,
   215, 217; and Canadian war crimes
   219, 222
McDonald, Lorne 104
Macdonald Maj. J.A. 155
Macdonald, Norma 13, 66, 103
McDougall, E. Stuart 194, 200;
   appointed to Tokyo trial 192;
   opinion of Webb 197
MacGeagh, Sir Henry 64
Mach, August 125, 129
MacKay, W.L. 14; at Meyer trial 71
McKee, Alexander 219
MacKeen, Dr R.A.H. 8, 77
MacKeen, H.P.: takes on Meyer case
   207–9, 211
Macklin, Brig. W.H.S. 7, 108, 155
McLean, Hector 16, 44

Maclean's magazine 207–8
McNaughton, Lt.-Gen. A.G.L. 223
Malmédy massacre 19, 45; U.S.
   investigation of contrasted with
   Canadian procedure 47, 103
Manchester, Robert: and Japanese
   trials 161, 188
Manual of Military Law 132
Maple Leaf 99, 104, 110, 159, 219–20
Martin, Edwin 218
Massey, Vincent xix, 105, 109, 155,
   254n.58; approves creation of No.1
   CWCIU 28; on UNWCC 32; urges
   war crimes investigations 33–4
Matthews, Brig. B. 28
Meitzel, Bernhard 87–8
Meyer, Hubert 205
Meyer, Kate 63, 91, 99, 101, 107, 210
Meyer, Kurt xi, 20, 25, 29, 46, 56, 65,
   102–155 passim, 223–4; early career
   of 18–21; interrogated by
   Macdonald 22–4; Jesionek implicates 26–8; Macdonald urges his
   trial 51–2; personality of 55–7; pre-
   trial conduct 58–62; on trial 62–78;
   takes the stand 79–87; addresses
   the court 99–100; in prison 206–7;
   petitions Department of Justice
   208–9; later career of 210–13; death
   of 214
Meyer case: as precedent 98
Meyer-Detring Col. 204–5
military law: described and contrasted with civil law 56; severity
   of German 135; in Japanese camps
   182. See also war crimes and laws of
   war
Milius, Karl Heinz 23–4, 62, 81
Mohnke, Wilhelm 12, 24, 87; career of
   18, 112; at Haut du Bosq 20; at

Fontenay-le-Pesnel 202–3; respon-
sibility for Le Mesnil-Patry 204;
avoids prosecution 215–16
Monoghan, T.C. 165
Montreal *Star* 176
Morden, Ken 36
Morden, W.D.S. 36, 42
Morrison, Capt. 7
Mortimer, Pte. 189
Moscow conference 5
Moss, Col. Thomas 161, 183, 188
Moss, J.A. 71
Mouen 58, 99; atrocity at 9, 57;
unresolved 43–4, 201
Mowat, Farley 222
Munro, Ross
Munshall-Ford, F.C. 161
Murchie, Lt.-Gen. J.C. 105, 108–10
Murdock, Scott 77
Murray, J.T.F. 164
Mutiny Act (1689) 56
Myatt, Victor 186
My Lai 226

Nazi Party 17, 18; and murdered
airmen 116–20, 126–34, 136–8
Neitz, Johann: trial of 122–4; release
of 209, 212, 213–14
Netherlands 14, 18, 191, 194
Newsom, G/C F.M. 120
Niemoeller, Martin 61
Niigata camp 159; described 188–9
Niimori, Genichiro: trial of 164–5
Nimmerfroh, Walter 41
9th Canadian Infantry Brigade 5, 21
Nippon *Times* 196
Nolan, Brig. Henry: appointed
prosecutor for Tokyo trial 192–3;
opening address 194–5; conducts
prosecution 195–6, 198

Norman, Herbert 193, 266n.68
Norris, J.A.: and Inouye trial 171
North Nova Scotia Highlanders 14,
21, 55; at Authie 5–6, 70–1
North Point camp 158, 166, 168
Number 1 Canadian War Crimes
Investigation Unit (CWCIU):
created 28–9; forms UK and NWE
detachments 35–7; investigations
described 37–8; March 1946 report
39–41; work made public 61;
dissolved 155. Individual cases
investigated: Berlin 38,
Buchenwald 39, Verneuil 39,
Dresden 40, Kalkar 40, Stalag
VIIB 40–1, Stalag IID 41
Nuremberg trial 55, 61, 98, 108;
Canada excluded from 51, 112,
254n.58; contrasted with Tokyo trial
191, 194; principles not applied to
Allies 225

O'Brien, T.W. 120
Oberweier trial 124–35
Ode, Tadashi 183
Oehlert Anna: defends Siebken and
Schnabel 204–5
Oeyama camp 179–82
Ofuna camp 178
Okuda, Hyoichi: trial of 188–90
Onami, Tomeiji 178
Opladen trial 136–53; validity of
questioned 154
Oppenheim, L.P. 132, 152
Orde, Brig. Reginald 53, 57, 102, 105,
120, 155; reviews charge sheet 58;
advises Macdonald 63–4; and
defects in war crimes regulations
64–5
Orr, Lt.-Col. Oscar 161, 165, 174, 191;

background of 160; works on
Japanese cases 183–7
Ossenbach, Wilhelm: described
138–40; and Opladen trial 149–52;
appeal 152–4; release 209, 212
Ottawa *Citizen* 199

Page, Maj. John 13, 35, 36; back-
ground of 8, 236n.22; protests
Canadian lack of participation in
UNWCC 33
Palm, Ob.Lt.: and Chateau d'Audrieu
41
Parker, W.R.: romance with Inouye
172–3
Patton, Gen. George S. 223
Patzig, Capt. 132–3
Payne, Ernie 6, 13
Payne, Sgt. John 168–9
Pearson, Lester: and war crime
sentence review 209
Peiper, Jochen 103
Penhale, Brig. M.H.S. 10
Permanent Court of International
Justice: Canada denied standing 32
Petch, Lt.-Col. Charles 70
Peterborough *Examiner* 111
Philippines 94, 192
Pickersgill, Frank 39
Plenter Dr: defends Ossenbach 150–1
Plourde, Capt. Frank 62, 98–9
Pollard, Lt.-Cpl. 79
Pootmans, R.J.: at Meyer trial 76
Pope, Gen. Maurice 111
Portal, Sir Charles 117
Power, Mary Violet: and Inouye trial
171–2
Pravda 197
prisoners of war: Grotius views on
xvi; first reports of killings of 6–10;

No. 1 CWCIU investigates 38–48.
See also German army and Japanese
army
Pritchard, R. John 187
Prussian Bureau of Investigation xvii
Puddicombe, Maj. George B. 183, 200;
background of 160; and Tanaka
trial 161–3; and Inouye trial 172–4
Putot-en-Bessin: battle of 6, 8, 44

Queen's Own Rifles of Canada 6, 25,
55

Rance, Sgt. Arthur 170, 174
Read, John 182; background of 31,
opposes war crimes investigations
32–3, 34, 241n.15; and defects in
regulations 64–5; and Meyer
commutation 105, 109, 254n.58
Red Cross parcels: stolen by
Tokunaga 168, 172; importance of
in camps 180–1, 185
Regina Rifles 63, 88–9
Reg. v. Finta (1994) 227
Reg. v. Smith (1900) 131–2
Reid, Capt. J.A.G. 168
Reitzenstein, Gerd von: and Chateau
d'Audrieu 41–2, 201–2
Renwick, J.A. 99
Rinko Coal Company 185–6
Ritchie, Justice R.A. 56, 208
Roberts, Maj. S. 88–9
Robertson, Norman 155; advised of
Read's opinion 33
Robichaud, Raymond 15–19, 37, 39,
63, 200; describes investigations 12;
transferred to No. 1 CWCIU 36;
and Meyer trial 89
Robinson, John Beverley xviii
Roland, Charles 166

Röling, B.V.A. 194

Roman, F/O Rudolph Anthony: and Neitz trial 122–4

Royal Air Force 117, 120: and post-war trials 201

Royal Army Medical Corps 161

Royal Canadian Air Force 201; crimes against airmen 3–4, 37, 118–20; to conduct its own trials 121–2; and Asian trials 191. Individual cases: Diest 119; Wassertrudingen 119; Woltersdorf 119; Frankenberg 120; Lüttringhausen 120, 201; Boesenberg, Hans Wilhelm 201; Frank, Josef 201; Hongue-Mare 201; Kuhn, Hans 201, 212; Lueftering Johann 201; Sommer, Max 201; Schnautz, Walter 212

Royal Canadian Mounted Police 170; officers attached to war crimes unit 7, 37

Royal Canadian Navy 40

Royal Rifles of Canada 166, 189, 195; at Hong Kong 157–8

Royal 22nd Regiment 'Van Doos' 41

Royal Warrant for War Crimes Trials (British) 64, 94; described 29, 240nn.46 and 47; rejected as a basis for Canadian trials 35; Inouye not subject to 174

Royal Winnipeg Rifles 55, 60; at Putot-en-Bessin 6, 44–5; at Chateau d'Audrieu 9

Rwanda 226

Sabourin, Romeo: and Buchenwald 39

St Laurent, Louis 64–5, 176, 209

Saint-Martin, Germaine 43

Saint Martin, Henri 43, 203

St Stephen's College: first reports of atrocity at 31; and Tokyo trial 195–6

Saito, Shunicki 159, 165; trial of 166–7; sentence reduced 176–7, 196

Sakai, Yusuke 162

Salesian mission: massacre at 161–3, 196, 222

Sanborn, Dick 177

Sanderson, Robert 220

Sato, Choichi: trial of 165

Sato, Katsuyasu: beatings by 188–90

Sayer, Ian 215

Schaefer, Ob.Lt. Robert 136, 138: orders killing of prisoners 139–53 *passim*

Schapp, Wilhelm: and Meyer appeal 102; and Opladen trial 140–1; defends Holzer 146–51; defence of duress 152–4

Scherer, Peter 125, 128–9

Scheumann, Adjutant 79, 86; and Abbaye Ardenne killings 59, 73–5, 82

Schnabel, Dietrich: trial of 203–5; execution of 206

Schumacher, Emma 200

Schumacher, Johann 200: trial of 125–35

Scotland, Lt.-Col. A.P. 103; assists in Meyer's interrogation 22–3; method of interrogation 47

Selwyn-Clarke, Dr 176

7th Canadian Infantry Brigade 6, 55, 63–4

Shamshuipo camp 164, 166

Shapcott, Brig. Henry 28, 159

Shepherd, Ed 186

Sherbrooke Fusilliers 5, 6, 21, 55

Shoji, Toshishige 224; trial of 163–4

Shutt, Major: and Le Mesnil-Patry
203–4
Siam-Burma Railway 195
Siebken, Bernhard 43, 45; background
of 202; on trial 203–5; execution of
206
Simonds, Lt.-Gen. Guy 108, 207;
sympathy with Meyer 209; and
Lister trial 217
Skutezky, Ernest 36, 119
Slaght, Arthur G. 155; appointed
honorary consul 30–1, 240n.3;
opposes Canadian participation in
war crimes trials 33–4
Smedmor, Capt. 55
Smith, Brig. J.. 94
Sogel incident 221
Somalia 227–8
South Saskatchewan Regiment 219
Sparling, Brig. H.A. 55; deliberations
96, 100
Stalag Luft III 3, 201
Stangenberg, Withold 202, 216;
witnesses Haut du Bosq kill-
ings 20–1
Steger, Fritz 79, 82–3
Stein, Charles: concern for Jews 31
Stenning, Lt.-Cdr. 180–1
Stern, Sigmund 26–7, 72
Stewart, Lt.-Col. J.C. 173
Stift, Dr Erich 81; interrogated 114
Stonborough, J.J. 36, 46, 54; at Meyer
trial 68–70, 76
Stormont, Dundas and Glengarry
Highlanders 77–9
Strathy, G/C.M.A.: drafts regulations
46
Stremme, Wilhelm 43–4
Strohm, Reinhard 128

Stun, Leopold: at Chateau d'Audrieu
42
Suarez, Francisco xv
superior orders, defence of: and
Oberweier trial 131–5; and
Opladen trial 152–4; and Tokunaga
169
Supreme Command for the Allied
Powers: establishes Japanese war
crimes trials 183–4; and high
defence standards 185–6, 192
Supreme Headquarters Allied
Expeditionary Force 9, 10–11, 24,
25, 33, 35; controls investigations 7–8; creates special inquiries
branch 11–12
Switzerland: investigates Chateau
d'Audrieu killings 10, 22–3, 51

Takahashi, Takeo: trial of 190
Takano, Junijiro 163
Tanaka, Ryosaburo: trial of 161–3
Tandy, J.J. 180
Tarleton, Brig. G.W.B. 8
Third Canadian Infantry Division
5–6, 21
Tiray, Dr: to investigate Abbaye
killing 59
Thomas, Osler 162
Thompson, Percy 180
Timmerman, Nelles 121
Titman, Gerald 188
Tojo, Hidecki 193, 197–9
Tokunaga, Isao 159, 166, 172, 196;
trial of 167–9; sentence reduced
176–7
Tokyo Shimbun 196
Tokyo trial: created by SCAP 192;
trials 193–8; impact of 198–9

Tombaugh, Col. Paul 11
Torbanisch, Friederich 19–20, 73, 91; statement at Meyer trial 69
Toronto *Globe and Mail* 3, 61, 68, 119, 158–9; and Meyer commutation 108–10; and Meyer's repatriation 210–11
'Totenkopf' 3rd SS Division 223
Treason Act (1351) 170, 174
Trist, Lt.-Col. 176
Tugby, Sgt.-Maj. Marcus: trial of 181–2
12th SS engineering battalion 9
12th SS Panzer Division (Hitler Jugend) 8–9, 12, 19, 21–8 *passim*, 67–101 *passim*, 222; at Authie and Buron 5–6, 14–16; organization of 17–18; reputation of 20; attitude of its soldiers 41–2; war diary unavailable to Canadians 42
12th SS reconnaissance battalion 8, 41–2
25th Panzer Grenadier Regiment 16, 18, 21–2, 26, 73
21st Army Group 7, 12, 25, 37
26th Panzer Grenadier Regiment 18, 20, 21, 112; and Le Mesnil-Patry killings 43
230th Infantry Regiment (Japanese) 163
229th Infantry Regiment (Japanese) 161

Uchida, Kanemasu 186–7
Union of Soviet Socialist Republics xvi, 5, 38, 82–3, 107, 112, 215; mistreatment of Soviet prisoners; objects to Canada on the Permanent Court 32; executes German war criminals 33; and Oneto incident 197
United Nations 225–6
United Nations War Crimes Commission 28, 33, 35, 112, 119; formed 5; Canada declines to participate 30; Canada joins 32
United States xvi, 5, 30, 32; outrage over Malmédy massacre 19; creates CROWCASS 33; assists Canadians 46–7; and command responsibility 94–5; assists Canada with Japanese cases 160, 182–3; and Tokyo trial 192–4; and Vietnam War 226

Vancouver *Sun* 111
Varley Lt.-Cpl. 167
Versailles 12, 24
Vico, Françine 76–7
Vico, Jean-Marie 15–16, 229; at Meyer trial 76–7, 89
Vietnam War 226
Vokes, Maj.-Gen. Chris 63, 102, 220, 223–4; background of 104–5; and commutation controversy 105–10; support for 111
Volkischer Beobachter 118
Volkssturm 137–8

Waffen SS 6, 8–9, 11, 12–16, 19; described 17; subculture of 20, 41–4; German sympathy for 61; described at Meyer trial 68–9; and veterans' group HIAG 214
Walker J.W. 36
Wall, de (solicitor): defends Weigel 150–1
war crimes: history of xv–xix; development of Allied policy and

attitudes towards 4–6, 11–14; and
Canadian investigations 28–9, 31–2;
discussed in Meyer summations
90–6; Japanese attitudes towards
157–60; why soldiers commit
221–3. *See also* laws of war
War Crimes Act (1946) 208
War Measures Act (1939) 35; conflicts
with regulations 64–5, 208
water torture: described 171–3
Webb, Sir William: president of
Tokyo trial 194, 197–8
Wehrmacht War Crimes Bureau 50–1
Weigel, Walter: implicated in killings
137–40; on trial 149–51; sentence
and execution 152–5
Werl prison 209–10, 212
Wermelskirchen 143, 151, 153
Wildermuth, Col.: views on war
crimes 50
Wilinski, Erich 201

Williams, Lt. Fred 78–9
Wimplinger, Michael 203
Windsor, Lt. Tom 78, 93
Winnipeg: courts martial held in 179–
82, 184
Winnipeg Grenadiers 199; at Hong
Kong 157–8, 176–7; and Winnipeg
trial 179–82
Witt, Fritz 21, 79: orders Meyer to
investigate killings 59, 82
Wongneichong Gap 163
Wormhout massacre 12, 215
Wright, Lt.-Col. Peter 62
Wunsche, Max 88

Yakabuki, Riki 165
Yamashita case (1945) 94–5, 98,
250n.62
Yoshida, Masato 186; on trial 188–9
Yugoslavian Civil War 226

1981 David F. Flaherty, ed., *Essays in the History of Canadian Law: Volume I*
1982 Marion MacRae and Anthony Adamson, *Cornerstones of Order: Courthouses and Town Halls of Ontario, 1784–1914*
1983 David H. Flaherty, ed., *Essays in the History of Canadian Law: Volume II*
1984 Patrick Brode, *Sir John Beverley Robinson: Bone and Sinew of the Compact*
      David Williams, *Duff, A Life in the Law*
1985 James Snell and Frederick Vaughan, *The Supreme Court of Canada: History of the Institution*
1986 Paul Romney, *Mr Attorney: The Attorney General for Ontario in Court, Cabinet, and Legislature, 1791–1899*
      Martin Friedland, *The Case of Valentine Shortis: A True Story of Crime and Politics in Canada*
1987 C. Ian Kyer and Jerome Bickenbach, *The Fiercest Debate: Cecil A. Wright, the Benchers, and Legal Education in Ontario, 1923–1957*
1988 Robert Sharpe, *The Last Day, the Last Hour: The Currie Libel Trial*
      John D. Arnup, *Middleton: The Beloved Judge*
1989 Desmond Brown, *The Genesis of the Canadian Criminal Code of 1892*
      Patrick Brode, *The Odyssey of John Anderson*
1990 Philip Girard and Jim Phillips, eds., *Essays in the History of Canadian Law: Volume III – Nova Scotia*
      Carol Wilton, ed., *Essays in the History of Canadian Law: Volume IV – Beyond the Law: Lawyers and Business in Canada, 1830–1930*
1991 Constance Backhouse, *Petticoats and Prejudice: Women and Law in Nineteenth-Century Canada*
1992 Brendan O'Brien, *Speedy Justice: The Tragic Last Voyage of His Majesty's Vessel Speedy*
      Robert Fraser, ed., *Provincial Justice: Upper Canadian Legal Portraits from the Dictionary of Canadian Biography*
1993 Greg Marquis, *Policing Canada's Century: A History of the Canadian Association of Chiefs of Police*
      F. Murray Greenwood, *Legacies of Fear: Law and Politics in Quebec in the Era of the French Revolution*
1994 Patrick Boyer, *A Passion for Justice: The Legacy of James Chalmers McRuer*
      Charles Pullen, *The Life and Times of Arthur Maloney: The Last of the Tribunes*
      Jim Phillips, Tina Loo, and Susan Lewthwaite, eds., *Essays in the History of Canadian Law: Volume V – Crime and Criminal Justice*

Brian Young, *The Politics of Codification: The Lower Canadian Civil Code of 1866*

1995 David Williams, *Just Lawyers: Seven Portraits*

Hamar Foster and John McLaren, eds., *Essays in the History of Canadian Law: Volume VI – British Columbia and the Yukon*

W.H. Morrow, ed., *Northern Justice: The Memoirs of Mr Justice William G. Morrow*

Beverley Boissery, *A Deep Sense of Wrong: The Treason, Trials, and Transportation to New South Wales of Lower Canadian Rebels after the 1838 Rebellion*

1996 Carol Wilton, ed., *Essays in the History of Canadian Law: Volume VII – Inside the Law: Canadian Law Firms in Historical Perspective*

William Kaplan, *Bad Judgment: The Case of Mr Justice Leo A. Landreville*

F. Murray Greenwood and Barry Wright, eds., *Canadian State Trials: Volume I – Law, Politics, and Security Measures, 1608–1837*

1997 James W. St.G. Walker, *'Race,' Rights, and the Law in the Supreme Court of Canada: Historical Case Studies*

Lori Chambers, *Married Women and Property Law in Victorian Ontario*

Patrick Brode, *Casual Slaughters and Accidental Judgments: Canadian War Crimes and Prosecutions, 1944–1948*

Ian Bushnell, *A History of the Federal Court of Canada, 1875–1992*